WESTMAR COLLEGE

ESSAYS ON
Wittgenstein's
Tractatus

LUDWIG WITTGENSTEIN
(circa 1908)

ESSAYS ON
Wittgenstein's
Tractatus

EDITED BY

IRVING M. COPI
University of Michigan

AND

ROBERT W. BEARD
Florida State University

THE MACMILLAN COMPANY
New York

Second Printing, 1967

Library of Congress catalog card number: 66-25586

THE MACMILLAN COMPANY, New York
COLLIER-MACMILLAN CANADA, LTD., Toronto, Ontario

PRINTED IN THE UNITED STATES OF AMERICA

Contents

v

Contents

Contents

Introduction

LUDWIG WITTGENSTEIN'S *Tractatus Logico-Philosophicus* was published over forty years ago, yet interest in it seems to be increasing rather than diminishing with passage of time. This is remarkable in view of the enormous impact it has already had on philosophical thought during the first half of the century.

The *Tractatus* profoundly influenced several major contemporary philosophical movements. Bertrand Russell has repeatedly acknowledged his indebtedness to Wittgenstein for some of the basic ideas of Logical Atomism—ideas that are embodied in the *Tractatus* and that are still being presupposed, criticized, or defended in current issues of leading philosophical journals. The earliest Logical Positivists, members of the Vienna Circle, devoted themselves for a time to the study of the *Tractatus*, though the extent to which they understood its fundamental teachings is a matter still being debated by philosophers today. Much of what is loosely called "Oxford Philosophy" or "Ordinary Language Philosophy" can be appreciated only as reaction to and struggle against the linguistic doctrines of the *Tractatus*. Still other analytical philosophers who are not to be identified as either logical atomists or positivists or ordinary language philosophers have been strongly influenced by the conception of philosophy set forth in the *Tractatus*.

Quite apart from the historical influence it has had the *Tractatus* is of interest and importance in its own right. There is room for disagreement, however, as to what is most important in it. What one holds to be of greatest significance in the *Tractatus* will depend in great measure upon one's interpretation of that work and one's assessment of the correctness of its doctrines. We have no intention in these introductory remarks of trying to settle any issues of interpretation or evaluation of specific doctrines. We are more interested in indicating the aims and scope of the work.

The significance of the *Tractatus* in the twentieth century may fruitfully be compared with that of Descartes' works in the sixteenth.

Each of the two men developed a genuinely philosophical response to an important contemporary intellectual achievement that was a turning point in the total culture of the West. Descartes responded to the new mathematical physics produced by Copernicus and Galileo which not only changed man's conception of the world in which he lived, but was destined to change the world itself with the technology it brought in its train. Wittgenstein responded to the new mathematical logic produced by Frege, Whitehead, and Russell which not only changed man's conception of the nature of mathematics and logic but promises (or threatens) to change the world with the new cybernetic devices of computers and automata whose design and construction is made possible by the new mathematical logic. It does not seem to have been sufficiently realized as yet that the mathematical logic to whose development Wittgenstein contributed, and the mathematical physics to whose development Descartes contributed, are of the same order of magnitude as revolutionary intellectual forces making for radical social change.

Any major breakthrough in the advance of science is bound to disrupt previously accepted ways of conceiving the world, even though the new conceptions permitted or required by it are not immediately clear. Descartes brought out clearly at least part of the world view implicit in the Copernican and Galilean scientific revolution by exploring the philosophical implications of their doctrines. He maintained that corporeality and quantity must be essential to the physical world in order for the new mathematical physics to apply to it. Wittgenstein brought out clearly at least part of the world view implicit in the Frege–Russell mathematical logic by exploring the philosophical implications of a relational logic involving quantifiers, variables, and truth-functions. He maintained that simple objects and their configurations must be the ultimate constituents of the world in order for the new mathematical logic to apply to it.

Each philosopher, moreover, attempted to delimit the realm of the new science of his day: each purported to draw boundaries to the claims that might legitimately be made on its behalf. Descartes maintained that though mathematical physics is supreme in describing the quantitative corporeal world, it can say nothing about the realm of the spirit. Wittgenstein maintained in the *Tractatus* that though "the conceptual notation of Frege and Russell" is supreme in describing configurations of things in the world, it can say nothing about the realm of value or even about its own status.

The *Tractatus* is a notoriously difficult book. Rudolf Metz wrote: "It is for the ordinary reader a book sealed with seven seals, of which the significance is only to be revealed to the most esoteric devotees, and which, as it seems to us, embodies a very peculiar combination of rigorous mathematical and logical thought and obscure mysticism." And according to Brand Blanshard: ". . . Wittgenstein . . . has the strange distinction of having produced a work on logic beside which the *Logic* of Hegel is luminously intelligible." A number of factors contribute to the obscurity of the *Tractatus*. It does not present a sustained exposition of its ideas but consists of numbered aphorisms whose order is vexed by a numerical key that is not even consistently followed by the author. In the *Tractatus* Wittgenstein seldom explains the historical or polemical context of his utterances, many of which require knowledge of their proper settings to be understood. Even if these incidental though formidable obstacles were removed, many passages of the *Tractatus* would remain difficult because of the new and strange philosophical ideas that they express. Small wonder that commentators and critics have not only disagreed vigorously as to the correctness of the doctrines of the *Tractatus* but have not even reached accord as to what those doctrines are.

The *Tractatus*, because of its difficulty, stands in need of clarification. The essays in this volume attempt to elucidate and to develop ideas stated very briefly and often very darkly in the *Tractatus*. They thus contribute to the needed clarification of the ideas of the *Tractatus*. Making these essays available in a single volume should help make the ideas of the *Tractatus* more accessible.

Except for the first essay, by Professor Ryle, which gives a brief, relatively non-controversial overview of Wittgenstein's life and work, the essays included here are reprinted in the chronological order of their first appearances. Their often conflicting accounts illuminate from quite different perspectives various difficult and obscure corners of the *Tractatus*. Some of these essays are vigorously polemical and contradict each other. They cannot, therefore, all be correct. But the final interpretation and evaluation of the *Tractatus* is still sufficiently distant to require that respectful attention be paid to these very diverse points of view.

As an aid to other scholars working in this field a comprehensive bibliography of works on the *Tractatus* has been appended.

ESSAYS ON
Wittgenstein's
Tractatus

Ludwig Wittgenstein[1]

GILBERT RYLE

AN original and powerful philosopher, Ludwig Wittgenstein, an
Austrian who finally became a naturalized British subject, came to
England shortly before the first World War to study engineering. In
1912, bitten by logical and philosophical problems about the nature
of mathematics, he migrated to Cambridge to work with Bertrand
Russell. During that war, he was in the Austrian army and ended up
a prisoner of war. In this period he wrote his one book, the famous
Tractatus Logico-Philosophicus, of which a not quite reliable English
translation was published in 1922. He taught in an Austrian village
school for some time, during which he came into close philosophical
touch with a few of the leading members of the Vienna Circle. In
1929 he came to Cambridge, where the importance of his ideas had
been quickly recognized. In 1939 he became Professor. For part of
the last war he was a hospital orderly at Guy's Hospital. In 1947 he
resigned his Chair. Besides the *Tractatus*, he published only one
article.

In the last twenty years, so far as I know, he published nothing;
attended no philosophical conferences; gave no lectures outside
Cambridge; corresponded on philosophical subjects with nobody
and discouraged the circulation even of notes of his Cambridge lectures and discussions. But with his serious students and a few col-
leagues, economists, mathematicians, physicists and philosophers,
he would discuss philosophical matters unwearyingly. Yet from his
jealously preserved little pond, there have spread waves over the
philosophical thinking of much of the English-speaking world.
Philosophers who never met him—and few of us did meet him—can
be heard talking philosophy in his tones of voice; and students who
can barely spell his name now wrinkle up their noses at things which

[1] From *Analysis*, vol. 12, no. 1, October, 1951, pp. 1–9. Reprinted by permission of
the editor and the author. A B.B.C. Third Programme talk, given on May 26, 1951.

had a bad smell for him. So what is the difference that he has made to philosophy?

It is vain to try to forecast the verdict of history upon a contemporary. I have to try to do this for one who has for about 30 years avoided any publication of his ideas. So what I offer is a set of impressions, interpretations, partly, of mere echoes of echoes.

From the time of Locke to that of Bradley philosophers had debated their issues as if they were psychological issues. Certainly their problems were, often, genuine philosophical problems, but they discussed them in psychological terms. And if they asked themselves, as they seldom did ask, what they were investigating, they tended to say that they were investigating the workings of the mind, just as physical scientists investigate the working of bodies. The sorts of "Mental Science" that they talked were sometimes positivistic, sometimes idealistic, according, roughly, as they were more impressed by chemistry than by theology or vice versa.

However, fifty years ago philosophers were getting their feet out of these psychological boots. For psychology had now begun to be done in laboratories and clinics, so arm-chair psychology became suspect. But even more influential was the fact that logical quandaries had recently been exposed at the very roots of pure mathematics. The mathematicians needed lifelines, which they could not provide for themselves. Logicians had to work out the logic of mathematics, and they could not base this logic on the findings of any empirical science, especially of so hazy a science as psychology. If logic and philosophy were not psychological enquiries, what were they?

During the first twenty years of this century, many philosophers gave another answer to this question, a Platonic answer. Philosophy studies not the workings of minds or, of course, of bodies either; it studies the denizens of a third domain, the domain of abstract, or conceptual entities, of possibilities, essences, timelessly subsisting universals, numbers, truths, falsities, values and meanings. This idea enabled its holders to continue to say that philosophy was the science of something, while denying that it was the science of any ordinary subject-matter; to champion its autonomy as a discipline, while denying that it was just one science among others; to give it the standing of a science while admitting its unlikeness to the sciences. Thus the question "What are philosophy and logic the sciences of?" received a new answer, though one with a disquietingly dreamlike ring. It was the answer given by Frege and by Russell.

In Vienna thinkers were facing much the same question, though from an opposite angle. Whereas here it had been widely assumed that philosophy was Mental Science, and therefore just a sister-science to physics, chemistry, zoology, etc., in the German-speaking world it was widely assumed that philosophy stood to the other sciences not as sister but as mother—or even governess. Somehow professors of philosophy there enjoyed such a pedagogic domination that they could dictate even to the scientists. *Of course* philosophers were the right people to decide whether the teachings of Darwin, Freud and Einstein were true.

Late in the nineteenth century Mach had mutinied against this view that metaphysics was a governess-science. By the early 1920s this mutiny became a rebellion. The Vienna Circle repudiated the myth that the questions of physics, biology, psychology or mathematics can be decided by metaphysical considerations. Metaphysics is not a governess-science or a sister-science; it is not a science at all. The classic case was that of Einstein's Relativity principle. The claims of professors of philosophy to refute this principle were baseless. Scientific questions are soluble only by scientific methods, and these are not the methods of philosophers.

Thus, in England the question was this. What are the special virtues which the natural and the mathematical sciences lack but logic and philosophy possess, such that these must be invoked when the former find themselves in quandaries? In Vienna the question was this. Given that philosophers cannot decide scientific questions, what are the logical virtues which scientific procedures possess, but philosophical procedures lack? The contrast between philosophy and science was drawn in both places. In Vienna, where the autonomy of the sciences was actually challenged, the object was to expose the pretensions of philosophy as a governess-science. Here, where, save for psychology, the autonomy of the sciences was not seriously challenged, it was drawn in order to extract the positive functions of logic and philosophy. Philosophy was regarded in Vienna as a blood-sucking parasite; in England as a medicinal leech.

To Wittgenstein the question came in its English form. And so he could not be called one of the Logical Positivists. Their polemics were not his; and his quest for the positive function of logic and philosophy was not, until much later, theirs. He was influenced by Frege and Russell, not by Mach. He had not himself felt the dead hand of professional philosophy which cramped, and still cramps, even scientific thought in Germany and Austria. He, conversely, himself helped to fix the logical lifelines for the mathematicians.

I want to show how Wittgenstein transformed and answered what was all the time his master-question, "What can philosophers and logicians do, and how should they do it?"

I have said that after a long imprisonment in psychological idioms, philosophy was, for a time, re-housed in Platonic idioms. But this was

3

only a temporary asylum. For after a short period during which philosophers tried not to mind the dreamlike character of the new asylum, something awoke them from the dream. Russell, in his enquiries into the logical principles underlying mathematics, found that he could not well help constructing statements which had the logically disturbing property that they were true only on condition that they were false, and false only on condition that they were true. Some of these self-subverting statements seemed to be inherent in the very basis which was to make mathematics secure. There was a major leak in the dry dock which Frege and he had built for mathematics.

Russell found a patch for the leak. Underlying the familiar distinction between truth and falsehood, there is a more radical distinction between significance and meaninglessness. True and false statements are both significant, but some forms of words, with the vocabulary and constructions of statements, are neither true nor false, but nonsensical—and nonsensical not for reasons of wording or of grammar, but for logical reasons. The self-subverting statements were of this sort, neither true nor false, but nonsensical simulacra of statements. Notice, it is only of such things as complex verbal expressions that we can ask whether they are significant or nonsense. The question could not be asked of mental processes; or of Platonic entities. So logic is from the start concerned, not with these but rather with what can or cannot be significantly said. Its subject-matter is a linguistic one, though its tasks are not at all those of philology.

In Wittgenstein's *Tractatus* this departmental conclusion is generalized. All logic and all philosophy are enquiries into what makes it significant or nonsensical to say certain things. The sciences aim at saying what is true about the world; philosophy aims at disclosing only the logic of what can be truly or even falsely said about the world. This is why philosophy is not a sister-science or a parent-science; that its business is not to add to the number of scientific statements, but to disclose their logic.

Wittgenstein begins by considering how a sentence, a map, a diagram or a scale-model can represent or even significantly misrepresent the facts. The isolated words 'London' and 'south' are not true or false. Nor can a single dot on a sheet of paper be an accurate or inaccurate map. The sentence 'London is north of Brighton' is true. The same words, differently arranged as 'Brighton is north of London', make a false statement. Arranged as 'South is London of Brighton' they make a farrago which is neither true nor false, but nonsense. For dots on paper to represent or misrepresent the direction of Brighton from London, there must be a dot for each town and they must be set out in accordance with some convention for points of the compass. For a statement, map or diagram to be true or false, there must be a plurality of words or marks; but, more, these bits must be put together in certain ways. And underlying the fact that the truth or falsity of the statement or map partly depends upon the particular way in which its bits are arranged, there lies the fact that whether a significant statement or map results at all, depends wholly on the general way in which the bits are put together. Some ways of jumbling them together are ruled out. What rules rule them out?

In the *Tractatus* Wittgenstein came to the frustrating conclusion that these principles of arrangement inevitably baffle significant statement. To try to tell what makes the difference between significant and nonsensical talk is itself to cross the divide between significant and nonsensical talk. Philosophizing can, indeed, open our eyes to these structural principles, but it cannot issue in significant statements of them. Philosophy is not a science; it cannot yield theories or doctrines. None the less it can be skilful or unskilful, successful or unsuccessful. It is in pursuing the activity itself that we see what we need to see. Rather like learning music or tennis, learning philosophy does not result in our being able to tell what we have learnt; though, as in music and tennis, we can show what we have learnt.

Now it is true that philosophical clarity is achieved in the acts of appreciating arguments rather than in propounding theorems. But it is false that all philosophical talk is nonsensical talk. Wittgenstein had himself said very effective things, and talking effectively is not talking nonsensically. What had brought him to this frustrating conclusion? When he wrote the *Tractatus*, he was, I think, over-influenced by his own analogies between saying things and making maps, diagrams and scale-models. Certainly, for marks on paper to constitute a temperature-chart, or for spoken words to constitute a significant statement, the dots and the words must be arranged according to rules and conventions. Only if the zigzag of dots on the nurse's graph-paper is systematically correlated with the thermometer-readings taken at successive moments of a day, can it represent or even misrepresent the alterations in the patient's temperature. Only if words are organized according to a number of complex general rules does a true or false statement result.

Suppose we now asked the nurse to depict on a second sheet of graph-paper, not the course of the patient's temperature, but the rules for representing his temperature by dots on graph paper, she would be baffled. Nor can the rules and conventions of map-making themselves be mapped. So Wittgenstein argued in the *Tractatus* that the philosopher or logician is debarred from saying what it is that makes things said significant or nonsensical. He can show it, but not tell it. After the *Tractatus* he realized that though saying things does resemble depicting things or mapping things in the respect for which he originally drew the analogy, it does not resemble them in all respects. Just as the nurse can tell, though not depict, how the temperature-chart represents or misrepresents the patient's temperature, so the philosopher can tell why, say, a scientist's statement makes or does not make sense. What alone would be absurd would be a sentence which purported to convey a comment upon its own significance or meaninglessness.

The *Tractatus* has two distinct but connected aims. The first, which I have crudely sketched, is to show both what philosophy is not, namely any sort of a science, and what it is, namely an activity of exploring the internal logic of what is said, for example, in this or that scientific theory. The second, which I shall not even try to sketch, is to show what sort of an enquiry Formal Logic is. This brings me to a general point about the *Tractatus*. Wittgenstein's first interest had been in the logic of mathematics and thence in the logical paradoxes which were the big leak in the dry dock that Frege and Russell had built. He was, therefore, equipped and predisposed to squeeze whatever can be significantly said into the few statement-patterns with which the logic of mathematical statements operates. He used its terminology, its codes, and its abacus-operations in his task of exploring various philosophical issues, and, above all, his own master-issue, that of the nature of philosophizing itself. In consequence, the *Tractatus* is, in large measure, a closed book to those who lack this technical equipment. Few people can read it without feeling that something important is happening; but few experts, even, can say what is happening.

But this is not the end of the story. Maybe it is only the preface. For, after lying fallow for some years, Wittgenstein returned to philosophy. His teaching in this period differs markedly from that of the *Tractatus*; it even repudiates parts of the *Tractatus*.

First, he no longer forces all expressions into the favoured few patterns of the logic of mathematics. With this goes a revolt against moulds of any sorts. The rubrics of logical systems and the abstract terms of philosophical schools are like the shoes of Chinese ladies, which deformed their feet and prevented them from walking on them. Philosophical elucidation is still inspection of expressions, but it is no longer inspection through the slots of a logician's stencil or through the prisms of a scholastic classification-system. His diction has reverted from that of a Russell discussing esoteric matters with mathematicians to that of a Socrates discussing everyday ideas with undoctrinated young men. Nor does he now elucidate only the propositions of the sciences. Like Moore, he explores the logic of all the things that all of us say.

Next, though I think that his master-problem is still that of the nature, tasks and methods of the philosophical activity, he no longer thinks that philosophers are condemned to trying to say the unsayable. But he now avoids any general statement of the nature of philosophy, not because this would be to say the unsayable, but because it would be to say a scholastic and therefore an obscuring thing. In philosophy, generalizations are unclarifications. The nature of philosophy is to be taught by producing concrete specimens of it. As the medical student learns surgery by witnessing and practising operations on dead and on live subjects, so the student of philosophy learns what philosophy is by following and practising operations on particular quandary-generating ways of talking. Thus Wittgenstein would rove, apparently aimlessly because without any statement of aim, from one concrete puzzle to its brothers, its cousins, its parents and its associates, demonstrating both what makes them puzzling and how to resolve them—demonstrating, but not telling; going through the moves, but not compiling a manual of them; teaching a skill, not dictating a doctrine.

One favourite procedure of his might be called the "tea-tasting method". Tea-tasters do not lump their samples into two or three comprehensive types. Rather they savour each sample and try to place it next door to its closest neighbours, and this not in respect of just one discriminable quality, but along the lengths of various lines of qualities. So Wittgenstein would exhibit the characteristic manner of working of a particular expression, by matching it against example after example of expressions progressively diverging from it in various respects and directions. He would show how striking similarities may go with important but ordinarily unremarked differences, and how we are tempted to lean too heavily on their similarities and hence to be tripped up by their latent differences.

For philosophers do not examine expressions at random. The quest for their internal logic is forced upon us by the fact that we find ourselves already caught up in unforeseen entanglements. Why do we slide into quandaries? Let me invent an example. We find ourselves talking as if like a train, so time itself might one day slow down and stop. We divide a train into coaches and coaches into compartments. We divide a month into weeks and weeks into days. When a train is passing me, some coaches are beyond me, some are still to come, and one compartment of one coach is directly abreast of me. I look at its occupants through the window. Surely time is like this. Last week has gone, next week is still to come, but I can exchange glances with the occupants of Now. So, as trains always slow down and stop somewhere, what makes time puff on so tirelessly? Might not Now be the last compartment of the last coach? Yet surely not; there would still be something behind it, if only the empty wind. You see that it is tempting, but also that it smells like nonsense to speak of the last compartment of time. Why may we say some things about time which are very much like some things that we legitimately say about trains, when to some of the proper corollaries of what we say about trains there correspond no proper corollaries about time? To answer this question, we should have to examine the functioning of whole ranges of things that we say about trains, rivers and winds; about moving shadows, rainbows and reflections; about perpetual motion machines, stars, clocks, sundials, and calendars; about the series of numbers, days of the week and minutes of the day. And then we may see why we slid and no longer incline to slide from the proper corollaries of familiar dictions about trains to corresponding corollaries of somewhat similar dictions about time. We see that we had overpressed certain analogies between ways of talking; and that we were so dominated by a favourite model, that we had gone on using it where it could no longer work. And now we know, in a way, what time is, though there is no shorter or better way of saying what time is than by going through again the same sort of process of linguistic tea-tasting.

I must conclude. Wittgenstein has made our generation of philosophers self-conscious about philosophy itself. It is, of course, possible for a person to be very thoughtful about the nature and methods of an activity, without being made any the better at performing it. The centipede of the poem ran well until he began to wonder how he ran. Maybe we have been made a bit neurotic about the nature of our calling. But Wittgenstein's demolition of the idea that philosophy is a sort of science has at least made us vigilant about our tools. We no longer try to use for our problems the methods of arguing which are the right ones for demonstrating theorems or establishing hypotheses. In particular we have learnt to pay deliberate attention to what can and cannot be said. What had, since the early days of this century, been the practice of G. E. Moore has received a rationale from Wittgenstein; and I expect that when the curtain is lifted we shall also find that Wittgenstein's concrete methods have increased the power, scope and delicacy of the methods by which Moore has for so long explored in detail the internal logic of what we say.

Review of 'Tractatus'[1]

FRANK P. RAMSEY

THIS is a most important book containing original ideas on a large range of topics, forming a coherent system, which whether or not it be, as the author claims, in essentials the final solution of the problems dealt with, is of extraordinary interest and deserves the attention of all philosophers. And even if the system be altogether unsound the book contains a large number of profound *obiter dicta* and criticisms of other theories. It is, however, very difficult to understand, in spite of the fact that it is printed with the German text and an English translation on opposite pages. Mr Wittgenstein writes, not consecutive prose, but short propositions numbered so as to show the emphasis laid upon them in his exposition. This gives his work an attractive epigrammatic flavour, and perhaps makes it more accurate in detail, as each sentence must have received separate consideration; but it seems to have prevented him from giving adequate explanations of many of his technical terms and theories, perhaps because explanations require some sacrifice of accuracy.

This deficiency is partly made up by Mr Russell's Introduction; but it is possible that he is not an infallible guide to Mr Wittgenstein's meaning. "In order to understand Mr Wittgenstein's book," says Mr Russell, "it is necessary to realize what is the problem with which he is concerned. In the part of his theory which deals with Symbolism he is concerned with the conditions that would have to be fulfilled by a logically perfect language." This seems to be a very doubtful generalization; there are, indeed, passages in which Mr Wittgenstein is explicitly concerned with a logically perfect, and not with any language, e.g. the discussion of 'logical syntax' in 3.325 ff.; but in general he seems to maintain that his doctrines apply to ordinary languages in spite of the appearance of the contrary (see

[1] From *Mind*, vol. 32, no. 128, October, 1923, pp. 465–78. Reprinted by permission of the editor and the estate of the author.

9

especially 4.002 ff.). This is obviously an important point, for this wider application greatly increases the interest and diminishes the plausibility of any thesis such as that which Mr Russell declares to be perhaps the most fundamental in Mr Wittgenstein's theory; that "in order that a certain sentence should assert a certain fact there must, however the language may be constructed, be something in common between the structure of the sentence and the structure of the fact".

This doctrine appears to depend on the difficult notions of a 'picture' and its 'form of representation', which I shall now try to explain and criticize.

A picture is a fact, the fact that its elements are combined with one another in a definite way. These elements are co-ordinated with certain objects (the constituents of the fact of which the picture is a picture). These co-ordinations constitute the representing relation which makes the picture a picture. This representing relation "belongs to the picture" (2.1513); this, I think, means that whenever we talk of a picture we have in mind some representing relation in virtue of which it is a picture. Under these circumstances we say that the picture represents that the objects are so combined with one another as are the elements of the picture, and this is the sense of the picture. And I think this must be taken to be the definition of 'represents' and of 'sense'; that is to say, that when we say that a picture represents that certain objects are combined in a certain way, we mean merely that the elements of the picture are combined in that way, and are co-ordinated with the objects by the representing relation which belongs to the picture. (That this is a definition follows, I think, from 5.542.)

Light may be thrown on the 'form of representation' by the following remarks made earlier in the book on the structure and form of facts. "The way in which objects hang together in the atomic fact is the structure of the atomic fact. The form is the possibility of the structure. The structure of the fact consists of the structures of the atomic facts" (2.032, 2.033, 2.034). The only point which I can see in the distinction between structure and form, is that the insertion of 'possibility' may include the case in which the alleged fact whose form we are considering is not a fact, so that we can talk of the form of the fact *aRb*, whether or no *aRb* is true, provided it is logically possible. It is to be regretted that the above definitions do not make it clear whether two facts can ever have the same structure or the same form; it looks as if two atomic facts might well have the same structure, because objects hung together in the same way in each of them. But it seems from remarks later in the book that the structure of the fact is not merely the way in which the objects hang together but depends also on what objects they are, so that two different facts never have the same structure.

A picture is a fact and as such has a structure and a form; we are, however, given the following new definitions of its 'structure' and its 'form of representation' in 2.15, 2.151. "That the elements of the picture are combined with one another in a definite way, represents that the things are so combined with one another. This connection of the elements of the picture is called its structure, and the possibility of this structure is called the form of representation of the picture. The form of representation is the possibility that the things are so combined with one another as are the elements of the picture." This passage is puzzling; firstly, because we have here two different definitions of the form of representation, and secondly, because it is not obvious how to interpret "this connection" in the first of the two definitions; it may refer to the definite way in which the elements are combined, or to the whole of the preceding sentence, i.e. "this connection of the elements" may be that their combination represents a similar combination of the things. On neither interpretation does the first definition seem to coincide with the second. We can only hope to decide between these possible meanings of 'form of representation' by considering the things which Mr Wittgenstein says about it. Its chief property, which makes it of fundamental importance in his theory, is that asserted in 2.17: "What the picture must have in common with reality in order to be able to represent it after its manner —rightly or falsely—is its form of representation." Further, "what every picture, of whatever form, must have in common with reality in order to be able to represent it at all—rightly or falsely—is the logical form, that is, the form of reality. If the form of representation is the logical form, then the picture is called a logical picture. Every picture is *also* a logical picture. (On the other hand, for example, not every picture is spatial.)" (2.18, 2.181, 2.182.) It appears, then, that a picture may have several forms of representation, but one of these must be *the* logical form; and that it is not asserted that the picture must have the same logical form as what it pictures, but that all pictures must have *the* logical form. This also makes more plausible the deduction that the logical form of representation cannot be represented; for that it was common to one picture and reality could afford no ground for supposing that it could not be represented in another picture.

Now it is easy to see a sense in which a picture may have the spatial and must also have the logical form, namely, by taking the form to be the (possibility of the) way in which the elements of the picture are combined. (One of the interpretations of the first definition given above.) This may be logical, as when the colour of a patch on a map represents the height above sea-level of the corresponding patch of country; the elements of the picture are combined as predicate and subject, and this represents that the corresponding things are also combined as predicate and subject. On the other hand, the form may be spatial, as when one dot being between two others represents that a certain town is between two others; but in this case we can also regard betweenness not as the way in which the dots are combined but as another element in the picture, which corresponds with itself. Then since betweenness and the dots are combined, not spatially, but as triple relation and its relata, that is logically, the form is logical. Here then we have something which may be spatial and must also be logical; but it does not follow that this is the form of representation, for the form of representation may be some more complicated entity involving this and so derivatively spatial or logical. If, indeed, the above were what were meant by the form of representation, then in saying that a picture must have the logical form Mr Wittgenstein would be saying no more than that it must be a fact; and in saying that we cannot represent or speak about the logical form of representation, no more than that we cannot talk about what makes a fact a fact, nor ultimately *about* facts at all, because every statement apparently about facts is really about their constituents. These things he certainly believes, but it seems to me unlikely that his complicated propositions about the form of representation amount to no more than this. Probably he is confused and does not use the term consistently; and if we revert to the second of the definitions given above, "The form of representation is the possibility that the things are so combined with one another as are the elements of the picture," we may discover another sense in which the picture has the form of representation in common with the pictured, namely, that the things with which its elements are co-ordinated by the representing relation are of such types that they *can* be combined in the same way as the elements of the picture; and so we arrive at the important principle that "the picture contains the possibility of the state of affairs which it represents" (2.203). It seems to me, for reasons explained later, that the independent acceptance of this principle will justify almost all the non-mystical deductions which Mr Wittgenstein makes from the necessity of something in common between the picture and the world, which cannot itself be represented; and that these deductions can so be given a firmer basis than is provided by the nature of this elusive entity, the form of representation, which is intrinsically impossible to discuss.

In order to obtain any further comprehension of what Mr Wittgenstein thinks a sentence must have in common with the fact which it asserts, or, indeed, of most of his book, it is necessary to understand his use of the word '*proposition*'. This is, I think, made easier by the introduction of two words used by C. S. Peirce. A word, in the sense in which there are a dozen words 'the' on a page, he called a *token*; and these dozen tokens are all instances of one *type*, the word 'the'. Besides 'word' there are other words which have this type-token ambiguity; thus a sensation, a thought, an emotion or an idea may be either a type or a token. And in Mr Wittgenstein's usage, in contrast, for instance, to Mr Russell's in *The Principles of Mathematics*, 'proposition' also has type-token ambiguity.

A *propositional sign* is a sentence; but this statement must be qualified, for by 'sentence' may be meant something of the same nature as the words of which it is composed. But a propositional sign differs essentially from a word because it is not an object or class of objects, but a fact, "the fact that its elements, the words, are combined in it in a definite way" (3.14). Thus 'propositional sign' has type-token ambiguity; the tokens (like those of any sign) are grouped into types by physical similarity (and by conventions associating certain noises with certain shapes) just as are the instances of a word. But a *proposition* is a type whose instances consist of all propositional sign tokens which have in common, not a certain appearance, but a certain *sense*.

As to the relation between a proposition and a thought Mr Wittgenstein is rather obscure; but I think his meaning is that a thought is a type whose tokens have in common a certain sense, and include the tokens of the corresponding proposition, but include also other non-verbal tokens; these, however, are not relevantly different from the verbal ones, so that it is sufficient to consider the latter. He says "It is clear that 'A believes that *p*', 'A thinks *p*', 'A says *p*', are of the form ' "*p*" says *p*' " (5.542), and so explicitly reduces the question as to the analysis of judgment, to which Mr Russell has at various times given different answers, to the question "What is it for a proposition token to have a certain sense?" This reduction seems to me an important advance, and as the question to which it leads is of fundamental importance, I propose to examine carefully what Mr Wittgenstein says by way of answering it.

First, it may be remarked that if we can answer our question we incidentally solve the problem of truth; or rather, it is already evident that there is no such problem. For if a thought or proposition token '*p*' says *p*, then it is called true if *p*, and false if $\sim p$. We can say that it is true if its sense agrees with reality, or if the possible state of affairs which it represents is the actual one, but these formulations only express the above definition in other words.

According to Mr Wittgenstein a proposition token is a logical picture; and so its sense should be given by the definition of the sense of a picture; accordingly the sense of a proposition is that the things meant by its elements (the words) are combined with one another in the same way as are the elements themselves, that is, logically.

13

But it is evident that, to say the least, this definition is very incomplete; it can be applied literally only in one case, that of the completely analysed elementary proposition. (It may be explained that an elementary proposition is one which asserts the existence of an atomic fact, and that a proposition token is completely analysed if there is an element in it corresponding to each object occurring in its sense.) Thus if '*a*' means *a*, '*b*' *b*, and '*R*', or more accurately the relation we establish between '*a*' and '*b*' by writing '*aRb*', means *R*, then that '*a*' stands in this relation to '*b*' says that *aRb*, and this is its sense. But this simple scheme must evidently be modified, if, for example, one word is used for 'having *R* to *b*' so that the proposition is not completely analysed; or if we have to deal with a more complicated proposition which contains logical constants such as 'not' or 'if', which do not represent objects as names do. Mr Wittgenstein does not make it quite clear how he proposes to deal with either of these difficulties. As regards the first, which he almost ignores, he may reasonably plead that it results from the enormous complication of colloquial language, which cannot be disentangled *a priori*; for in a perfect language all propositions would be completely analysed except when we defined a sign to take the place of a string of simple signs; then, as he says, the defined sign would signify *via* the signs by which it is defined. But the other difficulty must be faced, since we cannot be satisfied with a theory which deals only with elementary propositions.

The sense of propositions in general is explained by reference to elementary propositions. With regard to *n* elementary propositions there are 2^n possibilities of their truth and falsehood, which are called the truth-possibilities of the elementary propositions; similarly there are 2^n possibilities of existence and non-existence of the corresponding atomic facts. Mr Wittgenstein says that any proposition is the expression of agreement and disagreement with the truth-possibilities of certain elementary propositions, and its sense is its agreement and disagreement with the possibilities of existence and non-existence of the corresponding atomic facts. (4.4, 4.2.)

This is illustrated by the following symbolism for truth-functions. *T* stands for true, *F* for false, and we write the four possibilities for two elementary propositions thus:

p	*q*
T	*T*
F	*T*
T	*F*
F	*F*

Now by setting a *T* against a possibility for agreement and leaving a blank for disagreement we can express, for example, $p \supset q$, thus:

p	q	
T	T	T
F	T	T
T	F	
F	F	T

Or, adopting a conventional order for the possibilities, $(TT\!-\!T)$ (p, q). Evidently this notation does not in any way require p, q to be elementary propositions; and it can be extended to include propositions containing apparent variables. Thus p, q may be given not by enumeration but as all values of a propositional function, i.e. all propositions containing a certain expression (defined as "any part of a proposition which characterizes its sense" (3.31)); and $(\text{-}\,\text{-}\,\text{-}\,\text{-}\,\text{-}\,T)$ $(\bar{\xi})$, where the solitary T expresses agreement only with the possibility that all the arguments are false, and $\bar{\xi}$ is the set of values of fx, is what is written ordinarily as $\sim : (\exists x).fx$. So every proposition is a truth-function of elementary propositions, and many differently constructed propositional signs are the same proposition, because, expressing agreement and disagreement with the same truth-possibilities, they have the same sense and are the same truth-function of elementary propositions. Thus

$$q \supset p : \sim q \supset p \text{ and } \sim (\sim p \vee \sim p) \text{ are the same as } p.$$

This leads to an extremely simple theory of inference; if we call those truth-possibilities with which a proposition agrees, its truth-grounds, then q follows from p if the truth-grounds of p are contained among those of q. In this case Mr Wittgenstein also says that the sense of q is contained in that of p, that in asserting p we are incidentally asserting q. I think this statement is really a definition of containing as regards senses, and an extension of the meaning of assert partly in conformity with ordinary usage, which probably agrees as regards $p.q$ and p, or $(x).fx$ and fa but not otherwise.

There are two extreme cases of great importance; if we express disagreement with all the truth-possibilities we get a *contradiction*, if agreement with them all, a *tautology*, which says nothing. The propositions of logic are tautologies; and to have made clear this, their essential characteristic, is a remarkable achievement.

We have now to consider whether the above is an adequate account of what it is for a proposition token to have a certain sense;

and it seems to me that it certainly is not. For it is really only an account of what senses there are, not of what propositional signs have what sense. It enables us to substitute for ' "*p*" says *p*', ' "*p*" expresses agreement with these truth-possibilities and disagreement with these others'; but the latter formulation cannot be regarded as an ultimate analysis of the former, and it is not at all clear how its further analysis proceeds. We have therefore to look elsewhere for the answer to our question. Towards this answer Mr Wittgenstein does make a clear contribution; in 5.542, he says that in ' "*p*" says *p*' we have a co-ordination of facts by means of a co-ordination of their objects. But this account is incomplete because the sense is not completely determined by the objects which occur in it; nor is the propositional sign completely constituted by the names which occur in it, for in it there may also be logical constants which are not co-ordinated with objects and complete the determination of the sense in a way which is left obscure.

If we had only to deal with one logical symbolism I do not think there would be any difficulty. For, apart from variation in the names used, there would be a rule giving all propositional signs which, in that symbolism, had a certain sense, and we could complete the definition of 'sense' by adding to it these rules. Thus ' "*p*" says that $\sim aRb$' would, supposing us to be dealing with the symbolism of *Principia Mathematica*, be analysed as follows: call anything meaning *a*, '*a*', and so on, and call '*a*' '*R*' '*b*', '*q*'; then '*p*' is '$\sim q$' or '$\sim \sim \sim q$' or '$\sim q \vee \sim q$' or any of the other symbols constructed according to a definite rule. (It may, of course, be doubted whether it is possible to formulate this rule, as it seems to presuppose the whole of symbolic logic; but in any perfect notation it might be possible; for example in Mr Wittgenstein's notation with *T*'s and *F*'s there would be no difficulty.) But it is obvious that this is not enough; it will not give an analysis of '*A* asserts *p*', but only of '*A* asserts *p* using such-and-such a logical notation'. But we may well know that a Chinaman has a certain opinion without having an idea of the logical notation he uses. Also the evidently significant statement that Germans use 'nicht' for not becomes part of the definition of such words as 'believe', 'think' when used of Germans.

It is very hard to see a way out of this difficulty; one may perhaps be found in Mr Russell's suggestion in *The Analysis of Mind* (p. 250) that there may be special belief feelings occurring in disjunction and implication. Logical constants might then be significant as substitutes for these feelings, which would form the basis of a universal logical symbolism of human thought. But it looks as if Mr Wittgenstein believes in another kind of solution, going back to his earlier statement that the sense of a picture is that the things are so combined with one another as are the elements of the picture. The natural interpretation of this in our present context is that we can only represent that *a* does not have a certain relation to *b*, by making '*a*' not have a certain relation to '*b*', or in general that only a negative fact can assert a negative fact, only an implicative fact an implicative fact, and so on. This is absurd and evidently not what he means; but he does seem to hold that a proposition token resembles its sense somehow in this sort of way. Thus he says (5.512), "That which denies in '$\sim p$' is not '$\sim$', but that which all signs of this notation, which deny p, have in common. Hence the common rule according to which '$\sim p$', '$\sim \sim \sim p$', '$\sim p \vee \sim p$', '$\sim p . \sim p$', etc., etc. (to infinity) are constructed. And this which is common to them all mirrors denial." I cannot understand how it mirrors denial. It certainly does not do so in the simple way in which the conjunction of two propositions mirrors the conjunction of their senses. This difference between conjunction and the other truth-functions can be seen in the fact that to believe p and q is to believe p and to believe q; but to believe p or q is not the same as to believe p or to believe q, nor to believe not-p as not to believe p.

We must now turn to one of the most interesting of Mr Wittgenstein's theories, that there are certain things which cannot be said but only shown, and these constitute the Mystical. The reason why they cannot be said is that they have to do with the logical form, which propositions have in common with reality. What sort of things they are is explained in 4.122: "We can speak in a certain sense of formal properties of objects and atomic facts, or of properties of the structure of facts, and in the same sense of formal relations and relations of structures. [Instead of property of the structure I also say 'internal property'; instead of relation of structures 'internal relation'. I introduce these expressions in order to show the reason for the confusion, very widespread among philosophers, between internal relations and proper (external) relations.] The holding of such internal properties and relations cannot, however, be asserted by propositions, but shows itself in the propositions, which present the atomic facts and treat of the objects in question." As I have already said, it does not seem to me that the nature of the logical form is sufficiently clear to provide any cogent arguments in favour of such conclusions; and I think that a better approach to the treatment of internal properties may be given by the following criterion: "A property is internal if it is unthinkable that its object does not possess it" (4.123).

It is a principle of Mr Wittgenstein's, and, if true, is a very important discovery, that every genuine proposition asserts something possible, but not necessary. This follows from his account of a proposition as the expression of agreement and disagreement with

17

truth-possibilities of independent elementary propositions, so that the only necessity is that of tautology, the only impossibility that of contradiction. There is great difficulty in holding this; for Mr Wittgenstein admits that a point in the visual field *cannot* be both red and blue; and, indeed, otherwise, since he thinks induction has no logical basis, we should have no reason for thinking that we may not come upon a visual point which is both red and blue. Hence he says that 'This is both red and blue' is a contradiction. This implies that the apparently simple concepts red, blue (supposing us to mean by those words absolutely specific shades) are really complex and formally incompatible. He tries to show how this may be, by analysing them in terms of vibrations. But even supposing that the physicist thus provides an analysis of what we mean by 'red', Mr Wittgenstein is only reducing the difficulty to that of the *necessary* properties of space, time, and matter or the ether. He explicitly makes it depend on the *impossibility* of a particle being in two places at the same time. These necessary properties of space and time are hardly capable of a further reduction of this kind. For example, considering between in point of time as regards my experiences; if *B* is between *A* and *D*, and *C* between *B* and *D*, then *C* must be between *A* and *D*; but it is hard to see how this can be a formal tautology.

But not all apparently necessary truths can be supposed, or are by Mr Wittgenstein supposed, to be tautologies. There are also the internal properties of which it is unthinkable that their objects do not possess them. Sentences apparently asserting such properties of objects are held by Mr Wittgenstein to be nonsense, but to stand in some obscure relation to something inexpressible. This last seems to be involved by his reason for thinking that they are nonsense, which is that what they are meant to assert cannot be asserted. But it seems to me possible to give reasons why these sentences are nonsense and a general account of their origin and apparent significance, which have no mystical implications.

Sentences of this kind, which we call 'pseudo-propositions', arise in various ways depending on our language. One source is the grammatical necessity for such nouns as 'object' and 'thing', which do not like ordinary common nouns correspond to propositional functions. Thus from 'This is a red object' appears to follow the pseudo-proposition 'This is an object', which in the symbolism of *Principia Mathematica* could not be written at all. But the commonest and most important source is the substitution of names or relative names for descriptions. (I use 'relative names' to include '*p*', the expression for a given sense *p*; in contrast to a description of that sense, such as 'what I said'.) Usually this is legitimate; for if we have a propositional schema containing blanks, the significance of the schema when the blanks are filled by descriptions presupposes, in general, its significance when they are filled by the names of things answering to the descriptions. Thus the analysis of 'The ϕ is red' is 'There is one and only one thing which is ϕ; and it is red'; and the occurrence in this of 'It is red' shows that the significance of our proposition presupposes the significance of 'a is red', where a is of the type of the ϕ. But sometimes this is not the case because the proposition containing the description must be analysed a little differently. Thus 'The ϕ exists' is not 'There is one and only one thing which is ϕ; and it exists', but simply 'There is one and only one thing which is ϕ'; so that its significance does not presuppose that of 'a exists', which is nonsense, for its truth could be seen by mere inspection without comparison with reality, as is never the case with a genuine proposition. But partly because we sometimes fail to distinguish 'a exists' from 'The object meant by "a" exists', and partly because '— exists' is always significant when the blank is filled by a description, and we are not sufficiently sensitive to the difference between descriptions and names; 'a exists' sometimes feels as if it were significant. Mr Wittgenstein gives in to this deceptive feeling so far as to hold that the existence of the name 'a' shows that a exists, but that this cannot be asserted; it seems, however, to be a principal component in the mystical: "Not *how* the world is, is the mystical, but *that* it is" (6.44).

Our next example is provided by identity of which Mr Wittgenstein gives an important destructive criticism: "Russell's definition of '$=$' won't do; because according to it one cannot say that two objects have all their properties in common. (Even if this proposition is never true, it is nevertheless *significant*)" (5.5302). And '$a = b$' must be a pseudo-proposition since it is true or false *a priori* according as 'a', 'b' are names for the same or different things. If now we adopt the new convention that two different signs in one proposition must have different meanings, we get a new analysis of descriptions not involving identity. For $f(\imath x)(\phi x)$, instead of

$$(\exists c) : \phi x \supset_x x = c.fc,$$

we have $\qquad (\exists x).\phi x.fx : \sim (\exists x, y).\phi x.\phi y.$

And since $(\imath x)(\phi x) = c$ is analysed as $\phi c : \sim (\exists x, y).\phi x.\phi y$ we see that '$— = —$' is only significant when one blank at least is filled by a description. Incidentally this rejection of identity may have serious consequences in the theory of aggregates and cardinal number; it is, for example, hardly plausible to say that two classes are only of equal number when there is a one-one relation whose domain is the one and converse domain the other, unless such relations can be constructed by means of identity.

Next I shall show how this account applies to internal properties of the senses of propositions, or, if they are true propositions, the corresponding facts. '*p* is about *a*' is an example; its significance might be thought to follow from that of 'He said something about *a*'; but if we reflect on the analysis of the latter proposition we shall see that this is not the case; for it evidently reduces not to 'There is a *p* which he asserted and which is about *a*' but to 'There is a function ϕ such that he asserted ϕa', which does not involve the pseudo-proposition '*p* is about *a*'. Similarly '*p* is contradictory to *q*' might be thought to be involved in 'He contradicted me'; but it is seen to be a pseudo-proposition when we analyse the latter as 'There is a *p* such that I asserted *p*, he $\sim p$'. Of course this is not a complete analysis, but it is the first step and sufficient for our present purpose, and shows how '—is contradictory to—' is only significant when one blank at least is filled by a description.

Other pseudo-propositions are those of mathematics, which, according to Mr Wittgenstein, are equations obtained by writing '=' between two propositions which can be substituted for one another. I do not see how this account can be supposed to cover the whole of mathematics, and it is evidently incomplete since there are also inequalities, which are more difficult to explain. It is, however, easy to see that 'I have more than two fingers' does not presuppose the significance of '$10 > 2$'; for, remembering that different signs must have different meanings, it is simply '$(\exists x, y, z): x, y, z$ are fingers of mine'.

Just as the explanation of some apparently necessary truths as tautologies met with difficulty in the field of colour, so does the explanation of the remainder as pseudo-propositions. "This blue colour and that", says Mr Wittgenstein, "stand in the internal relation of brighter and darker *eo ipso*. It is unthinkable that *these* two objects should not stand in this relation" (4.123). Accordingly a sentence apparently asserting that one named colour is brighter than another named colour must be a pseudo-proposition; but it is hard to see how this can be reconciled with the indubitable significance of a sentence asserting that a described colour is brighter than another, such as 'My cushion at home is brighter than my carpet'. But in this case the difficulty could be completely removed by the supposition that the physicist is really analysing the meaning of 'red'; for his analysis of a colour comes eventually to a number, such as the length of a wave or what not, and the difficulty is reduced to that of reconciling the non-significance of an inequality between two given numbers with the significance of an inequality between two described numbers, which is evidently somehow possible on the lines suggested for 'I have more than two fingers' above.

Let us now pass to Mr Wittgenstein's account of philosophy. "The object of philosophy", he says, "is the logical clarification of thoughts. Philosophy is not a theory but an activity. A philosophical work consists essentially of elucidations. The result of philosophy is not a number of 'philosophical propositions', but to make propositions clear. Philosophy should make clear and delimit sharply the thoughts which otherwise are, as it were, opaque and blurred" (4.112). It seems to me that we cannot be satisfied with this account without some further explanation of 'clarity', and I shall try to give an explanation in harmony with Mr Wittgenstein's system. I think that a written sentence is 'clear' in so far as it has *visible* properties correlated with or 'showing' the internal properties of its sense. According to Mr Wittgenstein the latter always show themselves in internal properties of the proposition; but owing to the type-token ambiguity of 'proposition' it is not immediately clear what this means. Properties of a proposition must, I think, mean properties of all its tokens; but the internal properties of a proposition are those properties of the tokens which are, so to speak, internal not to the tokens but to the type; that is, those which one of the tokens must have if it is to be a token of that type, not those which it is unthinkable that it should not have anyhow. We must remember that there is no *necessity* for a sentence to have the sense it does in fact have; so that if a sentence says *fa*, it is not an internal property of the sentence that there is something in it somehow connected with *a*; but this is an internal property of the proposition, because the sentence could not otherwise belong to that proposition type, i.e. have that sense. So we see that the internal properties of a proposition which show those of its sense are not, in general, visible ones, but complicated ones involving the notion of meaning. But in a perfect language in which each thing had its own one name, that in the sense of a sentence a certain object occurred, would be also shown visibly by the occurrence in the sentence of the name of that object; and this might be expected to happen with regard to all internal properties of senses; that one sense, for example, is contained in another (i.e. one proposition follows from another) might always appear visibly in the sentences expressing them. (This is nearly achieved in Mr Wittgenstein's *T* notation.) Thus in a perfect language all sentences or thoughts would be perfectly clear. To give a general definition of 'clear' we must replace 'visible property of the sentence' by 'internal property of the propositional sign', which we interpret analogously to 'internal property of the proposition' as a property which a token must have if it is to be that sign, which, if the token is written, is the same as a visible property. We say then that a propositional sign is clear in so far as the internal properties of its sense are shown not only by internal properties of the proposition but also by internal properties of the propositional sign.

21

Frank P. Ramsey

(It may perhaps be confusion between the internal properties of the proposition and those of the propositional sign which gives rise to the idea that Mr Wittgenstein's doctrines are, in general, only asserted of a perfect language.)

We can easily interpret this idea of philosophy in terms of the non-mystical account of internal properties given above. First, we notice and explain the fact that we often apparently do or do not recognize that something has an internal property, although this is a pseudo-proposition and so cannot be recognized. What we really recognize is that 'The object or sense meant or asserted by the words before us has this property', which is significant because we have substituted a description for a name. Thus as the result of logical proof we recognize, not that *p* is a tautology which is a pseudo-proposition, but that '*p*' says nothing. To make propositions clear is to facilitate the recognition of their logical properties by expressing them in language such that these properties are associated with visible properties of the sentence.

But I think this activity will result in philosophical propositions whenever we discover anything new about the logical form of the senses of any interesting body of sentences, such as those expressing the facts of perception and thought. We must agree with Mr Wittgenstein that '*p* is of such-and-such a form' is nonsense, but ' "*p*" has a sense of such-and-such a form' may nevertheless not be nonsense. Whether it is or not depends on the analysis of ' "*p*" is significant', which seems to me probably a disjunctive proposition, whose alternatives arise partly from the different possible forms of the sense of '*p*'. If this is so, we can by excluding some of these alternatives make a proposition as to the form of the sense of '*p*'. And this in certain cases, such as when '*p*' is 'He thinks *q*' or 'He sees *a*', could be appropriately called a philosophical proposition. Nor would this be incompatible with Mr Wittgenstein's more moderate assertion that "Most propositions and questions, that have been written about philosophical matters, are not false, but senseless. We cannot, therefore, answer questions of this kind at all, but only state their senselessness. Most questions and propositions of the philosophers result from the fact that we do not understand the logic of our language" (4.003)

Lastly I wish to touch on Mr Wittgenstein's general view of the world. "The world", he says, "is the totality of facts, not of things" (1.1), and "it is clear that however different from the real one an imagined world may be, it must have something—a form—in common with the real world. This fixed form consists of the objects" (2.022, 2.023). It is an unusual view that any imaginable world must contain all the objects of the real one; but it seems to follow from his

22

principles, for if '*a* exists' is nonsense, we cannot imagine that it does not exist, but only that it does or does not have some property.

Mr Russell in his Introduction finds an acute difficulty in the fact that $(x).\phi x$ involves the totality of values of ϕx and so, apparently, that of the values of x, which according to Mr Wittgenstein cannot be spoken of; for it is one of his fundamental theses "that it is impossible to say anything about the world as a whole, and that whatever can be said has to be about bounded portions of the world". It seems doubtful, however, whether this is a fair expression of Mr Wittgenstein's view; for one thing, it suggests that it is impossible to say $(x).\phi x$, but only perhaps 'All *S*'s are *P*' taken as asserting nothing about the non-*S*'s, which he certainly does not maintain. It may, then, be interesting to consider what he says which gives plausibility to Mr Russell's interpretation. He does undoubtedly deny that we can speak of the number of all objects (4.1272). But this is not because all objects form an illegitimate totality, but because 'object' is a pseudoconcept expressed not by a function but by the variable x. (Incidentally I do not see why the number of all objects should not be defined as the sum of the number of things having any specified property and the number of things not having that property.) Also he says that "The feeling of the world as a limited whole is the mystical feeling" (6.45). But I do not think we can follow Mr Russell in deducing from this that the totality of values of x is mystical, if only because "The world is the totality of facts, not of things" (1.1). And I think that 'limited' gives the key to the sentence quoted above. The mystical feeling is the feeling that the world is not everything, that there is something outside it, its 'sense' or 'meaning'.

It must not be thought that the topics I have discussed nearly exhaust the interest of the book; Mr Wittgenstein makes remarks, always interesting, sometimes extremely penetrating, on many other subjects, such as the Theory of Types, Ancestral Relations, Probability, the Philosophy of Physics, and Ethics.

Review of 'Tractatus'[1]

THEODORE DE LAGUNA

IT is always well to have a theory pushed to extremes. Compromise may be wise in practice, but in abstract speculation it amounts only to a covering-over of the problems. The present work has the great merit of being uncompromising. It is the *reductio ad insanitatem* of the theory of logical atomism.

Very curious is the contrast between the temper of Mr Russell's introduction and that of Mr Wittgenstein's own text. The introduction is marked by the easy geniality which we expect from one who has lost his illusions and has found compensation for them in another quarter. There was a time when Mr Russell too felt that he could prove that two times two is four, and his great ambition was to construct a solid and secure logico-mathematical system. Now he thinks it ample praise to say of this book on logic that the theory which it sets forth is not at any point obviously wrong (p. 28). Mr Wittgenstein has not lost his illusions. On the contrary he is confident that he has attained his aim. He is willing to admit his deficiencies as a writer—his expressions may not always have hit the nail on the head —but he is sure that the truth of the thoughts which he has tried to express is "unassailable and definitive" (p. 29).

Mr Wittgenstein writes in crisp aphorisms, without paragraphing. In order to show the logical interconnection of his propositions, he numbers them in a very elaborate fashion. Thus proposition 5.2523 is the third comment on the second comment on the fifth comment on the second comment on the fifth main proposition. This would be very illuminating if it were not for two circumstances: first, that to follow the numbers is a constant distraction from the sense; and, secondly, that the writer himself sometimes gets mixed up. (Thus 4.0411 properly attaches to 4.04, not to 4.041.) Ordinary

[1] From *The Philosophical Review*, vol. 23, no. 1, whole no. 193, January, 1924, pp. 103–9. Reprinted by permission of the editor and Mrs Grace A. de Laguna.

paragraph-structure is almost as essential a part of our language-inheritance as sentence-structure; and it is to be hoped that Mr Wittgenstein's example will find few imitators.

The original text of the *Tractatus* is printed side by side with an English translation. The translation is slavishly literal, which was perhaps prudent. There are many petty errors; and there is also one of the first magnitude, for which, apparently, Mr Russell is responsible. He writes (p. 9): "Facts which are not compounded of other facts are what Mr Wittgenstein calls *Sachverhalte*, whereas a fact which may consist of two or more facts is called a *Tatsache*." The translator accordingly everywhere renders '*Sachverhalt*' by 'atomic fact', and '*Tatsache*' by 'fact'. But this is by no means the whole difference between them. A *Sachverhalt* is a logically possible condition of affairs, which may or may not exist in reality. A *Tatsache*, or fact, is the existence (or non-existence) of *Sachverhalte* (2; cf. 2.06). This distinction is maintained with general, though not perfect, consistency.

It is impossible for a reviewer to touch upon more than a few of the many important points with which Mr Wittgenstein's book is crowded. Let us begin with the most important, the logical atomism.

"The world is everything that is the case"; that is, it is "the totality of facts, not of things". The elementary objects, which exist eternally, are, apart from the facts in which they are connected together, endowed with only formal properties, i.e. with the capacity of entering into such connections. Facts—as we have just seen—are the existence or non-existence of elementary states of affairs. These are entirely independent of one another, just because they are elementary; and the fact is independent of all outside itself. The dropping-out of any one implies nothing as to the rest. Even a complete list of the facts in the world would not quite describe it; one would have to add—the fact (?)—that these were all the facts (1.11; but for a contrary view see 4.26). Curiously enough Mr Wittgenstein does not stop to consider whether the totality of facts is a legitimate conception, though he elsewhere suggests reasons for concluding that it is mere nonsense (4.1272).

That there are elementary facts, in which elementary objects are bound together, Mr Wittgenstein regards as certain, because otherwise there would be no distinction between truth and falsehood. If facts were not analysable into independent elements, we could not clearly assert them; and if there were no simple objects, no object could be denoted by a name in any proposition, unless the use of the name had been justified in a prior proposition. Even if every fact involved an infinite number of simple states of affairs, and each of these involved an infinite number of simple objects—which Mr

Wittgenstein apparently regards as a not impossible supposition—the simple would remain. (See 2.0211, f., 4.2211.) One might reply that so far as the possibility of clear assertion is concerned there might just as well be no simples, if there were an infinite number of them in every ordinary fact; and it is, of course, highly questionable whether each proposition has a truth or falsity—or even a meaning—all its own, independently of every other proposition.

The immediate consequence of this thoroughgoing atomism is sufficiently startling, though Mr Wittgenstein does not hesitate to embrace it. It is the essential invalidity of all attempts at prediction. The whole sum of past and present facts can not determine a single future fact. This, he observes in passing, is the true meaning of the freedom of the will. We have no means of knowing how we, or other men, will act, just as we have no means of knowing whether the sun will ever rise again. It is to be noted that the grounds alleged by Mr Wittgenstein apply to probable, as well as to certain, reasoning—though he himself does not make this clear. If facts consist of absolutely independent elements, we have not the slightest reason for supposing that the sun will rise upon another day.

Let us pass to the theory of symbolism. The significant proposition, or thought, is, according to Mr Wittgenstein, a *picture* of a fact—perhaps a correct one, perhaps an incorrect one, but still a picture. At first glance the proposition, spoken or written, may not seem to be a picture of the reality. But neither does a musical score appear to be a picture; yet that is what it is. "The gramophone record, the musical thought, the score, the waves of sound, all stand to one another in that pictorial internal relation, which holds between language and the world. . . . In the fact that there is a general rule by which the musician is able to read the symphony out of the score, and that there is a rule by which one could reconstruct the symphony from the line on the gramophone record and from this again—by means of the first rule—construct the score, herein lies the internal similarity between these things which at first sight seem to be entirely different" (4.041). Mr Wittgenstein adds: "In order to understand the essence of the proposition, consider hieroglyphic writing, which pictures the facts it describes. And from it came alphabetic writing, without the essence of the representation being lost" (4.016).

The theory is ingenious, but I venture to say it will not do. First, it makes the relation between thought and reality a symmetrical one—the possession of a common structure. The thought is to the reality exactly what the reality is to the thought. Secondly, there is no rule for translating from thought to reality or from reality to thought, and no one pretends to possess such a rule. Shall we say that we are to substitute for each element in the reality its symbol, and then connect these *as the objective elements are connected*? The question remains, how we are to secure this parallelism; and no answer is forthcoming. If the question is nonsensical, that is because the idea of such a translation is nonsensical. All our translation is from one language to another. Thirdly, the picture, even the portrait, asserts nothing. We may think or declare it to be a good or a bad likeness; but that is another matter. Finally, hieroglyphic writing, even in the primitive form of picture-writing, is not a picture of the facts which it describes. Like other language, it *predicates*. It has a logical structure, a syntax, such as a picture does not have.

Mr Wittgenstein's logical theory, in the narrower sense of the term, is a version of the so-called logic of propositions (as distinguished from the logic of classes or of properties). To my mind that is enough to condemn it. This sort of logic treats of reasoning in which propositions are dealt with without any reference to the things or properties which figure in them. They appear as units, p, q, r, or as combinations of such units effected by means of the operations denoted by 'and', 'or', 'neither . . . nor', etc.—truth-functions, as they are called. In Mr Wittgenstein's treatment the 'neither . . . nor' operation is made fundamental. He believes that all propositions are either simple or are built up in this fashion out of simple propositions; and since simple propositions are entirely independent of one another the only kind of inference that is left is the extraction of part of a given combination and asserting that part separately.

The whole procedure is utterly baseless. No scientific reasoning ever has the form of a syllogism in the logic of propositions. In science the particular qualities and relations of things always count. And there is not the slightest reason to suppose that any scientific reasoning is reducible to such a form. Of course no one will pretend to effect the reduction in any particular case. "Dear Sir," wrote the young Faraday, "The *oil* which you noticed yesterday turns out to be liquid chlorine." What combination of simple propositions is contained in that? Free as the logical atomists are to talk about simple propositions, they never cite one, except in the most doubtful way. From Mr Russell's standpoint this is perhaps not a serious difficulty. The elementary concept and proposition are for him like the electron—scientific hypotheses devised in order to explain the facts of experience. But for Mr Wittgenstein they are gospel-truth. According to him it is only as a truth-function of simple propositions about simple objects that a proposition can ever be understood. "Everything that can be thought at all can be thought clearly. Everything that can be said can be said clearly" (4.116). The correct conclusion would seem to be that we can never think or say anything at all.

A universal proposition, according to Mr Wittgenstein, arises through the simultaneous denial of a whole class of propositions, in which a given property is asserted. What it asserts, then, is that nothing has that property. If we object that we cannot think of all those propositions at once, so as to be able to deny them together, Mr Wittgenstein has ready the reply that a general description of the propositions in terms of the given property is all that is necessary (5.501). If the universal proposition is that which would be obtained by summating all the individual propositions and denying the sum, then it *is* the denial of the sum. My comment would be, first, that the description of the individual propositions in terms of the property contained in them is purely hypothetical, and that I see no reason for adopting such an hypothesis. Secondly, the universal proposition would *not* arise from the simultaneous denial, for it would require the additional statement that these were indeed all the propositions in which the given property can be asserted.[1]

The most remarkable feature of the *Tractatus* is the theory of the limits of expressibility in which it issues. This is an outgrowth of the picture-theory of the proposition, noticed above. According to Mr Wittgenstein, there are things which cannot be pictured at all. The spatial representation of a spatial reality may be as faithful as you please, but one thing it can not represent—the character of being spatial, which it has in common with the reality. It simply *exhibits* that. Even so the proposition "can represent the whole reality, but it cannot represent what it must have in common with the reality in order to represent it—the logical form. . . . The proposition *shows* the logical form of the reality. It exhibits it" (4.121).

The reader cannot but reflect that even on the basis of the picture-theory this conclusion is not unescapable. What one proposition exhibits, another might state. Mr Russell promptly suggests an endless hierarchy of languages, each of which expresses what the one below merely exhibits. But Mr Wittgenstein will allow no escape. "That which mirrors itself in language," he declares, "language cannot represent."

This contention leads almost at once to open absurdity; but, as we shall see, in this domain Mr Wittgenstein does not fear absurdity. He proceeds: "Thus a proposition '*fa*' shows that in its sense the object *a* occurs, two propositions '*fa*' and '*ga*' that they are both about the same object. If two propositions contradict one another, this is shown by their structure; similarly if one follows from another,

---

[1] On the other hand, the criticism suggested by Mr Russell (p. 22), that the totality of things in the world—which Mr Wittgenstein regards as nonsense—would seem to be involved in the class of propositions denied, is not sound. For only those things would be involved to which the given property could be intelligibly, whether truly or falsely, ascribed; and these, according to Mr Wittgenstein, would fall far short of including everything.

etc." (4.1211). Does it need pointing out that all this can be stated, and that in the very act of declaring that it is shown Mr Wittgenstein shows how to state it? I will merely add that if there is nothing in the statement beyond empty tautology, there is no more in the exhibition.

That which cannot be expressed in language is for Mr Wittgenstein the *mystical*, and he has a good deal to say about it. The soul, the will ("as the bearer of the ethical"), happiness, beauty—these do not belong to the world but to its limits. There can be no ethical propositions (6.42). Such matters are dumbly felt; and all the perplexities of metaphysics arise from trying to express them. The solution of the riddle is that there is no riddle, for no riddle can be put (6.5). Philosophy is not the science of these things. The only science is natural science. Philosophy is a discipline, the object of which is to make us see the vanity of all metaphysical speculation. Philosophy has no information to impart. "Concerning matters of which we cannot speak, we must be silent" (7). To anticipate an obvious objection, Mr Wittgenstein frankly acknowledges that what he has himself been saying is utterly senseless; but he hopes that it will be useful in an educational way—as a ladder to be kicked down when the summit of silence has been reached. Such candour is disarming, and no further comment seems to be called for.

I could single out a good deal in Mr Wittgenstein's book that seems to me to be very fine indeed; but I fear I have left small space for this. There are some remarks about the character of logical propositions and about logical pseudo-concepts which are well worthy of study; and the efforts toward a simplification of logical theory should meet with much sympathy. More than that, there is not a page which is not the product of hard thinking. The faults of the book are to my mind almost all illustrations of the weakness of a few initial assumptions. I do not think any serious student can work through the book the three or four times necessary to get a fair understanding of its drift, without being well repaid in stimulating suggestions.

Some Remarks on Logical Form[1]

LUDWIG WITTGENSTEIN

EVERY proposition has a content and a form. We get the picture of the pure form if we abstract from the meaning of the single words, or symbols (so far as they have independent meanings). That is to say, if we substitute variables for the constants of the proposition. The rules of syntax which applied to the constants must apply to the variables also. By syntax in this general sense of the word I mean the rules which tell us in which connections only a word gives sense, thus excluding nonsensical structures. The syntax of ordinary language, as is well known, is not quite adequate for this purpose. It does not in all cases prevent the construction of nonsensical pseudopropositions (constructions such as "red is higher than green" or "the Real, though it is an *in itself*, must also be able to become a *for myself*", etc.).

[1] From Aristotelian Society Supplementary Volume 9, *Knowledge, Experience and Realism*, Harrison and Sons, Ltd, 45, St. Martin's Lane, London, W.C.2, 1929, pp. 162–71. Reprinted with permission of the editor and Wittgenstein's literary executors.

"Wittgenstein disowned the following essay. He told me that he had returned to Cambridge thinking he would be able to do philosophy again, but after a time he dried up and had no ideas. Then came the invitation to write a paper for the Aristotelian Society, and he thought he would accept and try to write something, just to see whether anything came out that way. He described what he wrote as quite worthless. When the time of the meeting came he had recovered his capacity to think and told his audience that he would talk about something quite different, which he did: namely infinity. It was then, he said, that he first met Gilbert Ryle, whom he noticed listening 'with a *very* interested face'. In a letter to the editor of *Mind* Wittgenstein referred to this essay and called it 'weak'; and when Professor J. W. Scott asked him for a summary of it for his *Index to the Proceedings of the Aristotelian Society*, Wittgenstein wrote back begging him not to include any summary of it. It was Professor Scott's practice to make summaries himself if he could not get them from authors, but, he said, Wittgenstein wrote to him so earnestly that of course he did as he was asked to do. Again, in this letter, which is lost, Wittgenstein referred to the essay as 'weak and uncharacteristic'. I have consented to the reprint of the essay because I suppose that it will certainly be reprinted some time, and if that is to happen there had better be a statement indicating how little value can be set upon it as information about Wittgenstein's ideas. It was, I think, not normal for him to write when, as he put it, he had none."—G. E. M. ANSCOMBE.

Ludwig Wittgenstein

If we try to analyse any given propositions we shall find in general that they are logical sums, products or other truth-functions of simpler propositions. But our analysis, if carried far enough, must come to the point where it reaches propositional forms which are not themselves composed of simpler propositional forms. We must eventually reach the ultimate connection of the terms, the immediate connection which cannot be broken without destroying the propositional form as such. The propositions which represent this ultimate connection of terms I call, after B. Russell, atomic propositions. They, then, are the kernels of every proposition, *they* contain the material, and all the rest is only a development of this material. It is to them we have to look for the subject matter of propositions. It is the task of the theory of knowledge to find them and to understand their construction out of the words or symbols. This task is very difficult, and Philosophy has hardly yet begun to tackle it at some points. What method have we for tackling it? The idea is to express in an appropriate symbolism what in ordinary language leads to endless misunderstandings. That is to say, where ordinary language disguises logical structure, where it allows the formation of pseudopropositions, where it uses one term in an infinity of different meanings, we must replace it by a symbolism which gives a clear picture of the logical structure, excludes pseudo-propositions, and uses its terms unambiguously. Now we can only substitute a clear symbolism for the unprecise one by inspecting the phenomena which we want to describe, thus trying to understand their logical multiplicity. That is to say, we can only arrive at a correct analysis by, what might be called, the logical investigation of the phenomena themselves, i.e. in a certain sense *a posteriori*, and not by conjecturing about *a priori* possibilities. One is often tempted to ask from an *a priori* standpoint: What, after all, *can* be the only forms of atomic propositions, and to answer, e.g. subject-predicate and relational propositions with two or more terms further, perhaps, propositions relating predicates and relations to one another, and so on. But this, I believe, is mere playing with words. An atomic form cannot be foreseen. And it would be surprising if the actual phenomena had nothing more to teach us about their structure. To such conjectures about the structure of atomic propositions, we are led by our ordinary language, which uses the subject-predicate and the relational form. But in this our language is misleading: I will try to explain this by a simile. Let us imagine two parallel planes, I and II. On plane I figures are drawn, say, ellipses and rectangles of different sizes and shapes, and it is our task to produce images of these figures on plane II. Then we can imagine two ways, amongst others, of doing this. We can, first, lay down a law of projection—say that of ortho-gonal projection or any other—and then proceed to project all figures

32

from I into II, according to this law. Or, secondly, we could proceed thus: We lay down the rule that every ellipse on plane I is to appear as a circle in plane II, and every rectangle as a square in II. Such a way of representation may be convenient for us if for some reason we prefer to draw only circles and squares on plane II. Of course, from these images the exact shapes of the original figures on plane I cannot be immediately inferred. We can only gather from them that the original was an ellipse or a rectangle. In order to get in a single instance at the determinate shape of the original we would have to know the individual method by which, e.g. a particular ellipse is projected into the circle before me. The case of ordinary language is quite analogous. If the facts of reality are the ellipses and rectangles on plane I the subject-predicate and relational forms correspond to the circles and squares in plane II. These forms are the norms of our particular language into which we project in *ever so many different* ways *ever so many different* logical forms. And for this very reason we can draw no conclusions—except very vague ones—from the use of these norms as to the actual logical form of the phenomena described. Such forms as "This paper is boring", "The weather is fine", "I am lazy", which have nothing whatever in common with one another, present themselves as subject-predicate propositions, i.e. apparently as propositions of the same form.

If, now, we try to get at an actual analysis, we find logical forms which have very little similarity with the norms of ordinary language. We meet with the forms of space and time with the whole manifold of spatial and temporal objects, as colours, sounds, etc., etc., with their gradations, continuous transitions, and combinations in various proportions, all of which we cannot seize by our ordinary means of expression. And here I wish to make my first definite remark on the logical analysis of actual phenomena: it is this, that for their representation numbers (rational and irrational) must enter into the structure of the atomic propositions themselves. I will illustrate this by an example. Imagine a system of rectangular axes, as it were, cross wires, drawn in our field of vision and an arbitrary scale fixed. It is clear that we then can describe the shape and position of every patch of colour in our visual field by means of statements of numbers which have their significance relative to the system of co-ordinates and the unit chosen. Again, it is clear that this description will have the right logical multiplicity, and that a description which has a smaller multiplicity will not do. A simple example would be the representation of a patch P by the expression "[6—9, 3—8]" and of a proposition about it, e.g. P is red, by the symbol "[6—9, 3—8] R", where "R" is yet an unanalysed term ("6—9" and "3—8" stand for the continuous interval between the respective numbers). The system of co-ordinates here is part of the mode of expression; it is part of the method of projection by which the reality is projected into our symbolism. The relation of a patch lying between two others can be expressed analogously by the use of apparent variables. I need not say that this analysis does not in any way pretend to be complete. I have made no mention in it of time, and the use of two-dimensional space is not justified even in the case of monocular vision. I only wish to point out the direction in which, I believe, the analysis of visual phenomena is to be looked for, and that in this analysis we meet with logical forms quite different from those which ordinary language leads us to expect.

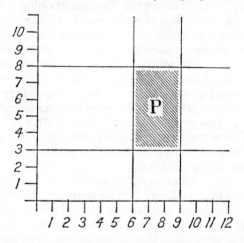

The occurrence of numbers in the forms of atomic propositions is, in my opinion, not merely a feature of a special symbolism, but an essential and, consequently, unavoidable feature of the representation. And numbers will have to enter these forms when—as we should say in ordinary language—we are dealing with properties which admit of gradation, i.e. properties as the length of an interval, the pitch of a tone, the brightness or redness of a shade of colour, etc. It is a characteristic of these properties that one degree of them excludes any other. One shade of colour cannot simultaneously have two different degrees of brightness or redness, a tone not two different strengths, etc. And the important point here is that these remarks do not express an experience but are in some sense tautologies. Every one of us knows that in ordinary life. If someone asks us "What is the temperature outside?" and we said "Eighty degrees", and now he were to ask us again, "And is it ninety degrees?" we should answer, "I told you it was eighty." We take the statement of a degree (of temperature, for instance) to be a *complete* description which needs

34

no supplementation. Thus, when asked, we say what the time is, and not also what it isn't.

One might think—and I thought so not long ago—that a statement expressing the degree of a quality could be analysed into a logical product of single statements of quantity and a completing supplementary statement. As I could describe the contents of my pocket by saying "It contains a penny, a shilling, two keys, and nothing else". This "and nothing else" is the supplementary statement which completes the description. But this will not do as an analysis of a statement of degree. For let us call the unit of, say, brightness b and let $E(b)$ be the statement that the entity E possesses this brightness, then the proposition $E(2b)$, which says that E has two degrees of brightness, should be analysable into the logical product $E(b)$ & $E(b)$, but this is equal to $E(b)$; if, on the other hand, we try to distinguish between the units and consequently write $E(2b) = E(b')$ & $E(b'')$, we assume two different units of brightness; and then, if an entity possesses one unit, the question could arise, which of the two—b' or b''—it is; which is obviously absurd.

I maintain that the statement which attributes a degree to a quality cannot further be analysed, and, moreover, that the relation of difference of degree is an internal relation and that it is therefore represented by an internal relation between the statements which attribute the different degrees. That is to say, the atomic statement must have the same multiplicity as the degree which it attributes, whence it follows that numbers must enter the forms of atomic propositions. The mutual exclusion of unanalysable statements of degree contradicts an opinion which was published by me several years ago and which necessitated that atomic propositions could not exclude one another. I here deliberately say "exclude" and not "contradict", for there is a difference between these two notions, and atomic propositions, although they cannot contradict, may exclude one another. I will try to explain this. There are functions which can give a true proposition only for one value of their argument because —if I may so express myself—there is only room in them for one. Take, for instance, a proposition which asserts the existence of a colour R at a certain time T in a certain place P of our visual field. I will write this proposition "R P T", and abstract for the moment from any consideration of how such a statement is to be further analysed. "B P T", then, says that the colour B is in the place P at the time T, and it will be clear to most of us here, and to all of us in ordinary life, that "R P T & B P T" is some sort of contradiction (and not merely a false proposition). Now if statements of degree were analysable—as I used to think—we could explain this contradiction by saying that the colour R contains all degrees of R and none of

B and that the colour B contains all degrees of B and none of R. But from the above it follows that no analysis can eliminate statements of degree. How, then, does the mutual exclusion of R P T and B P T operate? I believe it consists in the fact that R P T as well as B P T are in a certain sense *complete*. That which corresponds in reality to the function "( ) P T" leaves room only for one entity—in the same sense, in fact, in which we say that there is room for one person only in a chair. Our symbolism, which allows us to form the sign of the logical product of "R P T" and "B P T", gives here no correct picture of reality.

I have said elsewhere that a proposition "reaches up to reality", and by this I meant that the forms of the entities are contained in the form of the proposition which is about these entities. For the sentence, together with the mode of projection which projects reality into the sentence, determines the logical form of the entities, just as in our simile a picture on plane II, together with its mode of projection, determines the shape of the figure on plane I. This remark, I believe, gives us the key for the explanation of the mutual exclusion of R P T and B P T. For if the proposition contains the form of an entity which it is about, then it is possible that two propositions should collide in this very form. The propositions "Brown now sits in this chair" and "Jones now sits in this chair" each, in a sense, try to set their subject term on the chair. But the logical product of these propositions will put them both there at once, and this leads to a collision, a mutual exclusion of these terms. How does this exclusion represent itself in symbolism? We can write the logical product of the two propositions, *p* and *q*, in this way:

p	q	
T	T	T
T	F	F
F	T	F
F	F	F

What happens if these two propositions are R P T and B P T? In this case the top line "T T T" must disappear, as it represents an impossible combination. The true possibilities here are—

R P T	B P T
T	F
F	T
F	F

That is to say, there *is* no logical product of R P T and B P T in the first sense, and herein lies the exclusion as opposed to a contradiction. The contradiction, if it existed, would have to be written—

R P T	B P T	
T	T	F
T	F	F
F	T	F
F	F	F

but this is nonsense, as the top line, "T T F", gives the proposition a greater logical multiplicity than that of the actual possibilities. It is, of course, a deficiency of our notation that it does not prevent the formation of such nonsensical constructions, and a perfect notation will have to exclude such structures by definite rules of syntax. These will have to tell us that in the case of certain kinds of atomic propositions described in terms of definite symbolic features certain combinations of the T's and F's must be left out. Such rules, however, cannot be laid down until we have actually reached the ultimate analysis of the phenomena in question. This, as we all know, has not yet been achieved.

Logical Constructions (I)[1]

JOHN WISDOM

IN this paper I want (1) to tell you what I mean when I say "Pennies
are logical constructions", and (2) to find the analysis of that meaning. I want to translate "Pennies are logical constructions" as used by
me, and to analyse the fact I so express—or more strictly to find
what would be the analysis of the fact that pennies are logical constructions if it were a fact that pennies are logical constructions.

I. HISTORY

I shall not here try very hard to show that what I mean by logical construction is what Russell, Moore and Miss Stebbing mean. It is not
easy to know from Russell's language what he means by 'logical
construction' because he is confused in two respects: (1) He does not
distinguish between saying that a thing is a logical construction and
saying that it is an incomplete symbol. He says, e.g. "classes are, in
fact, like descriptions, logical fictions, or (as we say) 'incomplete
symbols' ".[2] As Miss Stebbing says, "Mr Russell cannot mean that
classes are incomplete symbols but that classes are *symbolized* by incomplete symbols and are therefore logical constructions".[3] (2) Russell fails to distinguish between a broad sense of incomplete symbol
and a narrow. He failed to notice that the sense in which "The King
of England", as used in "The King of England is happy", is an incomplete symbol, is very different from that in which the same phrase,
"The King of England", is an incomplete symbol as used in "The
King of England exists".[4] The phrase is an incomplete symbol in the

[1] From *Mind*, vol. 40, no. 158, April, 1931, pp. 188–216. Reprinted by permission of
the editor and the author.
[2] *Introduction to Mathematical Philosophy*, p. 182.
[3] *A Modern Introduction to Logic*, p. 157.
[4] This is an instantial sentence. I call a sentence instantial when it begins "There is"
or "There are" or is translatable into such a sentence, e.g. "Unicorns are imaginary",
"God exists", "There is an integer between 2 and 3".

first sentence merely because it does not name anything in Russell's sense but refers to something indirectly by one of its characteristics,[1] viz. that of *reigning over Englishmen*. The phrase is an incomplete symbol in the second sentence because it neither names nor refers to anything by one of its characteristics.[2] It is in terms of the second sense of 'incomplete symbol' that logical constructions are to be defined. Russell perhaps failed to notice the difference between the two senses partly because he did not notice that a phrase might be an incomplete symbol in one use and not in another.

Here is another example. Everyone will see the difference between the way in which Mr Hilaire Belloc uses 'llama' in

"The llama is a hairy sort of woolly fleecy goat
With an indolent expression and an undulating throat."

and the way in which I use it when I say "Yesterday the llama trotted up to me". In Mr Belloc's sentence "the llama" "stands for an abstraction" as we say. It stands for a typical llama. Typical of what? Typical of llamas. Mr Belloc's llama is a logical construction, and a logical construction out of llamas.

"But," it will perhaps be said, "why talk in this mysterious way. True, Mr. Belloc's use of the phrase 'the llama' is quite different from yours when you say of your pet llama, 'The llama trotted up to me this morning.' But it is quite simple. 'The llama', used Belloc's way, means 'Llamas' or 'Every llama', just as the phrase 'The heart' as used in medical text books means 'Every heart'."

The answer is that 'the llama' does *not* mean 'llamas' just as 'the heart' does *not* mean 'hearts'. 'The llama' (used Belloc's way) means 'llamas' only in the sense that whenever you utter a sentence beginning 'the llama' (used this way) you are expressing a proposition which could also be expressed by a sentence beginning 'llamas'. But 'the llama' does not mean 'llamas' in the sense that whenever you utter a sentence beginning 'the llama' you can substitute in that sentence 'llamas' for 'the llama' and still express the same proposition. To put it briefly: To say something about the llama is to say something about llamas but it is not to say the *same* thing about llamas as was said about the llama. To put it more exactly: Take any sentence "The llama R", where R is the whole of the sentence bar the words

---

[1] "The King of England exists (or does not exist)" does, of course, in a sense refer to something by one of its characteristics. But in a sense it does not. We may put the point another way. "The King of England is happy" is about the King of England. And "The King of England exists (or does not exist)" is in a sense about the King of England. But in a sense it is not. Compare Miss Stebbing, *A Modern Introduction to Logic*, p. 25. I cannot state clearly *here* what the distinction between these two uses of 'incomplete symbol' is. If I could I should not write this paper.

[2] Of course, if kings are logical constructions, then "the King of England" will be an incomplete symbol in the second sense in "The King of England is happy".

'The llama', i.e. R is the rest of the sentence. Then (1) the whole sentence "The llama R" expresses what can also be expressed by a whole sentence "Every llama S" and by a sentence "Llamas T"; *but* (2) S and T either are not R, or if they are R then R is used in one way in the original sentence, "The llama R", and in another way in the translation, "Every llama R". This alteration in the use of R occurs because "Every llama R" with R used as in "The llama R" does not express anything, i.e. is nonsense. We may express this by saying that 'every llama' is substitutable for 'the llama' (used Belloc's way) but not *simply* substitutable.

Take "The llama is a hairy beast". It is obvious that this can be translated "Llamas are hairy beasts". It is also obvious that "Llamas is a hairy beast" is nonsense. But is not this merely a matter of plurals? Take 'every llama' and the difficulty disappears. We write "Every llama is a hairy beast".

But the *use* of 'is a hairy beast' is different here from what it is in "The llama is a hairy beast". Consider "The gramophone was invented by Edison". This sentence means something which we can express by a sentence beginning 'Every gramophone'. But we cannot arrive at this translation by simply substituting in the original sentence the phrase 'every gramophone' for 'the gramophone'. For if we did we should obtain "Every gramophone was invented by Edison". This will not do. We are not saying this when we say "The gramophone was invented by Edison", although we are saying *something* about every gramophone. Again, consider "The llama was created by God for the benefit of man". This, though about every llama, cannot be written "Every llama was created by God for the benefit of man". In these two examples the fact that the subject-phrase 'every X' cannot be simply substituted for the subject-phrase 'the X' is obvious because, to obtain a translation of the original sentence beginning 'the X' which shall begin 'every X', we have not merely to use differently the original predicate phrase but we have to use a different predicate-phrase. It is when the original predicate-phrase is Grammatically Polygamous that it is not necessary to change *it* but only its *use*. And it is in this case that it is difficult to see that though sentences beginning 'the X', used Belloc's way, can be translated by sentences beginning 'every X', the one phrase is not *simply* substitutable for the other, i.e. not substitutable without change in the make-up or use of the original sentence.[1]

It is useful to compare the following case. "The Stuart family is

[1] We should distinguish between the use and the meaning of a word. 'Red' and 'green' have the same use in "This is red" and "This is green" though they have, of course, different meanings. On the other hand, the use of 'pleasant' is different in "Chocolate is pleasant" from what it is in "The experience of eating chocolate is pleasant". We tend not to speak of a word as ambiguous unless within the same use it

warlike" can be translated "Every Stuart is warlike". Here it seems to me quite clear that 'is warlike' is used in the second sentence (about individuals) in a way different from that in which it is used in the first sentence (about a family), although and *because* to say of a family that it is warlike *is* simply to say that its members are warlike. 'Is warlike' is grammatically polygamous.

I hope that it is now clear that when we say "The horse is herbivorous" we are not using 'is herbivorous' in the way it is used in "Every horse is herbivorous", although the latter sentence expresses what the former expresses. Similarly with "The llama is herbivorous" and "Every llama is herbivorous".

'Every llama', then, is substitutable for, but not simply substitutable for, 'the llama'. There is one more point. The translations—the sentences beginning 'every llama'—are a little less cryptic than the sentences beginning 'the llama'. This misuse of 'cryptic' it will be my business to explain in this paper. Now to say "The llama is a logical construction out of llamas" is just a misguided way of saying "(1) 'Every llama' is substitutable, but not simply, for 'the llama'; (2) substituted—'every llama'—sentences are less cryptic (in my sense) than the originals—'the llama' sentences".

The remark that the llama is a logical construction out of llamas is trivial because of at least three things. (1) Everybody knows not only that sentences beginning with 'the llama' (used Belloc's way) can be translated into sentences beginning 'every llama', but also just *how* to do the translation, i.e. just what other alterations to make in the sentence. (2) Everybody knows what we express by saying that the translations are less cryptic—everybody knows that the heart of the llama is in some sense "an abstraction". (3) The difference in crypticness is very slight.

On the other hand, "England is a logical construction out of Englishmen" is not trivial. For it means " 'Englishmen' is substitutable for but not simply substitutable for 'England', while the new sentences, beginning 'Englishmen' and having new predicate phrases, are less cryptic than those beginning 'England' ". This is not trivial. For (*a*) some people might doubt it; (*b*) it is very difficult to say what alteration must be made in a sentence beginning 'England' if we are to find a new sentence meaning the same but beginning 'Englishmen'. Thus "England declared war" cannot be translated "Englishmen declared war". Further, it can neither be translated "Englishmen decided to fight", nor be translated "The majority of Englishmen wished to fight". "Englishmen had selected a man (Minister

has more than one meaning. Cf. Miss Stebbing, "No word in isolation is properly ambiguous", *A Modern Introduction to Logic*, p. 21.

for War) who decided that they should fight" is nearer what is wanted. (*c*) When the translation is found it is markedly less cryptic.

The Trinity, no doubt, is a logical construction out of the Three Persons thereof. It is three because facts about it just *are* complicated facts about the Three Persons. It is one because it cannot be said to *be* the Three Persons. It is one because 'The Three Persons' is substitutable for 'The Trinity'. It is three because 'The Three Persons' is not simply substitutable for 'The Trinity'.

We must not say that a table *is* the string of events which make up its life-history. For then to say of a table that it collapsed is to say of a string of events that they collapsed. On the other hand, the fact that the table collapsed is perhaps nothing but the fact that a set of suitably inter-related events includes a collapse. We may claim that this is so and avoid the mistake of saying that a table *is* a string of events by saying that the table is a logical construction out of events. (I owe this point to Prof. Moore.)[1]

The llama is "an abstraction". You could never meet Mr Belloc's llama—only llamas. Similarly, you might meet Mr Ramsay Mac-Donald at the Regent Palace, but you could not, in the same sense, meet the modern politician there, and you could not in the same sense of 'meet', i.e. so as to say "How d'you do", meet the average man there.

Mr Belloc's use of 'the llama' is similar to the use of the expressions 'the average llama', 'the modern politician', 'the Englishman' (as used in "The Englishman's word is his bond"), 'the representative firm', 'the psychological individual', 'the economic man'. All these are logical constructions of a comparatively simple type. The llama *is* a logical construction of still simpler type. We can all see at once how to translate sentences about the average man. The representative firm is a trifle harder. Consider the sentence "The average man has an intelligence quotient of 60". This can be translated into a sentence beginning "every (or any) man". But of course it can *not* be translated "Every man has an intelligence quotient of 60". On the other hand, it *can* be translated "If you take every man's intelligence quotient and add them up and divide by the number of men the answer is 60".

To return to history. Russell made these two mistakes: (1) the substitution of incomplete symbol for logical construction, (2) the confusion of two senses of 'incomplete symbol'—the first a sense in which a symbol is incomplete if it does not name something, the second a sense in which a symbol is incomplete only if it neither names nor refers to something indirectly by one of its characteristics.

---

[1] More is said on this point in my *Interpretation and Analysis in Relation to Bentham's Theory of Definition. Psyche Miniatures.*

Moore saw Russell's mistakes and suggested the following definition: "Lions are logical constructions" means "There is a common usage of the expression 'is a lion' such that in that usage 'is a lion' is an incomplete symbol (in the second and drastic sense above)". I have not quoted words of Moore's, but I believe my words to be very like those Moore would have used. He has not used the expression 'logical construction' in his published writings. I have in lecture notes "classes are logical constructions = 'is a class' is an incomplete symbol". Moore's definition of incomplete symbol as quoted by Miss Stebbing is as follows: "S, in *this* usage, does occur in expressions which express propositions, and, in the case of *every* such expression, S never stands for any constituent of the proposition expressed". Df. This definition makes the articles 'a', 'the', and 'every' incomplete symbols. This could easily be corrected. It would be corrected if we added to the definition a clause expressing a point on which Moore always insists, viz. that if S is an incomplete symbol and forms part of some sentence, then the rest, taken as a whole, of that sentence is an incomplete symbol. With some amendment of this sort, Moore's definition would, I think, be at any rate nearly correct.[1] But though nearly correct it still has two defects: (1) 'stands for' is not unambiguous for every body, (2) it does not carry the analysis of incomplete symbol as far as it can be carried.

Miss Stebbing accepts Moore's definition of logical construction and incomplete symbol. I do not like her statement of the case which runs "Any X is a logical construction" = "X is symbolised by 'S' and 'an S' is an incomplete symbol". Df. For one thing, though this way of stating the definition brings out clearly the fact that it is a lion which is a logical construction and the phrase 'a lion' which is an incomplete symbol, it is bad grammar. For if X is a logical construction, then it suggests a lapse of logical grammar[2] to say that "X is symbolised by S".

Miss Stebbing and I both tried to analyse *stands for*,[3] and not without success. Also, unfortunately, not without mistake. Miss Stebbing says, "Thus an incomplete symbol is neither a name nor a descriptive phrase applying to any constituent of the proposition in whose verbal expression the incomplete symbol occurs". This seems nearly right, but, as Miss Stebbing agrees, no descriptive phrase ever does *apply to a constituent of the proposition in whose verbal expression it occurs.*

---

[1] "There is a common usage" is not enough. For every substantive there is a common usage, namely its usage in instantial sentences, in which it is an incomplete symbol.

[2] For some indication of the meaning of 'logical grammar' see note on theory of types (next instalment).

[3] *A Modern Introduction to Logic*, p. 155, note; and *Proc. Arist. Soc.*, N.S., 29, pp. 66–73.

While I lay myself open to the charge of using 'descriptive phrase' in a peculiar manner without explaining the new manner. For I say that an incomplete symbol is neither a name nor a descriptive phrase. And yet 'The King of England' in "The King of England does not exist" would ordinarily be called a descriptive phrase, while at the same time it is an incomplete symbol.

We may now set down the following clues as to the translation and analysis of "Pennies are logical constructions", as used by Russell, Moore and Miss Stebbing.

1. It is clearly a verbal proposition. And by that I do not mean an analytic proposition about the analysis of some characteristic such as *A father is a male parent*; I mean a proposition about words such as *'Cheval' means 'horse'*. On the other hand, as Mr Mace has pointed out to me, it is a verbal proposition which is more important than a translation such as *'Rich' means 'wealthy'*. It is a remark about how the subject-phrase 'pennies' is used in non-instantial sentences. It is important to philosophy[1] because it tells how the sentence is and is not related to facts. And thus provides clues to and prevents mistakes about the analysis of those facts.

It follows from (1) that (2) *Pennies are logical constructions* (or *logical fictions*) does not mean or entail *Pennies are imaginary*. Nor would *unicorns are logical fictions* entail *unicorns are imaginary or fictitious*. Unicorns and phoenixes are of course imaginary. We may, if we like, express this fact by saying *"Unicorns and phoenixes are fictitious"*. But we cannot express it by "Unicorns and phoenixes are logical fictions". For *Unicorns are fictions* is a proposition about the contents of the world, i.e. an instantial proposition, while *Unicorns are logical fictions* is a proposition about words, i.e. a verbal proposition.

And it follows from (1) that (3) *Pennies are logical constructions* does not entail and is not entailed by *Pennies are ideal constructions* in the sense in which Prof. Stout speaks, in *The Groundwork*, of my ideal construction of a gold house for Smith. We may assert *Utopias are ideal constructions*, but this would neither entail nor be entailed by *Utopias are logical constructions*. For the former is a psychological proposition while the latter is a verbal proposition which could be expressed by " 'Utopias' is not a genuine descriptive phrase".

And it follows from (1) that (4) *Pennies are logical constructions* would neither entail nor be entailed by *Pennies are hypothetical entities*, in the sense in which electrons used to be, physical objects would be on Dr Broad's Sensum theory, and unconscious thoughts and feelings are. An unconscious thought is a hypothetical entity because (1) it never is observed, (2) the hypothesis that there are such

[1] See Susan Stebbing, *A Modern Introduction to Logic*, pp. 116, 117.

things accounts for certain facts which we do observe, and thus has some probability. We may, if we like, express a belief that pennies are hypothetical entities in this sense by saying "Pennies are inferentials". Inferentials are Jeremy Bentham's inferred entities.

Now (1), (2), (3) and (4) are also true of what *I* mean by 'logical construction'.

II. SUMMARY

The following is a summary of the rest of the paper. It is not an exact summary, but it is nearly so.

1. "Pennies are logical constructions" means " 'Pennies' as we all use the word in non-existential sentences, e.g. 'Pennies are stamped with the King's head', is a Specious subject-phrase in those sentences". And this means that any sentence with 'pennies' as subject-phrase[1] is not an Ostensive sentence.[2]

2. "S is an Ostensive sentence" means that one of two things is the case.[3] It means that S either (1) expresses an elementary fact, E, and Sketches it, or (2) expresses a non-elementary fact, F, and Indicates each elementary fact which is a Main Prop in a Support of F.

3. E is a support of F if and only if F is either a fact of the form *Something which has φ has ψ* or a fact of the form *The thing which has φ has ψ* or a fact of the form *Everything which has φ has ψ*, while E is a molecular fact *This has φ and this has ψ*.

This has ψ is said to be the Main Prop in the support E.

4. "S Sketches, E, an elementary fact" means "Every element in S names one element in E, and every element in E is named by one element in S, and the arrangement of the elements in S shows the arrangement of the elements in E".

5. "S Indicates, E, an elementary fact" means "S is not a sketch of E, but if for the subject-phrase of S a name be put, then the resultant sentence S′ sketches E".

So the analysis of *"Pennies are logical constructions"* is *Any non-instantial Sentence with 'pennies' as subject-phrase neither expresses an elementary fact, E, and sketches it, nor expresses a non-elementary fact, F, and indicates each elementary fact which is a main prop in a support of F.*

---

[1] The subject-phrase is the part of the sentence before the verb. The predicate-phrase is the part after the subject-phrase.

[2] Every sentence suggests an analysis of the fact it expresses. But the suggestion of a non-ostensive sentence is misleading. Philosophy is concerned with the analysis of facts—a doctrine which Wittgenstein has lately preached and Moore long practised. It is consequently important to philosophers to know whether and in what degree a sentence is ostensive.

[3] I have *not* said that it means one of two, i.e. is ambiguous.

In this summary there are at least these six words which need more exposition—'sketch', 'name', 'show', 'elementary', 'non-elementary', 'express', and 'support'. The meanings of 'express' and 'name' I can only point to and cannot analyse. The meanings of the others I hope not only to point to but also to analyse.

III. FACTS AND ELEMENTS

The word 'fact' will be used in this paper in an ordinary way. When I speak of an ordinary use of an English word I do not mean a common use among philosophers but a common use today among people who speak English. Here are four examples of the way in which I shall use fact. (1) ". . . the fact that two men were in the wildest struggle"; (2) ". . . to say nothing of the fact that I shall probably be sick"; (3) "Perhaps this inborn reserve was explained by the fact that, although they had travelled round the world since childhood, they hailed originally from a bleak, wild, marshy country . . ."; (4) " 'We're living in nineteen-thirty. Why not remember that?' 'I was going to remind you of that fact'."[1]

'The Elements of a fact' has a meaning in this paper which can be pointed out as follows. Consider the fact that (1) George is happy, (2) George hates Geoffrey, (3) This is red, (4) This is on that. George and the predicate *happy* are elements in fact (1); George, Geoffrey and the relation *hates* in fact (2); This and *red* are elements in fact (3); and This, that and *on* in fact (4). George is a Constituent of fact (1) and *happy* a Component of it. George and Geoffrey are constituents of fact (2) and the relation *hates* a component of it. This is a constituent of fact (3) and *red* a component. This and that are constituents of fact (4) and *on* a component of it.[2]

Again, consider "Some dogs are sleepy", "Every dog is sleepy", "The dog is sleepy". The facts so expressed may also be thus expressed: (1) "Sleepy characterizes something characterized by being a dog"; (2) "Sleepy characterizes everything characterized by being a dog"; (3) "Sleepy characterizes the thing characterized by being a dog".[3] *Sleepy* and *being a dog* are constituents of each of these facts and the tie *characterizes* is a component.

This last point distinguishes the second group of facts from the first. *Characterizes* is not an element in the first group of facts. What is expressed by "This is red" is of course equipollent[4] to what is

---

[1] *Strand Magazine*, December, 1929, pp. 372, 373, 378, 396.

[2] The constituents of a fact are sometimes universals, as in *Red entails extended*. But a particular cannot be a component.

[3] I owe this formulation to Prof. G. E. Moore.

[4] Two propositions are equipollent if the one entails the other and the other the one. See Johnson, *Logic*, vol. 1, p. 140.

expressed by "This is characterized by red". And what is expressed by "This is characterized by red" is of course equipollent to what is expressed by "This is characterized by characterized by red". But these equipollencies are not identities. For when we say "This is red" we do not mean what we mean when we say "This is characterized by characterized by red". It is true that the fact expressed by "This is red" is not merely two things *this* and *red*. It is these two stuck together and stuck together in a certain way. As Mr Russell said, a fact has a *sense*. It has a logical arrangement. But the arrangement is not an element in it. To say of a thing that it is a house is not to say of it only that it is a set of bricks. It is to say that it is a set of bricks arranged in a certain way. But the arrangement is not part of what the house is made of. A family is not Bill, Betty and Bob. It has an arrangement. Betty is Bill's wife and Bob the child of both. But blood ties are not members of families. Following Mr Johnson I shall confine the phrase 'characterizing tie' to what arranges the elements of a fact. The confusing thing about the characterizing tie is this: if it arranges the elements of a fact F_1, then there is an equipollent fact F_2 with that tie as an element, and its elements arranged by that very tie.

Mr Johnson says: "The general term 'tie' is used to denote what is not a component of a construct but is involved in understanding the specific form of unity that gives significance to the construct; and the specific term 'characterizing tie' denotes what is involved in understanding the junction of substantive with adjective. The invariable verbal expression for the characterizing tie is the verb *to be* in one or other of its different modes. To think of 'a tall man' or of 'a cold sensation' is to think of 'a man as being tall', 'a sensation as being cold'. Here the word 'being' expresses the characterizing tie, and the fact that in some cases the word may be omitted is further evidence that the tie is not an additional component in the construct, but a mere formal element, indicating the connection of substantive to adjective. This is its peculiar and sole function."[1]

As to Mr Johnson's language here—(1) He is using 'component' as I have been using 'element'. (2) It is surely misleading to talk of the tie as *indicating* the connection of substantive with adjective. That psychological function belongs to the verb 'to be'. The tie is what is indicated. It *is* the connection of substantive with adjective, and it has a logical or formal function.

As to what Mr Johnson means—I see it all plainly except what he says last, which I think untrue. For the characterizing tie is *sometimes* an element in a fact. It is an element in the fact *This is characterized by red*. And it is an element in each of the facts in the second

[1] Johnson, *Logic*, vol. 1, p. 10.

group of facts above. What we express by "Every dog is sleepy" is what we express by "*Sleepy* characterizes whatever *being a dog* (i.e. canine) characterizes". Again, what we express by "There are no dogs" is what we express by "*Being a dog* does not characterize something". Of this more later.

The use of 'Fact', then, in this paper is a well-known *Strand Magazine* use. It is an analysable notion, but with the tools at present to hand I cannot express the analysis grammatically and unambiguously. If I can say "It was because X was P at t", e.g. he was drunk at noon, then I can say, "It was due to the fact that he was drunk at noon". If I can say, "It was because X was R to Y at t", e.g. this was on that at noon, then I can say, "It was due to the fact that X was R to Y at t". The X's and Y's and P's and R's are Elements in the facts. The X's and Y's are Constituents. The P's and R's are Components. Besides elements in facts there are "Directors" for facts.

The Director for the first kind of fact, X was P at t, is the Characterizing Tie. The Director for the second kind of fact, X was R to Y at t, may be called the Connectional Tie.

There is a fact when and only when one or more things are tied to one another.[1] A fact may be one thing tied to another by the characterizing tie, e.g. *This is red*. Then it is a One-Termed Fact. The characterizing tie is a dyadic tie—it involves two things. A fact may be one thing and another (a relation) and another thing, tied by a connectional tie, e.g. *This is on that*. Then it is a Two-Termed Fact. The tie in this case is triadic. A fact may be one thing and another thing and yet another thing and a relation, tied by a connectional tie. Then it is a Triadic Fact. The tie in this case is tetradic. A fact may be . . . and so on.

The Elements in a fact are the things which are tied. The Constituent of a one-termed fact is the thing which is characterized. A many-termed fact always contains an element which is a relation, and the Constituents of a many-termed fact are those things between which the relation may be said to hold. The Components of a fact are those elements which are not constituents.

We shall speak of the elements, constituents and components of series, such as the series of your ancestors; of systems, such as your family; and of sentences.

---

[1] Bradley's argument—the one which is usually called his argument against relations—has brought out the fact that we cannot analyse what is meant by saying of one thing that it is united or tied to another. We can only point to cases of one thing's being united to another. We may express this by saying that the conception of unitedness is ultimate. I cannot *tell* you what is meant by saying of one thing that it is united to another. I can only point to what is meant.

It is a mistake to express this by saying that there is "in every fact something which eludes analysis". For (1) unitedness is not *in* a fact. (2) We are not hunting its analysis, therefore it doesn't elude us.

The word 'sentence' will be used in a peculiar way throughout this paper. In ordinary language if I write on one piece of paper "This is red" and on another piece of paper "This is red" I am writing the same sentence twice. This is because in the ordinary use of language a sentence is not one particular series of inter-related marks rather than another, but (roughly) a class of all those series of inter-related marks which are similar to a given series. Thus the sentence "This is red" is all series of marks similar to the series "This is red", written here. Now 'sentence' is so used in this paper that if I write the same sentence twice I write two sentences. The two series of marks which are the results of my two acts of writing are two sentences. A sentence (ordinary use) is a logical construction out of sentences (in this paper's use).

This point Ramsey has made clear, see *Mind*, N.S., vol. 32, p. 468 [pp. 12–13].

Strictly, of course, even if we use 'sentence' in the way just pointed out, we cannot say that a sentence is a fact—not even the fact that certain marks are related in such and such a way. And neither systems, my family, nor series, the Kings of England, are facts. Still, because of the peculiarly intimate relation which holds between a sentence and the fact that the marks which make it up are arranged in the way they are, and between a series and the fact that its terms are arranged in the way they are, and between a system and the fact that its elements are arranged in the way they are, I shall insist on saying that they are all unities and that facts are too. Facts, sentences, series and systems all have internal structure. A family is not merely a set of people—it is the inter-relationship of a set of people. A sentence is not merely a set of marks—it is the inter-relationship of a set of marks. Further, facts, sentences, series and systems all have ties.

But not in exactly the same sense. For it will turn out that a fact is not grammatically of the same type as a sentence or a system. This means that what is said of the one can never be correctly said *in the same sense* of the other. Consequently they are not unities in the same sense. Consequently, if later I were to define what is meant by saying of two unities that they are identical in structure, the definition would not apply in exactly the same sense to facts, sentences and systems. A separate definition would strictly be required for each. It will be best at present to manage in the following way. A sentence, in the sense in which I said I was going to use it, was a particular occurrence—a noise, or a scratch on paper. Now whenever there is a sentence in this sense there is a fact which is related to it in a peculiarly intimate way—the fact namely that the elements of the occurrence are arranged in the way they are. Let us, till further notice, mean by a sentence such a fact as that.

IV. WITTGENSTEIN AND PICTURING

I shall now try to point out what I mean by sketching, with the help of what Mr Wittgenstein has done to point out the very similar relation of *picturing*.[1]

Mr Wittgenstein writes:

4.01. "The sentence is a picture of reality. The sentence is a model of the reality as we think it is."

4.011. "At the first glance the sentence—say as it stands printed on paper —does not seem to be a picture of the reality of which it treats. But nor does the musical score appear at first sight to be a picture of a musical piece; nor does our phonetic spelling (letters) seem to be a picture of our spoken language. And yet these symbolisms prove to be pictures—even in the ordinary sense of the word—of what they represent."

4.012. "It is obvious that we perceive a sentence of the form aRb as a picture. Here the sign is obviously a likeness of the signified." (Compare also 'Q x Q' in chess.)

4.014. "The gramophone record, the musical thought, the score, the waves of sound, all stand to one another in that pictorial internal relation, which holds between language and the world. To all of them the logical structure is common."

4.016. "In order to understand the essence of the sentence, consider hieroglyphic writing, which pictures the facts it describes."

2.14. "The picture consists in the fact that its elements are combined with one another in a definite way."

2.15. "That the elements of the picture are combined with one another in a definite way, represents that the things are so combined with one another.

This connection of the elements of the picture is called its structure."

2.131. "The elements of the picture stand, in the picture, for the objects."

4.04. "In the sentence there must be exactly as many things distinguishable as there are in the state of affairs, which it represents."

3.2. "In sentences thoughts can be so expressed that to the objects of the thoughts correspond the elements of the sentence."

3.201. "These elements [of sentences] I call simple signs."

3.202. "The simple signs employed in sentences are called names."

3.203. "The name means the object. The object is its meaning."

According to Wittgenstein, then, a sentence, if it is to picture a fact or state of affairs, must have elements such that a one to one correspondence holds between the elements of the sentence and the elements of the fact.

But besides naming the objects and relations which are elements in

---

[1] I put the word 'sentence' where the translation of *Tractatus Logico-Philosophicus* puts 'proposition'. It is quite possible that Mr Wittgenstein would not accept my translation 'sentence'. My description of what I mean by 'sketching' must therefore run "the relation which *would* be similar to Mr Wittgenstein's picturing *if* he accepted 'sentence'".

the fact, it must show what it can never say, namely, the logical form of the fact. Thus to quote Wittgenstein:

4.025. "The translation of one language into another is not a process of translating each sentence of the one into a sentence of the other, but only the constituent parts of sentences are translated."

4.121. "Sentences cannot represent the logical form: this mirrors itself in the sentences."

4.022. "The sentence *shows* how things stand, *if* it is true."

We gather that when a sentence pictures a fact, then (1) elements in the sentence name elements in the fact: for each element in the fact there is an element in the sentence which is its name and vice versa, and (2) the sentence shows the form of the fact.

When a mirror mirrors a scene, then (1) for each coloured patch in the reflection there is a coloured patch in the scene, and vice versa, and (2) the form of the scene is also the form of the reflection—if the coloured patches in the scene run red, green, blue then the coloured patches in the reflection run red, green, blue—in the same order (though the other way round). And even if the mirror distorts there will still be these two facts about the relation between the reflection and the scene. Similarly, if we translate our English into French there will still be these two facts about the relation between the sentence and the case.

I try to give a more definite description of the meaning of 'to picture' by comments on what Wittgenstein says.

Wittgenstein says that sentences picture facts. But hardly any, if any, sentences in any ordinary language do picture facts. Wittgenstein does not want to assert that they do. He is trying to point out an ideal to which some sentences try to attain. He should, I think, have drawn our attention to the fact that some sentences do not try to attain to this ideal. If we consider (1) in what respects those sentences which do try to attain to this ideal fall short of it, and (2) in what respects those sentences which do not try to attain to this ideal differ from those which do, we shall see the ideal more clearly.

Suppose I see a red patch and utter to myself the sentence of which many of us have had such high hopes—"This is red". Even this sentence fails in at least one respect, and perhaps in three or more, to attain to the ideal—to picture a fact. For the sentence contains three elements, "This", "is", "red", while the first fact contains two—what is named by "This" and what is named by "red"—or better, something or other which is characterized and something or other which characterizes. It is true that the fact is not merely two things, this and red. It has a logical arrangement. But the arrangement is not an element in it. A house is not a set of bricks. It has an arrangement—spatial. But the arrangement is not part of what it is made of.

It is clear that with suitable conventions we could write instead of "This is red", "(This) red". And that would be an improvement. Because 'is' is a mark more like 'This' and 'red' than is '(   )'. And this unlikeness in look keeps one in mind of its unlikeness of function. It is clear that with suitable conventions we could write instead of "This is red", "This red". Here we rely not on brackets round 'This', much less on an extra word such as 'is', but on the spatial arrangement of the marks to show the logical arrangement of the elements in the fact. If we had the suitable conventions and did write "This red" in the way suggested we should have a sentence which pictured a fact—provided two things which I fear may be so are not so. I fear that "This is red" may always mean "This has some determinate shade which is a shade of red".[1] Let us, however, suppose that I use "is red" not to mean "has some shade which is a shade of red" but to mean some perfectly determinate shade.

I have a similar fear about 'This'. If I speak not to myself but to someone else and say "This is red" I use "This" as meaning something like "The thing to which I am pointing".[2] It is to be hoped that sometimes when I talk to myself I use it to mean something. My last sentence is not a joke. I do not mean by it that it is to be hoped that I use 'This' as I use 'something'. Nor that it is to be hoped that I am not always talking nonsense when I begin a sentence with 'This'. It means that it is to be hoped that sometimes there is something such that I am using 'this' as a name for it.

To sum up. If we write instead of "This is red" "This red" and 'red' names a shade and 'This' names the something which is of that shade, then "This red" as so used would picture a fact.

If instead of "This is bigger than that" we write "This bigger that", and 'bigger' names a relation and does not mean 'some relation which is a species of bigger', and 'this' and 'that' are names, we again have a sentence which pictures a fact.

But now take a sentence which does not try to picture a fact. Take "The son of the brother of the mother of the boy kissed the girl with almond eyes". This sentence does not picture a fact. The sentence "This is the son of the brother of the mother of the boy, and this kissed the girl with almond eyes" more nearly pictures a fact. And the sentence "This is the son of that, and that is the brother of the mother of the boy, and etc." still more nearly. Owing to the paucity in language of words like 'this' and 'that' we must now invent new ones—'thet', 'thot' and 'thit'—and proceed as follows: "This is the son of that, and that is the brother of thet, and thet is the mother of the boy,

---

[1] See Moore, *Proc. Arist. Soc.*, supplement, vol. 3, pp. 99 ff.; and supplement, vol. 7, pp. 171 ff.; and Langford, *Mind*, Oct., 1929, pp. 436 ff.

[2] I do not feel sure of this.

and this kissed the girl with almond eyes". Next: "This is the son of that, and that is the brother of thet, and thet is the mother of thot, and thot is a boy, and this kissed the girl with almond eyes". Lastly, we have "This is the son of that, and that is the brother of thet, and thet is the mother of thot, and thot is a boy, and this kissed Sylvia". This sentence very nearly pictures a fact.

And if we eliminate words which merely emphasize spatial order and write "This son that, and that brother thet, and thet mother thot, and thot boy, and this kissed Sylvia" we have a sentence which pictures a fact.

Each sentence we have considered we altered till it was "identical in form with" some fact. Then it pictured the fact. Identity in form is the first condition of picturing. We shall find that it is not the last.

If a sentence is to picture a fact, then it must be related to that fact rather in the way in which a picture is related to what it is a picture of and a reflection to what it is a reflection of. The sentence must be identical in structure with the fact it pictures. But, of course, a sentence even in our extraordinary sense is not a picture, much less a reflection,[1] in the ordinary sense of 'picture'. Apart from the more obvious objections to such a view the following should be noted: (1) A sentence is not identical in structure with the fact it expresses in the sense in which a reflection, a picture, a diagram or a map is identical in structure with what it reflects, pictures, represents, or maps. A paragraph or account of a state of affairs *is* identical in structure in this sense with the state of affairs of which it is an account. A sentence is not like a map, but like one of the facts which make up a map,[2] such as that this dot is above that. This fact is of the same form as the fact about the inter-relationship of two towns which it is used to represent. (2) A sentence is not *usually* identical in form with the fact it expresses but only with something at a different logical level. "This red" is identical in form not with the fact expressed by "This red" but with the fact expressed by "This characterized (by) red". (3) The elements of a reflection are patches and the elements of a scene are patches. They are of the same order. The elements of sentences are marks (patches, unities), but the elements of the facts they try to picture are often not unities but particulars and universals, and therefore of a different order. (4) The elements of the scene which are reflected in the reflection are not the ultimate elements of that scene. For a patch has elements—its shade and the particular which has that shade.[3] (5) A sentence requires a speaker. A picture, it is true,

---

[1] Mr Wittgenstein does not say that a sentence is a reflection.

[2] Of course, a map is *not* made up of facts. To say it is is bad grammar. It is a logical construction out of facts.

[3] See R. F. A. Hoernlé, "Concerning Universals", *Mind*, April, 1927, p. 202; and Broad, *The Mind and its Place in Nature*, pp. 48 and 588.

requires an artist, and a diagram a draughtsman. In this they are more like a sentence than a reflection is. And though the use of dots in a diagram and splotches in a picture is not quite that of words in a sentence, yet the uses are very similar, and with a little leniency we may count objection (5) only against the view that a sentence is a reflection. Let us now consider these points.

V. IDENTITY OF FORM

First as to identity of logical form.[1] Even the best sentences are identical in form with a fact in only a rather unexciting way—not like a map and a country. A sentence is identical in form with a fact if and only if they contain the same number of elements. This entails that if the one has an *n*-adic component the other has, and that if one has an *n*-adic tie the other has. In this sense a one-termed fact is identical in form with any other one-termed fact, and not with anything else. And *n*-termed facts are identical in form only with *n*-termed facts. Thus *George hates Geoffrey* is identical in form with *Amelia loves Annabel*, with *The Earth attracts the moon*, and with, among other two-termed facts, the fact that a certain mark is next another, e.g. 'George' next 'Geoffrey'. On the other hand, it is not identical in form with the three-termed fact *The moon is between the earth and the sun. George stuck a knife in Geoffrey* is identical in form with *The moon is between the earth and the sun.* And the fact that '*This*' *is next* '*red*', as it is if I write "This red", is identical in structure with *George hates Geoffrey* and with *Selfridge's is in Oxford St.*, and with, among other two-termed facts, the fact *This is characterized by red.* And the fact that 'hates' is between 'George' and 'Geoffrey', as it is if I write "George hates Geoffrey", is identical in form with the fact that the relation *hates* is between (in a new non-spatial sense of 'between' in which it stands for the connectional tie) George and Geoffrey. Thus the sentence "George hates Geoffrey" is identical in form not with the fact *George hates Geoffrey* but with *George is connected by* hates *to Geoffrey.* I call this last fact the First Derivative of *George hates Geoffrey*.

VI. EQUALITY OF LEVEL

So we come to our second point—that a sentence is usually of a different logical level from that of the fact it pictures.

Supposing I am a gunman and wish to convey quietly to you the news that I have murdered Al Capone. On the table I place a glass, a dish and a knife. I place them in this order—(1) glass, (2) knife,

[1] Susan Stebbing, *Modern Introduction to Logic*, pp. 51–3.

(3) dish. I do this instead of placing marks like (1) "I", (2) "murdered" and (3) "Capone" in that order on a piece of paper. There is a temptation to say that the first "sentence", the crockery arrangement, and the second sentence, the arrangement of marks, are identical in form with the fact they both express. But they are not; as will be seen if we compare them with two better sentences. Supposing I merely place a glass *on* a dish or the mark "I" *next* "Capone".[1] These two "sentences" are identical in form with the fact they express; in these two sentences the components, viz. *on* and *next*, correspond to the component, viz. the relation *murdered*, of the fact they express. In the first two sentences their *constituents*, viz. the knife and "murdered", correspond to the *component* of the fact they express. These two facts, the first two sentences, are not, therefore, identical in form with the fact which they express; they are, however, identical in form with what I call its First Derivative.

What is meant by saying of one fact that it is identical in form with the First Derivative of another? Suppose we have a fact *George hates Anne*. Then there is another fact, *George is a referent*[2] *of hates*, and *Anne is a relatum of hates*. This second fact is the First Derivative of the first. Symbolically, if we have $(xy)R$ then we have $(xR)r_1$ and $(Ry)r_2$. "F is the First Derivative of F^1" means "The components of F^1 are the constituents of F and the ties of F^1 are the components of F".

No ordinary sentence attempts to do more than be identical in structure with the first derivative of the fact it expresses—for all ordinary sentences differ from the glass on the dish in that they contain a word, and thus a constituent, corresponding to the component of the fact they express. Even if we write "This red" instead of "This is red" we have a sentence which is identical in structure not with the fact it expresses but with that fact's first derivative. On the other hand, if I introduce a convention so that I write "This that" instead of "This on that" I get a sentence identical in form with the fact it expresses; for the component *next* of my "This that" sentence corresponds to the component of the fact. It is clear, therefore, that in this respect relational sentences are in a better case than predicational[3] sentences. We may now write down—If a fact is to picture a fact it must be identical in form with that fact or its first derivative.

VII. NAMING AND SHOWING

More than this is required. We must deal with our fifth point—the necessity of an artist. Just as an arrangement of splotches of paint on

[1] As Mr Mace says, "Like a puzzle picture".
[2] In A has R to B, A is referent and B is relatum.
[3] Relational sentences are sentences expressing many-termed facts. Df. Predicational sentences are those expressing one-termed facts. Df.

earth might by chance be identical in structure with a scene in heaven without being a picture of it, so might an arrangement of marks happen to be identical in structure with a fact without picturing it. Just as we require someone to make the splotches with intent to paint the scene, so we require someone to make the marks with intent to express the fact. A sentence requires a speaker. We may now write down: If a fact, F, is to picture a fact F^1, then (1) F must be identical in form with F^1 or with its first derivative, and (2) someone must be using F to express F^1.[1]

Now when one fact, F, is identical in form with another, F^1, or its first derivative, and is used by a speaker to express F^1, then a selection from a certain set of triadic relations is liable to hold between the elements and ties of F, the speaker, and the elements and ties of F^1. These relations cannot hold unless F is identical in form with F^1 or its first derivative. It is in terms of these relations that we must define *picturing*.

Which selection from these relations shall hold between F, a speaker, and F^1, depends upon whether F is (*a*) identical in form with F^1 or (*b*) with its first derivative. Suppose you express F^1 by F and (*a*) F is identical in form with F^1, e.g. you put a glass on a dish to express the fact that I have killed Al Capone. Then (1) you use one constituent of F, viz. the glass, for one constituent of F^1, viz. me, and the other constituent of F, viz. the dish, for the other constituent of F^1, viz. Capone. This particular kind of "using" relation which holds between you and me and the glass I call Naming. Then (2) you use the component of F, viz. the relation *on*, for the component of F^1, viz. the relation *killed*. I call this using of a component for a component Docketing, although it is very similar to naming. Then (3) you use the tying of the elements of F, viz. triadic tying, for the tying of the elements of F^1, viz. triadic tying. This kind of using I call Identically-showing.[2] Suppose you express F^1 by F and (*b*) F is identical in form not with F^1 but with its first derivative, e.g. you put down first a glass then a knife and then a dish to express the fact that I have killed Capone. Then (1) you use one constituent of F, viz. the knife, for the component of F^1, viz. killed. I call this using of a constituent for a component Labelling, although it is very similar to naming and docketing. Then (2) you again name the constituents of F^1 by constituents of F. Then (3) you use the relating of the *constituents* of F, viz. the triadic spatial relating, betweenness, for the tying of the elements of F^1, viz. triadic tying. This kind of using I call Non-identically showing.[3] It is here that we speak of the spatial

---

[1] Whenever these two conditions are fulfilled, F is a sketch of F^1.

[2] It may also be called "formally showing".

[3] It may also be called "materially showing".

arrangement of the constituents of the sentence showing the logical arrangement of the elements of the fact. The use of the tying (or relating) of the elements (or constituents) of F to show the tying of the elements of F^1 is markedly different from the use of the elements (or constituents) of F to name or docket or label the elements of F^1. It is not that the tie (or component) of F is used to stand directly for the tie of F^1, nor even merely that the n-adicness of the one indicates the n-adicness of the other. It is like this: The fact that F has the elements (or constituents) it has enables the hearer to know what elements F^1 has; and the fact that these elements (or constituents) of F are tied (or related) in the order they are tells the hearer in what order those elements of F^1 are tied. Thus, with one convention about what the order of the elements in a sentence tells, to put a glass on a dish tells the hearer that I have killed Al Capone, but with another convention, one according to which sentences were like mirror images, the hearer would learn from that sentence, the glass on the dish, that Al Capone had killed me—a very different thing.

These definitions are, of course, far from satisfactory. Even if they give the correct analyses of the five relations, the words in which those analyses are expressed are not unambiguous. The words "used for" are very dangerous. So I propose to supplement these analyses by descriptions of the relations. (1) *Names*, *labels*, and *dockets* are all species of one relation, *used by someone to stand directly for*, while *identically shows* and *non-identically shows* are both species of another relation *shows*. (2) *Showing* holds only when the sentence is identical in form with the fact it expresses. (3) Only the relating or tying of one thing to a second can show the relating or tying of a third thing to a fourth. And if the relation or tie which is shown is n-adic, then the relation or tie which is showing is n-adic. Only a *fact* can show the sense (or tying) of a fact. (A set of words cannot show the sense of a fact—only an arrangement of words can do this.) A fact can only *show* the sense of the fact it expresses.[1] It cannot state it.[2] (I think we might have a sentence which states the sense of a fact which it does not express. Thus "This is characterized by red" seems to state the

---

[1] Wittgenstein says, *Tractatus Logico-Philosophicus*, 4.022, "The sentence shows how things stand if it is true." And adds, mistakenly, it seems to me, "And it says that they do so stand."

[2] If I write a letter in haste I may either let the letter show my haste—by the scrawliness of the writing—or add a postscript stating my haste. But was I in haste when I wrote the postscript? This postscript (so they say) cannot state. If I want to state that I was in haste when writing the postscript I must add a postscript to the postscript. Mr Wittgenstein says (*Tractatus* 3.332), "No proposition can say anything about itself, because the propositional sign cannot be contained in itself (that is the 'whole theory of types')." To me it looks fishy. If I write "this is in haste" in a letter 'this' refers to all the writing on the notepaper. Of course a proposition cannot be a proposition *with regard* to itself, i.e. cannot be an element of itself.

sense of the fact which not it but "This is red" expresses.)[1] (4) The relation *showing* is triadic—it involves three terms—a sentence, a speaker, and a fact.

(5) *Standing directly for* is a triadic relation between a speaker, a constituent (or component in the case of docketing) of the sentence he utters and an element of the fact he expresses. Thus if I say "This on that" the relation holds between me and "this" and what I use "this" as a name for, and between me and "that" and what I use "that" as a name for. On the other hand, though if I say "The bay beat him" the descriptive phrase "the bay" may be said to stand for something—viz. the winning horse—yet the relation here expressed by "stand for" is tetradic and involves the four terms, me, the phrase 'the bay', the quality *bay*, and the horse to which the quality applies. It is therefore not the relation with which we are concerned. (6) This relation holds between an element of a sentence, an element of a fact, and a speaker, if and only if the sentence is identical in form with the fact it expresses (or its first derivative, of course). Thus each constituent of "That kissed Sylvia" (the sentence above) stands for an element in the fact it expresses. But no constituent of "the boy kissed the girl" stands for a constituent of the fact it expresses. (7) The relation has five determinates,[2] and which of these shall hold between a mark which is a constituent of a sentence and an element of the fact the sentence expresses is determined by (*a*) whether the sentence is (α) predicational, or (β) relational, and by (*b*) the place of the mark in the sentence, i.e. whether (α) the sentence being predicational the mark is first or last, and whether (β) the sentence being relational the mark is first, second or third. Thus suppose we have the predicational sentence "This is red" and the predicational sentence "Red is a quality" the use of red in these two sentences is somewhat different. Again, if I write "This overlaps that" and "That overlaps this" then I use 'this' in two rather different ways.[3] And if I say "*Overlaps* is a determinate of *has some spatial relation*" I use 'overlaps' differently. We may then use a sign to stand directly for something in five ways. We may use it (i) in a predicational sentence for the component; (ii) in a relational sentence for the relation; (iii) in a relational sentence for the relatum; (iv) in a relational sentence for the referent; (v) in a predicational sentence for the constituent (or subject). (8) When a word is used in either of the last three ways it is called by Mr Russell and Mr Johnson a "proper name" or sometimes simply a "name".

---

[1] It will, however, be psychologically impossible to explain in language to someone who does not know how sense is shown in language, how sense is shown in language. Because without knowing this he will not understand the language of our explanation.

[2] Apart from docketing, which occurs when a component, not a constituent, stands or a component.

[3] Consequently there are two slightly different uses of 'name'.

Miss Stebbing and Miss Whetnall would call it a demonstrative symbol. Mr Johnson points out that "proper name" in this new sense is an ideal limit to which proper names in the ordinary sense of 'Jack' and 'Jill' approximate, while uniquely descriptive phrases such as "The boy who broke his crown" do not.[1] Miss Stebbing accepts Mr Johnson's account, but prefers the word 'demonstrative symbol'. I cannot quote in full her description of the relation she expresses by 'is a demonstrative symbol for'. She says that a demonstrative symbol is a symbol which stands for an object with which we are directly acquainted and that it indicates an object without ascribing characteristics. She writes "A says: 'That Church is very large.' B replies: 'That is not a Church, it is the Pitt Press Buildings.' Here B is aware of the referent pointed to by A, but refuses to accept the description implicit in the phrase 'That Church' which A uses to indicate the referent. . . . If A now retorts, 'It looks like a church', here 'it' simply demonstrates . . . ."[2] I should accept this as a good account of what I mean by 'naming'. I shall call symbols which are used in any of the five ways mentioned above to stand directly for something Demonstrative.

If a fact (a sentence) F is to picture a fact, F^1, then (1) it must be identical in form either (*a*) with F^1 or (*b*) with the first derivative of F^1; and (2) if (*a*) there must be someone who is using each constituent of F to name just one constituent of F^1 and is so naming *each* constituent of F^1, and is using the component of F to docket the component of F^1, and is showing the tying of the elements of F^1 by the tying of the elements of F, while if (*b*) there must be someone who is using a constituent of F to label a constituent of F^1, and each other constituent of F to name just one constituent of F^1, and is so naming *each* constituent of F^1, and is showing the tying of the elements of F^1 by the relating (component) of the constituents of F.

Condition (2) entails condition (1). We may therefore eliminate the latter. We then have the definition of *sketch of*. That is to say "F is a sketch of F^1" means there is someone who is using F to express F^1 and using it either as indicated in (2*a*) above or as indicated in (2*b*) above.

Condition (2), though sufficient for *sketching*, is insufficient for *picturing* in Wittgenstein's sense. *Sketching* is adequate for the definition of logical constructions. What I say therefore, till page 216 [p. 65], since it is concerned with picturing, but not with sketching, is irrelevant to the definition of logical constructions and may be skipped. In my opinion it is, however, useful in causing one to become clear about logical constructions.

[1] *Logic*, vol. 1, p. 80.
[2] *A Modern Introduction to Logic*, p. 15, and chap. iii.

VIII. ORDER AND ULTIMACY

So we come to our third and fourth points, namely—(*a*) that the sentence and the fact shall be of the same Order, and (*b*) that the fact shall be of the First Order, i.e. such that its elements are its ultimate elements.

Suppose I am happy—then there is a fact and a unity. Suppose someone uses 'this' as a name for my happiness, and says "This is good". The sentence "This is good" as so used does not picture a fact because its constituents do not label the "ultimate elements" of a fact. The "ultimate elements" of *This is good* include me and the predicate *happy*. Now these are not elements of the fact *This is good* in the sense we have been using 'elements'. They are elements only in the sense that they are elements of an element in our sense. Let us use the expression 'factor' to mean 'either an element or an element of an element or an element of an element of an element or etc.'. We may now pursue our enquiry in the following language. "This is good" does not picture a fact because its constituents do not label the ultimate factors in a fact. What is meant by 'the *ultimate* factors in a fact'? It may be suggested that the ultimate factors in a fact are the factors which are simple or have no parts (in the widest sense of part). But this is a mistake. Remember our improved sentence "This red". The elements of this sentence as improved by us stand directly for ultimate factors in a fact. But it is quite uncertain whether the particular for which 'This' is a demonstrative symbol has parts or not—it may have an infinite number of parts. McTaggart's theory of the infinite divisibility of substance is not incompatible with the theory of atomic facts. On the other hand, though what 'this' names may have parts, the parts must be all of the same logical type, and if what 'this' names is a particular then all the parts must be particulars. This is because to say of a factor that it is ultimate is to say of it that it is a block, and not a unity or construct. To say of a factor that it is ultimate is not to say that it has no parts but it is to say that it has no elements. A particular is not a unity, nor is a perfectly determinate shade of red—they may have parts but they have no elements. They are homogeneous wholes—they are blocks.

If we attempted to tell of the structure of the world and made a list of sentences of the form "This is P" where 'This' named a unity as in "This is good", much about the structure of the world would have been left unsaid.[1] For if each *this* were a unity each would have a

---

[1] I define the Naturalistic Fallacy thus—Let α be the set of possible atomic facts. Let π be the set of components of members of α. Then "Henry is committing the Naturalistic Fallacy" means "Henry is either asserting that good is or contains a member of π, or is asserting that good is *p*, where *p* in point of fact either is or contains a member of π".

structure. And about this structure nothing would have been said.

I have defined the ultimate factors of a fact as those factors which are not unities. But I have never made clear what is meant by "unity". You do not know what is meant by the expression "elements of a unity" because it is grammatically polygamous. We may say, without talking nonsense: (1) "A fact is a unity"; (2) "An event is a unity"; (3) "A society is a unity"; (4) "A machine is a unity". "Fact", "event", "society" and "machine" are words of different grammatical levels. Consequently there are four uses of 'unity', each of a different grammatical level, and there are of course as many uses of 'element' as there are of 'unity'. To avoid a grammatical lapse we must adopt one and only one of the uses of 'unity' and 'element'. One is tempted to define the ultimate factors in a fact as those which are not unities at any grammatical level. But the conception of a grammatical level can be defined only in terms of logical constructions. Now the conception of an ultimate factor does not involve that of logical constructions in its analysis. Consequently, though it is true of every ultimate factor in a fact that it is not a unity at any grammatical level we must not *define* ultimate factor that way. We must proceed as follows:

Take the use of 'element' in which what 'This' names and 'red' labels are elements in the fact expressed by "This red",[1] and use 'element' in that way *throughout* these definitions. Then we have: (1) the Factors of a fact are the elements of the fact and the elements of the elements of the fact and the elements of the elements of the elements of the fact, and so on. (2) The Ultimate factors of a fact are those factors of the fact which have no elements. (3) A First Order Fact is a fact the elements of which have no elements. (They are therefore also its ultimate factors.) (4) A Second Order Fact is a fact the elements of the elements of which have no elements. (5) An n-Order Fact is a fact the elements of the elements of the elements (and so on $n - 1$ times) of which have no elements. (6) Two facts are Equiordinal if they are both of order n.

Since the only things which can have elements in the sense required are facts we can make the following statements: (1) A fact is a First Order Fact if and only if it is a fact which is not about facts—or, more strictly, no elements of which is a fact. (2) A fact is a Second Order Fact if and only if it is about first order facts—or, more strictly, has an element which is a first order fact. (3) A fact is of Order-n if it is about a fact of order $n - 1$. (4) Two facts are Equiordinal if they are both of order n.

Here I must anticipate an objection which might be urged against

---

[1] If we have a sentence "SP" we can be sure that S is an element of the fact expressed by "SP" only if we know that "SP" sketches the fact it expresses.

these definitions. It might be said—"Consider the fact expressed by 'This adjoins that' where 'This' and 'that' do not name particulars, as 'This' does in 'This red', but patches. Here, then, what 'this' names is a patch. Now you yourself have admitted that a patch is a unity, and have claimed that such a fact as is expressed by 'This adjoins that' is not a first order fact (see p. 205 (3) [p. 54 (3)]) but a second order fact. But a patch is not a fact and therefore has not elements in the sense in which a fact has elements. A fact about a patch, therefore, is not about a fact and not about something which has elements in the sense of 'has elements' in terms of which you defined first order facts. Such a fact therefore on your definitions is not a second order fact but is a first order fact."

With the logical equipment at present to hand, I cannot explain clearly the mistake involved in this argument. I shall, however, deny here two of its premisses. (1) The patch is not, in the strict sense of element, described above, an element in the fact expressed by "This adjoins that".[1] And *This adjoins that* is not about the patch in the sense of 'about' used in the definitions above and *is* about a fact—the fact expressed by "This black" (here 'This' is used to name a particular and is therefore not used as it is in "This adjoins that"). It is not necessary, therefore, for me to hold that it is of the first order, even if a patch has not elements. It is true that "This adjoins that" *apparently* expresses a fact about a patch and there is a sense of 'about' in which this fact can correctly be said to be 'about a patch'. Nevertheless, "This adjoins that" *really* expresses a fact about a fact.[2] We may say that the fact *This adjoins that* is about a patch but is "really about" a fact. Now, "really about" is what means what was meant by 'about' in the definitions. Compare here—*England declared war* is about England but is "really about" Englishmen, although we must not translate "England declared war" by "Englishmen declared war"—remember the llama. I cannot analyse the distinction between *about* and *really about* until I have analysed the meaning of 'logical construction'. (2) It is not true that the patch "has no elements" in the sense those words have in the definitions. It is true that to say of a patch "This has elements", using 'has elements' as we do of facts, would not express a true proposition, since it would not express one at all, i.e. be nonsense. But it is also true that to say of a patch 'This has not elements', using 'has not elements' as we do of the elements of *This red*, does not express a true proposition, since it does not express one at all. It is not true, therefore, that according to the definitions above I must say that *This adjoins that* is a first order fact. For

---

[1] "This adjoins that" does not strictly sketch a fact unless we either (1) use 'This' to name a fact (not a patch), or (2) use 'This' to name a particular (not a patch).

[2] And really, really, expresses an event about an event.

a first order fact must be defined as follows: Let F be a first order fact and E be one of its elements. Then "E has elements" must express a false proposition.[1] A first order fact must not be defined as follows: Let F be a first order fact and E be one of its elements. Then "E has elements" must not express a true proposition, i.e. must express a false one *or* not express one at all.

The analysis of first order facts is not in terms of logical constructions. Thus this analysis is not logically dependent upon logical constructions. But it is difficult to understand the words used to express this analysis clearly enough to be able to tell of what order a given fact is until the words 'logical construction' are understood. Thus, the understanding of the statement of the analyses is psychologically dependent upon logical constructions.

We may say, if we like, that a fact is of the *n*th order if it is either really and apparently about facts of order $n - 1$, or really about facts of order $n - 1$, but apparently about something else which is "equivalent to but not identical with" facts of order $n - 1$. We may say, if we like, that a fact is of order n if its elements are unities, at some grammatical level, i.e. in some logical language, of order $n - 1$. But these statements, though true, do not give the analysis of *fact of order n*. And these statements will not be properly understood by one who does not understand 'logical constructions'. This does not matter (even psychologically) because to understand 'logical construction' it is necessary to understand only 'sketching'—not 'picturing'.

CONCLUSION

To sum up: (1) Two facts F and F^1 may or may not be of the same form or equitermed. (2) F and F^1, even if equitermed, may or may not be equilevel. (3) F and F^1, even if equitermed and equilevel, may or may not be equiordinal. (4) F and F^1, even if equitermed, equilevel, and equiordinal, may or may not be of the first order.

"F is a sketch of F^1" means "There is someone who is naming each constituent of F^1 by a constituent of F, and is either (α) showing the tying of the elements of F^1 by the tying of the elements of F and docketing the component of F^1 by the component of F, or (β) showing the tying of the elements of F^1 by the relating of the elements of F and labelling the components of F^1 by a constituent of F".

"F is a sketch of F^1" entails that F is equitermed either with F^1 (if alternative (α) is realized) or with the first derivative of F^1 (if alternative (β) is realized).

And when anyone uses a fact F, which is identical in form with

---

[1] Better: Then "E has not elements" must express a true proposition.

another, F^1, or the first derivative of F^1, to express F^1, then F is a sketch of F^1.

To deal with lies and mistakes a slight modification is necessary. "F (a sentence) is a sketch" means "If the speaker of F is speaking truly then there is a fact F^1 such that the speaker of F is naming each constituent of F^1, etc."

"F is an outline of F^1" means "F is a sketch of F^1 and the elements of F^1 are not its ultimate factors", e.g. "This is good" outlines a fact.

"F is a picture of F^1" means "F is a sketch of F^1 and the elements of F^1 are its ultimate factors".

"F is a perfect picture of F^1" means "The elements of F^1 are its ultimate factors and F and F^1 are equitermed, equilevel and equiordinal".

NOTE (1964): "This article was not intended to give an explanation of what Wittgenstein meant."—John Wisdom.

An Epistle[1]

On the Subject of the Ethical and Aesthetic Beliefs
of
HERR LUDWIG WITTGENSTEIN
(*Doctor of Philosophy*)
to
RICHARD BRAITHWAITE, Esq., M.A.
(*Fellow of King's College*)

JULIAN BELL

TIMID, I venture on a doubtful field,
The heaviest weapon in our verse to wield;
Presume with Dryden's couplet to engage
The wild philosophers in all their rage.
Well knowing how I merit the reproach
In learned fields, unlearned, to encroach;
Well knowing that, a puny Jonah, I
The great Behemoth of the seas defy;
Whose learning, logic, casuistry's so vast,
He overflows the metaphysic waste.

Yet still I hope a line or two may stick,
And that, like Jonah, I shall make him sick.
If, Richard, this analogy alarms,
I do but fight the foe with his own arms;
Whose tortuous mind we often see compare
An opera to begetting of a chair.
(This process may propriety confuse,
But it's a metaphor I've heard him use.)
  My own beliefs are trite and few, as fit

[1] From Sherard Vines (ed.), *Whips and Scorpions: Specimens of Modern Satiric Verse, 1914–31*, London: Wishart, 1932, pp. 21–30. Reprinted by permission of the publisher and Mr Quentin Bell.

The narrow compass of a rustic wit:
Good Sense and Reason; for the rest I hope
Voltaire had owned them, and adorned them Pope:
The rational Common Sense, the easy rule,
That marked for centuries the Cambridge school.
In Rabelais abbey may I graduate,
In Epicurus garden, Candide's mate;
Tho' life looks silly, laugh that it's no worse,
With Herrick, love my mistress and good verse.
We know what's what, and that, so Butler[1] says,
For metaphysic is the highest praise.
If further you should ask, I take my stand
On principles we all can understand
And think one certain truth we yet shall find
'Value is known and found in States of Mind'.
Then, if your question you again repeat,
Why should I rush upon a clear defeat;
Since my opponent, logic being his trade,
Will sure confute me, or if not, evade?
To such a question I might well reply
Let him first mind his trade, then so will I.
But who, on any issue, ever saw
Ludwig refrain from laying down the law?
In every company he shouts us down,
And stops our sentence stuttering his own;
Unceasing argues, harsh, irate and loud,
Sure that he's right, and of his rightness proud.
Such faults are common, shared by all in part,
But Wittgenstein pontificates on Art.

So, Richard, chivalry is my excuse,
I but defend a violated Muse:
What though she has been rather used to rape,
Is that a reason monsters should escape?
But this most urges me, and lulls my fear,
That he declares all reasoning useless here.
Either we know, or nothing can be known;
He's right, and we are different in the bone:
With privileged omniscience soaring high
He sees the Universe before him lie;
Each whirling, lost electrons motion planned
He reads as easy as a watches hand.
Seeing at once each individual fact,

[1] Hudibras, not Analogy.

68

Knowing the consequence of every act,
Plotting a graph on spaces winding curves,
Conscious that instant if one atom swerves.
Knows too the black depths of the human mind,
Motive and thought their name, shape, cause assigned;
The highest ecstasy, most black despair,
Moments when beauty lights the laden air;
Moments when lovers part, or when they meet,—
Omniscient Wittgenstein grows indiscreet:
Knows every stray reflection, joke and whim,
Hopes, fears and fancies, all are known to him.
Yet, though he searches every thought and shape
The flying values from the net escape.

He tells us so; and yet it seems to me,
(Perhaps its only my simplicity)
That perfect map, where everything is shown,
Remains as yet, even to him, unknown.
Ludwig's omniscient; well, I would be civil,
But is he God Almighty, or the Devil?
Still let me state his case as best I can
Before his logic and his facts we scan;
And, whether we may think them false or true
At least the Devil here shall get his due.
    On the world's walls the fluttering Values beat—
—Like drunken mot'rists skidding down a street—
Unknown, touch'd, tast'd, heard, smell'd, undescried,
The Values ring the bell, but stay outside.
All statements men can make, or false or true,
Have facts for predicate, and object too.
This being admitted, it is clearly seen
All statements about Value nothing mean.
His case, if rightly I have understood,
Is he talks nonsense when he talks of Good.
And what there is of fairest and of best
Remains by human language unexprest.
Thought cannot think of, Science cannot show
The element of value here below.

And yet, should I suggest that right and wrong
Are silly burthens of a foolish song;
All actions, thoughts and feelings much the same,
And Value nothing but an empty name:
Or, venturing to try the stuff on art,

Say that his whistlings better than Mozart;
Say Milton should with Humbert go to school
Say Arnold were, by Brémond's side, a fool:
Why, if such statements nonsense are alone,
Do they seem even sillier than his own?
    For he talks nonsense, numerous statements makes,
Forever his own vow of silence breaks:
Ethics, aesthetics, talks of day and night,
And calls things good or bad, and wrong or right.
The universe sails down its charted course,
He smuggles knowledge from a secret source:
A mystic in the end, confessed and plain,
The ancient enemy returned again;
Who knows by his direct experience
What is beyond all knowledge and all sense.

Accept his statements, and what can we find
In all this mystery, but a State of Mind?
Valued by him, and doubtless rightly so,
But fact one day psychology will know.
It seems the great logician has forgot
That either these things are, or they are not;
Even for the mystic does this rule persist,
His visions, if they do exist, exist;
Subject as much to science scrutiny
As copulation or the rule of three.
His visions, in that universal view,
Were shown—and in asylum case books too.

How many saints and sages past have raved
The self same nonsense to a world unsaved.
Since of the truth but portions are our own
How can we know aught *must* remain unknown?
Still science marches on with steady feet,
The map grows yearly more and more complete;
And proves the visions that a saint believed
The sick illusions of a mind deceived.

But in these matters, as he has confest,
Reason's worth little, even at the best.
Agreed: from which I should have thought it clear
The perfect place for tolerance was here.
Let each one choose, but for himself alone,
Nor busy prophets cast the foremost stone.

But Ludwig will have none of this, and would
Issue pope's orders what is bad, what good.
   Reason dismist, how can he get his way?
He may command, but we need not obey.
His only method then is to persuade;
He should have come to us to learn his trade.
Persuasions, verse's great prerogative,
By which the poets love, and sometimes live.
Values that all philosophers escape
The poets catch, and give them form and shape.
His words t'express his meaning were too weak,
But what if Racine, Milton chose to speak?
In ten neat syllables forever lies
All heroes feel, all knowledge of the wise:
Where Dryden's couplets march with ringing stride
There is no value missed, or left outside.
But let us once more to his creed return,
Its essence scan; what is it, but to burn?
Religion once again shall raise its head—
A general resurrection of the dead:—
A battered harlot, who, though old, has found
A silly priest, whose lechry thinks her sound.
We, like good rationalists, have never been
Tempted by Jesus, or by Magdalene.

The murder's out; if now we disagree
Cast into darkness, millstones and the sea.
So he persuades us, but he well may find
The world has got itself another mind,
Since Calvin saved our souls with rack and flame,
And Calas died to save a Catholic's name.
He'd raise religion; has he never thought
How Voltaire laughed God, once and all, from court?
When fiends arise, the water that we take
And sprinkle on them comes from Ferney's lake.
   To us today what can Religion give,
What secrets can it teach us, how to live?
What is the offer that old Blockhead makes
To calm our minds, unriddle our mistakes?
On Moscow's walls religion stands decreed
The people opium: he who runs may read.
But honest minds, of thinking unafraid,
By no desires and by no passions swayed,
With self-reliant courage that can face

Life's brevity, the silences of space:
Sure to all problems by which men are tried
Good sense alone the answer can provide:
Reject such prophets, whose hell painted grave
But fills with misery the short time we have.

   Then, Richard, why must we, who know it vain,
Seek value in his tortured maze of pain;
When in mere common nature we can find
Every delight of body and of mind.
I pity Ludwig while I disagree,
The cause of his opinions all can see,
In that ascetic life, intent to shun
The common pleasures known to everyone.
Round his brains' convolutions wildly hurled
The secrets hidden from a sober world,
Both good and evil, ecstasy and sin,
He does not seek without, but finds within.
Therefore to him the plan was void and null,
Therefore the world seemed valueless and dull.
He makes a virtue of his own defects,
And what he cannot understand, rejects.
For had he ever used his hands or eyes
He might have turned from learning to be wise.

   If once in closing winter he had seen,
When crisp air rings as the hard frost bites keen,
The blue sky faintly veiled with hoary white,
And on the elms the golden leaves hang light;
Seen from a ploughland slope clearly revealed
The wood's bright colours, crimson hedgèd field;
With farm and church th' enormous plain extends
To low-hung mists, where the horizon ends;
And moulded hills and flashing river lie
Like a great map beneath the vaulting sky.
With sparkling blood our quickened pulses beat,
And all earth's beauty lies before our feet.
Yet, should it rain, should even a cloud arise,
The vision leaves our souls, the scene our eyes:
Should indigestion, or a cold, attack,
We curse the frost, and see the world in black.
On matter all our highest good depends.
And, matter failing, every value ends.
The world is ours, with all its kingdoms brave
No more exists of what we want to have.

   My case were won, the question had not been

An Epistle

If Ludwig ever had fair Chloe seen.
Had mark'd a gestures or a movements grace,
Or seen warm firelight flick'ring on her face;
He'd owned that here all Good, all Beauty lies,
Nor sought a world transcending Chloe's eyes.
Yet, like her flowers, of common earth she's made,
She too is mortal, and she too must fade;
And matters victory is easy told;
Chloe, for all her beauty, must grow old.
The landscape changes with the changing year,
The music ends, the visions disappear;
The wrangle of philosophers must cease,
And even Wittgenstein must hold his peace;
To self-same darkness they and we descend
And Ludwig's one with Chloe in the end.

Richard, my sermon's old, my moral trite,
Yet, at the last, will you not own I'm right?
The issue's simple, as it seems to me
Between good sense, sainted insanity;
To alter facts till facts our passions fit,
Or face the truth, and make the best of it.

(*The author wishes to make it clear that this satire is not intended as a personal attack, nor as a criticism of the purely logical and philosophical achievements of Dr Wittgenstein, but solely as a criticism of certain views on art and morals advocated by him three years ago.*)

Are there Ultimate Simples?[1]

JULIUS R. WEINBERG

IN the course of modern philosophy, there have been several attempts
to demonstrate the existence of ultimately simple objects by purely
logical methods. One of the most recent of such attempts forms part
of the foundation of Wittgenstein's logical doctrine. As Wittgenstein has, until quite recently, been considered the authoritative
source of Logical Positivism, an examination of his supposed demonstration of logical simples is propaedeutic to an evaluation of the
method of the school.

The doctrine of logical simples is fundamental to the philosophy
of Logical Positivism. The two principal aims of that philosophical
movement are: to present science with a secure logical foundation,
and to eliminate metaphysics from all significant discourse.[2] In order
to do these things it is necessary to show by logical analysis that there
is only one complete analysis of any given proposition, and that this
analysis is absolutely terminated in the discovery of elementary propositions which are directly and solely concerned with immediate
experience. The doctrine that ultimate simples exist is required to
insure the completeness and uniqueness of any given analysis. The
doctrine can either be assumed, or demonstrated, or introduced as an
arbitrary postulate (convention) to be justified by the success of the
system employing it, but it is evidently essential to Logical Positivism.
For we can see the possible consequences of logical analysis in case
it is not introduced.

To found science on a logical, empirical basis and to eliminate
all trans-empirical concepts as being non-significant, it is necessary,
as remarked above, to prove (1) that there is only one complete

---

[1] From *Philosophy of Science*, vol. 2, no. 4, October, 1935, pp. 387–99. Copyright
© 1935, The Williams & Wilkins Co., Baltimore, Md. 21202, U.S.A. Reprinted by
permission of the author and the copyright holder.

[2] *Wissenschaftliche Weltauffassung, Der Wiener Kreis*, Wien, 1929, pp. 15 ff.

analysis of a proposition and, (2) that this analysis has a theoretically ultimate limit in empirical reality. Now, if many distinct analyses were possible, or if there were no limit to a given analysis, then the theses of Logical Positivism could not be demonstrated. Even though a given analysis of propositions reduced them to propositions exclusively concerned with empirical reality, another possible analysis might very well lead to propositions which were not exclusively concerned with the empirical reality. Similarly, if there were no ultimate limit to analysis, although a given analysis led solely to the empirical reality when carried out to any previously assigned point, further analysis beyond this point might reveal non-empirical reality. Both of these apparent possibilities have to be excluded.

The doctrine of logical simples implies that there is only one complete analysis of propositions, and that this analysis terminates in the empirically grounded elementary propositions. There are three definite steps which conjointly establish the thesis. These are: (1) the demonstration that any proposition is a truth-function of the elementary propositions, and conversely that from any set of elementary propositions, a given truth-function can be constructed; (2) the demonstration that apparent exceptions to this (1) do not exist; (3) the demonstration that the elementary propositions entail logical simples.

Propositions ostensibly compounded out of other propositions are always truth-functions of the latter. Consider the proposition P which is an ostensible compound of p, q, r, . . . P is either a truth-function of p, q, r, . . . or it is not. If it is a truth-function, it can be reduced to p, q, r, . . . , and conversely from p, q, r, . . . P can be constructed. Wittgenstein accomplishes this by an amazingly simple, yet very effective, device. The truth-connectives holding among any group of propositions are: "not", "and", "or", "implies", "is equivalent to", "not both", "neither—nor", "one but not both", "one and not others", etc. Now all of these can be defined in terms of one and the same operation. We may choose "equivalence"[1] or "mutual rejection"[2] or "incompatibility"[3] as the primitive operation. Wittgenstein chooses mutual rejection and defines all the logical truth-operations as compounds of mutual rejection or the "stroke", "/". Thus P/Q is "neither P nor Q". P/P then becomes "not-P", "P or Q" becomes $(P/Q) / (P/Q)$, etc. In general, then, any truth-function of the elementary propositions is a successive and varied application of '/' to the elementary propositions.[4] The

[1] Tarski, A., "Sur le terme primitif de la logistique", *Fundamenta Mathematicae*, vol. 4, pp. 196–200, 1924.

[2] Sheffer, H. M., *Trans. Amer. Math. Soc.*, vol. 14, pp. 481–8, 1913.

[3] Nicod, J., "A reduction in the number of primitive propositions of logic", *Proc. Camb. Phil. Soc.*, vol. 19, pp. 32–41, 1917.

[4] Wittgenstein, L., *Tractatus Logico-Philosophicus*, London, 1922, prop. 6.001.

demonstration that all propositions are truth-functions of elementary propositions then becomes quite simple. At this point an elementary proposition may be considered simply as one which does not ostensibly contain other propositions, whereas a non-elementary proposition is one which does ostensibly contain other propositions.

Now if all the truth-functions are variations of one and the same function, namely the stroke, it is clear that any non-elementary proposition is a compound of other propositions formed by means of the stroke and can be reduced to elementary propositions simply by omitting the principle strokes, then the strokes of lesser scope, etc., until the elementary propositions are obtained.

There are certain apparent exceptions to the assertion that propositions occur in others only as bases of stroke-functions.[1] For this assertion is equivalent to the doctrine that there are only finite truth-functions, i.e. extensional functions, of propositions, whereas it seems as if other functions of propositions might occur. In particular, it seems as if infinite truth-functions and intensional functions might occur. For example, the idea of universal quantification, i.e. "for every X, ØX obtains", does not seem to be developable from a set of elementary propositions by means of the stroke. There would then be infinite truth-functions which could not be reduced to elementary propositions. Again, the occurrence of a proposition P in the assertion "P contains an apparent variable" seems to be a case of P's occurrence in a larger proposition other than as the base of a truth-operation. The same obtains for "John believes P".

Wittgenstein, to whom this whole analysis is due, has shown that these apparent exceptions cannot stand the test of analysis. Universal quantification is an ambiguous idea, which when rendered unambiguous, does not constitute an exception. For a finite number of cases, "for every X" becomes equivalent to "this X and that X etc." An infinite number of cases of propositions does not occur because the idea of infinity is not applicable to propositions. It is not, in fact, a logical idea at all, but belongs rather to mathematics.

The intensional function remains to be dealt with. A propositional sentence has two aspects between which Wittgenstein radically distinguishes. As it is spoken, thought, or written, it is a series of noises, a psychological process, or a series of marks. It is, that is to say, a fact in its own right. As it is used to represent some fact, no account is taken of its own factual nature, but, by means of it, another fact is represented. Now it is easy to see that it is only with the latter aspect that we are concerned when we speak of "the proposition" or

---

[1] Wittgenstein, op. cit., prop. 5.54: "a proposition occurs in another proposition only as the base of a truth-operation".

"the symbol" in its occurrence as a part of another "proposition" or another "symbol". Hence P, as proposition, is intended when we say that P occurs in a truth-function, whereas P, as a fact, is intended when we say "P contains an apparent variable" or "John believes P". These two aspects of the propositional sentence have not the least to do with one another. The "intensional" exceptions do not actually constitute genuine exceptions.[1] From these considerations we are naturally led to the idea that there are only two kinds of propositions, elementary and non-elementary (the latter being simple truth-functions of the former), and further that the elementary propositions constitute the ultimate basis of all significant discourse. It could, of course, be urged that the elementary propositions might themselves be functions of other propositions. But, while this view does not lead to contradictions, it produces practical difficulties which are equally vicious. Assuming that the number of propositions is definitely limited, the truth of a given proposition would then become dependent upon itself, since it would become, in part at least, a truth-function of itself. On the other hand, if no limit to the number of propositions is assumed, the truth of any proposition would depend on the truth of others in an unending regress. In this case, the truth would never be finally determined.

In other words, since the truth of a compound proposition depends upon the truth of its constituent propositions, there must be some proposition whose truth depends upon agreement with reality rather than upon the truth of constituent propositions. Otherwise, truth would either be dependent on itself or upon an infinite regress. Hence, if truth exists at all, there must be elementary propositions. This is a final conclusion to which almost everyone would give assent. And if this were the whole of Wittgenstein's argument, no difficulties would arise.

Wittgenstein, however, believes that the nature of elementary propositions requires the assumption of logical simples. It is this part of his doctrine that requires examination. The argument purporting to demonstrate the existence of logical simples runs as follows: "If the world had no substance (i.e. simple objects) then whether a proposition had sense would depend on whether another proposition was true. It would then be impossible to form a picture of the world (true or false)."[2] The significance of this argument depends on the explanations of terms given in various parts of the *Tractatus*. The principal terms requiring explanation are "object", "fact", "proposition", "true and false", and "sense of a proposition".

A proposition always enunciates the existence or non-existence

[1] Wittgenstein, op. cit., prop. 5.542.
[2] Wittgenstein, op. cit., prop. 2.0211–2.0212.

of a fact. Logical analysis should find its ultimate data in elementary propositions and the facts which they represent. Names and other ingredients of symbolism interest the logician merely as material for constructing propositions and not on their own account, because names, etc. have their sole significance as articulate parts of propositions. The same consideration obtains for objects and facts. Objects as such are purely formal entities which constitute the constituents of facts. They can only be conceived in the context of some facts or others. On the other hand, some description of objects and names is necessary in order to understand the nature of the facts and propositions constructed out of them. An object may, therefore, be described as whatever is a distinguishable part of one or more facts. A fact is simply a combination of objects. This circular description is unavoidable and does not, it is admitted, explain very much. It does serve to point out the independent and complete character of the fact as contrasted with the dependent and incomplete nature of objects. The proposition has already been explained as a picture or representation of a fact. If the fact exists, the proposition is said to be true, and if not, false. The sense of the proposition is what exists if the proposition is true. Obviously, a false proposition can have sense. These explanations suffice for the discussion of Wittgenstein's argument.

One further principle is required. "Every statement about a complex can be analysed into a statement about its constituents and into those statements which completely describe the complex."[1] This seems to mean that whenever a statement occurs in which there is the name of a complex, a translation of that statement into another statement (or several other statements) is possible such that the name of the complex gives way to a concatenation of the names of its constituent parts. By virtue of the considerations in the third paragraph of the present essay, one and only one analysis of a given complex is possible.[2] We may now consider the demonstration that simples are necessary. Wittgenstein supposes that the assertion that a proposition has sense is incompatible with the assertion that the proposition contains names which are reducible without limit to other terms. This is clear from the direct form of the demonstration. In the indirect form given in the *Tractatus* the argument is: If the world has no simples, then, if any proposition has sense, another proposition is true, and if any proposition has sense implies another proposition is true, then it is impossible to form a picture of the world, i.e. no proposition has sense. In the direct form: It is possible to form a picture of the world implies it is false that *any proposition has sense*

[1] Wittgenstein, op. cit., prop. 2.0201.
[2] See also Wittgenstein, op. cit., prop. 3.25.

implies another proposition is true, and if it is false that *any proposition has sense implies another proposition is true* then the world has simples.

We may now elucidate the argument. If the world had no simples then propositions containing names of complexes would be transformed into other propositions asserting that the elements of the complex were united in such and such a way. These elements are *ex hypothesi* not simples but complexes in their own right. The sense of any one proposition about complexes would depend on the truth of those propositions into which it would be transformed. This process of transformation would proceed without end. Hence, there would be no connection between the propositions and their extra-propositional referents. This implies that no connection between the pictures of the world and the world itself exists. Hence picturization of the world is out of the question and this is equivalent to the assertion that propositions have no sense. The denial of simples is, therefore, logically incompatible with the assertion that propositions have sense.

In the direct form, the argument has the form: If propositions have sense independent of other propositions, then there are simples. It remains to ask whether this is a demonstratively certain proposition. If there is a logical connection between propositional sense and the existence of simples, the argument is a *petitio.* If not, the argument is an *ignoratio.*

A consideration of what Wittgenstein means by the sense of a proposition shows that the argument is not an *ignoratio elenchi.* The sense of a proposition is the possibility that the fact to which it refers (i.e. the fact which it pictures or represents) exists. In order that a proposition have sense, it is necessary to establish a bi-unique isomorphic correspondence between the proposition and its referent. That is, the terms of the proposition must be correlated with the elements of the fact, and the form of representation of the proposition must be identical with the structure of the fact. In other words, in order to have representation of one thing by another there must be an identity of the arrangement of the elements of the one and the arrangement of the elements of the other and a one-one correlation of the elements of these respective things.[1] From this it is clear that the sense of propositions is essentially connected with the nature of facts. The argument is, therefore, not an *ignoratio.*

But, inasmuch as the kind of correspondence required in Wittgenstein's conception of sense is possible only on condition of a correlation of simple names, simply arranged, with simple objects, simply arranged, the conception of sense implicitly contains the

[1] *Tractatus,* 3.21, 2.13, 2.15, 2.18, 4.0312.

assumption of simple objects. In other words, what is to be proved has been implicitly assumed, because what has to be proved is the existence of simples which depends upon the existence of a proposition with a significance independent of other propositions, and this last depends upon the existence of simples. Hence, the argument is a *petitio principii* in the form in which it was given.[1]

We are now prepared to consider whether the argument can be construed so as to avoid the trivial appearance that it has presented thus far. Or rather, let us enquire whether there is any other argument in the *Tractatus*, explicit or implied, that would necessarily establish the existence of simples. There seems to be such an argument, but it can be shown to be quite inadequate to demonstrate what it attempts to demonstrate.

We turn to the definition of fact given in Wittgenstein's work. We found that the argument for simples depended upon 'sense'. It was shown that 'sense' in such an argument was either irrelevant or arbitrarily defined in lieu of further information. Perhaps the conception of 'fact' will supply this need, and will show that only one conception of 'sense' is possible, because only one conception of fact is possible. This, if true, would remove any appearance of triviality, and would present at the same time an independent argument for the existence of simples.

"A fact is a combination of objects (entities, things)."[2] There are, of course, facts (Tatsachen) composed of other facts, but these divide into independent facts (Sachverhalte), and we shall henceforth be exclusively concerned with the latter. A fact, then, is not a simple entity, but always a complex of objects. Objects, on the other hand, are conceivable solely as possible constituents of facts. The objects contain the possibility of those facts of which they are possible constituents. In the fact there is no further entity by virtue of which the objects are, as it were, held together. The objects simply combine immediately with one another to form a fact, and this combination is internal to the objects. The objects, that is, "hang into one another" in the fact. The specific mode of combination, the way in which the objects hang together, may be called the structure of the fact.

What, now, can be deduced from the definition given? If a fact is a combination of objects, it is necessary that it be a specific combination in order that the fact be a specific fact. The combination will be singular, since it is necessary only to have *one* mode of combination of two or more objects in order to have *a* fact. Hence, the simplest kind

---

[1] It is true that all formal reasoning is a begging of the question if something about the world is in question. To say that a reasoning is formally rigorous is therefore, to deny that anything about the world has been established thereby.

[2] *Tractatus,* 2.01.

of facts conceivable will be singular, specific modes of combination of objects. Furthermore, in order that the combination of objects in the fact be singular and specific, it is necessary that the objects be irreducibly simple, for a singular and specific mode of combination could not obtain among objects which were complex. A singular, specific mode of combination among complexes is a contradiction in terms. If, then, there are facts in the sense defined, there will necessarily be irreducibly simple constituents of facts. And, of course, if there are not facts in the sense defined, it is difficult to conceive what kind of complexes facts may be. Facts, therefore, are either definite or ambiguous combinations. Wittgenstein would unquestionably regard an 'ambiguous combination' as a contradiction in terms,[1] and it is evident that a 'specific singular combination among complexes' is a contradiction in terms. Hence, if there are facts, there must be specific facts, and if there are specific facts, there must be absolutely simple constituents of facts. This, apparently, is the argument which underlies the one which we considered above. We may, therefore, consider it exclusively, and enquire as to its validity.

It is, evidently, an argument from definition. As it stands it is formally valid, but still trivial, because purely verbal. In order to render it free from this charge, it would be necessary to show: 1. that it is really possible to define what is meant by 'a fact', and 2. that the definition which has been given in the *Tractatus* is the only legitimate definition possible.

Let us consider (2) first, because it leads into (1) more understandably than in the logically more correct order of these requirements. How could we demonstrate the exclusive correctness of the definition? There appears to be only one way, namely the method of intuitive induction. Just as we grasp the essence of triangularity from an examination of several triangles, so we should be able to grasp the essence of 'fact' from an examination of several facts. If by this method we find one fact that satisfies our definition, we know that the definition contains a sufficient condition of 'being a fact', and if we also grasp the one and only essential of 'being a fact' from an examination of several facts, and find that this essential is in our definition, we also have the necessary condition.

The successful application of intuitive induction in this case depends (1) on whether there is a common characteristic of facts in virtue of which they are facts, i.e. on whether all facts share an essential characteristic called 'being a fact', and (2) on whether, assuming that there is such a characteristic, it can be introduced into discourse as the definiens of a definition.

---

[1] *Tractatus*, prop. 5.5423: "To perceive a complex means to perceive that its constituents are combined in a definite way."

This remains an open question since there are no known arguments to support an affirmative answer and many that support a negative one.

Principal among the arguments on the negative side is the difficulty of conceiving how facts which have neither constituents nor components in common could have anything in common. If, e.g., fact F' has a, b, etc. as constituents and R as component, and F" has m, n, etc. as constituents and S as component, F' and F" have nothing specific in common. What is the justification for calling a, b, m, n, by the common name 'object' and R, S by the common name 'structure'? In order to construct a definition it is necessary to use these common terms, but the terms have no apparent connotation, since they denote things with nothing in common.[1] If these terms have no connotation, they cannot be used in a definition that must present an essential characteristic. And, in another place, Wittgenstein, himself, has said that 'object' is a pseudo-concept and occurs in discourse solely as a variable name.[2] It seems reasonably clear that this renders definition of 'being a fact' impossible, and it throws considerable doubt on the existence of this essential characteristic.

Intuitive induction may discover the essence of 'being a fact', but this essence cannot be expressed. As a consequence, the argument from the definition is meaningless. That is to say, if the definition cannot be given, deductions from it cannot be given. If it is necessary intuitively to grasp what it is to be a fact, then it is also necessary intuitively to grasp what it is to be a simple constituent of a fact. There would then be no argument for simples, but everything of this kind would have to depend upon intuition.

If, however, it is possible to define fact, if the use of the words 'object', 'structure', etc. do have some connotation, it is still difficult to see how the definition could be justified. How, in other words, assuming *some* definition to be possible, could we prove that one particular definition alone was possible? Intuitive induction would not serve us in this case. We can conceive of many definitions of fact which are not self-contradictory. It seems quite impossible to demonstrate that one alone is correct. No logical principles would serve to do it. Direct examination of facts will not suffice. Experiment and problematic induction are obviously useless for such a task.

We are forced to conclude that the possibility of defining 'fact' is questionable, and that even if we disregard this questionable point and proceed to construct a definition, there is no way to demonstrate the exclusive correctness of it. Other definitions are always possible, and there will be no way to judge which among them is exclusively

---

[1] Equivocation in Aristotle's sense. Cf. *Categories*, 1.1cc.
[2] *Tractatus*, 4.1272.

correct. We can make deductions from these definitions, but since the definitions are quite arbitrary, deductions from them will have merely a verbal force.

What, then, must be said about the possibility of demonstrating the two principal theses of Wittgenstein's Logical Positivism? First, can the exclusively empirical reference of all significant discourse be demonstrated by any logical methods? Secondly, is it possible to demonstrate the ultimate empirical reference of discourse without self-contradiction? This question cannot be adequately treated here. The contradiction arises because after we have demonstrated that the ultimate reference of discourse is exclusively empirical, we are forced to account for our demonstration which obviously cannot itself have an empirical reference.

At first sight, it would seem possible to show that, even without the apparently indemonstrable doctrine of ultimate simples, propositions must be possibly true or false in order to have any significance, and that the only decisive criterion of truth or falsity is an experiment.

But that an experiment is an exclusively empirical test remains to be proven, and cannot be assumed or arbitrarily introduced as being empirical by definition. The elements of theory and implicit beliefs which cling to every experiment in natural science have to be eliminated by some method or other. This would be particularly hard to accomplish in the case of a microscopic experiment. It frequently happens that we think we have verified a proposition, when we have really only confirmed the consequence of a theory. It is such a case as this one which should make us extremely skeptical of equating experimental and empirical criteria of meaning.

The argument that the "sense" of a proposition in the widest sense of the word must ultimately be determined by extra-propositional considerations (i.e. the facts, whatever they may be), is not subject to the same criticisms levelled against Wittgenstein's particular argument. It is clear that any infinite regress in which propositions always depend on other propositions in respect either of meaning or truth leads to absurd results. This merely establishes the fact that propositions have an ultimately extra-propositions reference. From this, nothing can be determined concerning the nature of this reference. This argument does not suffice, therefore, to prove the empirical character of propositional meaning. The stronger argument of Wittgenstein would, if it were valid, suffice to demonstrate that conclusion. But, as we saw, this was not the case.

The only safe judgment in regard to this matter at the present stage of logical investigation seems to be: That some propositions have not been shown to have an exclusively empirical reference and that consequently we do not have the right to regard metaphysics as meaningless, because non-empirical, until we have shown that every non-metaphysical proposition is purely empirical.

NOTE (1964): "There are a number of misconceptions in my essay which should be corrected. The first of these is that the ultimate end of analysis is empirical reality. I do not know what Wittgenstein supposed the ultimately simple objects were, but I now see that it was rash to assume that they would be empirically accessible. The second error was to attribute to Wittgenstein the idea that quantified propositions are equivalent to *finite* conjunctions, disjunctions, etc. The third error was to think of Wittgenstein as a logical positivist. There are doubtless other misconceptions but I have accepted the invitation of the editors to reprint this essay because I still think it contains some points of value. The mass of literature which has appeared since 1934 on Wittgenstein's philosophy has clarified many points about which all of us were puzzled, but the picture of Wittgenstein's earlier thought which emerges from all these critiques and elucidations is not as flattering as were earlier portraits made by enthusiastic disciples. Nevertheless, my debt to the stimulus afforded by reading the *Tractatus* as a young man remains and I am glad to have the opportunity to acknowledge it here."—*Julius R. Weinberg*.

Structure in Sentence
and in Fact[1]

WILLIS MOORE

LUDWIG WITTGENSTEIN and certain of his friends and followers have
offered an interesting answer to the question of the relation "one
fact (such as a sentence) [must] have to another in order to be capable
of being a symbol for that other".[2] The answer in brief, as Russell
puts it, is that, "in order that a certain sentence should assert a certain fact there must . . . be something in common between the structure of the sentence and the structure of the fact".[3] Wittgenstein
himself in the *Tractatus* usually denominates this common element as
logical structure. The sentence is said to *picture* its fact; it *reflects,
mirrors, shows* or *exhibits* by means of its own structure the structure
of the fact it is about. Critics and interpreters generally agree with
Russell's broad characterization of the theory but disagree greatly as
to the exact nature of this postulated common structure. Consequently, the evaluation of the theory which this paper proposes to
make must include an examination of its several alternative interpretations.

At least one logical positivist calls this common element *grammatical* structure. Mrs S. K. Langer writes: "The sentence may denote
any fact which has a structure similar to that which we call the syntax. If we know the grammatical structure, i.e. the relation which the
parts of the sentence bear to each other, then we know that the
possible denotations of the sentence as a whole are limited to those
things which have an analogous structure."[4] Such passages as the

[1] From *Philosophy of Science*, vol. 5, no. 1, January, 1938, pp. 81–8. Copyright ©
1938, The Williams & Wilkins Co., Baltimore, Md. 21202, U.S.A. Reprinted by permission of the author and the copyright holder.
[2] Russell, Bertrand, *Introduction* to Wittgenstein's *Tractatus Logico-Philosophicus*,
p. 8.
[3] Ibid., p. 8.   [4] *The Practice of Philosophy*, pp. 112–13.

following from the *Tractatus* might seem to support this interpretation: "One name stands for one thing, and another for another thing, and they are connected together, and the whole, like a living picture, presents the atomic fact".[1] "That the elements of the picture are combined with one another in a definite way, represents that the things are so combined with one another. This connection of the elements of the picture is called its structure. . . ."[2]

Both Russell[3] and Schlick[4] have cautioned against the confusion of what they call *grammatical* and *logical* structure. Mrs Langer may be making some such mistake in interpreting Wittgenstein, but the view is worth examining anyway. The first question is as to the nature of *grammatical* structure. For the purposes of this analysis we shall take Russell's explanation offered in *Our Knowledge of the External World*.[5] That which remains constant in the series of sentences beginning with "Socrates drank the hemlock" and ending with "Coleridge ate opium" is what will serve as an example of the structure or form as distinguished from the content of a sentence. These sentences have in common a certain arrangement of certain types of words. Symbols for an actor, an act, and an object acted upon appear, as read or as spoken, in the order named. This structure we call, in grammatical terms, the active voice type.

Now, is it true that this structure is common to these sentences and the facts they express? First, can the objects meant by the symbols, namely, the actor, act, and object acted upon, be wholly or in part the element common to sentence and fact? They do appear in the fact but clearly do not appear in the sentence. The constituents of the sentence are *symbols* for actor, act, etc., but not the things symbolized. Furthermore, the *particular* actors, acts, etc., by definition are not parts of the structure; and how an actor or an act in general could appear either in sentence or in fact is incomprehensible to me.

A more likely supposition as to the nature of grammatical structure is that it is the configuration of the elements of the sentence, their different meanings serving merely to distinguish one from another. In the written sentence the order is spatial; as read off or spoken it is temporal. Can either of these be the structure said to be common to a sentence and its fact? Assuredly in some cases the spatial arrangement of the sentence elements *could* be similar to that of the fact. For example, in the sentence, "John sits next to James", we could be picturing the spatial relationship of John to James, where James is to the right of John. But the obvious fact that the spatial arrangement of elements could be (and generally is) different in the sentence

---

[1] Op. cit., 4.031.   [2] Ibid., 2.15.
[3] *Introduction to Mathematical Logic*, p. 199.
[4] University of California Lectures, 1931–2.   [5] Pp. 42 ff.

and its fact shows this factor to be an accidental feature of symbolization. The sentence, "Socrates drank the hemlock", is one such contrary example. Could Socrates in the fact be to the left of the act and
the act to the left of the hemlock? To ask the question is to reveal the
ridiculousness of the hypothesis.

Similarly, there is no *necessary* agreement between the temporal
order of the elements of the sentence as read or spoken and the
elements of the fact. Does Socrates in the fact appear first, followed
by the act of drinking and the hemlock in the order named? Obviously neither spatial nor temporal configuration of sentence elements is necessarily a reflection of a like configuration in facts. This
is not to deny the existence of such structures, or even the occurrence
of types of such, in either sentence or fact. Nor is it to deny the possibility of either one of these occasionally directly reflecting what
appears in fact. These resemblances, exemplified in our early written
language, are not logically necessary to expression or communication.
The propositional sign, as a complex fact, necessarily has some
structure or other, and man has learned to utilize this aspect of the
sign to symbolize certain aspects of facts, even in some instances
similar structural elements; but such symbolization is entirely arbitrary, within the bounds of the conventional system.

Our conclusion must be that if grammatical structure is wholly or
in part spatial or temporal configuration of distinguishable sentence
elements it cannot be the factor necessarily common to a sentence
and what it is about. Any other interpretation of what is meant by
grammatical structure would, I am sure, be subject to the same
conclusion.

Wittgenstein in various passages in the *Tractatus* calls this common
element the "form of representation", or "the logical form of representation".[1] "Form of representation" he defines as "the possibility
of structure".[2] What he seems to mean by this is that for one fact to
picture another it must be able to exhibit the same mode of relation,
e.g. a spatial fact can be represented by a spatial picture, a coloured
one by a coloured picture, a logical one by a logical picture.[3] But, all
pictures are also logical pictures and language is in terms of such.[4]
Therefore, it would seem that every picture would have this necessary element in common with any fact. So, to say that a sentence has
in common with what it pictures the possibility of logical structure is
to say nothing of any significance; for what it has in common with all
facts (including all other sentences) can in no way explain how it can
represent some particular fact. Logical form, as the mere *possibility*
of logical structure, is not, then, the factor Wittgenstein intends.

[1] Op. cit., 2.17, 2.18, and 2.2.   [2] Ibid., 2.033 and 2.15.
[3] Ibid., 2.171.   [4] Ibid., 2.182.

The language of the *Tractatus* sometimes suggests that this factor is a "law of projection" or "rule of translation" for projecting or translating a fact from one medium to another.[1] In this rule or law, so it appears, lies the internal similarity holding between picture and pictured. But, if this be true this common element certainly is not, as elsewhere stated, reflected by or mirrored in a fact. The law itself is not *in* the fact or the sentence. Nor is this factor as usually described such that it needs a law or rule to reveal it. Now there *is* a law of translation which enables a person to know what a propositional sign is about and a rule which a speaker or writer of one must follow if he expects to be understood; but these amount to no more than being conventional in the use of sensible objects as signs. Using these objects in communication as others do is difficult to construe as some element common to sentence and fact, or as one revealing such an element.

A more reasonable interpretation is the one given by Moritz Schlick.[2] He contended that for Wittgenstein logical structure has at least two aspects discernible in all sentences, namely, *multiplicity* and *order*. This interpretation is based upon numerous passages from the *Tractatus* of which the following are representative: "In the proposition there must be exactly as many things distinguishable as there are in the state of affairs, which it represents. They must both possess the same logical (mathematical) multiplicity."[3] "The propositional sign consists in the fact that its elements, the words, are combined in it in a definite way."[4] The first passage describes *multiplicity*; the second *order* or configuration.

It is significant that Wittgenstein illustrated what he took the relation between sentence and fact to be by means of an analogy with that holding between a line on a phonograph record and the stream of sound it records.[5] In what sense might this line and its stream of sound exhibit the same multiplicity and order of elements? We might at first perceive no similarity. One of the states of affairs concerned is a fine engraved line of varying patterns of indentation, appearing on a dark disk; the other is a stream of tones varying in pitch, intensity, colour, etc. More careful examination, however, reveals common features. If the recording is a good one the record will show a perceptible variation in these marks for every perceptible variation in the stream of sound. The two states of affairs exhibit the same number of variations, i.e. have the same logical multiplicity. Furthermore, they also show identical patterns of variation—for example, a deep indentation followed by two shallower ones on the record corresponds to an intense tone followed by two less intense ones in the

[1] Op. cit., 4.014. [2] University of California Lectures, 1931–2.
[3] Op. cit., 4.04. [4] Ibid., 3.14. [5] Ibid., 4.0141.

stream of sound. So, in a fairly simple sense, the line on the record and the sound it records do exhibit an identity of structure. In this case the common element is sensibly discernible.

This description of the relation holding between a line on a record and the sound recorded is, I believe, accurate. If logical structure consists in multiplicity and configuration of distinguishable elements, then the line and the sound certainly have them in common. The problem lies, however, in the application of the analogy. Is the *sentence-fact* relation the same as the *phonograph record-sound recorded* relation? Wittgenstein assumes that it is.

We can deal briefly with the aspect of logical structure called *configuration* or *order*. If by such is meant the sort of thing just described as an arrangement of distinguishable elements in line and sound then we have already rejected it as a necessary common element as between sentence and fact. In the line and sound it is merely spatial and temporal configuration of elements, the same thing dealt with above as a possible interpretation of *grammatical* structure. What was said there holds here of *logical* order. Such spatial or temporal configuration as appears in a sentence is either non-significant or simply a conventional device for indicating something about a fact. What *is* thus indicated, whether or not it be a similar structure in the fact, could as well be indicated by some different configuration of elements, or even by a word or phrase.

Logical multiplicity, however, cannot be so easily disposed of. We must return to our typical sentence, "Socrates drank the hemlock", and re-examine it and the fact it represents to settle the question this analogy raises. Does this sentence have the same logical multiplicity as its fact exhibits? First, what *is* the multiplicity of the sentence, i.e. what is the number of distinguishable elements that compose it? This question is not easy to answer. Must we count the letters? The dozens of variations in the marks lower in level than letters? Or if we ascend to the level of words, do we count the word *the*? Does the tense of the verb count? Or the direction of the act, however indicated? But let us pass over these difficulties, assuming for simplicity's sake that there are three elements present in the sentence, a symbol for actor, one for act, and one for object acted upon. Turning now to the scene pictured by the sentence—do we find there this same multiplicity of elements? The answer will depend largely upon what we take to be the fact represented. The scene I imagine as a result of reading this sentence is much more complex than the sentence. For example, I cannot imagine it without thinking some sort of container for the hemlock. If this scene suggested (which is probably no more complex than the scene in the presence of which the proposition was originally conceived) is what is meant by the fact represented by the

91

sentence, then their multiplicity is not identical. The sentence is always the result of a narrow selection from a complex fact. Both the borders of the fact and the number of elements within those borders seem to be relative to the purpose and other factors in the mind of the perceiver of the moment.

If, however, by the fact represented is meant only those elements of the richer context strictly indicated (denoted) in the sentence, then by sheer definition the sentence and its fact have the same multiplicity. But such an identity of structure would not be analogous to that present in a phonograph record line and its sound. In this latter case a perceiver can read the multiplicity of the sound from the line and that of the line from the sound. The same is not true of the sentence and its fact. One cannot read the multiplicity of the sentence from its fact but only that of the fact from the sentence. In a sense the line does *mirror* the multiplicity of the sound, and vice versa; but the sentence can hardly be said to do so with regard to the multiplicity of its fact. Rather it *defines* this multiplicity. An analogy better suited to the sentence-fact situation, as here interpreted, than that of the phonograph record-sound recorded type is that of the use of lights in a theatre so arranged and operated as to throw into relief on the stage first one set of figures and then another at the will of the person controlling the lights. The lights correspond to the sentence and the figures on the stage to the fact expressed by the sentence. The sentence is, thus, in a sense, the creator of the multiplicity of its fact, not a reflection of it. At any rate, I think we must conclude that, on either interpretation of what is meant by the fact represented, the sentence-fact relation is not analogous to the one used by Wittgenstein for purposes of illustration.

But, for the sake of the argument, let us assume all that Wittgenstein claims here, that the picture and the pictured have a definite and an identical logical multiplicity. Even so, would this knowledge alone enable us to understand why this picture pictures this particular fact rather than some other? Certainly not. Two sentences could have exactly the same multiplicity of elements and yet represent two facts which differ in every respect except this one, that they, too, have the same number of distinguishable elements. Conversely, two facts with identical multiplicity, if differing at all in content, must be represented by two sentences rather than one. Clearly the phenomenon of representation by sentences is not explained by a mirroring of structure if by such is meant multiplicity of distinguishable elements.

Those who support this theory would probably contend that identity of multiplicity alone does not explain representation but that this together with order can do so. Unless by *order* is meant something other than configuration of elements this contention has already been dealt with. It is difficult to see how order and multiplicity taken together constitute the element common to sentence and fact if actually order is seldom so found, and never necessarily so, and, further, if multiplicity, instead of being common to the two, is rather *defined* in the one by the other.

What must we conclude as to this theory? If a sentence did represent its fact as a line on a record records its sound, we probably should have to agree with Wittgenstein's contention. But the situations are only loosely analogous. The line on the record bears a mechanical, causal relation to its sound. Man produces the record by taking advantage of concomitant variations in natural processes. Two facts that vary together thus *do* have an "internal similarity" of the sort postulated by Wittgenstein. Sentences, on the other hand, bear a different relation to their facts. The relation is not *internal* but rather one determined by a factor external to the two facts concerned. This third factor is the mind for which the two facts are associated. The sentence *means* its fact; the line on the disk *records* its sound. By virtue of *meaning*, any element of one fact can come to stand for, and represent, any element of another fact, even including its structure. It is not necessary for one fact to reproduce or exhibit the structure of another in order for a mind to see the one through the other.

There *is* a valuable aspect to Wittgenstein's theory and that is its stress upon the necessity for complexity in a sign that is to represent, rather than simply to denote a complex fact. Representation, so the view holds, differs from denotation. The former can present new facts, by means of rearrangement of old elements, while the latter can only indicate the old. The possibility of complexity of a sign allows for a new dimension in language above simple denotation. But I doubt that this aspect of the theory is new. It is probably as old as Aristotle.

A final doubt must always confront a critic. Can he be sure that he has properly interpreted the theory criticized? It is possible, in this instance, that by *logical structure* Wittgenstein meant something not even hinted at in the paper. If such be the case then these conclusions probably miss their intended mark; but this is a risk men universally must accept when they turn critics.

Some Problems Connected with Language[1]

MAX BLACK

INTRODUCTION

THE widespread recognition of the importance in philosophy of an investigation of language is largely due to the influence exerted by Wittgenstein's *Tractatus Logico-Philosophicus*. The central thesis of that book is summarized in the statement that "all philosophy is 'critique of language' ".[2] Critical examination of the language we use is no longer to be regarded as a precautionary measure against ambiguity, vagueness and rhetoric, as a mere preliminary to the serious business of philosophy. In the new interpretation, philosophy or, to be more exact, the subject which replaces the "inextricable tangle of problems which is known as philosophy",[3] is identical with the investigation of language. This programme has been elaborated in great detail by the movement sometimes known as "Logical Positivism", of which Carnap is a leading representative. In the book from which the last quotation was taken Carnap urges that "once philosophy is purified of all unscientific elements, only the logic of science remains".[4] The "logic of science" would not commonly be thought to mean the same as "the critique of language". But Carnap explains that by the "*logic* of science" he means "the syntax of the *language* of science".[5] By the "language of science" again he means not the technical vocabulary of scientists but the "universal" language in terms of which *every* fact, whether of common knowledge or of scientific knowledge in a narrower sense, can be expressed. The

---

[1] From the *Proceedings of the Aristotelian Society*, N.S., vol. 39, Harrison and Sons, Ltd, 44–7, St Martin's Lane, London, W.C.2, 1939, pp. 43–68. Reprinted by permission of the editor and the author.

[2] *Tractatus Logico-Philosophicus*, 4.0031.

[3] R. Carnap, *Logical Syntax of Language*, 279.　　[4] Ibid.　　[5] Loc. cit., 281.

95

differences in method and purpose between Carnap's "logical syntax of the language of science" and Wittgenstein's[1] "critique of language" are less important than the agreement that "language" is the whole subject-matter of philosophy. A similar view is implicit in Ayer's remark "that philosophy provides definitions"[2] or Wisdom's remark that "all philosophic statements *mention* words".[3] But of those who have been influenced by the *Tractatus*, Schlick has expressed the importance in philosophy of an examination of language with most emphasis. "The whole history of philosophy", he says, "might have taken a very different course if the minds of the great thinkers had been more deeply impressed by the remarkable fact that there is such a thing as language."[4]

If attention to the existence of language may change the course of the history of philosophy and philosophy is to be confined to the investigation of language it would seem desirable to have a plain statement of the character of such an enquiry and the respects in which it differs from empirical investigations of the same subject-matter. And since views of this sort are derivative from the doctrine of the *Tractatus*, it would be a matter of more than historical interest to have an unmetaphorical statement of what the doctrines of that book are taken to be. Such a statement is not available;[5] the voluminous commentary on Wittgenstein's doctrines (occupying by now a bulk many times greater than that of the original) is remarkably sparing in exegesis. The larger part of this paper is accordingly occupied by exposition and criticism of Wittgenstein's views. The first section explains the more elementary portions of his analysis of language. In the second section objections on the ground of internal inconsistency are answered. The third section discusses the extent to which the analysis is applicable to any languages currently in use and the paper ends with some brief remarks on the general character of philosophical investigations of language.

A. THE ANALYSIS OF LANGUAGE

Wittgenstein's analysis of language, according to Russell, "is concerned with the conditions which would have to be fulfilled by a

---

[1] Throughout this paper, references to "Wittgenstein" mean references to the opinions expressed in his *Tractatus*. It is hardly necessary to add that its author's views may have changed in the interval of sixteen years since his book was published.

[2] *Language, Truth and Logic*, 55 (and *passim*).   [3] *Psyche*, 13, 155.

[4] *Gesammelte Aufsätze, 1926–1936*, 153. (The quotation is from a lecture delivered in the University of London in 1932.)

[5] But cf. the following:

    (*a*) Russell's Introduction to the *Tractatus*.

    (*b*) Ramsey's critical notice, *Mind*, 32 (reprinted in *The Foundations of Mathematics*).

    (*c*) J. Weinberg, *Examination of Logical Positivism*, chs. 1, 2.

logically perfect language".[1] On this interpretation "ordinary" language is inaccurate in two respects. It allows nonsensical combination of symbols and, secondly, contains symbols which are vague and ambiguous.[2] The function of the philosopher is to construct a new language in which these defects have been repaired by the provision of precise symbols and explicit rules for their combination.

While this view of the character of Wittgenstein's investigation (which may have been suggested by Russell's own attempts to construct a logically perfect language) is supported by a few of the remarks made in the *Tractatus*, the main trend of the book is against it. Passages such as the following: "all propositions of our colloquial language are actually, just as they are, logically completely in order"[3] and, again, "every possible proposition is legitimately constructed"[4] can be brought to refute Russell's interpretation, and in support of the view that Wittgenstein was interested in "colloquial" language, "just as it is". If the philosophical investigation of language is concerned with language in its present condition the interest of its conclusions is, as Ramsey pointed out,[5] greatly increased. But Wittgenstein is not clear on this point. He is willing to say "we must employ a symbolism" [i.e. a *new* symbolism] "which excludes them" [i.e. confusions between symbols arising from the physical resemblance of their perceptible signs] "by not applying the same sign in different symbols and by not applying signs in the same way which signify in different ways. A symbolism, that is to say, which obeys the rules of logical grammar—of logical syntax."[6] Such a symbolism, however, *would* be an "ideal" language (or a step towards an ideal language) in Russell's sense.

Such contradictions in Wittgenstein's own formulations of the character of his method, are symptomatic of an attempt to satisfy incompatible demands and will be the basis of the criticisms elaborated in section C of this paper. But they are suppressed and superficially resolved in the *Tractatus* by the use of the pair of technical terms, "sign" and "symbol".

The distinction between these two terms is connected, but not identical, with the distinction between "token" and "type" introduced by Peirce.[7] It will be remembered that the object of introducing the latter distinction was to avoid the appearance of contradiction in such a sentence as "The book was fifty thousand words long but he used only five thousand words in writing it".[8] This is done by saying

---

[1] *Tractatus Logico-Philosophicus*, Introduction, 7.   [2] Russell, op. cit., 8.
[3] *Tractatus Logico-Philosophicus*, 5.553.   [4] Ibid., 5.4733.
[5] *Foundations of Mathematics*, 271 [p. 10].
[6] *Tractatus*, 3.325.
[7] Cf. L. S. Stebbing, "Sounds, Shapes and Words", Aristotelian Society Supplementary Volume 14, 4.   [8] Cf. Stebbing, ibid., for Peirce's example.

that the word "word" is used in two different senses: (*a*) in such a way that the two shapes "and" and "and" in this line are *two* words, (*b*) in such a way that there is the *one* word "and" in the English language. The next step is to call the shapes (or corresponding sounds) *token*-words[1] "of" a (single) *type*-word. Each type-word in a language, say W, has then a correlated set of sounds and shapes, say C_W, consisting of all the tokens "of" that type.

By analysing the different senses in which the word "word" is used in English, Stebbing arrives at a partial analysis of the meaning of "tokens of the same type". "Tokens of the same word", she says, "*must* have some degree of similarity with other tokens of the same word."[2] This is unhelpful, for all sounds have "some degree of similarity" and two tokens of different words may have a greater degree of similarity than two tokens of the same word. Stebbing wishes to exclude the suggestion that tokens of the same type belong to *that* type in virtue of having the same meaning attached to them.[3] The relations which determine that certain sounds and shapes belong to the same set C_W associated with one type-word W are, on Stebbing's view, sensible relations, e.g. that of differing from certain sounds or shapes, the "norms", by not more than specified degrees of intensity, pitch or spatial quality, etc. The tokens "fair" and "fair" used to mean blond and impartial respectively are counted as tokens of the same type-word.[4]

Wittgenstein, on the contrary, uses the word "symbol" in order to designate tokens arranged in sets *in accordance with the meaning which is attached to them*. The word "sign" he uses with type-token ambiguity: sometimes to mean a token, as when he speaks of the "sensibly perceptible sign (sound or written sign)",[5] or says that "the sign is the part of the symbol perceptible by the senses",[6] sometimes to mean a type, as when he says " 'A' is the same sign as 'A' ".[7] The phrase "belonging to the same symbol" on the other hand is used only for tokens (but only for *some*) which are used in the same way. Tokens belonging to different types may accordingly belong to the same symbol and vice versa. "In the language of everyday life it very often happens that the same word signifies in two different ways— and therefore belongs to different symbols—or that two words which signify in different ways are apparently applied in the same way in the proposition."[8] But "signs which serve *one* purpose are logi-

---

[1] A "token-word" is, of course, not a special *kind* of word.   [2] Op. cit., 12.
[3] For this view see A. M. MacIver, "Token, Type and Meaning", *Analysis*, 4, 58–64.
[4] Stebbing, op. cit., 12. For the purpose of the present discussion it is of no great importance whether Stebbing's analysis is accurate. Probably considerations of identity of meaning play *some* part in determining common uses of the phrase "the *same* word". But it is convenient to *define* the token-type distinction without reference to meaning.
[5] *Tractatus*, 3.11.   [6] Ibid., 3.32.   [7] Ibid., 3.203.   [8] Ibid., 3.323.

cally equivalent [i.e. belong to the same symbol], signs which serve *no* purpose are logically meaningless [belong to no symbol]".[1]

We can now reconcile the apparent contradiction involved in maintaining that colloquial language is "logically completely in order" while recommending an *improved* notation. In colloquial language we have two systems of classification of tokens: (*a*) according to types, (*b*) according to symbols. The former is largely, though not entirely, conventional (or as Wittgenstein elsewhere calls it, "accidental"); the latter is the expression of "logical structure". It is because we confuse grammatical distinctions with those of logic that changes in the signs used may be advisable. But any such change is a practical device to prevent confusion, like changing the names of London streets—a "mechanical expedient" for facilitating the recognition of logical relations between symbols. "Whenever we make up 'ideal languages' it is not in order to replace ordinary languages by them; but just to remove some trouble, caused in somebody's mind by thinking that he has got hold of the exact use of a common word."[2] How logical, as distinct from grammatical, structure can be made more explicit is discussed later in this paper.

The distinctions between token and type, on the one hand, and again between sign and symbol will be found relevant to the detailed description of Wittgenstein's analysis of language, which now follows.

Wittgenstein expresses the result of his examination of language by using a number of technical terms, of which "name", "proposition", "structure", "saying" and "showing" are those with which this paper is primarily concerned. It will be found that none of these can be defined or adequately described in isolation. Like the primitive notions of an uninterpreted formal geometry, their meanings are determined by exhibiting their mutual relations in a set of what is sometimes called "implicit definitions".

A "proposition" (type-sense) is any symbol which has meaning independently of other symbols. It is composed of "names",[3] but names, unlike propositions, must occur in combination with other names (and logical connectives) in order to convey a complete meaning. "Only the proposition has sense; only in the context of a proposition has a name meaning."[4] Those propositions whose truth-value is independent of the truth-value of any other propositions are called

---

[1] Loc. cit., 5.47321. It is to be noticed however that synonyms are not necessarily regarded as cases of the same symbol. In 3.341 there is reference to "all symbols which can fulfil the same purpose". Nor do all the names of a single object belong to a single symbol. It seems that criteria of sensible resemblance between the associated tokens play *some* part in determining the use of the word "symbol".

[2] From notes of lectures delivered by Wittgenstein at Cambridge, 1933–4.

[3] *Tractatus*, 4.21, 4.22.   [4] Ibid., 3.3.

"elementary".[1] "Elementary propositions" constitute as it were the atoms out of which all other propositions are constructed by means of logical operations. The unit of language, like that of matter, has, as the physicists would say, a "fine structure". Every proposition is composite; "it has something in common with *other* symbols";[2] and its elements, the "names", "are combined with one another in a definite way".[3] The way in which the elements are connected in the elementary proposition is called its "structure".[4] The "names" are the smallest units of meaning; they are the "simple signs"[5] which cannot be analysed further by definitions.[6]

We come now to the correlation between language and that to which language refers. In this three aspects can be distinguished: the reference of names, the reference of propositions and the correspondence between structure in the proposition and structure in that to which propositions refer.

(1) Names stand for "objects", and the meaning of a name is the "object" to which it refers.[7] (2) Propositions represent "possible states of affair"[8] and in order to verify a proposition "we must compare it with reality".[8] (3) The structure of the proposition repeats the structure of the state of affairs which it represents: the names in the proposition are combined in the same way as objects in the corresponding possible state of affairs.[9] In particular the "multiplicity" of both must be the same: "In the proposition there must be as many things distinguishable as there are in the state of affairs which it represents."[10]

In explaining the meanings of the technical terms he introduces Wittgenstein constantly suggests that he is using "language" in such a way that to say there is a language implies that there are *users* of the language. Thus "the meanings of the simple signs (the words) must be explained to us [i.e. by those who use them] if we are to understand them".[11] Moreover, the criterion of the kind of symbol to which a token belongs is the way in which the token (and the corresponding type) *are used*. "In order to recognize the symbol in the sign we must consider the significant *use*."[12] And again "What does not get expressed in the sign is shown by its application. What the signs conceal, their application declares."[13]

In this brief outline I have tried to keep as closely as possible to Wittgenstein's own words and I have deliberately omitted the more complex parts of the theory (e.g. the discussion of non-elementary propositions, of mathematical equations, of symbols other than names and propositions).

[1] *Tractatus*, 4.21 et seq.   [2] Ibid., 5.5261.   [3] Ibid., 2.14.
[4] Ibid., 2.15.   [5] Ibid., 3.202.   [6] Ibid., 3.26.
[7] Ibid., 3.203.   [8] Ibid., 2.202.   [9] Ibid., 3.21, 4.0311.
[10] Ibid., 4.04.   [11] Ibid., 4.026.   [12] Ibid., 3.326.
[13] Ibid., 3.262.

In criticizing Wittgenstein's analysis it is important to remember its purpose. It is primarily directed towards establishing a single negative thesis ("Mein Grundgedanke" as Wittgenstein calls it) "that the *logic* of the facts cannot be represented".[1] By the phrase "logic of the facts" in this context is meant a system of relations between that "structure" in "states of affairs" which is repeated in the structure of propositions. Wittgenstein makes a sharp distinction between "saying" (or "asserting") and "showing". Propositions *assert* the existence of a state of affairs,[2] but they "*show* the logical form of reality. They exhibit it."[3] Now much of the *Tractatus* is concerned with remarks about the logical structure of symbols so its method must, on its own principles, consist of "showing". But this seems to involve the unintelligibility of the *Tractatus* itself, since "what *can* be shown *cannot* be said".[4]

The charge of internal contradiction based upon this distinction between "saying" and "showing" has been so commonly levelled against the *Tractatus* that it will be convenient to answer it at once before proceeding to consider the applicability of Wittgenstein's categories of "name", "proposition" and "structure".

B. IS THE TRACTATUS SELF-CONTRADICTORY?

It has been widely assumed that in maintaining that it is logically impossible to "say" anything about logical structure Wittgenstein is implying the incommunicability of facts about structure and hence the meaninglessness of his own remarks in the *Tractatus*. Russell, for instance, in objecting that "after all, Mr Wittgenstein manages to say a good deal about what cannot be said"[5] is clearly taking *what can be said* to be identical with *what can be conveyed by means of language* or *what has meaning*. Wittgenstein provides support for this interpretation in the much-quoted passage with which his book ends: "My propositions are elucidatory in this way: he who understands them finally recognizes them as senseless . . . whereof one cannot speak thereof one must be silent."[6] It is this passage more than any other which leads Carnap to regard the *Tractatus* as a series of "more or less vague explanations which the reader must subsequently recognize as pseudo-sentences and abandon".[7] Ramsey adopts the same view in his expression of worry at the suggestion that philosophy is nonsense—"we must then take seriously that it is nonsense, and not pretend, as Wittgenstein does, that it is important nonsense".[8]

---

[1] Ibid., 4.0312.
[2] Ibid., 4.22.
[3] Ibid., 4.121.
[4] Ibid., 4.1212.
[5] Introduction to *Tractatus*, 22.
[6] *Tractatus*, 5.64, 7.
[7] *Logical Syntax of Language*, 283.
[8] *Foundations of Mathematics*, 263.

These critics have taken a single provocative remark too literally. The statement on which the charges of self-contradiction are based itself contains a contradiction. A "senseless" proposition is not a proposition at all and it is logically impossible that whatever we "understand" should, whether "finally" or at any other time, be revealed as senseless. Either there *was* nothing to understand and we were uttering nonsensical collocations of sounds, or we *did* understand and something *was* communicated.

Closer attention to the remainder of Wittgenstein's argument would show that he is using the crucial words "saying" and "showing" in a technical sense which deviates from the sense which would commonly be attributed to them. It is characteristic of Wittgenstein's sense that the phrase *p can be said* is restricted to the cases where *p* is an empirical proposition. This is demonstrated by the following three statements about mathematics and logic: "The propositions of mathematics are equations and therefore pseudo-propositions"[1]—"The logic of the world which the propositions of logic *show* in tautologies mathematics *show* in equations"[2]—"The propositions of logic therefore say nothing (They are the analytical propositions)."[3] It appears, then, that to say that *p* "says" something is to say that *p* is empirical; to say that *p* "shows" but does not say anything is to say that *p* is not empirical. In the respect of "saying nothing" propositions about logical structure, the propositions of philosophy, are in no worse case than the "propositions" of mathematics or logic. Now Wittgenstein could not intend to deny that mathematical equations may convey "information" of a certain sort to those who meet them for the first time, but he is concerned to stress the difference between this kind of information and that conveyed by empirical propositions. He is not saying that logical structure is ineffable but he is drawing attention to a difference in usage between two kinds of propositional symbols. Reserving the word "sense" for empirical propositions is a provocative (and as it seems, misleading) way of emphasizing this difference.[4]

Not only does Wittgenstein not imply the self-defeating doctrine that his own propositions are nonsensical; he supplies us with sufficient clues on which to base a more positive notion of the methods used in exhibiting relations of logical structure. One such method can

---

[1] *Tractatus*, 5.2.   [2] Ibid., 6.22.   [3] Ibid., 6.11.

[4] The use of a common word in a new and rather shocking context is an important factor in the *succès de scandale* of Wittgenstein's book. Contrast the rhetorical force of "my propositions are senseless" with "my propositions are not empirical". An important case where the use of a common word in an unusual sense produces confusion is that of "tautology". This word is applied to certain described kinds of truth function, but it has no *explanatory* force. Cf. Hahn, *Logique, Mathématiques et Connaissance de la réalité*, 31, for a "tautological" theory of the nature of mathematics, wrongly based on the *Tractatus*.

be illustrated by explaining the analysis of a proposition asserting that some combination of signs is nonsensical, e.g. the proposition *"The Good is less identical than the Beautiful is nonsense"*.[1]

The grammatical form of this sentence is that of "A is B", where A is some complex object and B is a property of that object. But "The Good is less identical than the Beautiful" does not express a proposition. By adjoining the eight signs we have failed to assert anything. The word nonsense is not a property of a complex (for there *is* no complex); it is more like a signal that we have not succeeded in framing a proposition. The failure of the attempt makes more vivid, "shows" us, the way in which the signs "Good", "is", "less", etc., are used in the language in which they occur.[2]

Propositions such as that used as an example differ from *empirical* propositions in which any or all of the same words may occur. They belong to the category of rules for the manipulation of signs in the language (or deductions from such rules): they may convey information of a certain kind about rules but it is not the kind of information that is conveyed by empirical propositions. In the latter we *use* signs to make extra-linguistic reference: in the statements of logical syntax we use signs in another way in order to reveal and emphasize the kind of ways in which it is permissible in language to use them.[3]

On some such lines as these it would be possible to give more elaborate analyses of the various types of statements which belong to logical syntax.

C. THE APPLICABILITY OF WITTGENSTEIN'S ANALYSIS

Wittgenstein's account of "name", "proposition" and "structure" has been compared in this paper to a formal geometry whose primitive notions are defined by their mutual relations as expressed in a system of "implicit definitions" or axioms. When a formal geometry comes to receive a specific interpretation, i.e. to be applied to a definite subject-matter, it is necessary to supplement the axioms by "applicative definitions" or *Zuordnungsdefinitionen* of each of the notions involved. If our analogy holds and Wittgenstein's account of

---

[1] An example used in the *Tractatus*, 4.003. The account which now follows is not to be found in the *Tractatus*.

[2] Or rather it tells us how they are *not* used.

[3] Cf. the difference between the record of a "move" in chess (say 1. P-K4) and the statement of an impossibility (say that there cannot be ten queens of the same colour simultaneously on the board). The latter is about the way in which the pieces may or may not be moved, the former tells us how they *were* moved. The latter is settled before the game begins (belongs to the definition of the game), the former conveys information about the particular game recorded.

Max Black

language is to be more than an exercise in formal mathematics, it will be necessary to supply criteria for the application of words like "name", "sign", "symbol", etc., to any particular language in which we may be interested. In trying to discover how the "names" and "logical structure" of a language like English are to be recognized we shall see the limitations of Wittgenstein's theory.

First as to names. To those who are familiar with general linguistic theory the hierarchical pattern of Wittgenstein's analysis will not be a novelty. The categories of "name", "proposition", "structure of proposition" are parallel to the linguistic categories of "word", "sentence" and "sentence-structure". The student of linguistic theory finds it hard to define these words or to explain unambiguously how they are to be applied in any given language.[1] He is guided by physical characteristics of the tokens used in the language (e.g. by intonation, the isolation of syllables by pauses, etc.). But Wittgenstein has to use criteria which take account of physical characteristics (viz. those which assign tokens to types) without coinciding with the criteria used by the linguistic theorist. For whereas the linguist is searching for something like a minimum unit of *speech* (the "word"), the philosopher needs a minimum unit of *meaning*. Thus the symbol *uncle*, which is a unit for linguistics, will be decomposed in Wittgenstein's scheme by the analysis of the propositions in which it may occur. Only when such re-translation has proceeded so far that each propositional sign appears overtly as a complex of elementary propositions none of which can be further decomposed, shall we be in the position to point out those simple signs which are the "names" in Wittgenstein's sense.

If we try to apply this programme seriously to any given "language" (e.g. the brand of English spoken by members of the Aristotelian Society) we shall be faced in our search for names by a difficulty unknown to the linguist. In searching for units of speech the latter confines himself exclusively to the phonemes[2] and compounds of phonemes actually current in the language he is investigating: his task is that of selection and classification. But in the analysis of propositions into complexes of elementary propositions we shall need to invent signs as our analysis proceeds. It is not possible to produce a single "name" in Wittgenstein's sense from our current vocabulary. Nor have we definite criteria for deciding whether any examples which might be produced in fact satisfy the requirements.[3]

---

[1] Cf. R. Bloomfield, *Language*, 178–9, for a discussion of the meaning of "word".

[2] A smallest recognizable significant feature of speech.

[3] We can prove that some examples will not satisfy the requirements (by producing analyses of the propositions in which they occur): we cannot prove that a given symbol *does* satisfy the requirements.

It must not be forgotten, of course, that most languages use non-visual significant features in symbolism, e.g. stress and intonation. The poverty of the printed or written word leaves a loophole for anybody who wishes to argue that language consists of units of meaning —let us continue to call them "names"—while defining these units of meaning only in terms of tokens already used in the language under examination. He might draw, for defining characteristics of his units, upon those significant features of speech which are not explicitly represented in writing. In "inventing" signs, he might proceed to argue, what we are doing is adding a class of shapes to an already existing class of tokens having other physical characteristics and already constituting a type in the language.

A defence on these lines becomes less plausible when regard is paid to the part played by *context* as an element of significance in language. This is most clearly seen by considering the use of demonstratives. In using a sentence like "This is my fountain pen", where I accompany the utterance of the word "this" by showing you my fountain pen, the words used are insufficient to express a proposition unless accompanied by the appropriate demonstration. To my hearers, then, the propositional sign is constituted by seeing my pen as well as by hearing the noises I utter. Only by accepting this would it be possible to maintain that part of Wittgenstein's analysis which demands that complexity in the state of affairs referred to should be reflected in the propositional sign which refers. For I may use the same set of words "This is my fountain pen" on two separate occasions to refer to two different objects. I am then making two *different* assertions, viz. in the one case that my fountain pen is my fountain pen, in the other that some other object, say my hat, is. Since I use the same words on both occasions, the perceptible tokens which allow my hearer to recognize the difference in the two sentences must be diverse on the two occasions. The visual appearance of my fountain pen and my hat respectively must therefore be counted as tokens of the propositional sign. A similar analysis could be made of the use of all sentences whose meaning is supplemented by the circumstances in which they are uttered.

The fact that we systematically make use in this way of features of the context to supplement the meaning of sounds or shapes which would otherwise fail to express complete propositions will supply the believer in simple signs with further materials for his case. He might argue with some plausibility that, in certain circumstances, when we use the noise "this" to refer to a coloured expanse in the visual field, it is the appearance of the visual expanse to the hearer in a certain relation to the sound which is heard at the same instant which constitutes the "name" of the expanse itself.

Such a view involves an awkward extension of the sense of the word "token" to include in addition to the regular use of shapes and sounds, the contextual use of appearances of an object to refer to the appearance itself or the object of which it is an appearance. The extension of the narrower sense of the term "token" is made in the interests of preserving in the propositional-token a *perceptible* complexity corresponding to the complexity of the corresponding referent. The appearance of the fountain pen (together with the accompanying sound) is to count as a "name" for the pen because we want each object to have its own different but perceptible name.

This desperate expedient will not always serve. Consider the sentence "Today is Monday" which expresses different propositions according to the day on which it is uttered. What is it in the context that determines the hearer to understand that when I now say "Today is Monday" I assert that December 12th and not some other day is Monday? Surely only the fact that I utter the form of words on December 12th and not on some other day. But the fact that I utter the words today is not a perceptible feature of the linguistic situation. To urge in this case that there are *perceptible* differences in the two linguistic situations constituted by the utterance on different occasions of the same form of words "Today is December 12th" is utterly implausible. The natural method of describing the situation is to say that we use sentence-tokens belonging to the *same* sentence-type on the two occasions to express two different propositions. That this can be done is no more mysterious than is the fact that we can use the same key to open the front door each day. To suppose that the sentence-tokens *must* be unlike would be like arguing that we must use a different key every time we unlock the door.

To sum up this part of our discussion. Suppose we define a language as a logical construction out of the significant *perceptible* tokens used by a certain group of speakers in accordance with certain rules. Among these tokens will be some which we can distinguish as word-tokens and propositional-tokens. Propositional-tokens expressing elementary propositions will be a sub-class of all the propositional-tokens in the language: Let us call them elementary propositional-tokens. Let us call word-tokens which occur as parts of elementary propositional-tokens by the title of name-tokens. Each "name" in Wittgenstein's sense is a logical construction out of a class of name-tokens. Whenever x is a name let "C_x" denote the set of the name-tokens in terms of which x is the logical construction. Then we maintain that there will be *some* values of x, say a and b (with $a \neq b$), such that C_a and C_b contain some common members, i.e. difference in the "name" does not imply mutual exclusion of the correlated sets of name-tokens. Moreover, we have no criteria for determining whether any suggested class C of tokens is the correlated class C_x of name-tokens of some name x.

THE NOTION OF "STRUCTURE" IN WITTGENSTEIN'S ANALYSIS

I have already pointed out that recognition of the structure of a proposition depends upon ability to identify the elements (names) which are the proposition's constituents. Thus the difficulties in finding applicative definitions for the term "name" automatically involve difficulties in finding applicative definitions for the term "structure". The latter, however, is even less well defined than the former and needs separate attention.

I propose to refer first to the use made by Russell and subsequent writers of the notion of "logical form" and then to point out the modifications from it contained in Wittgenstein's notion of "logical structure".

It is convenient to quote Russell's own account of the notion of "logical form". "In every proposition . . . there is, besides the particular subject-matter concerned, a certain *form*, a way in which the constituents of the proposition . . . are put together. If I say *Socrates is mortal, Jones is angry, the sun is hot*, there is something in common in these three cases, something indicated by the word *is*. What is in common is the *form* of the proposition, not an actual constituent."[1] To this Stebbing adds the comment that "the form of a proposition is what remains unchanged although all the constituents of the proposition are altered".[2]

It is noteworthy that neither Russell nor Stebbing provides a *definition* of logical form. Both assume that there is such a thing. Russell asserts not only that each proposition has a logical form but that a number of propositions have the same form in common. Similarly, Stebbing asserts, without proof, that if each constituent of a proposition were replaced by some other term *something* would remain constant. The absence of a definition would not matter if some criteria were given for determining the logical form of a given proposition. Criteria for the *identity of logical form* in two or more propositions are easier to find than criteria for determination of the logical form of a single proposition. Let us examine for identity of logical form the three propositions used as examples in the passage quoted from Russell.

Identity of logical form in two propositions demands, as a partial condition, equality of the number of constituents in each. But none of the three propositions in question are incapable of further analysis

[1] *Our Knowledge of the External World*, 62.   [2] *Modern Introduction to Logic*, 125.

and it is not at all probable that the fully analysed propositions would be found to have the same number of constituents. To say that the three propositions have the same form is like saying that the mathematical equations $(3x + 7)^2 + 9 = 0$ and $(5x^3 + 4x + 5)^2 + 11 = 0$ have the same mathematical form. Certainly each of these equations contains the square of an algebraic polynomial plus a constant and in this respect are similar, but the fact that the expressions squared are different in the two cases prevents us from asserting identity of form. In the mathematical case, moreover, the equation skeleton "$(\ldots)^2 + --- = 0$" can be preserved, whatever expressions are substituted at the places indicated by "$\ldots$" and "$---$" But the propositional skeleton "$(\ldots)$ is $(---)$" will not be preserved when the proposition is analysed. In general, therefore, recognition of identity of form in two or more propositions involves knowledge of the full analysis of the propositions. In exceptionally favourable cases, however, close similarity in two propositions may permit us to assert identity of logical form in ignorance of the analyses of the propositions. We can say that "John loves Mary" and "Tom hates Margery" are identical in logical form because the corresponding terms are of exactly the same kinds.

In comparing the logical form of two completely analysed propositions, the only features of the propositions which are relevant are (a) one-one correspondence of the terms in both, (b) identity of arrangement of the terms, as shown by the disposition of the logical constants, (c) identity of category of corresponding terms. By saying that two terms are of identical categories we mean that they are both either particulars or both propositional functions with the same number and types of arguments.

To these conditions Wittgenstein adds that corresponding terms must be of the same *kind* in the sense of making sense or nonsense in the same contexts. It is in this respect that his notion of "logical structure" differs from Russell's notion of "logical form". Thus the criteria for identity of logical structure are even more difficult to apply than those of logical form.

The conceptions of logical structure and logical form are probably derivative from the psychologically more primitive notion of *visual* form, and there is consequently a tendency to confuse the former with the latter. Consider, for example, the representation of the simplest integers in the following notation:

I II III IIII IIIII IIIIII IIIIIII . . .

Here the tokens display certain obvious relations of visual form. But in the sense in which Wittgenstein wishes to speak of structure exactly the same (logical) structure is embodied in the notation

1 2 3 4 5 6 7 . . .

(or rather in the propositions in which they occur). And exactly the same logical structure would be displayed by *any* system of signs used in the same way.[1] For the purpose of determining logical structure it is, for instance, a matter of complete indifference whether we represent certain features of states of affairs by spatial *arrangement* rather than by sounds or shapes. Hence the unimportance in theory of attempts to "improve" symbolism: tokens of *any* properties whatsoever can be used as the material for a complete language. The function of resemblances between propositional signs (e.g. between "*aRb*" and "*bRc*") is the *practical* one of reminding users of the language of the relations between the logical structures of the corresponding propositions. Accordingly, there need be nothing in common between the physical structure of the system of tokens used in the language and the "states of affairs" to which the language refers.

On this view of the matter, the difficulties of discovering relations of logical structure in a given language are of the same nature as those involved in finding "names". "Names" are so defined that no physical characteristics of tokens are a clue to their identification. And the same is true of "logical structure". "What signifies in the symbol is what is common to all those symbols by which it can be replaced."[2] So long as we define identity of symbols in terms of identity of their associated sets of tokens, we shall be bound to say that synonymous symbols (whether names or propositions) need have no common features. If it is objected that propositions may nevertheless have a structure which is not exhibited in the physical relationships of their associated sets of tokens we must ask for a *definition* of this alleged structure. It is not sufficient to say that the structure *is* the common feature of all symbols which can fulfil the same purpose; it must first be demonstrated that there *is* such a common feature.[3]

CONCLUDING REMARKS CONCERNING THE APPLICABILITY OF WITTGENSTEIN'S ANALYSIS

It is impossible to obtain from the *Tractatus* exact criteria for the application of the fundamental terms "name" and "structure". I suggest that this is due to the attempt to stretch a spatial analogy (which is legitimate in certain restricted methods of symbolism) in such a way as to apply to *every* language. It is possible to construct a

---

[1] How to decide *when* two systems of signs are used "in the same way" is precisely the difficulty.

[2] *Tractatus*, 3.344.

[3] Cf. the argument that all objects which can open a door must have common features. This is plausible so long as we think of keys. But what is there in common between a key, a door handle, and a battering ram? Only that they can fulfil the same purpose.

symbolism in which practically every term of Wittgenstein's analysis can be exactly applied. Consider, for example, a "world" composed of points and bars, as shown in the following figure. Each dot is an "object", each continuous linkage a "state of affairs".

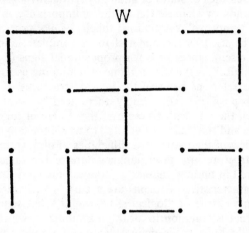

Fig. 1

Consider next a "language" as shown in the following figure, where each dot represents the corresponding dot in Fig. 1, each bar the corresponding bar in Fig. 1.

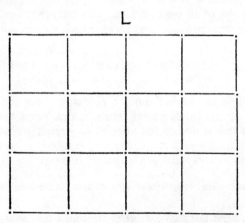

Fig. 2

The next figure shows an *asserted* (false) proposition in this language.

P

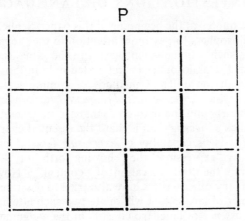

Fig. 3

In this symbolism there *is* something in common between a proposition and its referent for the state of affairs and the correlated propositional-token are geometrically congruent. I am suggesting that the attempt to use this type of symbolism as a pattern for symbolism in general is responsible both for the lack of definition of the fundamental terms in Wittgenstein's analysis and for the resulting mysticism. Immediately we allow, in our special symbolism, the system L to be *any* system of signs which can "adequately" represent W, we are led first to allow topological distortion of the symbolizing diagram (by stretching the elastic medium on which we suppose it inscribed) then to replace the dots and bars by words or other shapes until we arrive at a system of signs having no *geometrical* resemblance to W. If we persist in saying that every such system of symbols must have the same structure we are using the word "structure" in a new but undefined sense. To say that all systems which represent W *must* have the same structure is to say no more than that all systems which represent W must represent W.

It is characteristic of "philosophical" investigations of language to insist that the propositions expressing the product of the investigation are necessary. We have seen Wittgenstein insisting that equivalent symbols *"must"* have the same multiplicity. I believe the alleged "necessity" of such declarations is connected with a determination to stretch a term like "multiplicity" until it becomes a universal category. I will conclude this paper by saying a little more about the nature of attempts to discover the "essential" characteristics of language.

D. THE CHARACTER OF "PHILOSOPHICAL" INVESTIGATIONS OF LANGUAGE

In a passage quoted at the beginning of this paper, Schlick was found inviting philosophers to pay more attention to the "remarkable fact that there is such a thing as language". In the same lecture Schlick explains that the philosopher is "interested only in those characteristics which all the different methods of communication have in common and which are the *essential characteristics* of Language". He wants "to understand the nature of language in general".[1] The upshot of Schlick's investigation is that "the essential characteristic of language . . . is its capability of *expressing* facts",[1] providing we understand by "expression" the "showing forth" of "logical structure" and not the communication of "content".[2] Now it will be found that many other writers have also tried to describe the "essential" character of language. I will quote two such attempts:

". . . the *essence* of language consists in the assigning of conventional, voluntarily articulated sounds, or their equivalent, to the diverse elements of experience."[3]

". . . the *essence* of language lies in the intentional conveyance of ideas from one living being to another through the instrumentality of arbitrary tokens or symbols agreed upon and understood by both as being associated with the particular ideas in question."[4]

A further remark of Butler's where he says that he is trying to formulate "the essentials, the presence of which constituted language while their absence negatives it altogether"[5] provides a clue to the character of enquiries which terminate in dicta such as these about the essence of language. For the essential characteristics, "the presence of which constitute language", are simply the *defining* characteristics of language. Wittgenstein, Schlick, Sapir and Butler are engaged in providing definitions, or explicit rules for the use of, the *word* "language".

The last remark may easily be misleading and needs to be corrected by the following considerations.

(1) Philosophers are not puzzled about the meaning of the word "language" in the way that a foreigner who did not know English might be. Philosophers know how to use the word "language"; they wish nevertheless to make the rules for its use more explicit or to reduce the variety of different ways in which it is used to a single pattern.

---

[1] *Gesammelte Aufsätze*, 155.
[2] Schlick was strongly influenced by Wittgenstein's views. But he gives us no more definite an account of "logical structure" than is found in the *Tractatus*.
[3] Sapir.   [4] Samuel Butler, *Essays on Art, Life and Science*.
[5] Ibid., 184.

(2) The "philosophical" definition of "language" is not arbitrary: there are correct and incorrect definitions (or more correct and less correct definitions). The test of correctness is agreement with the usage of the language in which the word occurs. But the rule for using the word "language" is not a statement *about* the way in which the word is used in the language in question. The latter is, of course, an empirical statement.[1] We must distinguish between rules *of* usage and statements *about* the usage. A rule in chess is not a statement about the behaviour of chess players. If it were we could never formulate the rules of a game which had not yet been played. Nor is a "rule", whether in a game or in language, a command or prescription as some philosophers who have been impressed by the differences between rules and statements have supposed. (For *who* commands, and what are the penalties for disobedience?) It would be nearer the mark to regard a rule in chess as a description of ways in which the pieces might be moved. Similarly, we can regard a definition such as

" 'owl' = 'kind of large-headed small-faced hook-beaked large-eyed soft-plumaged nocturnal bird of prey' "

(Oxford Dictionary)

as a rule for the mutual substitution of the two expressions united by the sign of equality. Like other descriptions, a "rule" is a sentence-fragment to which we can add other sentence-fragments in order to produce sentences expressing propositions.

Thus from the rule

$$\text{``}A\text{''} = \text{``}B\text{''} \quad . \quad . \quad . \quad . \quad (r)$$

we can form the sentence

"Most educated speakers of the class C
   in situation S
(e.g. Englishmen who speak English correctly)
   substitute "A" for "B" and vice versa" . . . (s).

Now the sentence s expresses an empirical proposition. And s is formed from r in a regular way which could be followed in manufacturing a corresponding s for *each* rule of substitution r. The test of a proposed rule r is the truth of the corresponding empirical proposition expressed by the corresponding sentence s.

If this account is accurate, the philosopher of language, though the products of his analysis are not empirical propositions but recommended rules for the use of the word "language," may nevertheless need to employ empirical methods in searching for the rules.

[1] Cf. Broad, Aristotelian Society Supplementary Volume 15, 107.

(Just as somebody who did not know the rules of chess might find it necessary to observe the behaviour of chess players in order to arrive at the rules of chess.) The empirical methods will not coincide with those at present used by students of linguistic theory because they will be concerned with relations of meaning and not of linguistic structure in a narrower sense. It is certain that language is a great deal more complex than the accounts supplied by any of the authors mentioned in this paper would suggest. The defect in their answers is not in the character of their method but in the fact that their fragmentary and approximatory conclusions are presented as if they were complete analyses.

The Picture Theory of Meaning[1]

EDNA O'SHAUGHNESSY

ISAIAH BERLIN has recently discoursed on the proneness of philosophers to adopt as a paradigm one type of sentence-fact relation, and then Deflate other sentences to sentences of the chosen sort, or, alternatively, Inflate other facts to facts of the chosen sort. In his view, one of the causes of this persistent propensity is the Correspondence Theory of Language, 'the assumption that words are names and that it is not truth, so much as meaning, that is a form of correspondence between symbols and things' (*P.A.S.* 1949–50, p. 180). One form which the Correspondence view of meaning takes is the Picture Theory. I shall explore the logic of 'picture', and of related notions like 'map', 'reflection' in the hope of showing what the Picture Theory is and why it *must* be a misdescription of 'how words mean'. Some philosophers hold the Picture Theory outright. Others, although they do not say explicitly that names of things are like pictures of things, or that sentences picture facts, yet describe language in terms that properly describe not language but pictures. I shall mostly draw examples from three sources: Russell, Wittgenstein's *Tractatus*, and Wisdom's articles on 'Logical Constructions'. For ease of statement and with no commitment to any use beyond that introduced, pictures, maps, sentences, etc., will be said to be signs that signify. A sign will be composed of elements. What the picture, etc., depicts, the signified, will also be said to be composed of elements.

A picture, for example, might have as its elements splodges of paint; if what it signifies is a landscape, the signified might have as elements stones, leaves, trees. It is possible to set up a correspondence between elements of the sign and elements of the signified: the brown

[1] From *Mind*, N.S., vol. 62, no. 246, April, 1953, pp. 184–201. Reprinted by permission of the editor and the author.

strokes correspond to the tree trunks, the green dots to leaves. However, a picture is not a jumble of variegated paint patches. To show trees in a forest the browns and greens must be disposed on the canvas in a particular arrangement, an arrangement similar to the arrangement of the leaves and the tree trunks they represent.

This elicits three characteristics of the relation which holds between picture and pictured. The elements of a picture represent elements in the pictured. The arrangement of the elements in the picture shows the arrangement of the elements in the pictured. To each element in the picture there corresponds an element in the pictured. There are further features of 'picture' which influence elucidations of 'word' or 'sentence' in picture terms.

There is no differentiation of function among the elements of a picture. One patch of paint does not do this, and another that. All elements of a picture bear the same relation to the elements of the pictured: that of 'representing'. Further, the terms between which the relation of picturing holds, the picture and the pictured, are both entities in the sense that, unlike dreams or the meanings of words, they are among the furniture of the world. When a picture stands in a relation to something which is not a thing, we no longer speak of it as picturing that thing. It illustrates a story; *The Old Wives' Tale* is not a thing and it is that which is illustrated; or it is a graph of a temperature; a record of nervous impulses in the brain; a spatial interpretation of a symphony. Not only must both picture and pictured be entities, but they must also be entities in what—for want of a better word—I call the same *genre*. A picture is a visual pattern and can picture only what is visually accessible. A still-life of a duck cannot show the taste of the bird as it may show its markings. The sense in which a picture shows a tasty bird is the sense in which I see a tasty bird, that is, I see a bird which looks as if it would be succulent to the taste. I cannot *see* the taste of a bird any more than a picture can show it. As Wittgenstein says: '2.171 The picture can represent every reality whose form it has. The spatial picture, everything spatial, the coloured everything coloured, etc.' Of course, picture and pictured cannot be in the identical *genre*. If they were, the one would be a replica, a duplicate, or a model of the other and not a picture of it. To be a picture something must be omitted, but what remains can show only features of the scene in the same *genre* as itself, i.e. certainly spatial and possibly coloured features.

It is now possible to summarize features we may expect in a description of language which uses the picture as a model. Elements of the sign will stand for, and be in one to one correspondence with, elements in the signified. The arrangement of elements in the sign will show the arrangement of the elements in the signified. There will be no diversity of role among the elements of the sign. Sign and signified will be entities in the same *genre*.

Look now at a description of language in picture terms. Wittgenstein says: '4.01 The proposition is a picture of reality. 4.0312 The possibility of propositions is based upon the principle of the representation of objects by signs. 3.21 To the configuration of the simple signs in the propositional sign corresponds the configuration of the objects in the state of affairs.' As in a picture, so in a proposition. '4.0311 One name stands for one thing, and another for another thing, and they are connected together. And so the whole, like a living picture, presents the atomic fact.'

The *Tractatus* also satisfies the model's demand that sign and signified be in the same *genre*. It achieves this by equating the sign (the proposition) to the signified (the fact). '2.1 We make to ourselves pictures of facts. 2.141 The picture is a fact.' Russell, in *Our Knowledge of the External World*, is constrained 'to preserve the parallelism in language as regards facts and propositions' (p. 63) and to talk of the one as he talks of the other for the same reason. In addition propositions and facts must become entities. '3.1431 The essential nature of the propositional sign becomes very clear when we imagine it made up of spatial objects (such as tables, chairs, books) instead of written signs.' Here Wittgenstein thinks of propositions and—since propositions coincide with facts—of facts as a complex of objects. So does Wisdom: 'It is true that the fact expressed by 'This is red' is not merely two things *this* and *red*. It is these two stuck together and stuck together in a certain way' (*Mind*, 1931, p. 197 [p. 48]). Again, Wisdom writes—note the italics and initial capital substituted for the significantly omitted 'that'—'suppose I say "Some dogs are sleepy" and speak truly. Then there will be one or two facts out in the big world of this sort: *This is a dog and this is sleepy, That is a dog and that is sleepy, Thet is a dog and etc.*' (*Mind*, 1931, p. 473). That on this model facts are things is here even plainer.

Different philosophers may make different use of the picture model. They may pick on different features or stop short where another might go on. Wittgenstein asserts a correspondence between elements of the sign and elements of the signified ('3.2 In propositions thoughts can be so expressed that to the objects of the thoughts correspond the elements of the propositional sign.') but does not go on to assert that this correspondence is one to one. There are elements in the sign, e.g. the logical constants, which do not represent, that is, do not stand for objects. Nor, in consequence, does he assign the same role to all elements in the proposition. Wisdom, on the other hand, adopts these two features of the picture model. There must be an isomorphism of elements in the proposition and the fact—this is what he means by 'identity of form'; and all elements in the proposition stand for elements in the fact. Wisdom says they are all Demonstrative Symbols in Stebbing's sense—('A demonstrative phrase is like a bodily gesture, it points at something for consideration.' *A Modern Introduction to Logic*, p. 15)—that is, they all perform the same function.

At once, for views like these there are difficulties. Consider first those created by the notion that elements of the sign stand for elements in the signified. Take the phrase 'The river' in 'The river is long'. For what could it stand? The river? But then, since all words in the sentence stand for an object, for what does 'long' stand? The river too? But this is absurd. Shall we say then that 'The river' stands for the river without its length, and 'long' stands for its length? This is to take the road that will end at the bare particular. Or shall we say that 'The river' stands for the river with all its properties and 'long' stands for its length, i.e. one of its properties? This makes all relations internal. Clearly, a 'stand for' account of the function of the words in a sentence will not do. Equally clearly, theories of meaning which say: The name means the object, even if they do not acknowledge it, use 'mean' with the logic of 'stand for'. And how can it apply at all to conditional sentences or negative sentences? Does 'not' name an element in the world? If it does, how odd an element; if it doesn't, how do we describe the difference between 'This is red' and 'This is not red'? 'This' confesses Wisdom (*Mind*, 1932, p. 461) 'is the sleeping dog negation and we hurry past. . . .'

Again, how can the view that the arrangement of elements in the sign shows the arrangement of elements in the signified account for statements, which, though they have a different arrangement of elements, yet express the same fact? May not 'This is red and round' and 'This is red and this is round' state the same fact? Either it must be claimed that no two sentences can ever express the same fact—which is to deny a use to 'same fact'—or it must be admitted that the arrangement of elements in the sentence does not always show the arrangement of elements in the fact, that some sentences are better at doing this than others, e.g. that 'This is red and this is round' more nearly shows the arrangement of elements in the fact than the misleadingly telescoped 'This is red and round'. And then the suspicion arises that no ordinary sentence intimates really well the structure of the fact, that only some as yet undisclosed sentences could do this, perhaps, or is it that no *sentence* can be used to do this at all?

Consider next difficulties created by the transformation of facts into things. There is a modicum of plausibility in 'The fact *Sophia hit me* is in the world'; there is no semblance of it in 'The fact *Something hit me* is in the world'. While the first fact is composed of *Sophia* and *me* in a certain relation, what would be the elements of the second fact? *Something* and *me*? But what sort of thing is *something*? Sentences like 'Everything which is round is red', 'The thing which is round is red' pose the same problem as will any sentence not composed of names of objects and simple verbs. Clearly, a philosopher committed to treating facts as things must discard embarrassing elements like *something, everything, the thing which*, etc. Consider, for instance, the devices Wisdom resorted to. His first stratagem is to introduce the new relation of 'referring'. He separates the fact *expressed* by these embarrassing sentences from the facts to which they *refer*. The facts referred to are always of the satisfactory concrete sort. 'Suppose I say "Some dogs are sleepy" and speak truly. Then there will be one or two facts out in the big world of this sort: *This is a dog and this is sleepy. That is a dog and that is sleepy. Thet is a dog and etc.* What I refer to by my sentences are these facts. What I express by my sentence is *the* fact that there are such facts as these.'

This is unsatisfactory: the fact expressed still contains deplorable elements. Wisdom's second expedient is to jettison both the relation of 'expressing' and his self-devised 'referring'. He invents a new one—'locating'. Sentences now simply locate facts. The difference between 'Sophia hit me' and 'Something hit me' is now describable as a difference in completeness of location. 'Sophia hit me' precisely locates the fact *Sophia hit me*. 'Something hit me' partially locates the facts *Sophia hit me, Amos hit me, Martha*. . . . The facts are all composed of tangible elements with no difficult *somethings*, or *everythings* occurring in them. Thus we find old facts discarded, like the fact that someone hit me, and new facts invoked, like *Sophia hit me, Amos hit me, Martha*. . . . We find that the intimate link between sentence and fact has been broken, and in its place a loose union between a sentence and countless other facts. Would one not have thought that 'Someone hit me', if related to any fact, would be related to the fact that someone hit me, and not to *Sophia hit me, Amos hit me, Martha* . . .?

Finally, consider one of the consequences of the assimilation of sentences to facts. '3.1432 We must not say "The complex sign '*aRb*' says '*a* stands in relation *R* to *b*' "; but we must say, "that '*a*' stands in a certain relation to '*b*' says that *aRb*".' Normally we should say that it was a fact *about* the sign 'aRb' that 'a' stands in a certain relation to 'b', not that the sign 'aRb' *is* that fact. This way of converting sentences into facts creates a difficulty: in conversion, an n-termed sentence becomes an n + 1-termed fact. Consider 'Sophia hates Amos'. This becomes the fact '*Hates*' *is between* '*Sophia*' *and* '*Amos*', which has the consequence that it is impossible to gear the form of a sentence to the form of the fact. The sentence 'Sophia hates Amos' is not identical in form with, i.e. has not the same number of elements as, the fact *Sophia hates Amos*. For the sentence is the fact *'Hates' is between 'Sophia' and 'Amos'*, i.e. it has four elements while *Sophia hates Amos* has only three. This view brings with it the consequence that all ordinary sentences have, for fact-stating purposes, one word too many!

All these difficulties strengthen the suspicion that pictures are, as a model for sentences, unfortunate. In some cases, e.g. negative sentences, there is no fit; in other cases, e.g. sentences containing words like 'something', contriving is needed to achieve a fit, and in even the best cases the fit is uncomfortable—it is time to examine closely pictures and sentences. To bring out their logic I propose also to examine reflections and maps.

Reflections, pictures, and maps share a feature of fundamental importance. They are icons.[1] An icon is a sign which has at least one of the properties of that for which it is a sign, and signifies in virtue of such a property. In a drawing of a cat with her small kitten, more of the picture will be occupied by the cat than the kitten; the relative dimensions of the cat and the kitten are repeated in the picture of the cat and the kitten. Reflections, pictures, and maps duplicate the spatial properties of that which they reflect, picture or map.[2] Sentences, on the other hand, are not icons. In the sentence 'The cat is bigger than the kitten', 'cat' is in the same type as 'kitten'. To convey our meaning we have no need to write 'THE CAT is bigger than the kitten'.

The next difference to notice between icons and sentences is important. Icons show, sentences state. A reflection in water shows the trees on its bank, a picture shows a girl holding a cat, a map shows the course of a river. A sentence states that the tree is on the river bank, that the girl holds a cat, that the river flows from north to south.

Before continuing it may be worthwhile to examine briefly a sense of 'show' which in this context is confusing. It is a sense different from the sense in which for example a picture of a girl holding a cat has been said to show a girl holding a cat. In the new sense of 'show' a picture of a girl holding a cat may show something other than a girl holding a cat; it may, in this sense, show the influence of a school of painting or that the artist's technique has improved. This sense of 'show' is applicable to sentences too. A sentence may show care in construction or that its writer spells poorly. It seems to me clear that 'show' in this sense of 'reveals' is not of direct interest to us. From now on I ignore it to discuss 'show' only in the sense in which an icon, but not a sentence, may show.

[1] I adapt this term from C. S. Peirce.
[2] This is inaccurate. It fails to take account of the effects of, e.g., perspective or projection. So to take account would complicate but not, I think, alter the description.

To continue, then, with the comparison of showing and stating. Both relations are resoluble into two components. Showing consists in representing and arranging, stating in referring and describing. Here the similarity ends. It is possible to point at a reflection in a river saying 'Look at the tree in the water'. Similarly, of a picture we may say 'This'—pointing at a line in a drawing—'is the tree trunk', or of a map 'Here's Oxford and there's Woodstock'—indicating two dots with the finger. But we cannot say as we indicate one of the words in a sentence 'This is a tree'. The fact that icons are like what they signify is acknowledged by our willingness to say that the icon *is* what it signifies.

There is no locution alternative to 'is' for the relation between the elements of a reflection and the elements of what it reflects. Its elements are trees, clouds, leaves. We do not say that a reflection represents or stands for or denotes or refers to the scene it reflects. Perhaps this is so because it is a causal phenomenon and these relations all imply an agent who uses the sign to represent, stand for, denote, or refer to the signified. The image on a television or cinema screen is spoken about in a similar way. 'Look, there's Philip Harben' and not 'Look, that represents, or stands for, etc. Philip Harben'. Of a picture, on the other hand, in addition to saying that a curved stroke is the tree trunk, we may say that it represents the tree trunk. Similarly, of a map, the dot which is Oxford may also be said to stand for Oxford. Instead of writing: The elements of an icon stand for, represent, or are, elements in the signified, let us use the single relation of representing and say: The elements of an icon represent elements in the signified. Now, showing is not merely representing. The elements of an icon must be in a certain arrangement. The lines which represent the trunk and the speckles which represent the leaves will not make a picture of a tree unless (roughly) the lines and speckles are arranged so that the speckles are on top of the lines. Thus the arrangement of the elements in the icon must be similar to the arrangement of the elements in what it signifies.

Now contrast showing, which we have resolved into representing and arranging, with stating. The elements of a sentence, viz. its words, neither are, nor do they stand for, or represent what they signify. 'Tree' is not a tree in the way that a drawing of a tree is a tree, and nor does 'tree' represent a tree in the way that a drawing does. Words have meaning—unlike strokes and lines—and are used (this is two of many chosen because we are concerned with sentences in their fact-stating use) to refer to and characterize things. 'The tree is bare' both refers to a tree and describes it as bare. In 'The tree is bare', 'The tree' refers to an object and 'is bare' describes that object. So to apportion the function of 'The tree' and 'is bare' is not, of course, quite correct as Strawson pointed out in *On Referring* (*Mind*, 1950). 'The tree' is descriptive as well as referential, as we see if we contrast it with 'It' in 'It is bare'.

Although stating, like showing, resolves into two components, the relations between stating, referring, and describing are different from the relations between showing, representing, and arranging. To begin with, referring and describing are not the counterparts of representing and arranging. Rather do both referring and describing correspond to the one relation of representing. Some elements of a sentence refer, some describe, some do both; all the elements of an icon represent. Arranging is an ordering of elements all of which represent, but describing is not an ordering of elements all of which refer. Describing is on a par with referring in the way in which arranging is not with representing.

Next, showing bears a relation to representing different from the relation that stating bears to describing and referring. A sentence states, but its elements cannot state. An icon shows—and so do its elements. Compare the sentence 'My cat sits on its cushion' with a picture of a cat on a cushion. If from the drawing I erase the cushion I leave a picture of a cat. The removal of 'sits on his cushion' from the sentence leaves, not a sentence, but a phrase. In other words, elements which represent also show; but elements which refer or describe do not also state. Not only do all the elements of an icon signify in the same way, but the icon signifies the way all its elements do. In contrast, a sentence states, but does not, as its elements do, refer or describe.

Finally we must notice that showing is not first representing and then arranging. Representing is simultaneous with arranging. Stating, on the other hand, is first referring and then describing, or perhaps first describing and then referring. The order in a sentence *may* contribute to fixing its meaning, but difference in meaning may be achieved by means other than difference in word order by, e.g., case inflection. The order found in a spatial icon, however, must contribute to fixing its significance. The order of words in a sentence is a conventional order of presentation; the spatial ordering of the elements in a reflection, picture, or map, is an iconic order of representation.

By now it is clear that it is a mistake to think that showing is composed of representation and arrangement in the way that stating is reference and description. We now see that not only is showing unlike stating, but also that representing and arranging are related to showing in a way unlike the way in which referring and describing are related to stating.

There are further differences between icons and sentences. If all the elements in the sign represent elements in the signified, it is possible to set up a correspondence between the elements of each. In the case of a reflection the correspondence is clearly one to one. As Wisdom put it: 'When a mirror mirrors a scene then for each coloured patch in the reflection, there is a coloured patch in the scene and vice versa. . . .' A reflection may be blurred as in rippled water, or distorted as in a concave mirror; these are respectively a defect of clarity and a peculiarity in projection. It cannot, however, omit detail. To each element in the scene there must correspond an element in the reflection. This does not hold good of pictures. Though it is still the case that a correspondence can be set up between the elements of a picture and the elements of the pictured, the correspondence need not be one to one. A portrait may be faithful to the last detail, but it may not. It may be a sketch, or an outline drawing, or even a composition design, showing only broad masses and omitting detail completely. Similarly, a map may omit detail, and in so far as it does, it ceases to be in one to one correspondence with that of which it is a map. For example, a map of England may show every English river, or it may show instead merely the main rivers. Reflections, pictures, maps, form a series of decreasing iconicity, i.e. they differ in the number of features they must have in common with what they signify. Language, though its mode of signification is conventional and not iconic, contains a few iconic devices like 'creak', 'buzz', 'tinkle'. These are similar in sound to the sounds they may be used to refer to. Even though it is only the elements of a reflection, and not of a picture or map, which must be isomorphic with the elements of the scene, it is still in general true that the elements of an icon can be set in correspondence—though not always in one to one correspondence —with the elements of that of which it is an icon. This is so because *all* the elements of an icon represent. We saw above that the elements of a sentence have no function analogous to representing. At best, referring is its analogue—and not all words refer. Since the elements of a sentence do not represent elements in the signified, *a fortiori*, the elements of a sentence do not correspond to elements in the signified.

The elements of icons and sentences differ in another respect. The elements of a sentence are part of a vocabulary, the elements of an icon are not. Whether we take as elements of an icon lines, dots, and patches, or meaningful combinations of such lines, dots, and patches, the point still holds. If the lines, etc. are themselves to be taken as elements, then, as they have no constant significance, they cannot constitute a vocabulary, as the items in a vocabulary must be usable with the *same* meaning on different occasions. A 2 cm. line could be used to represent the side of a fan, a mouth, etc. If meaningful combinations of lines, dots, etc., i.e. such combinations as represent a recognizable object, are taken as elements, the elements of an icon still cannot form a vocabulary as they cannot be used in many situations: being themselves icons, they represent a specific object. A sketch of a face, for example, has a specific shape and a specific arrangement of features; it represents *that* face and no other. As iconicity decreases so the possibility of a vocabulary increases.

Maps, which are less iconic than pictures and reflections, have the beginnings of a vocabulary. Dots stand for towns, crosses for churches, etc., and the dots and crosses are used with the same significance in different instances. Since the signs may stand for other things in another map the vocabulary is relative to each map. Each map needs therefore a legend to interpret its signs. It would be possible to have a standard set of symbols for map-making, so that no key—for this purpose—was necessary. In practice some cartographic symbols are standard and others vary from map to map. They still constitute a vocabulary whether they have a constant significance merely for a particular map, or whether they are general cartographic conventions.

However, not all the elements in a map are items in a rudimentary vocabulary. Lines standing for rivers and sea-fronts are not so for the reasons that the elements of a picture are not. A map stands midway between a picture and a language. Its more iconic elements are like picture elements; its less iconic and therefore more conventional elements are like language elements. The fact that maps and languages have a vocabulary is connected with another difference. A conventional sign does not, like an icon, show what it signifies. There is nothing in the sign 'cat' to show that it signifies a cat, as there is in a drawing of a cat. We have to learn the meaning of 'cat' in a way we do not have to learn the meaning of a drawing. We learn to read (significant idiom) a map because it is to some extent conventional.

Consider now the question of entities. That sentences, unlike icons, do not signify *qua* entity can be brought out by comparing a sentence with an icon. Take a picture of a cushion between a cat and a mouse, and the sentence 'This adjoins that'. To speak of the sentence as the fact that 'Adjoins' is between 'this' and 'that' (3.1432 . . . That 'a' stands in a certain relation to 'b' says that aRb) is to regard it as three marks in ink in the way that a picture of a cushion between a cat and a mouse is three marks in ink. But a sentence does not signify because it is a pattern of marks—its physical appearance is irrelevant in the sense that there is no correlation between appearance and function, e.g. homonyms look alike but have different meanings, a sentence looks no different from its component words, yet signifies differently, and so on. It is just because the sentence, unlike the picture, does not signify *qua* collection of ink marks, that we do not talk

124

about it as the sentence 'Adjoins' is between 'this' and 'that' (cf. the picture of the cushion between the cat and the mouse). Nor is what is stated, a fact, on a par with the scene reflected, person pictured or country mapped. Facts are not things. Anyone who holds that they are must do violence to the concept of fact. By this I mean that they must misuse the term 'fact', for I take the question of whether a fact is a thing, or an event or a true statement, to be the question of whether the idioms appropriate to the one are appropriate to the other. Though the fact and thing idiom merge, e.g. De Gama discovered the Canaries, Poirot discovered the facts, facts and things may be overlooked, concealed, unearthed, etc., the merging is minute compared to the vast terrain of each which remains separate. Facts cannot be broken or identified, they neither exist nor do they not exist. Yet they seem so brute, so inescapable, surely they are out there in the world—just like the table? But the table is not a fact, nor is the table is brown, nor the table being brown. That the table is brown is (or rather may be) a fact—and there are no 'thats' in the world.

We must now consider one last difference of great importance between icons and sentences. As icons signify by being like what they signify, their range of signification is limited. The special restriction of a reflection to what is in spatial proximity to it is unconnected with its iconicity, and due solely to the fact that it is a causal phenomenon. Both reflections and pictures, however, can show only spatial and coloured relations, i.e. they can show only what is in (what I earlier called) the same *genre* as themselves. A song or a taste can be neither reflected nor pictured. Maps, being less iconic and more conventional, may show the spatial relationships of a greater variety of things than reflections or pictures, e.g. although we cannot picture the equator, we can mark it on a map. A map's range of signification expands in other directions too. As well as geographical maps, there are political maps, rainfall maps, ethnological maps. This increase in scope depends upon and is accompanied by an increase in conventionality. Since language is wholly conventional it has an unlimited range. It is restricted to no *genre* spatial or otherwise. To show you how someone looks I can paint a picture; to show you how she sounds I must sing, not paint; in words I can tell you both how she looks and how she sings. It is the strength of the icon that it signifies with great specificity. It is its weakness that it can signify only what is like itself. Language can describe anything bar the ineffable—and even this it characterizes as such.

It seems to me that this review of reflections, pictures, maps and sentences, reveals two vastly different modes of signification: the iconic and the conventional. Earlier we summarized the demands of the picture model. We can now see them as demands which can only be fulfilled by a *misdescription* of language. They demand, in effect, that language signify iconically. But since language does not signify in virtue of properties it has in common with what is signified—it is not an icon—any description of it which describes it as iconic misdescribes it. It is clear that sentences do not show, but state, that arrangement, which is an essential factor in iconic signification, need not occur in conventional signification, that the elements of a sentence do not stand for objects but (may be used to) refer to or describe objects. And since the words in a sentence do not stand for objects, they cannot be in correspondence, let alone one to one correspondence, with objects. Nor can a language fulfil the demand that the sign be in the same *genre* as the signified since it does not signify in virtue of being itself like what is signified and nor, in the case of language, can the sign and the signified be treated as things. A sentence and a picture differ in the very respects in which—if the one is to be a model for the other—they would have to resemble one another.

It now becomes clear too why, on the picture model, sentences always have a word too many. An icon needs no mark for what it shows by likeness. A drawing of one thing adjoining another needs a mark for one thing and a mark for the other, but no mark for the relation of adjoining. This it shows by the spatial placing of the marks for the two things. A sentence needs a mark where a picture does not: it cannot show that this adjoins that, but must *say* so. (Wittgenstein was wrong in saying: '4.1212 What *can* be shown *cannot* be said.') Say we drop the mark for *adjoins* and write 'This that' in place of 'This adjoins that'. How would we indicate that this adjoins as opposed to surpasses or divides into that? Again, words like 'a', 'the', 'which', 'all', 'some', 'three', do a job which, as opposed to iconic, is characteristically linguistic. Since a language has a vocabulary, i.e. is composed of signs which may be used on different occasions to talk about different things, some device is needed to show which thing is being talked about on any given occasion. To say merely 'Cats on cushions' would not tell whether it is the cats (my neighbour's and my own), all cats, some cats, or no cats, that are on cushions. The function of 'the', 'all', 'some', 'no', is not to destroy the non-existent correspondence which holds between a sentence and a fact but to help identify which cats are being spoken about. Indeed, any censure of a word on the ground that its occurrence in a sentence wrecks the isomorphism between language and reality must be mistaken—language does not try so to correspond, and nothing, therefore, can cause it to fail to do so.

Why are negative statements, conditional statements, disjunctive statements, etc., not describable in picture terms? The reason is that they are the very statements which have no pictorial counterparts. I can say that a cat is black and I can picture a black cat. But whereas I can also tell you that it is not black, I cannot picture this. To say that a cat is not black is not to say of what colour it is; but if I paint I must paint a cat of *some* colour. And how could we show in a picture that all cats are black, that *the* cat (as opposed to *a* cat) is black? The sentences which do not yield to the picture model are just those which cover a region no picture could picture. Variations in tense—we can picture a black cat but how could we picture a cat that was or will be black?—is another example. And were a picture theory to succeed in the fact-stating sphere, some other account would still be needed for commands, questions, prayers, promises, hopes, wishes, fears. If we consider how small a proportion of actual discourse is composed of simple sentences of the cat-on-the-mat type, we see what a small part of language this model could even purport to elucidate.

Of course, iconic and conventional signs are not wholly diverse. At the least they share the grammar of 'sign'. For instance both sorts signify well or ill. A portrait can be faithful, true to the original, or show a face as other than it is; a map can be accurate or inaccurate; a sentence, when used informatively, true or false. All are further alike in that they can signify in various 'projections'. A concave mirror will in a regular manner distort what it reflects; a picture may be cubist or pointillist in its form of representation; maps can be in different projections, e.g. Mercator's; and a tale can be told in the first person singular, or in an impersonal reporter's idiom, in Freudian terms, etc. As well as variation in projection there is variation in style. By this I mean that there may be differences not due to any regular transformation. Idiosyncratic omissions, high-lighting of one detail rather than another, occur in stories, and also in pictures, e.g. a caricature, and in maps, e.g. a diagram. Again, pictures, maps, sentences, are all alike in this: to know if they are faithful, adequate, true, whether they distort or not, something other than themselves must be examined, that which they purport to reflect, picture, map or describe. It is also true that iconic signification slides into linguistic. Historically a large number of our conventional signs have come ultimately from pictographs. The prejudice that what has a common source has common properties may lead us to think icons and linguistic signs more alike than they are. Thus Wittgenstein could say: '4.016 In order to understand the essence of the proposition, consider hieroglyphic writing, which pictures the facts it describes. And from it came the alphabet without the essence of the representation being lost.' Picture languages embody the transition from iconic to conventional, having signs at once both (hieroglyphs for instance). Such signs may be representational to a larger or smaller extent. The human figure with protruding ribs that represents famine or the weeping eye that stands for sorrow are stylized pictures, ideographs, representing simple abstract ideas. If a drawing of an eye comes to represent not only ideas suggested by eyes but also all homonyms of 'eye', then a sign of purely phonetic value has emerged, and the picture has become conventionalized. All this fills in the fissure between iconic and conventional signification.

Nonetheless, although an icon and the elements in it represent, neither the proposition nor its parts represent. A picture has parts which are little pictures, that is, an icon stands for something just as its elements do. But with a sentence the case is different. Parts of a sentence are not themselves sentences and though its elements may refer to or describe something the sentence itself cannot. Put in this way, it is clear that it is a possible description of the search for a correlate of a sentence to parallel the correlates of the words in a sentence, to say that it is an assimilation of stating to showing. This is, among other things, to imagine that just as the icon, like its elements, represents something, so the sentence, like its elements, refers to something. We see too why the picture can be a model for words as well as sentences. Since the elements of a picture are themselves pictures one could think that words are pictures, as well as that a sentence is a picture. Thus we might say that 'the name like the picture is an imitation of the thing' (*Cratylus* 430) or that 'The proposition is a picture of reality' (*Tractatus* 4.12).

Consider the 'picture' elucidation of names. This may be put as 'The name means the object, the object is its meaning'. To say this is to use 'means' with the logic of 'stand for' or 'represent', i.e. to construe words on the iconic model. The attendant puzzle: 'If the word means *this* object, perhaps the one by which it is ostensively defined, how can it mean any other object?' comes from trying to fit an essentially linguistic attribute into an iconic description. If an icon represents *this* object, it can represent no other. A painting of a red rose shows a rose of a determinate shade and a particular shape and the picture cannot picture a rose of any other colour or shape. An icon must always be specific. A language on the other hand has signs that can be used with the same meaning on different occasions. Thus to ask: 'How if the word means this object can it mean another?' is first to assimilate words to icons and then to demand that an icon signify linguistically. This is to ask of a sign that it at once 'mean' the object (signify *specifically*) and have meaning (signify so that there are *general* directions for its use). The complaint that words are too indeterminate in their signification—which often accompanies the thesis that the name means the object—can be viewed as a complaint that words are not iconic enough in their signification. The ideal name would picture, say, a particular.

Although the Picture Theory brings with it puzzles that even its holders recognize as insoluble, it nevertheless seems to have the virtue of dealing adequately with two questions, which may, as a result of certain philosophical views, become problems: How is it that we immediately understand a sentence we have never heard before? How can a false sentence have meaning?

We understand a new combination of words for the same reason, we might say, that we comprehend a picture on seeing it for the first time. No explanation is necessary in either case; the picture 'speaks' for itself, it shows what it pictures; the sentence speaks for itself, it 'shows' its sense. The parallel is most clearly stated by Wittgenstein '4.01 The proposition is a picture of reality. 4.02 This we see from the fact that we understand the sense of the propositional sign, without having had it explained to us. 4.021 The proposition is a picture of reality for I know the state of affairs presented by it, if I understand the proposition. And I understand the proposition without its sense having been explained to me. 4.022 The proposition *shows* its sense. 4.027 It is essential to propositions that they can communicate a new sense to us.' This seems to explain how it is that we can understand a new sentence, but does it really? A sentence does not show its meaning—consider the impenetrability of a sentence in an unmastered language. To understand a statement we must first have learnt the language in which it is made—but in the sense in which there are foreign languages there are no foreign pictures. Only if learning was unnecessary for languages too would Wittgenstein be right in saying '4.03 A proposition must communicate a new sense with old words. The proposition communicates to us a state of affairs, therefore it must be essentially connected with the state of affairs.' We do not understand a sentence on first hearing it because it is *essentially* connected with reality; a sentence is *conventionally* connected with reality. '4.012 It is obvious that we perceive a proposition of the form *aRb* as a picture. Here the sign is obviously a likeness of the signified.' But a sentence, unlike a picture, is not a likeness of the signified, so that this must fail to explain how we find a new sense in old words. Indeed, the picture view itself creates the need for an 'explanation'. This is the puzzle, this time with sentences instead of names, of how if the sign means *this*, can it ever mean anything else? As before, the puzzle pivots on saying that the sign is an iconic sign and then wishing that it would function as a linguistic sign.

The Picture Theory appears also to explain how a *false* sentence can have meaning. We can come to be perplexed about the meaning of false sentences as a result of a view such as Russell's that 'the

129

components of the fact which makes a proposition true or false . . . are the *meanings* of the symbols we must understand in order to understand the proposition' (*Philosophy of Logical Atomism*). This view apparently accounts for the meaningfulness of true propositions, for in this case the fact 'corresponds in a way that makes the proposition true'. Suppose it is a fact that this is red and I say: 'This is red', then 'this' means *this* and 'red' means *red*. But what if I say: 'This is blue' when in fact this is red? 'This' means *this* but what now does 'blue' mean? What component in the fact that this is red *can* blue mean? Either we must say that since *blue* is not a component of the fact—viz. this is red—which makes 'This is blue' false, 'blue' has no meaning, or we must say that 'blue' means *red*—in 'the false way'. Neither pleases. It seems better to press the model further and say that just as a picture shows what it pictures even when it does not picture any actual thing so a sentence shows what it means even when it does not mean any actual fact. '4.061 If one does not observe that propositions have a sense independent of the facts, one can easily believe that true and false are two relations between signs and things signified with equal rights. 2.22 The picture represents what it represents independently of its truth or falsehood, through the form of representation. 2.221 What the picture represents is its sense. 4.022 The proposition *shows* its sense.' Since, as was pointed out earlier, a proposition can show only what is *other* than its sense this account of the meaningfulness of false sentences is not correct. Nevertheless, by making meaning independent of truth or falsity it does come nearer a right description.[1]

Finally, let us notice it is not for nothing that philosophers thought 'there will always be a certain fundamental identity of structure between the fact and the symbol for it'. The truth in this is that a sentence 'S' cannot be used to state in any way inadequately the fact that S. 'S' may default in the statement of a fact F only if 'S' is other than 'F'. 'S', for example, may state approximately the fact that F, where 'S' is an approximation to 'F', e.g. 'There are two thousand men on strike' says in round figures or is a less precise statement of 'There are 1763 men on strike'. Take another case. 'S' may state without detail the fact that F, where 'S' is a sentence giving less information than 'F', e.g. 'She walked up the hill' states a bare, a plain, an unvarnished fact compared with 'She walked slowly up the hill singing all the way'. A hesitation can of course appear whether 'S' states the fact that F in a less detailed way than 'F', or whether 'S' and 'F' state different facts. Does 'She walked up the hill with Roderick' add a detail to the fact that she walked up the hill or state a further fact about her? There seems to be a tendency to give the

[1] See Strawson: "On Referring", *Mind*, July, 1950.

answer that 'S' adds a detail to 'F' if 'S' and 'F' are linguistically similar, and to give the opposite answer, to say 'F' states a new fact, if 'S' and 'F' are linguistically different. 'She walked up the hill with Roderick' adds a detail to the fact that she walked up the hill. '*Roderick* was her escort' supplies a fact additional to the fact that she walked up the hill.

The important point for us is that the question whether 'S' states the fact that F loosely or approximately, in less or in great detail, cannot arise unless 'S' is different from 'F'. It makes no sense to ask whether 'The cat is on the mat' is an approximate, a plain, a full, or an adequate statement of the fact that the cat is on the mat. If 'S' is identical with 'F', i.e. when 'S' states the fact that S, then 'S' states altogether adequately the fact that S, is, if you like, in perfect correspondence with the fact it states. But if, in such a case, we put it this way, we must mean by correspondence no more than that it makes no sense to question the fitness of 'S' to state the fact that S. Sentences and facts cannot correspond in any way that suits the needs of a Correspondence Theory of Language.

NOTE (1965): "While discriminating modes of signifying may be a useful enterprise towards clarifying the question 'What is meaning?' it seems to me that the paper as a whole is wrong-headed.

"It implies that the Picture Theory of Meaning is an error, even a simple error. This is a failure to realize that it is a great philosophical view that develops the general problem. Furthermore, the agglomeration of different modes of signifying described in the paper is only a small part of what the Picture Theory of Meaning contains. The forces which lead to it are many and strong; of course, Wittgenstein has set these out incomparably in the opening passages of the *Philosophical Investigations*."—Edna O'Shaughnessy.

'Tractatus' 3.1432[1]

ELLIS EVANS

3.1432. We must not say, "The complex sign '*aRb*' says '*a* stands in relation R to *b*'"; but we must say, "*That* '*a*' stands in a certain relation to '*b*' says *that aRb*".

IN a recent article,[2] Mrs Daitz says that this assimilation of the *fact* that in '*aRb*', '*a*' stands in a certain relation to '*b*', to the *sign* '*aRb*' creates a difficulty: for the sign then becomes a four-element fact, whereas what the sign says, i.e. that *aRb*, has only three elements. For instance, the sentence 'Sophia hates Amos' becomes the four-element fact that 'hates' is between 'Sophia' and 'Amos': whereas the fact *Sophia hates Amos* has only three elements. Thus, she concludes, Wittgenstein's view has the consequence that such sentences have one element too many for fact-stating purposes.

Now the four elements into which Wittgenstein converts '*aRb*' are evidently the three signs and their order. That is to say, the fact that the sign is what it is, is the fact that it contains '*a*', that it contains '*b*', that it contains 'R', and that it contains them in the order '*aRb*'. But when Wittgenstein says, that the fact that '*a*' stands in a certain relation to '*b*' says that *aRb*, I think he means, that it is the last of those four facts about '*aRb*' that lets '*aRb*' say that *aRb and not for instance that bRa*. He has just been talking (3.1431) about the mutual spatial position of the elements of the propositional sign. Here, I think he is pointing out that the position of the elements of the sign '*aRb*' is symbolic. (I am assuming of course that he did not have a symmetrical relation in mind.) He is saying that it is that particular arrangement of those elements that signifies that *aRb* (and not that *bRa*).

---

[1] From *Mind*, N.S., vol. 64, no. 254, April, 1955, pp. 259–60. Reprinted by permission of the editor and the author.
[2] Edna Daitz, "The Picture Theory of Meaning", *Mind*, April, 1953, pp. 184–201 [pp. 115–31].

I take his account of what we must *not* say as follows. If, in describing how the symbolism of '*aRb*' works, we say merely that '*aRb*' says '*a* stands in R to *b*', we have not shown what it is about the sign '*aRb*' that indicates how, in the fact that *aRb*, the three elements corresponding to '*a*', 'R', and '*b*' are combined. In our statement of what '*aRb*' says, namely '*a* stands in R to *b*', we have reproduced the order of the signs in '*aRb*'. But that order is symbolic: thus we have reproduced a covert symbolic element in '*a* stands in R to *b*', and thus '*aRb*' has not been completely analysed. We have said that '*a*' means *a*, that 'R' means R, and that '*b*' means *b*, and we have said it in that order: but we have not shown that it is the fact that those signs are in that order that allows us to say that '*aRb*' says '*a* stands in R to *b*' and not '*b* stands in R to *a*'. Consequently the complete analysis should show that it is the order of the terms in '*aRb*' that determines that '*aRb*' says that *aRb* and not that *bRa* or some other structure of the elements corresponding to '*a*', 'R' and '*b*' (if such be possible).

Wittgenstein says that we must not take the *complex sign* as saying that *a* stands in R to *b*. I take this as meaning that we must not say that the *group* says that, but that the *grouping* says that, the way the elements of the complex sign are ordered. To the individual elements of the sign, correspond the elements of the fact: but it is the *order* of the elements of the sign that corresponds to the *structure* of the elements of the fact. To take Mrs Daitz's example, 'Sophia hates Amos' indicates that Sophia hates Amos rather than that Amos hates Sophia in virtue of the order of the words concerned. Wittgenstein would have said, I think, that the fact that Sophia hates Amos contained four elements: the two people, the hating, and the structure of these, i.e. that it is Sophia and not Amos that is doing the hating and Amos and not Sophia that is receiving it. The individual words correspond to those first three elements, and the order of the words to the fourth.

When Mrs Daitz says that the fact *Sophia hates Amos* contains only three elements, it rather looks as if she is seeing only the three elements corresponding to the three words in her italicized sentence, and neglecting the element in the fact that Sophia hates Amos which corresponds to the *order* of the words in her italicized sentence. But if that element did not exist, then, to the fact that 'hates' is between 'Sophia' and 'Amos', nothing in the fact that Sophia hates Amos would correspond: and it would consequently be possible to express that fact, the fact that Sophia hates Amos, by using the same words in different order. But that is not the case.

On this interpretation, Mrs Daitz, in bringing against Wittgenstein the point that the fact *Sophia hates Amos* has three elements,

whereas the sentence 'Sophia hates Amos' has four (in Wittgenstein's view), does precisely what Wittgenstein is saying we shouldn't
do. She neglects one feature of the symbolism of 'aRb' while unconsciously conceding its existence by reproducing it in her reference
to the fact stated by 'aRb'. When referring to that fact, she uses the
formulation "the fact *Sophia hates Amos*", thus reproducing the
order of words in the sentence 'Sophia hates Amos' whose meaning
she is referring to. Wittgenstein has thus already dealt with the point
she brings against him: his remark is designed to counter the view
that such facts as *Sophia hates Amos* contain only three elements, by
showing that the language in which they are expressed contains a
symbolic element which is sometimes unrecognized.

Pictures and Form in Wittgenstein's 'Tractatus'[1]

B. F. McGUINNESS

WITTGENSTEIN'S *Tractatus* is a series of propositions numbered in such a way as to indicate their respective importance within the whole and their logical dependence upon one another.[2] That a system of numeration so troublesome for an author to devise will give many useful indications to the interpreter, is a truth that has only to be stated to be acknowledged. It may fairly be assumed, for example, that the propositions beginning with the number 6 represent what he regarded as the chief results of his enquiry: this assumption is confirmed by the frequent echoes to be found in these propositions of what W said in the *Vorwort*.

The structure of the 6's is roughly as follows:[3] in 6 itself the general form of a proposition is announced. By this is meant the form that any expression which is to be a proposition must have: the 4's and 5's have been largely devoted to showing that this form will be identical with the form that any truth-function must have (4's) and to showing what form it is that any truth-function must have (5's). It is then shown, in the 6.1's, that the propositions of logic are tautologies, which say nothing and have no content. In the 6.2's it is

[1] From *Filosofia e Simbolismo*, *Archivio di Filosofia*, Fratelli Bocca Editori: Roma, 1956, pp. 207–28. Reprinted by permission of the editor and the author.
[2] *Tractatus Logico-Philosophicus*, by Ludwig Wittgenstein, London, Kegan Paul, 1922: KP (Italian translation: by G. C. M. Colombo, S.J., Milan, Fratelli Bocca 1954: FB). I am indebted to Fr. Colombo for the suggestion that I should write article and for frequent discussions: in this latter point I am also indebted to my colleague in Oxford, Mr D. F. Pears.

W explains his system of numeration in a footnote printed on KP, p. 30, FB, p. 164. In the remainder of this article simple numerals will indicate propositions of the *Tractatus*.
[3] By "the n's" I shall mean those propositions that begin with the number or numbers n.

137

shown that the propositions of mathematics are likewise pseudo-propositions: the essential thing here is that mathematics is a *part* of logic, as W says twice (6.2, 6.234). In the 6.3's W deals with the apparent a-priority of at least some parts of natural science. His conclusion here is in accord with Einstein's dictum about Geometry: some propositions of "science" are necessarily true, in the sense that they are necessary consequences of our choice of a particular method of describing the world: but these say nothing about the world. There will be other propositions in science that do say something about the world (6.3431) but these will not be necessarily true and are the only "scientific propositions" properly so called.[1] The 6.4's and 6.5's discuss those questions to which natural science doesn't even seem to give an answer. Ethics is clearly one field of such questions, and W claims that there are *no* ethical propositions. On other matters, such as the freedom of the will, the "meaning" of life and "the riddle" (perhaps this is the felt contingency of the world) there *can be* no questions, because there are no propositions that would be their answers. Finally W recommends philosophical analysis (to borrow a later term) as a cure, and mystical feeling as a substitute, for metaphysics. The book closes with the often-quoted warning not to try to put the data of this feeling into words (7): *Wovon man nicht sprechen kann, darüber muss man schweigen.*[2]

---

[1] This remark seems to me to follow not only from 6.34 but from the requirement of consistency with 4.111 from which it may be inferred that propositions which have content and are not *a priori* are coextensive with natural science. However it may well be felt that there is a lack of clarity in the 6.3's concerning the existence within what we normally call natural science of a distinction between *a priori* pseudo-propositions and real non-*a priori* propositions, and a complete absence of any indication how to assign a given proposition to one or other of these two classes. It may be questioned whether any very precise indications *could* be given.

[2] The sequence of the last four propositions is interesting and may briefly be commented on here. 6.522 alludes again to "the mystical" which is however something inexpressible. 6.53 describes "the correct method" of philosophizing—that is, philosophical analysis resulting in the demonstration of the meaninglessness of metaphysical propositions. 6.54 is another well-known proposition in which he describes his own propositions as nonsensical, and compares them to a ladder which one who has climbed it must throw away. A consideration of the context illuminates both 6.54 and 7: W is reproaching himself for not following the only strictly correct philosophical method. Instead of saying things like, "What is mystical is not what the world is *like*, but that there *is* a world", he ought to have confined himself to the demonstration of the senselessness of metaphysical propositions—the attempt to *say* anything about what is mystical—and to the silent practice of mysticism. Thus he does not wish others to produce "propositions" like his but to engage in a quite different activity. It is in virtue of this fact—that they lead to something quite different from themselves—that his propositions resemble a ladder. Remarks such as that logic is a mirror-image of the world (6.13) or that the existence of the world is mysterious (6.44) do not themselves convey a correct view of the world, since such a view will not consist in holding any propositions, but they may help others to attain such a view—provided those others see what is wrong with these propositions themselves (this, I think, is part of the force of "*überwinden*" in 6.54). These propositions (for it is to such that 6.54 principally applies, in my view) are right in what they deny—that logic is a theory, or that the

Pictures and Form in Wittgenstein's 'Tractatus'

The assessment of what is "important" in the *Tractatus* will vary with judgment, interest and taste: about what the author regarded as his conclusions, he himself has left us in no doubt: they can be seen from the foregoing summary. He has examined the "propositions" of logic, mathematics, natural science, and traditional philosophy (principally metaphysics and ethics), and he has shown that of all of them only the non-*a-priori* parts of natural science have a claim to the title of "proposition", the others are either contentless like those of logic, or nonsensical like those of metaphysics.[1]

This sketch of W's conclusions contains, of course, nothing new; but the consideration of them within the sequence of thought of the 6's and of the terms in which W actually puts them brings out two aspects to which I should like to draw attention. First is the way in which all these conclusions are announced as conclusions about the features of certain propositions or pseudo-propositions. This, of course, is not a property peculiar to the 6's, since throughout the Tractatus "*Satz*" is by far the most common technical term. It is not the terms used in them, we might say, but the sorts of combinations of terms of which they consist that characterize logic, mathematics and metaphysics, just as the world is the totality of facts, not the

[1] The distinction between a "proposition" that says nothing but is without content and even senseless (*sinnlos*), and one that is nonsensical (*unsinnig*), comes out very clearly not only from the well-known passage (4.461–4.4611) where tautologies and contradictions (!) are said to belong to the former but not to the latter class, but also from 5.5303:"Roughly speaking, to say of *two* things that they are identical is nonsense, and to say of *one* thing that it is identical with itself says nothing." It is true that the particular example of an *Unsinn* given here raises some difficulties, since it implies that, where *a* and *b* are two things, "*a = b*" is not a contradiction (otherwise, by 4.4611, it would not be an *Unsinn*); but if so, it should seem that "*a = a*" is not a tautology (a result that would also follow from the truth that a tautology is a particular kind of truth-function). If, however, "*a = a*" is not a tautology, why should not it too be an *Unsinn*? It is a weak defence to say that in a language properly adapted to the expression of thought (that is how I interpret "*Begriffsschrift*") the sign of equality would disappear. In my view W ought to have said that this sign did lead to sense when put between expressions one of which was a description, but would always lead to *Unsinn* when placed between names. This raises the question whether it is possible for one thing to have two names. None of this, however, affects the truth that W here draws a distinction between "*nichtssagend*" and "*unsinnig*".

nature of the world is mysterious—but wrong in what they seem to assert. Even construed as denials, they ought more properly to be put in the form of demonstrations that certain "propositions" about logic or the world are senseless, for when there is a "subject" about which nothing can be said, one ought *not* to *say* that nothing can be said about it, *but* one ought to say *nothing* about it and make others do likewise.

It will be clear that at the end of the *Tractatus* W is not saying that he has reached no results, for results, though unimportant ones, are what he lays claim to in the *Vorwort*: rather he is concerned lest his method shall have seemed to give a new handhold to metaphysical reflection about the world and about logic: it has been his principal aim to remove the temptation to such speculation, but in doing so he has attempted to do justice if not to the truth, at least to the legitimate feeling that underlay this temptation. It is by this generosity that he has incurred the danger against which he here attempts to guard.

totality of things (1.1). R. Carnap has suggested (in *The Logical Syntax of Language*, London, 1937, p. 303) that, in the formal mode of speech, this sentence would run: "Science is a system of sentences, not of words.")[1]

That all the conclusions are expressed as conclusions about propositions is chiefly interesting here because of its connection with the second aspect of those conclusions that I have in mind, an aspect which brings us directly to the particular subject of this paper: namely that all of them are thought either to follow from or to be comments on the discovery of the general form of a proposition. The central parts of the 6's are intended to show that the propositions of logic, mathematics and the *a priori* parts of natural science are *not* results of the application of the operation of simultaneous negation to elementary propositions. The 6.4's start with the consideration that since what is good or bad is the existence of a state of affairs, an ethical proposition, if there were such a thing, would be the assertion of a proposition (compounded exclusively of elementary propositions) about the interior of the world (so to speak) plus an assertion *that* the truth of this assertion was a good or bad thing. As such it would involve the formation of a proposition out of elementary propositions by the use of operations other than of simultaneous negation. But the general form of a proposition does not permit this: ergo. Thus to think of something as good (if "think" is the right word) is not to assert anything about a state of affairs, but to have a distinct feeling about a state of affairs. Suppose a certain state of affairs which seems good to one man and bad to another: for each it will have the same *structure*, but the dimensions of it will seem larger to the one than to the other: thus the happy man's world will be (or

---

[1] 6.53 says, it is true, that in a metaphysical proposition there are certain signs to which no meaning (*Bedeutung*) has been given, but it may fairly be assumed that W has in mind words which in certain uses do have *Bedeutung*, but which are used in metaphysical propositions in a way in which they have none. His own favourite example of such a word is "*identisch*": the reason why "Socrates is identical" is nonsense, he says (5.4733, cf. 5.473), is that we have given no meaning to the word "identical" as a *property-word* (the word "*Eigenschaftswort*" is *gesperrt* in the text, which helps to make our point).

Further support for the view that metaphysics is characterized not by the use of meaningless words but by the use of meaningful words in nonsensical combinations comes from 3.323–3.324 where it is pointed out that our vernacular language gives rise to the confusion of which philosophy is full by, for example, allowing "identical" to look like a word for a property. Also from 4.003 where it is said that most of the questions raised and the propositions asserted by philosophers are rooted in misunderstandings of the logic of our language. It seems to me clear that the introduction of meaningless names would not naturally be the result of such misunderstandings, and that the example given of an extremely obviously nonsensical question (whether the good is more or less identical than the beautiful) is nonsensical because of the way the words are used rather than because of the words that are used. At any rate, the parallel, with the nonsense-example "Socrates is identical", suggests that what is wrong here is the misuse of "identical".

could be) of exactly the same structure as that of the unhappy man, but it will have, as it were, larger dimensions.[1] The structure of the world is expressible in language, these "dimensions" are not. The 6.5's chiefly deal with what are felt to be questions, even though we cannot think of any propositions that would be their answers.

Enough will have been said to make clear the importance of "the general form of a proposition" in the sequence of W's thought as he has presented it to us. Briefly the difficulties with which this confronts us are the following: in the first part of the *Tractatus*, notably in the 3's and early 4's, we seem to be told that the essence of a proposition is to be a picture, while in the later parts we are told that its essence is to be a truth-function, that is to say a result of applying the operation of simultaneous negation to elementary propositions. The "picture theory" requires further elaboration, and the truth-function account of what it is to be a proposition seems to involve a circularity by presupposing a prior understanding of what it is to be an elementary proposition. But a more serious difficulty is that the

---

[1] This is the best sense that I can at the moment see for 6.43. It might seem more consistent with 5.6–5.62 to understand talk about "the limits of the world" in 6.43 in such a way that by altering the limits of the world was meant altering the objects named and the elementary propositions possible within a man's own private language ("that language which I alone understand", as the translation should read at 5.62*). In that case, the happy man (the man who thinks things good) would see more (or less or different) things than the unhappy man. There might be enough agreement between their private languages to permit the sort of communication we now have (this is a problem that will in any case arise for W, given the superficial meaning of the 5.6's), but the analysis of a given proposition in the public language into the elementary propositions of each man's private language will be different. Thus a change *of* a man's world, as opposed to a change *in* it, would be a change of the objects that constituted the form of his world, and thus a change of the analysis in his language of some propositions of the public language: a change of "the limits of his world" (5.6). On this view, if men could see the world in the same way they could all see that it was good (or bad).

There are two difficulties for this interpretation: first 2.022–2.023, from which it appears that all possible worlds have their objects (and thus, in one sense, their limits 5.5561) in common. Against this must be set 5.123, which speaks (presumably allegorically) of the *creation* of objects by God, and seems to envisage the possibility of His including or omitting certain objects from creation. It may be thought that the objects that form the limits of a man's world, also limit the worlds that he can at that time think of as possible. It is conceivable *that* he should change, but he can not conceive *how* he might. This would be of a piece with the inexpressibility of an ethical viewpoint. The second difficulty is that in 6.43 W speaks of the world's waxing or waning *as a whole* (my italics). It seems to me that this last phrase is more suited to my interpretation (where it is, as it were, the dimensions of every single fact that change) than to the mere adding, subtracting or change of some, not necessarily all, objects.

In either case it is to be noted that living the good and living the bad life are matters of *viewpoint*. This, I think, is also the lesson of 5.621–5.63. "The world and life are one. I am my world."

*(Note added in 1964). I no longer believe that there is a reference to a private language at 5.62: cf. the version in the translation by Mr Pears and myself (Routledge, 1961), "of that language which alone I understand". As far as it goes, this change of view renders unnecessary the argument of footnote [1] and confirms my 1956 interpretation of 6.43.

two accounts seem to be quite separate things, and, if this is so, cannot both be adequate accounts of what it is to be a proposition.[1]

That a proposition is a picture is first absolutely asserted in the 4's, at 4.01–4.012 and 4.021: unless it were a picture it could not assert anything (4.03) nor be true or false (4.06). Thereafter, apart from passing references at 4.462 and 5.156, the notion of the proposition as a picture disappears from the *Tractatus*. It has of course been previously implied, most clearly at 3.42 and 3–3.1, but also by the almost exact parallelism between the 2.1's, which discuss pictures, and the 3.1's to 3.4's, which discuss propositions. Russell in his introduction to the *Tractatus* (KP, p. 8, FB, p. 136) says that W is concerned with "the question: what relation must one fact (such as a sentence) have to another in order to be *capable* of being a symbol for that other. . . . In order that a certain sentence should assert a certain fact there must, however the language may be constructed, be something in common between the structure of the sentence and the structure of the fact. This is perhaps the most fundamental thesis of Mr Wittgenstein's theory." W himself puts this at 4.03, by saying that the essential connection that a proposition must have with a state of affairs, in order to communicate that state of affairs to us, is that it must be its logical picture. The particular aspects of being a picture that are stressed in the 4.0's are: being such that signs within the proposition deputize for (*vertreten*) objects (4.0312) and being logically articulated and composite (*logisch gegliedert, zusammengesetzt*: 4.032). There must be composition within the proposition, and composition of such a kind that a mere list of the names occurring within it is not sufficient to characterize it, rather each of them has a different rôle within the proposition, though all of them have the rôle of deputizing for objects.[2] In fact the notion of deputizing for an object is inseparable from that of playing a particular rôle in a proposition or picture.[3] It seems then that the essence of a pro-

---

[1] The existence and importance of this problem were first, to my knowledge, pointed out and many directions for its solution (on which I have drawn freely) given by Miss G. E. M. Anscombe in lectures at Oxford.

[2] We may here draw attention to a passage to which we must return: 3.14–3.142, of which 2.14–2.141 is a parallel. It is by being articulated that a proposition is a fact, *the* fact that its elements, the words, are related to one another (*sich zu einander verhalten*) in the way they are. And it is by being a fact that a proposition is distinguished from the set of names occurring in it.

[3] I think this is why W says: "The elements of a picture are, *in the picture*, deputies' for objects' (2.13) and "A name is a deputy, *in a proposition*, for an object" (3.22, my italics in both cases). In any case 3.3 and 3.314 explicitly say that a name and an expression respectively have meaning only in the context (*Zusammenhang*) of a proposition.

These passages show, it seems to me, that what it is for a sign to be a deputy for an object is to be understood in terms of what it is for a fact to represent another fact, and not conversely. Ramsey in his review of the *Tractatus* (*Mind*, 1922, reprinted in *The Foundations of Mathematics*, p. 271 [p. 10]) maintained the opposite view, citing 5.542 (where W speaks of "a co-ordination of facts by means of a co-ordination of

position includes the deputizing for objects of its names and that this in turn involves that the proposition is articulated or composite in a way that a set of names is not. It is not my intention here to try to give all the reasons which may have led W to such conclusions, but it may be worth pointing out that one important premiss is the possibility of understanding a proposition or putting together a picture without knowing whether it is a true proposition or picture (4.021, 4.03).[1]

That the proposition or picture should consist of elements which deputize for objects, and that it should be compounded out of these elements in a quite definite way (so that a different composition would result in a different proposition), these are necessary conditions for the proposition to assert any fact, but more is required if it is to assert *the* fact that it does assert. It must be composed of elements that deputize for the objects whose combination is that fact; and those elements must have the same relation to one another as the objects have in the fact.[2] This requirement, which is brought out very clearly in the 2's and 3's, is the requirement of an identity of form (2.17) between the picture and the pictured. It will be clear that, since our interest is in the general form of a proposition, any remarks about the form of a proposition are important for us.

We meet the form of a fact in 2.033, of a picture in 2.15 (*die Form der Abbildung*) and of a proposition in 3.312 and 3.315. The first two have much in common but leave certain obscurities, which with the help of the third which is somewhat different we may be able to resolve.

Both for facts and for pictures the notion of form is introduced *via* the notion of structure. The structure of a fact or picture is the way in which its elements hang together (2.032, 2.15 . . . *Dieser Zusammenhang* . . .): The form is the possibility of the structure (2.033, 2.15). It is first of all necessary to see that two facts or pictures are of different *structure* if their objects (or elements) are arranged in the same way, but are different objects; in such a case however they will have the same *form*. Thus a fact and its picture may have the same form (must have, indeed) but cannot have the same structure.[3] Each

---

[1] I suspect that the same premiss is used in the proof of atomism. 2.0212 runs: It would then be impossible (sc. if there were no objects) to *essay* a depiction of the world. (This is a possible translation of "*entwerfen*", and the only one that fits the context, in my opinion.)

[2] It is sometimes suggested that an atomic fact is uniquely determined by the objects that occur in it: cf. Colombo, FB, p. 40. It seems to me that in this case a class of names would be sufficient to assert a fact, contrary to 3.142.

[3] This interpretation of "*Struktur*" was suggested by Ramsey in his review on the

---

their objects") as a proof that W regarded "deputizing" as the more intelligible notion, and "representing" as explicable in terms of it.

fact that we are aware of has its own structure: that *these* objects stand in *this* arrangement constitutes *this* structure. The structure of the fact that John loves Mary is the fact that John stands in the relation of loving to Mary. It will be obvious from this example that to assert the existence of the structure is nothing other than to assert the fact, and it will also seem that to say that a fact has a certain structure is to say nothing beyond what one has already said in asserting the fact. It does not seem to me, however, that this triviality is an objection to my interpretation of "*Struktur*". W says of *Form* that the logical form of reality cannot be represented in or expressed by a proposition, but is exhibited or shown by a proposition (4.12's passim, 6.124). A rough paraphrase of this for our purpose would be: the logical form of a proposition and of the fact that it states is perceived *eo ipso* by anyone who understands the proposition: but since, in order to understand any proposition P_n about a proposition p, you must already understand p, therefore the proposition P_k ascribing a certain logical form to p is bound to be otiose. It is evident that the same will hold of propositions about the structure of a proposition: indeed we find W using the fact that a proposition shows its own *structure* as a sort of illustration of the fact that it *shows* (rather than represents) the logical form of reality. "4.1211 Thus a proposition '*fa*' shows that in its sense the object *a* occurs." The occurrence of the particular object *a* is surely a feature of structure rather than of form.[1] Although it touches a more general question than we are here concerned with, the reader may wish to consider the suggestion that we feel a need to speak of structure and form only because our everyday speech disguises our thoughts (4.002), fails to make *obvious* the structure of our thoughts and of the facts that we state, though *implicitly* (*stillschweigend* 4.002) we do grasp those structures. Thus when we speak of the structure of the fact that

---

[1] It is perhaps worth saying that I cannot use 4.122 to prove my point, since the structures he there speaks of are those of complex facts (*Tatsachen*) and he speaks as if the *structure* of a *complex* fact is something that corresponds to the *formal properties* of an *atomic* fact.

---

grounds that it could be seen from the structure of propositions when one followed from the other (5.13, cf. 5.2, 5.22). Also 4.1211 says that the structure of two propositions shows when they contradict one another: if contradiction could be seen from the *forms* of propositions, then *p* would be the contradictory of not-*q*. However 5.131 says that if one proposition follows from another, this is expressed by relations in which their *forms* stand to one another.

I can reconcile this with Ramsey's view and mine, about the contrast between "*Struktur*" and "*Form*", only by saying that if one proposition follows from another, then there must be *at least* a relation between their forms—though there must be more as well. When one proposition follows from another, there will always be between the forms of the two a relation much closer than that between *p* and not-not-*q*. But, however close the formal relations between two propositions, it is always possible that, because of some difference in the objects named (a difference of structure, not of form), they should be logically independent of one another.

John loves Mary, as if this were something different from the fact that John loves Mary, we are really thinking of a translation of the *statement* that John loves Mary into a more explicit language (*eine Zeichensprache, die der logischen Grammatik . . . gehorcht* 3.325).

How, then, are we to understand the statement that the form of a picture or fact is the possibility of its structure? My view will be conveyed by the following analogy: suppose a system within which three or more of the letters *a, b, c* and *d* in immediate succession (repetitions being allowed), immediately preceded by the sign (") and immediately followed by the sign ("), constitute a well-formed formula. Within such a system "*aba*" and "*aca*" will be structures, and they can be said to be of the form "*a a*", on the grounds that they are possible ways of turning "*a a*" into a well-formed formula. We may wish to say instead that they are of the form "*a ( ) a*" or "*axa*", a suitable rôle, that of a variable, having been ascribed to the letter *x* or the signs ( ). Alternatively, on similar grounds, we may wish to say that they are of the forms "*xyx*" or "*xyz*" or finally " . . . *xyz* . . ." The last alternative is of course equivalent to saying that they are well-formed formulae. But probably, if we had to choose which of all the possible candidates was *the* form of these structures, we should say that "*xyz*" was.

The application of the analogy will be obvious: that John loves Mary is (let us suppose) a fact, so it is a structure.[1] It is of the form "that *x* loves *y*" or of the form "that *x* loves but is not identical with *y*" or of the form "that *x* stands in a relation to *y*" or of the form "that something is true of an ordered couple of objects" or of the form "that something is true of one or more objects".[2] Of course *all* facts are of the last of these forms. The fact or the structure that John loves Mary can be said to be of each or all of these forms, for each of them defines a range of facts and states of affairs that may or may not hold, such that one fact or state of affairs among these, one possible instantiation of each of these forms, is: that John loves Mary. If we had to say which of all these was *the* form of the fact John loves Mary, we should probably say that "that *x* stands in a relation to *y*" (with a stipulation that we wished to indicate that range of facts which resulted if identical substitutions for *x* and *y* were excluded) was *the* form.[3] To avoid difficulties arising from the particular example and irrelevant to the general case, let us say that

---

[1] The last paragraph but one will make clear how saying that it *is* a structure is identical with saying that it *has* a structure.

[2] We cannot say, however, that it is of the form "that someone loves someone else" or of the form "that one thing stands in a relation to another" for these are themselves facts, or could conceivably be so. Just as "*a a*" is not a well-formed formula in my analogy, so in the *Tractatus* the form of a fact is not itself a fact. Otherwise it could itself be asserted by a statement, contrary to the 4.12's.

[3] For the stipulation, cf. the 5.53's.

the form *par préférence* of the fact that *aRb* (where *"a"*, *"R"* and *"b"* designate constants, though W would not put it in this way) is *"$\Phi(x, y)$"*.[1]

At first sight it may seem that a slightly different account has to be given of the form of a picture, as this is described in the 2.1's. 2.15–2.151 seem to mean the following: the structure of a picture (namely the fact that its elements are related to one another in a definite way: which fact, by 2.14, is identical with the picture itself) sets forth (*stellt vor*) that things are related to one another in this way: the picture's form of depiction (by which W means: that it is possible for the elements to stand in this relation to one another) is at the same time the possibility that objects should stand in this relation to one another. 2.151 may seem puzzling, but it should be evident that if form is the possibility of structure (2.033, 2.15) and if picture and fact are to have their form in common (2.17, 2.2, etc.), then to say that the one structure is possible will be to say also that the other is. Thus the structure or the fact that the part of the picture which deputizes for *a* (let us call this part: *"a"*) stands in a certain relation to *"b"* sets forth the structure or the state of affairs that *aRb*. Further, if it is possible for *"a"* to stand in a certain relation to *"b"*, then it is possible that *aRb*, and conversely.[2]

In reality, 2.15–2.151 agree very well with my previous account of

---

[1] For the use of *"Φ"* as opposed to *"R"* in the indication of *forms*, cf. 3.333, 4.24.

There is evidence in pre-*Tractatus* MSS., to which I shall return, that W at one time spoke of two kinds of indefinable symbol, Names and Forms, understanding by the latter symbols for relations and properties. If we followed this way of speaking we could say that the fact that *aRb* was of the form *"xRy"* rather than *"$\Phi(x, y)$"*. But we have already seen that there are many different, because more or less general, "forms" of a particular fact. It might well be that *"xRy"* was *a* form of the fact that *aRb* but not *the* form in the sense in which W was speaking of a unique form at 2.033.

"x loves *y"* has a good claim to be *the* form of the fact that John loves Mary, but this is because, since "loves" is not an indefinable it confers logical (by which I mean inferential) properties on any proposition in which it occurs—e.g. whatever *x* and *y* may be, if *x* loves *y*, then *x* does not hate *y*. It cannot be for this sort of reason that W thought of *indefinable* relational symbols as "forms".

One reason for regarding *"R"* in *"aRb"* as a form but not *"a"* or *"b"*, where all designate constants, is that, unlike a name, the symbol for a particular relation determines how many and what type of other symbols there must be in an elementary proposition. Thus knowing that the symbol for a particular relation occurs in a proposition tells us more about the form of that proposition, than knowing that a particular name does so.

[2] For further propositions where W says or implies that the existence of a picture guarantees the possibility of the state of affairs represented, see 2.203, 3.02, 3.4.

The particular way in which I have described the setting forth of a state of affairs by a picture is derived from 3.1432, a proposition which occurs more than once in pre-*Tractatus* MSS. On the analogy of that proposition it should seem that there will not be an element of the picture which deputizes for *R*. *"a"* and *"b"* are elements of the picture and deputize for *a* and *b*. That *"a"* has a certain relation to *"b"* sets forth that *a* has a certain relation to *b*, but there is no object *R* and no picture-element *"R"*. See discussion below and note 1, above.

The further question arises and must be discussed, whether *"a"* stands to *"b"* in the

the form of a fact. Since a picture *is* a fact (2.141) it has a certain form, say "that x is to the left of y" or "that x stands in a relation to y", and since there are just as many elements in the picture as there are objects in the fact it represents,[1] therefore this form will also be that of the fact. And this is indeed the case, for the fact that a is to the left of b has the form "that x is to the left of y" or "that x stands in a relation to y". Both fact and picture are possible instantiations of this form.

We can also explain why W speaks of "the form of depiction" of a picture, rather than simply of its form. The reason is that a picture may have many alternative "forms" some of which may be irrelevant to its rôle as a fact that depicts. For example, a picture showing forth that aRb might contain as a deputy for a, a complex pattern of strokes, $A1, A2, \ldots An$ in that order, whereas a was a simple and undefinable object. Let us call $A1, A2, \ldots An$ in that order "a". Clearly one way of giving the structure of the picture will be "that $A1, A2, \ldots An$ in that order have a certain relation to 'b' ", the corresponding form being: "that $x1, x2, \ldots xn$ in that order have a relation to y". Another way of giving its structure and form will be: "that 'a' has a certain relation to 'b' ", and "that x has a relation to y", respectively. Now, though both structures and both forms in a sense belong to the picture, it is clearly in virtue of the latter pair that it is called a picture of the fact that aRb (where a and b are indefinables): being of the latter form is a necessary and sufficient condition for it to be a possible picture of, a possible way of depicting, the fact that aRb. So this is the form of depiction of the picture. A picture as a fact has many forms, its form of depiction is that form which includes all and only (or at any rate only) what the picture has in common with the fact it represents. We shall automatically arrive at this form if we recognize into what elements the picture *qua* the picture that it is must be divided.[2] Conversely we can say that *the* form of a fact (we

---

[1] This is the first feature of pictures that W mentions, at 2.13, and therefore, by implication, a very significant one. He stresses it again, of course, e.g. at 4.0312. I think that whatever may be true of the propositions and pictures that we are used to, it can be *shown* that the *thoughts* (cf. the 3's) which they express must possess the same multiplicity as the facts they state or represent. For one suggestion about the premisses that may have led W to his view cf. note 1, p. 143, and the text to it.

[2] This is one reason why the depicting relation, that is to say, the coordinations of the elements of the picture with things, belongs to the picture (2.153–2.1514). To recognize what picture it is, we must know what count as its elements when it is regarded as a picture, and what these elements stand for.

---

same relation that a is said to stand in towards b. 3.1432 appears to go against, and (on a certain interpretation of the German word "so") 2.15 seems to support, this view. Even if the elements of the picture and of the fact stood in the same relation to one another (as would be the case if the fact that "a" was to the left of "b" set forth that a was to the left of b), the structure of the picture would be distinct from that of the fact, since the elements of the two are different.

were seeking previously a criterion for *the* form) is the least that a fact must, or the most that it can, have in common with a fact which is to depict it.

The alternative in this last suggestion will help us to show that there is a range of generality or specificity within the form of depiction itself. A picture which represents that a is to the left of b by putting "a" to the left of "b" has as its form of depiction "that x is to the left of y" and is a spatial picture (2.171), and has spatial form (2.18) in common with reality. On the other hand, a picture which represents that a loves b by putting "a" to the left of "b" has as its form of depiction "that x stands in a relation to y" and is a logical picture, having logical form in common with reality (cf. the 2.18's). It will be clear that a spatial form of depiction is one kind of, and thus presupposes, a logical form of depiction (2.182). It should seem that generally in a spatial picture or model there will be grounds for saying that the relation in which the elements of the picture stand to one another is the same as the relation in which the objects in the fact which it shows forth stand to one another, while in a logical non-spatial picture this is not so. This will perhaps explain the discrepancy, remarked in note 2, p. 146, above, between 3.1432 where W is speaking of propositions, i.e. logical pictures, and 2.15 where he may have principally spatial pictures in mind.

There is one difficulty, alluded to in notes 1 and 2, p. 146, above, that must be mentioned here. In some unpublished writings prior in date to the *Tractatus*,[1] W spoke of symbols for properties and relations as *forms*, in contrast to the symbols for objects, which were *names*. Some may see the persistence of that terminology in 2.0251: Space, time and colour (colouredness) are forms of objects, though I find that proposition obscure. Certainly, such symbols are not thought to be names: I think this is clear from 3.1432 (see note 1, p. 146) and 4.24 (where "f" and "Φ" are functions of names, not themselves names). This latter proposition occurs precisely in a context in which W asserts that an elementary proposition is a complex or concatenation of names. We must assume that, e.g., "R" in "aRb" is not itself a name but that its occurrence between them is (part of) the way in which the names "a" and "b" are connected to form the proposition: there is thus no *object* corresponding to "R".[2] We have

---

[1] The MSS. in question are: "*Notes on Logic*", 1913, listed by Colombo in his Bibliography (FB, p. 316), and "*Notes dictated to G. E. Moore in Norway*", April, 1914. I have been enabled to consult the latter through the kindness of Miss G. E. M. Anscombe, one of Wittgenstein's literary executors. (Note added in 1964): Versions of these notes have now been published in L. Wittgenstein, *Notebooks 1914–1916*, Blackwell, 1961.

[2] It has been thought that 4.123 affords proof that properties also are objects. But W expressly points out there that the word "object" is improperly used there. That he does so does not however prove *our* point, since the impropriety may be due to the fact

explained how this way of speaking may be accommodated in our account of form: a particular relation may be called a characteristic of the structure *or* of the form of a fact: when a picture shows forth a fact by putting its elements into the *same* relation as the objects in the fact, then we may say that that particular relation is a characteristic of the form of depiction of that picture. Otherwise the form of depiction of a picture in which the elements stand in a particular two-termed relation will be "that *x* has a relation to *y*". The *Tractatus*, however, raises a new problem: for it seems to imply that not all predicates of *n* places are of the same logical form, whereas we have assumed the contradictory of this. The implication arises from the talk about the form of an object 2.0141, and 2.0233 (cf. 2.0121 and 2.0131). If two objects have different logical forms, then there are states of affairs in which the one can figure and the other cannot, in the way that a colour can be bright and a weight cannot. So we might think that there would be on the one hand objects which could have with one another only certain two-place relations, and on the other hand two-place relations which could hold only between certain ranges of objects. Thus the form of depiction of a picture showing forth that *aRb* would be *either* "that *x* has a relation to *y*" or "that *x'* has a relation to *y'*" *or* . . . different styles of variable being used according to the different types of object and relation involved in the state of affairs pictured. We should have different types of the same multiplicity, or on the same level, and a ramified theory of types. Words like "object" would be typically ambiguous.

At the very least it must be said that W overlooks or neglects this. All his examples of type-differences, of differences of logical form, are of the order of the difference between *n*-placed predicates and *n* + 1-placed predicates,[1] or between propositions, facts and things. He says, at 3.331 (cf. 3.333), that the *whole* "Theory of Types" is contained in the observation that a propositional sign cannot be its own argument. Confusions arise (3.323) because what is really a relational word looks like a property-word (cf. 5.4733): he never mentions that ordinary language doesn't distinguish between *property*-words of different type, though this, one would imagine, would be a more abundant source of confusions. His example of a conceivable special

[1] In the "*Notes dictated to G. E. Moore*" (see note 1, p. 148) things, properties and relations are called "types": at *Tractatus* 5.5351 they are called "prototypes" (*Urbilder*).

---

that a certain blue colour is a complex with logical, inferential, properties, rather than to the fact that it is a property.

The temptation to think of properties and relations as objects arises from W's talk about the proposition as a concatenation of names; it is hard to see how "*fa*" could be so described, unless "*f*" too were a name. However at 4.24 W seems to rule this out, so he must be thinking that "*fa*" is the limiting case of a concatenation of names.

form of elementary proposition is one containing a sign for a twenty-seven-place relation (5.5541).

In view of this silence, and this preference for a certain kind of example, I am tempted to conclude that W did not recognize difference of type or logical form within objects properly so-called, properties, or n-placed relations. His main interest, as in the 4.04's, was in multiplicity. The proposition which seems to suggest a contrary view need not necessarily do so: "2.0233 Two objects of the same logical form are distinguished from one another (if we ignore their external properties) only in that they are different". This is a general remark asserting that distinguishability demands *a*) external properties or *b*) difference of logical form: there is no absolute implication that objects ever do differ in logical form from one another.[1] This will give us a true "logical atomism" with no two particulars differing in type, no difference of type, for example, between mental and physical particulars: neutral monism.

We may now turn to the description of the form of a proposition in the 3.31's, which suggested and now confirms our account of the form of a fact or picture. He is speaking of what he calls an expression or symbol. This is something that characterizes (3.31) and presupposes (3.311) the form of a number of propositions. It is exhibited or presented by the general form of a class of propositions (3.312), that is to say by a propositional variable (3.313). We are told in 3.315 how such a variable may be constructed: we are to put a variable in place of some constituent part of the proposition, e.g. "*aRx*" for "*aRb*". By so doing we shall have determined a class of propositions: all those that assert that *a* has the relation *R* to a thing. But of course *what* propositions belong to this class will depend on the meaning we attach to "*a*" and "*R*". We can of course put variables in the place of any sign to which we have arbitrarily assigned a meaning: thus we should obtain the expression or symbol "*xRy*", and finally, when all such signs have been replaced, we obtain the expression "$\Phi(x, y)$", which characterizes the class of all two-termed relational propositions. This, W tells us, corresponds to or, as I should say, presents to us, a logical form, a logical prototype (*Urbild*). What class of propositions this symbol determines does not depend on any arbitrary

---

[1] It seems to me that some support is given to this view by the consideration that it makes the form of one object give us knowledge of all states of affairs that are possible (cf. 2.014–2.0141). That in turn makes it easier to understand how one proposition "gives us" the whole of logical space, 3.42. If there was a type of object whose form was unknown to us, then (it should seem) we could very well understand a single proposition, or very many propositions, and yet be unaware of many of the possibilities and impossibilities that make up logical space.

It may be thought, however, that the 5.55's go against this point.

My view also depends upon finding a satisfactory interpretation of 2.0251, which I have not been able to do.

assignment of meaning.[1] It would be idle to pretend that the selection of a particular typographical sign, such as "$\Phi(x, y)$", for a variable was non-arbitrary: I have introduced it into my account of 3.315 purely for expository convenience. It is by our arbitrary convention that this sign designates the class of two-termed relational propositions: what is not arbitrary is that any propositional sign which expresses such a proposition (or in other words: which states that one object has a relation to another) will consist in the fact that one name is put in a relation to another. *Any* way of putting one name into relation with another *could* (by an arbitrary convention) express this same proposition: and nothing save such a fact or what was recognized as being linguistically equivalent to such a fact could express that proposition. Further, any object whatever could be a name (3.3411), therefore the general form of this class of propositions (3.312) is "that x has a relation to y" which we choose to express by the variable: "$\Phi(x, y)$".

Thus the fact that aRb is depicted by the fact that something deputizing for a (whether an element of a picture or, less generally, a name in a propositional sign) stands in a certain relation to something deputizing for b. Fact, picture, proposition and thought have the same form "that x stands in a relation to y". The existence of the picture or proposition guarantees the possibility of the fact—it shows that there *can* be facts of this form by *being* a fact of this form.

It might be thought that I have erred, or even that W erred, against the principle that a picture cannot depict its form of depiction (2.172–2.174) and that we cannot represent the logical form of a proposition of a fact *by* a proposition (4.12–4.121). However the full subtlety of his position is brought out by the fact that I have not erred in this way. I have not *explained* what the logical form of anything is, I have merely produced other things of the same logical form, thus presupposing that the logical form of the fact I began with and the logical form of the facts I produced were equally easy to grasp. To say that "John loves Mary" is of the form "$\Phi(x, y)$" is merely to say that we *could* have used any of the following signs to assert that John loves Mary: "aRb", "bRa", "ab", "ba", "$aRSb$" . . . and in general any sign consisting in the fact that one object is put into relation with another. If, however, we used a sign of which this was not true, then we should be said to be asserting that John loved

---

[1] This interpretation demands that the sign "R" in the propositional sign "aRb" shall have a meaning (*Bedeutung*). It might therefore be argued that "R" must be a name and R an object, contrary to my conclusions above. 3.314 however implies that expressions other than names have *Bedeutung*. Likewise at 3.333 W speaks of the *Bedeutung* of functions, while at 4.24 he distinguishes functions from names.

Mary only if we were prepared to adopt instead some sign of which it was true.[1]

The general form of a *class* of propositions (3.311–3.312), for the expression of which we are given instructions in 3.315, is obviously something more specific than the general form of a proposition. Nor can we reach an expression for the latter by further conversion of symbols with arbitrarily assigned meaning into variables, since "$\Phi (x, y)$" is already a completely variable expression. Nor can we hope to give *a priori* a list of all the special forms of propositions (5.554, 5.555), that is to say of all the classes of propositions, that there are: we cannot say *a priori* that we shall need or that we shall not need a sign for a 27-termed relation—experience will decide (5.5541). It remains for us to determine what can be seen to be necessarily true of every proposition from the examples of the form of a proposition that have already been given, or are implicit, in the *Tractatus.*

Two closely interconnected features of a proposition are of over-riding importance here: First that a proposition is a fact and has the form of a fact, second that a proposition is composite (*zusammengesetzt* 3.1431, 4.032, 5.5261; *gegliedert* 4.032; *artikuliert* 3.141, 3.251): a propositional sign consists not in a set of names (3.142) but in some fact about certain names.[2] All propositions, then, will have the form: "that such and such is the case" or in other words "that such and such is true of such and such objects". Now these are pre-

---

[1] For the importance of "possible ways of symbolizing" cf. 3.3421. The last sentence of this paragraph requires more explication and argument than can be given here.

[2] Facts, as opposed to objects, must be composite: what is a fact is that something is true of some objects. But why should what asserts a fact be composite? Clearly it will be so, if every proposition contains (or must be translatable into something containing) words whose function is to stand for objects without implying, by their occurrence in the proposition, any fact about those objects. Thus if in a fully analysed proposition there must be names that deputize for objects (*der Prinzip der Vertretung* 4.0312), then every proposition must be composite (4.032).

Whenever the occurrence of a word in a proposition implies a certain fact about an object, we *can* replace that proposition by another one in which that fact is explicitly stated, in a way which Russell in his article "On Denoting" (*Mind*, 1905) was the first to point out. Application of this method wherever possible will produce fully-analysed propositions containing names (3.24).

It can also be seen that such an analysis *must* be possible if we are capable of forming propositions which are *essentially* connected with the states of affairs they inform us of and thus are capable of communicating "a new sense with old words" (4.027–4.03). In other words analysis of all propositions into elementary propositions must be possible if we can understand a proposition without knowing whether it or any other proposition is true. (2.0211, cf. note 1, p. 143, and the text to it.)

W appears to have thought it obvious that this condition was fulfilled. It could easily be maintained however (to mention but one counter-example) that no ethical proposition could be understood without prior knowledge of several matters of fact.

Finally it must be noted that the assertion at the head of this note, that facts are composite and objects simple, is itself thought to be established by these considerations about sense and understanding.

cisely the accounts of the general form of the proposition that are given at 4.5 and 5.47 respectively, only that the intervening argument allows further conclusions to be drawn, which are then stated, without a repetition of the premisses, in the early 6's.

The chief point made in the 4.1's to 4.5's is that every fact is either an atomic fact (*Sachverhalt*) or consists in the existence or non-existence of certain atomic facts.[1]

Thus every proposition either asserts that an atomic fact exists, in which case it is an elementary proposition,[2] or it is equivalent to the assertion or denial of some set of elementary propositions. Obviously the former alternative is a limiting case of the latter, so we can describe the general case by saying that every proposition is some truth-function of elementary propositions (5).

If an atomic fact were defined as a fact that does not consist in the existence or non-existence of other facts, the above argument would be logically impeccable. W however assumes that an atomic fact so defined will at the same time be a combination of objects (2.01), or in other words that an elementary proposition will consist of names in immediate combination (4.221). It might well be thought that there must indeed be elementary propositions in this sense, but that there are propositions compounded out of these in such a way that they are not merely truth-functions of elementary propositions. W does not allow this possibility: as he says at 5.54, in discussing the general form of a proposition he has assumed that propositions occur in other propositions only as bases of truth-operations. All cases of intensional inoccurrence, such as the propositions that someone knows a certain proposition to be true, or that such and such a state of affairs is bad and ought to be remedied, are ruled out in advance: it is hard not to find this exclusion somewhat arbitrary.[3] It may be argued on epistemological grounds that there must be elementary propositions; it cannot be argued on logical grounds that all propositions are truth-functions of them. This assertion seems rather to be an arbitrary definition or a metaphysical thesis.

It is these conclusions which give content to the assertion at 4.5

---

[1] Cf. 2.06: The existence and non-existence of atomic facts is reality.

[2] This term is introduced at 4.21.

[3] W gives some justification for the exclusion of former example at 5.542, claiming that "*A* says *p*" is of the form " '*p*' says *p*", so that we are dealing not with the co-ordination of a fact and an object, but with the coordination of two facts *via* the coordination of their objects. This seems to mean that we are saying (1) that a conformation of a certain kind is occurring in the man's mind (cf. "*Gegenstände des Gedankens*" at 3.2. Perhaps W is thinking of the words of the proposition going through the man's mind). (2) that this conformation says that . . . The chief objection to this account is that in order for the words or whatever it may be in the man's mind to project the possible state of affairs he has to "think the sense of the proposition", cf. 3.11. I do not say this is a refutation of W, but it points to a serious lacuna in his argument.

B. F. McGuinness

that the general form of a proposition is expressed by the variable (4.53): *"Es verhält sich so und so"*—which we must translate "Such and such combinations (scil. of objects) hold".[1] I.e. every proposition asserts or denies some combinations of objects, or in other words the existence or non-existence of some atomic facts. Thus every proposition is a truth-function of elementary propositions. At the same time every proposition, since it is a fact, will itself consist in certain combinations of objects: *"Es verhält sich so und so"* is a form of which a proposition and the fact it states are two different possible specifications.[2]

By 5.47, where the next reference occurs, this description of propositional form in general can be carried further, since W is in a position to show that all truth-functions of elementary propositions can be arrived at by the application of one fundamental truth-operation (see the 5.5's). The operation in question is the joint negation of a set of propositions: any alternation, conjunction, implication, equivalence or negation of elementary propositions can be represented as a joint negation. He further holds that anyone who is capable of asserting a proposition is thereby capable of asserting, and also of denying, a set of propositions. Thus, if you grasp any one proposition, you thereby grasp all the possible ways in which complex propositions can be constructed out of elementary propositions.[3] Since all propositions are truth-functions of elementary propositions, the general form of propositions can be given by describing the operation which produces any truth-function.

[1] Colombo's *"Le cose stanno così e così"* makes this point (FB, p. 219). "Such and such is the case" in KP obscures it. W thinks it worthwhile to *explain* (2) that what is the case is the existence of atomic facts (*Sachverhalte*) and *ein Sachverhalt = dass sich die Sachen (Dinge Gegenstände) so und so zu einander verhalten*. Cf. the frequent use of *sich verhalten* to describe the rôle of objects in an atomic fact: 2.031, 2.14, 2.15–2.151, 3.14, see also 5.5423.

I do not wish to imply that for W all propositions were ultimately relational, though it would have given greater simplicity to his theories if this were so: in *Der Logische Aufbau der Welt* (Berlin, 1928) Carnap developed many of W's theses in a manner which did involve this assumption. W explicitly rejected it in "Notes on Logic" (see note 1, p. 148) and seems still to do so at 5.553. 2.01, etc., when taken in conjunction with 4.24 imply the doctrine, however odd it may sound, that a proposition such as *"fa"* asserts a *"sich verhalten"* or *"Verbindung"* of the object *a*.

[2] We do not however generally represent the fact that certain objects do not stand in a certain relation by the fact that certain signs do not stand in a certain relation. Instead we use a sign of negation. This may seem to be a difference in form between a complex proposition and the fact that it states.

Cf., however, 5.512 where W says that the general rule for forming the negation of a proposition "mirrors negation". I take this to mean that in virtue of this general rule there can be said to be an identity of form even between a negative proposition and the fact it asserts.

[3] To take simple examples: *"p"* itself is the negation of the negation of *"p"*, *"p ⊃ q"* is the joint negation of *"p"* and the negation of *"q"*.

Space compels me to present in a rough and undocumented fashion what I take to be W's argument here.

Now this is precisely the programme announced at 5.47 and the result produced at 6. We have seen that proposition and fact alike are essentially composite (*zusammengesetz*); a fact does not consist of a set of objects, nor a proposition of a set of names—each consists in something's holding of some objects or names. Thus when a man apprehends such composition, he apprehends that something holds or is true of some objects, and this (in the terminology of 4.24) is the apprehension that a function is satisfied by certain arguments. But the apprehension that any proposition is true implies the capacity to conceive that it should be false, and indeed to conceive that all of any set of propositions are false, which in turn involves the capacity to construct any truth-function whatever of propositions. Thus ability to employ the fundamental logic operation is a necessary condition of the apprehension of any form of composition. It is at the same time a sufficient condition—that is to say, if a man can negate elementary propositions, he can obviously frame them.

These considerations make 5.47 comprehensible: ". . . Where composition is to be found, argument and function are to be found also, and where these are, all the logical constants are implicit.— You might say: the sole logical constant is what all propositions, by their nature, have in common with one another. This, however, is the general form of a proposition." It is also clear how, at 6 and 6.001, W is able to regard a description of this logical operation as a sufficient characterization of the general form of the proposition. It is significant that the first point about this that he chooses to stress is that it gives us the only way in which one proposition can be formed from another (6.002).

We are thus brought back to our starting-point in the 6's and our first aim has been achieved—namely to show the unity of W's account of a proposition and its form throughout the *Tractatus*. This was part of the general work of exegesis, which, particularly for this book, has to precede criticism. For that reason we have often delayed over particular propositions on our way. At the end however it may be possible to draw some general conclusions.

The following seem to be the most questionable among the premises that led W to the wholesale devaluation of ranges of propositions that we find in the 6's.

1: that there are elementary propositions in which names deputize for objects. More explicitly this is the thesis that all propositions which presuppose a fact can be so re-formulated as to state that fact rather than to presuppose it. (Some indication of W's reasons for this view are given in my notes 1, p. 143, and 2, p. 152, above.)

2: that the objects referred to in such propositions are of one type. More explicitly: that the occurrence of apparent type-differences between objects referred to in a pair of propositions shows that at least one of those propositions is not fully analysed. (I have argued that W did hold this view in note 1, p. 150, and the text to it.)

3: that the truth or falsehood of any complex proposition is wholly determined by that of the elementary propositions occurring in its analysis. (This is what I have called the rejection of intensional inoccurrence, and I have argued, in note 3, p. 150, and the text to it, that W gives no good reason for it.)

Even if these premisses be rejected, there is one lesson, which seems to me of great epistemological importance, to be drawn from what we have seen of W's account of propositions. I mean his insistence on the truth that having a thought, seeing a picture or entertaining a proposition is not merely a means towards the apprehension of a fact, but is itself the apprehension of a fact. There could be no process by which people were taught to apprehend a fact, since all instruction takes place through the presentation of facts to the pupil. Likewise there can be no true explanation of our ability to apprehend a fact: we must regard it simply as an inexplicable human capacity (perhaps a way of thinking similar to this is discernible at 4.002). The considerations thus vaguely indicated seem, or seemed to W, to suggest that in our ability to apprehend a fact we have a sort of *a priori* knowledge, which there is no way of expressing. In our awareness of the essence of a proposition we are aware of the essence of a fact and thus of the essence of the world (5.4711). Further, in our knowledge of any fact there is implicit all our *a priori* knowledge of logical truth (5.47, cf. 3.42), and W certainly thinks that logic shows us or mirrors for us something about the world (5.511, 6.12, 6.124, 6.13).

I have suggested above that the rejection of ethical propositions seems arbitrary, if all that supports it is the fragmentary argument against intensional inoccurrence that W gives. But perhaps its true basis is the inexpressible metaphysic constituted by our intuition (if I may use the word) of what it is to be a fact: ethical "facts" do not measure up to its standards. If this is so, then it seems likely that W will prove guilty of circularity in the following way: his metaphysic of silence is supported by the logical and epistemological doctrines which precede the 6's, but these themselves depend at their crucial points on that metaphysics. But I must leave this suggestion to be explored by the reader.

On Wittgenstein's 'Solipsism'[1]

JAAKKO HINTIKKA

THE main difficulties people have had in trying to understand Wittgenstein's pronouncements on solipsism in the *Tractatus Logico-Philosophicus* (London, 1922) are connected with the proposition 5.62 of the book. This proposition has recently been quoted by Professor J. O. Urmson[2] in the following form:

> In fact what solipsism *intends* is quite correct, only it cannot be *said*, but it shows itself. That the world is *my* world shows itself in the fact that the limits of language (*the* language, which I alone understand) means the limits of my world.

The clause in the brackets is, beyond reasonable doubt, a mistranslation. The German original reads: ". . . die Grenzen *der* Sprache (der Sprache, die allein ich verstehe) die Grenzen *meiner* Welt bedeuten." The joker here is the word 'allein'. In all the relevant examples that I have seen quoted in the dictionaries, this word is used to qualify the word it *follows*. The same is the case with all the other (relevant) instances of 'allein' that I have come across in the *Tractatus* (cf. 2.224 and 5.631). One of the dictionaries (Sanders, *Wörterbuch der deutschen Sprache*) states that one of the nearly synonymous words *nur, bloss, einzig* is used instead of *allein* (to mean 'alone') in all the contexts where the position of the word could make it ambiguous. The parenthetical clause would be a case in point if 'allein' there meant 'alone'.

It is obvious, then, that a correct translation of the words in the brackets is "the only language that I understand". In fact, this is the way Russell reads the passage (see his introduction to the *Tractatus*, p. 18); and it is essentially the way the passage is rendered in English in the copy of the book I have at my disposal (third impression, 1947).

---

[1] From *Mind*, N.S., vol. 67, no. 265, January, 1958, pp. 88–91. Reprinted by permission of the editor and the author.
[2] J. O. Urmson, *Philosophical Analysis*, Oxford, 1956, p. 135.

The removal of this mistake is not without interest, for the incorrect translation of 5.62 was the only passage of the *Tractatus* which would have forced one to conclude that Wittgenstein held something like solipsism in the usual sense of the word. In the passage I have quoted he says that what solipsism *intends* is correct; and many readers have taken this to mean that Wittgenstein in the *Tractatus* accepted ordinary solipsism. I shall suggest, however, that the passage is to be understood in a different way. What Wittgenstein thought solipsism *intends* to say is entirely different from what philosophers usually take it to say. When he says that solipsism is correct he means his peculiar interpretation of solipsism which can only be understood in the context of the other doctrines of the *Tractatus*.

This is shown, I think, by the way Wittgenstein presents his remarks on solipsism and argues for them in the *Tractatus*. His alleged solipsism turns on the claim that the limits of language are the limits of the world. What, then, is meant by this? What, in particular, is meant by the limits or boundaries (*Grenzen*) of the world? The answer is given on the page of the *Tractatus* which precedes the first remarks on solipsism: "Empirical reality is limited by the totality of objects. The boundary appears again in the totality of elementary propositions." And what is the relation of this 'boundary' to logic? Again we find an explicit answer in the *Tractatus*: Logic cannot anticipate what objects and what elementary propositions there are in the world. Although logic is prior to every 'how', it is not prior to 'what' (5.552). "We cannot therefore say in logic: This and this there is in the world, that there is not." (Cf. 5.61 and 5.557.) Questions of this kind are only decided by the application of logic, and this application cannot be anticipated by purely logical means (5.557). Although logic is prior to every representation of *how* the world is, its limits can in this special sense be said to coincide with the limits of the world.

The way Wittgenstein argues for this view is seen from 5.5–5.557. The basic reason for his view is that *if* the totality of elementary propositions could be discussed in logic, we should be able to tell *a priori* once and for all what the forms of all elementary propositions are. And this is taken by him to be impossible. (Cf. 5.55–5.551.)

But what does this have to do with solipsism? In view of the way Wittgenstein was seen to argue for his view, we can answer: *nothing*, as long as we do not grant him a further consequence of the view we have discussed so far. This further doctrine is *prima facie* very peculiar, for it in effect identifies the subject (the *metaphysical* subject, Wittgenstein says) with the sum total of his language. To be more accurate, Wittgenstein identifies the limits of one's language with the limits of one's self. The motives of this apparently strange doctrine are clear from Wittgenstein's remarks. What he is concerned with is not the empirical subject but the 'metaphysical' subject discussed in philosophy. In other words, he is interested only in what can be said to be mine *necessarily*; for otherwise he would only be doing empirical psychology. But the only necessity there is, according to the other doctrines of the *Tractatus*, is the empty tautological necessity of logic. There is nothing, therefore, in the world which can be said to be mine in the relevant sense of the word. If I can say that something is mine, it immediately follows that this something can possibly be yours, too.[1] In particular, it follows from the doctrines I explained above that there is no part of the world of which it can be said that it necessarily is. "No part of our experience is . . . *a priori*" (5.634). Hence, "in an important sense, there is no subject"; the 'thinking, imagining subject' does not do as the metaphysical subject (5.631).

The only boundaries I cannot possibly transcend are those of my language. Whatever we think can be expressed in language; there is no way of getting 'beyond' language. "What we cannot think, that we cannot think; we cannot even *say* what we cannot think" (5.61). Hence, the only way of drawing the limits of the metaphysical subject seems to be to identify them with the limits of my language.

The fact that Wittgenstein's 'metaphysical' subject is a complex not unlike a totality of propositions is also seen from his analysis of the form of words "*A* believes that *p*". The analysis in 5.541–5.5421 is calculated to show that "*A* believes that *p*" is really of the form "'*p*' says *p*". In other words, to say that a person believes that *p* is to say (or, rather, to show) that the propositional sign '*p*' (which is a fact) represents or mirrors the fact that *p* (see 5.542). The original form of words which *prima facie* is about the person *A* in this way turns out to be about a *proposition* which is somehow connected with *A*. This proposition is taken by Wittgenstein to be a part of the "subject" *A*; for otherwise the complexity of '*p*' (or, under an alternative reading, the multiplicity of propositions believed by *A*) would not show that the subject (the soul) is complex, as claimed by Wittgenstein in 5.5421.

Unless the 'linguistic' nature of Wittgenstein's 'metaphysical' subject is recognized, it is open to a serious *prima facie* criticism. It has been argued[2] that Wittgenstein overlooks the possibility (and necessity) of a subject's direct self-consciousness. As a criticism of Wittgenstein's way of illustrating his point by comparing the world to the field of vision, it has been pointed out that while it is not essential for the eye to see itself through the constitution of the field of vision,

---

[1] Cf. *Philosophical Investigations*, 253 (p. 91): "In so far as it make ssense to say that my pain is the same as his, it is also possible for us both to have the same pain."

[2] See Francesco Barone, 'Il solipsismo linguistico di Ludwig Wittgenstein', *Filosofia, Rivista trimestrale*, vol. 2 (1951), no. 4, pp. 543–70, especially p. 560.

it is (allegedly) essential for thinking to have consciousness of itself. Whatever is the ultimate force of this objection, it cannot be made within our interpretation of Wittgenstein's doctrines. If the 'metaphysical' subject is a totality of propositions, it *cannot* refer to itself, for it follows from the other doctrines of the *Tractatus* that no proposition can refer to itself (cf. 3.332).

Perhaps a more natural way of saying that Wittgenstein identified the metaphysical subject with a totality of propositions would be to say that he identified it with a totality of *thoughts*; for "the thought is the significant proposition". There is, however, nothing private and nothing psychological about Wittgenstein's notion of a thought. Like Frege's *Gedanke*,[1] it can be shared by different people. In the *Tractatus* the propositional signs are completely public, and so is that which "does not get expressed in the signs"; for if it were private, it could not be "shown by their application" (3.262). And the limits of the metaphysical subject cannot be the limits of one's actual thoughts, for there is nothing necessary about *that* limitation. The only necessary limits are the general limits of possible thoughts, i.e. the limits of language in general.

This is the basis of Wittgenstein's 'solipsism'. Having identified the metaphysical subject with the totality of one's language and the limits of language with the limits of the world, he could say that the limits of the (metaphysical) subject are the limits of the world.

"I am my world." We must not fail to see, however, that the motives of this version of solipsism have little to do with what is ordinarily called 'solipsism'. For instance, it has nothing to do with the classification of elementary propositions into 'mine' and 'yours'. Wittgenstein's point is that if we can speak of such a distinction at all, then the distinction is irrelevant; for if we can speak of the distinction, it is automatically contingent. Hence, it appears rather far-fetched to see in Wittgenstein's 'solipsism' an anticipation of the troubles of the logical positivists about 'other minds'.[2] One can say that the reason why Wittgenstein claimed that solipsism is essentially correct is diametrically opposed to the reason usually given for solipsism. What is usually taken to be the claim of solipsism is the *impossibility* of getting 'beyond the boundaries of myself'. Wittgenstein's solipsism is based on the exactly opposite claim that all the ordinary boundaries of myself are completely *contingent* and hence irrelevant 'for what is higher'.

How little Wittgenstein's identification of one's self with the logical limits of one's language (which are nothing but the limitations of

---

[1] See *Translations from the Philosophical Writings of Gottlob Frege*, edited by Peter Geach and Max Black, Blackwells, Oxford, 1952, p. 62.
[2] Cf. Urmson, op. cit., p. 135.

language in general) has to do with solipsism is perhaps seen by observing that essentially the same identification was used by Charles Sanders Peirce for the opposite purpose. In his early discussion of the 'consequences of the four incapacities' (The *Journal of Speculative Philosophy*, 1868; *Collected Papers*, 5, 264–317) Peirce came to identify, for reasons of his own, 'my language' with 'the sum total of myself'. From this he concluded that "the individual man, since his separate existence is manifested only by ignorance and error, so far as he is anything apart from his fellows, and from what he and they are to be, is only a negation". This is ordinarily neglected because man "persists in identifying himself with his will, his power over the animal organism, with brute force"; a remark which compares in an interesting way with the proposition 5.631 of the *Tractatus*.

The similarities, and dissimilarities, between Wittgenstein and Peirce should make us take seriously the former's claim that, under his interpretation, "solipsism, strictly carried out, coincides with pure realism".

NOTE (1964): I understand that my reading of 5.62 is borne out by notes in Wittgenstein's own hand, discovered by Dr C. Lewy in a copy of the *Tracatus* he had been using.

'Tractatus' 5.542[1]

IRVING M. COPI

IN the *Tractatus* Wittgenstein held that "Propositions are truth-functions of elementary propositions" (5). He acknowledged that a difficulty is posed by ". . . certain propositional forms of psychology, like 'A thinks, that *p* is the case', or 'A thinks *p*', . . ." in which ". . . it appears superficially as if the proposition *p* stood to the object A in a kind of relation" (5.541). Wittgenstein's resolution of this difficulty was formulated in what J. O. Urmson describes in *Philosophical Analysis* (p. 133) as "a passage of almost impenetrable obscurity".

5·542 But it is clear that "A believes that *p*", "A thinks *p*", "A says *p*", are of the form "'*p*' says *p*": and here we have no co-ordination of a fact and an object, but a co-ordination of facts by means of a co-ordination of their objects.

It will be convenient to follow Wittgenstein in using the letter "*p*" without quotation marks to refer to a fact (as in 5.43 ". . . a fact *p* . . .") and in using the letter "*p*" with quotation marks to refer to a proposition (as in 5.12 ". . . a proposition "*p*" . . .", and also in 5.123, 5.1241, 5.1311, 5.152, 5.44, 5.512, 5.513; but cf. 4.24, 5.141, and 5.541). For definiteness and simplicity attention will be confined here to atomic facts and elementary propositions. The fact *p* is a combination (2.01) or configuration (2.0272, 3.21) of entities or things (2.01, 2.0121, 2.0124, 2.013) or objects (2.01, 2.0141, 2.0272, 2.03, 2.031, 4.2211): $o_1, o_2, \ldots, o_k$. The proposition "*p*" is a combination (3.14) or configuration (3.21) or connection or concatenation (4.22) of exactly the same number (4.0311, 4.04) of elements (3.2) or words (3.14, 4.026, 4.03) or signs (4.0312) or simple signs (3.201, 3.202, 3.21, 4.026) or symbols (3.31) or simple symbols (4.24) or

[1] From *Analysis*, vol. 18, no. 5 (N.S., no. 65), April, 1958, pp. 102–4. Reprinted by permission of the editor.

163

primitive signs (3.26) or expressions (3.31, 3.318) or names (3.202, 3.26, 4.0311, 4.22, 5.55): n_1, n_2, . . ., n_k. Each name n_1 signifies (3.323), represents (3.22, 3.221, 4.0312), stands for (4.0311), names or has for its meaning (3.203) the co-ordinated (2.1514, 5.526) or corresponding (2.13) object o_1. It is in virtue of this co-ordination of their constituent parts and the similarity of their (logical) form or structure (2.15, 2.171, 2.18, 3.21, 4.014, 4.12) that the proposition "p" asserts (4.03, 6.1264), communicates (4.027, 4.03), describes (4.023), expresses (3.251), models (4.01), pictures (4.01, 4.011, 4.021, 4.032, 4.06), presents (4.021, 4.0311, 4.1), shows (4.461), signifies (4.061), or says (3.1432, 4.0621, 4.465, 5.542) the fact p.

Therefore, according to the *Tractatus* (especially 4.0311 and 4.04), whatever says a composite must be itself composite. But any fact p is composite. Hence any A that believes, thinks, judges, or says p must be composite. And since an object cannot be composite (2.021) but must be simple (2.02), A is not an object. An A that says p is a fact, the fact *that* A, and is therefore a configuration of objects a_1, a_2, . . ., a_q. These considerations serve to explain Wittgenstein's assertion that in "A believes that p", "A thinks p", etc., we have no co-ordination of a fact and an object. A is not an object at all, hence not an object co-ordinated with the fact p.

There is more to be explained in the passage cited. Urmson suggests (p. 133) that Wittgenstein ". . . appears to assimilate belief to the uttering of a sentence, so that Jones's belief *is* the set of words he utters and 'Jones believes that p' can therefore be said to be of the form ' "p" says p' . . .". But the word "belief" in ". . . Jones's belief . . ." is ambiguous, meaning either *what* he believes or his believing. (Different interpretations parallel different versions of the extensionality thesis set forth by Russell and Carnap. The first is like Carnap's suggestion on page 248 of *The Logical Syntax of Language* that "Charles says (writes, reads) A" can be translated into "Charles says 'A' ", and that "Charles thinks . . . A" can be translated into "Charles thinks 'A' ". The second is like Russell's suggestion in Appendix C, on page 661 of Volume I of the second edition of *Principia Mathematica*, that the series of words uttered is ". . . part of the series of events which constitutes the person".) But it cannot be the former, because if Wittgenstein had meant that, he would have analysed "A thinks p" not into " 'p' says p" but into "A says 'p' ". The ambiguity of Urmson's formulation is thus easily resolved.

But I do not think that Wittgenstein would have agreed with Urmson's suggestion that ". . . Jones's belief *is* the set of words he utters . . .". For the *Tractatus* implies a quite clear distinction between a thought and a mere "set of words" (3.14, 3.141, 3.142), and even between a thought and a configuration of words: "In the proposition the thought is expressed perceptibly through the senses" (3.1) and "The sign through which we express the thought I call the propositional sign. And the proposition is the propositional sign in its projective relation to the world" (3.12, but cf. 3.5 and 4).

One of the facts co-ordinated in "A thinks p" is the fact A (i.e. the fact *that* A). What is the other? In "A thinks 'p' " or "A says 'p' " the other fact would be the proposition or propositional sign 'p'. But in "A thinks p" the other fact is p itself (i.e. the fact *that p*). Since the co-ordination between the two facts A and p is "by means of a co-ordination of their objects", it would seem that for A to think or believe p, among the objects $a_1, a_2, \ldots, a_q$ that constitute the fact A there must be k objects $a_{p1}, a_{p2}, \ldots, a_{pk}$ that are co-ordinated with the k objects $o_1, o_2, \ldots, o_k$ that constitute the fact p. Since it is this sort of co-ordination of the names $n_1, n_2, \ldots, n_k$ in "p" with the objects $o_1, o_2, \ldots, o_k$ in p that permits "p" to say p, Wittgenstein was justified in saying that "A believes that p", "A thinks p", "A says p", are of the form " 'p' says p".

A possible objection to this interpretation of 5.542 is that people have false beliefs as well as true ones, and that only a true belief can be a belief in a fact. But the term 'fact' is ambiguous: there are both possible facts (Sachverhalten) and actual facts (Tatsachen). Thus "What is the case, the fact, is the existence of atomic facts. (Was der Fall ist, die Tatsache, ist das Bestehen von Sachverhalten)" (2). A true belief is in an actual fact (Tatsache) whereas a false belief is in a possible but non-actual fact (Sachverhalt). The truth of the belief but not its actuality is involved in this distinction. For the same objects are combined in a possible atomic fact (Sachverhalt) as in the actual fact (Tatsache), and it is in terms of these objects that the belief statement must be analysed ("Every statement about complexes can be analysed into a statement about their constituent parts, and into those propositions which completely describe the complexes" (2.0201)). A true belief that p will be a configuration of (possibly non-verbal) names that corresponds to the actual configuration of the objects they designate; whereas a false belief will be a configuration of (possibly non-verbal) names that corresponds to a non-actual but merely possible configuration of the objects designated by them.

Objects, Properties, and Relations in the 'Tractatus'[1]

IRVING M. COPI

FEW recent works in philosophy compare with Wittgenstein's *Tractatus* either in obscurity of style, range of influence, or depth of insight. Considering its difficulty, scandalously few studies of it have been published. Recent articles by Mrs Daitz[2] and Mr Evans[3] emphasize that further study is needed, for in my opinion certain key passages of that work are to be understood in ways quite different from those suggested by Mrs Daitz and Mr Evans.

1. THE 'TRACTATUS' AND ORDINARY LANGUAGE

In Mrs Daitz's criticism of Wittgenstein's "assimilation of sentences to facts" (p. 188 [p. 119]) she writes that "This view brings with it the consequence that all ordinary sentences have, for fact-stating purposes, one word too many!" (p. 189 [p. 120]). This criticism is damaging if the *Tractatus* is intended as an account of ordinary sentences, for not all of its assertions are true of ordinary sentences—as Mrs Daitz correctly maintains. On the other hand, if the *Tractatus* is *not* intended as an account of ordinary sentences, then it is no objection that its assertions are not true of ordinary sentences. One might with equal justice condemn a Latin grammar because its assertions are not true of Chinese sentences.

[1] This paper was written while the author was a John Simon Guggenheim Memorial Fellow. From *Mind*, N.S., vol. 67, N.S., no. 266, April, 1958, pp. 145–65. Reprinted by permission of the editor.
[2] Edna Daitz, "The Picture Theory of Meaning", *Mind*, April, 1953, pp. 184–201 [present volume].
[3] Ellis Evans, "Tractatus 3.1432", *Mind*, April, 1955, pp. 259–60 [present volume].

Although scores of his propositions contain special symbols and are concerned with special symbolisms, Wittgenstein certainly says *some* things about ordinary sentences. For example, he remarks that "Colloquial language is a part of the human organism and is not less complicated than it", and goes on to say that "The [tacit conventions][1] to understand colloquial language are enormously complicated" (4.002). He admits that the picture theory of meaning does not seem to be immediately applicable to ordinary language, "At the first glance the proposition—say as it stands printed on paper—does not seem to be a picture of the reality of which it treats . . ." (4.011).

Wittgenstein does not seem to maintain a completely consistent attitude towards ordinary language. Apparent approval is suggested by "All propositions of our colloquial language are actually, just as they are, logically completely in order" (5.5563). But the reverse is expressed by "In the language of everyday life it very often happens that the same word signifies in two different ways. . . . Thus there easily arise the most fundamental confusions (of which the whole of philosophy is full)" (3.323, 3.324). Ordinary language is said to be obscure and misleading: "That the propositional sign is a fact is concealed by the ordinary form of expression, written or printed . . ." (3.143). "From it [colloquial language] it is humanly impossible to gather immediately the logic of language. . . . Language disguises the thought" (4.002).

The tendency to reject ordinary language seems to me to predominate. Wittgenstein was concerned with the construction of "an adequate notation" (6.122), writing: "In order to avoid these errors [the most fundamental confusions (of which the whole of philosophy is full)], we must employ a symbolism which excludes them. . . . A symbolism, that is to say, which obeys the rules of *logical* grammar—of logical syntax" (3.325). Symbolic logic was hailed as a start in the right direction: "The logical symbolism of Frege and Russell is such a language, which, however, does still not exclude all errors" (3.325). The *Tractatus* contains several definite proposals for improving that symbolism by altering it in the direction of greater artificiality. For example "Identity of the object I express by identity of the sign and not by means of a sign of identity . . ." (5.53). "I write therefore not 'f(a,b).a = b', but 'f(a,a)' . . ." (5.531). Wittgenstein concluded that: "The identity sign is therefore not an essential constituent of logical notation" (5.533). "And we see that apparent propositions like: "a = a", . . ., cannot be written in a correct logical notation at all" (5.534).

---

[1] Departures from the Kegan Paul translation are marked by square brackets. The changes which appear in numbers 4.002, 4.0311, and 4.0312 were suggested by Professor Ryle.

I understand Wittgenstein to be primarily concerned with specifications for an artificial symbolic language which would conform to "the rules of logical grammar" and thereby exclude "fundamental confusions (of which the whole of philosophy is full)". Or, as Russell says in his Introduction, ". . . he is concerned with the conditions which would have to be fulfilled by a logically perfect language" (p. 7). If this interpretation is correct, then to point out that Wittgenstein's assertions are not true of ordinary sentences is no criticism of his doctrines. And to point out that his assertions are true of this or that ordinary sentence is altogether beside the point. For this reason Mrs Daitz's and Mr Evans's extended discussion of the sentence "Sophia hates Amos" seems to me wholly irrelevant to any appraisal of Wittgenstein's doctrines.

In the following sections it will be instructive to set forth some of the reasons why such a sentence as "Sophia hates Amos" cannot be an elementary proposition in the sense of the *Tractatus*.

2. WITTGENSTEIN'S RESTRICTED PICTURE THEORY OF MEANING

Wittgenstein expounds a "picture theory of meaning" for propositions, writing: "The proposition is a picture of reality . . ." (4.01, 4.021). "The proposition only asserts something, in so far as it is a picture" (4.03). "Propositions can be true or false only by being pictures of the reality" (4.06).

The pictorial nature of propositions was not simply *assumed*. It was *inferred* by Wittgenstein from what he regarded as an essential characteristic of propositions, that a person who knows the language can understand a proposition he has never seen or heard before. "It is essential to propositions, that they can communicate a *new* sense to us" (4.027). The inference was given three different formulations. First: "In order to understand the essence of the proposition, consider hieroglyphic writing, which pictures the facts it describes. And from it came the alphabet without the essence of the representation being lost. This we see from the fact that we understand the sense of the propositional sign, without having had it explained to us" (4.016, 4.02). Second: "The proposition is a picture of reality, for I know the state of affairs presented by it, if I understand the proposition. And I understand the proposition without its sense having been explained to me" (4.021). Third: "A proposition must communicate a new sense with old words. The proposition communicates to us a state of affairs, therefore it must be *essentially* connected with the state of affairs. And the connection is, in fact, that it is its logical picture" (4.03).

These various formulations of Wittgenstein's argument clarify the intended scope of his picture theory of meaning. His conclusion asserts the picture theory of meaning for composite signs only, that is, for propositions or propositional signs, but not for simple signs or words.

Nowhere does Wittgenstein assert or suggest that simple signs, words, or names are pictures. By implication, the picture theory is denied for non-composite signs when it is said that pictures must be composite: "The picture consists in the fact that its elements are combined with one another in a definite way" (2.14). The one argument intended to establish the picture theory for propositions cannot possibly be applied to words, for its premiss attributes to propositions a characteristic that is explicitly denied to single words. Propositional signs are said to be pictures because ". . . we understand the sense of the propositional sign, without having had it explained to us" (4.02). But "The meanings of the simple signs (the words) must be explained to us, if we are to understand them" (4.026).

For these reasons I think it incorrect to interpret the *Tractatus* as presenting a picture theory of words. Even apart from the foregoing considerations, it is surprising that Mrs Daitz should assert of "the 'picture' elucidation of names" that it "may be put as 'The name means the object, the object is its meaning' " (p. 198 [p. 128]). Wittgenstein's proposition 3.203 ("The name means the object. The object is its meaning.") clearly formulates a *denotation* theory of meaning for names. It asserts that for a name to have a meaning there must exist an object that it names. But it has nothing to do with *pictures*. In fact, since a picture has a meaning even if there exists no object that it pictures, a picture theory of meaning for names is incompatible with a denotation theory of meaning for them. Thus Wittgenstein's proposition 3.203 implies the denial of the picture theory of meaning for names, and is not a "way of putting" that theory. Therefore even had Mrs Daitz succeeded in showing that ". . . the Picture Theory . . . *must* be a misdescription of 'how words mean' " (p. 184 [p. 115]), she would not thereby have damaged the *Tractatus*. For there Wittgenstein does not assert that the picture theory describes 'how words mean', but in effect denies it.

Wittgenstein's picture theory of meaning is even further restricted. Intended for propositions only, it applies not to *all* propositions, but to elementary propositions alone. Different passages suggest more or less clearly that elementary propositions only are pictures. The implicit arguments vary in the degree of their cogency, but it seems worthwhile to indicate at least three of them.

First, in explaining how propositions can have sense Wittgenstein is led to assert that *what* they picture or present are atomic facts:

"One name stands for one thing, and another for another thing, and they are connected together. And so the whole, like a [tableau vivant], presents the atomic fact" (4.0311). In a later passage he remarks that: "The simplest proposition, the elementary proposition, asserts the existence of an atomic fact" (4.21). Granted that propositions which are pictures assert atomic facts, and that propositions which assert atomic facts are elementary propositions, it follows that propositions which are pictures are elementary propositions.

A second argument involves as premiss: "The elements of the picture stand, in the picture, for the objects" (2.131). Now all the elements of an elementary proposition stand for objects, because "The elementary proposition consists of names" (4.22) and "In the proposition the name [stands for] the object" (3.22). But non-elementary propositions are ". . . truth-functions of elementary propositions" (5, see also 5.3, 5.54, 6.001). And "All truth-functions are results of the successive application of a finite number of truth-operations to elementary propositions" (5.32, see also 5.234, 5.5). Hence non-elementary propositions contain truth-operations or logical constants. But those truth-operations or logical constants do not stand for objects: "My fundamental thought is that the 'logical constants' do not [stand for objects]" (4.0312). "And if there were an object called '$\sim$', then '$\sim\sim p$' would have to say something other than 'p'. For the one proposition would then treat of $\sim$, the other would not" (5.44). In short, non-elementary propositions contain elements which do not stand for objects, but all elements of pictures must stand for objects, therefore non-elementary propositions cannot be pictures. Hence Wittgenstein intended his picture theory of meaning for elementary propositions only.

A third argument concerns the numbers of elements in pictures and in what they picture. Mrs Daitz correctly reports that "Wittgenstein asserts a correspondence between elements of the sign and elements of the signified . . ." (p. 186 [p. 117]). But it is not true that he ". . . does not go on to assert that this correspondence is one to one" (p. 186 [p. 117]). The one to one nature of the correspondence is definitely asserted: "In the proposition there must be exactly as many things distinguishable as there are in the state of affairs, which it represents. They must both possess the same logical (mathematical) multiplicity . . ." (4.04). That pictures and states of affairs pictured have the same multiplicity follows from Wittgenstein's earlier remarks that "To the objects correspond in the picture the elements of the picture" (2.13) and "The elements of the picture stand, in the picture, for the objects" (2.131). An elementary proposition and the state of affairs it represents have the same multiplicity, hence the elementary proposition can be a picture: "One name stands for one thing, and another for another thing, and they are connected together. And so the whole, like a [tableau vivant], presents the atomic fact" (4.0311). The preceding remark holds for elementary propositions, since "The simplest proposition, the elementary proposition, asserts the existence of an atomic fact" (4.21). However, the alleged one to one correspondence obviously fails to hold for non-elementary propositions. To any proposition '*p*' there corresponds the logically equivalent non-elementary proposition '$\sim\sim p$'. Identically the same fact is asserted both by '*p*' and by '$\sim\sim p$' for as Wittgenstein argues: "That from a fact *p* an infinite number of *others* should follow, namely $\sim\sim p$, $\sim\sim\sim\sim p$, etc., is indeed hardly to be believed" (5.43). Since '$\sim\sim p$' contains more elements than '*p*', they do not have the same multiplicity. Hence if non-elementary as well as elementary propositions had the same multiplicity as the facts they assert, there would follow the absurd conclusion that one and the same fact must contain different numbers of objects. The present argument is in effect a *reductio ad absurdum* proof that the picture theory of meaning is intended for elementary propositions only.

When understood in this restricted sense, the picture theory of meaning is not damaged by the usual 'refutations' of its critics. For example, Mrs Daitz argues persuasively that ". . . negative statements, conditional statements, disjunctive statements, etc., [are] not describable in picture terms", and that they are ". . . statements which have no pictorial counterparts" (p. 196 [pp. 126–7]). But these are non-elementary propositions, to which Wittgenstein's picture theory was not meant to apply.

Mrs Daitz bases another 'refutation' of the picture theory of meaning on an alleged fundamental difference between pictures and languages: ". . . in the sense in which there are foreign languages there are no foreign pictures" (p. 199 [p. 129]). The implications of this alleged fundamental difference are clear: ". . . we comprehend a picture on seeing it for the first time. No explanation is necessary . . .; the picture 'speaks' for itself, it shows what it pictures . . ." (p. 199 [p. 129]). But "A sentence does not show its meaning—consider the impenetrability of a sentence in an unmastered language. To understand a statement we must first have learnt the language in which it is made . . ." (p. 199 [p. 129]).

Mrs Daitz believes these implications to refute the doctrines of the *Tractatus*: "Only if learning was unnecessary for languages too would Wittgenstein be right in saying '4.03 A proposition must communicate a new sense with old words. The proposition communicates to us a state of affairs, therefore it must be essentially connected with the state of affairs.' We do not understand a sentence on first hearing it because it is *essentially* connected with reality; a sentence is *conventionally* connected with reality" (p. 199 [p. 129]).

Before examining this 'refutation', two remarks are in order. First, Wittgenstein knew very well that foreign languages must be learned before propositions expressed in them can be understood. When he wrote "I understand the proposition, without its sense having been explained to me" (4.021), he was clearly presupposing a mastery of the language. For of the proposition (sentence, statement) he wrote "One understands it if one understands its constituent parts" (4.024), and he insisted that the meanings of those constituent parts must be *learned*: "The meaning of the simple signs (the words) must be explained to us, if we are to understand them" (4.026). Hence Wittgenstein does not deny "the impenetrability of a sentence in an unmastered language".

And second, Wittgenstein does not deny that "a sentence is *conventionally* connected with reality", though he would insist that that is not the whole story. "In our notations there is indeed something arbitrary, but *this* is not arbitrary, namely that *if* we have determined anything arbitrarily, then something else *must* be the case. (This results from the *essence* of the notation)" (3.342). Wittgenstein explicitly denies that the connection between propositions and reality must be either wholly essential or wholly accidental (conventional), writing "A proposition possesses essential and accidental features . . ." (3.34). The connection between words and objects is conventional or arbitrary, and must be learned. But the connection between the structure of a proposition and the structure of the fact asserted by it is not wholly conventional. One essential connection, their having the same logical (mathematical) multiplicity, has already been mentioned and will be discussed further in the following section.

Mrs Daitz's criticism involves the following argument: Since there are foreign languages but no foreign pictures, understanding a picture requires no previous learning, whereas understanding a proposition does require previous learning; hence no proposition is a picture. There are two presuppositions underlying this objection. The first can scarcely be challenged: there are foreign languages, so understanding a proposition requires previous learning.

The second presupposition is that there are no foreign pictures, so understanding a picture requires no previous learning. In sharp contrast to the first, this second presupposition is very questionable. *Are* there no foreign pictures? *Do* we comprehend *any* picture on seeing it for the first time? Is no explanation of any picture ever necessary? Does the picture 'speak' for itself to every beholder, regardless of his ignorance in matters of style and idiom? Just to ask these questions is to expose the error of Mrs Daitz's second presupposition.

There may be *some* pictures whose content or subject matter is immediately evident to anyone who looks at them. But many pictures require much learning for their interpretation. These include maps, diagrams, political cartoons, cubist paintings, and pictures in religious symbolism; all unintelligible to the uninitiated. Even perspective had to be learned. It seems, therefore, that the alleged fundamental difference between pictures and propositions involves a fundamental mistake. It is simply false that ". . . in the sense in which there are foreign languages there are no foreign pictures" (p. 199 [p. 129]).

The present objection to the picture theory of meaning rests on two presuppositions. The first is admitted to be a truism, but the second is patently false. These remarks are not intended to demonstrate the truth of the picture theory of meaning. They are intended to show only that the usual refutations of it are not convincing.

3. RELATIONS

Around the beginning of the present century many philosophers were concerned with problems involving relations. In his *Principles of Mathematics* Russell carefully examined Bradley's well-known argument against relations, and concluded that "the endless regress, though undeniable, is logically quite harmless" (p. 100). Bradley is nowhere mentioned in the *Tractatus*, nor are his views referred to explicitly, but Wittgenstein there develops a theory of relations that permits another and quite different reply to Bradley's argument. That reply is intimately connected with his picture theory of meaning, which must now be examined in greater detail.

Wittgenstein declares an atomic fact to be a "combination" or "configuration" of objects (2.01, 2.0272). A picture is a fact (2.141); "The picture consists in the fact that its elements are combined with one another in a definite way" (2.14). The mode of combination of elements of a picture represents the mode of combination of objects in the atomic fact that is pictured by it: "That the elements of the picture are combined with one another in a definite way, represents that the things are so combined with one another" (2.15). Similarly, an elementary proposition is "a connection, a concatenation, of names" (4.22). It too is a fact: "The propositional sign consists in the fact that its element, the words, are combined in it in a definite way. The propositional sign is a fact" (3.14). It is the mode of union of its constituent elements that makes it a picture and determines the *sense* of a proposition: "The proposition is a picture of its state of affairs, only insofar as it is logically articulated" (4.032). "One name stands for one thing, and another for another thing, and they are connected together. And so the whole, like a [tableau vivant], presents the atomic fact" (4.0311, see also 3.1431). As in the case of pictures and their elements, the mode of combination of names in a propositional sign represents the mode of combination of objects in the atomic fact that is asserted by it: "To the configuration of the simple signs in the propositional sign corresponds the configuration of the objects in the state of affairs" (3.21). In brief, an atomic fact, which consists of objects related to each other, is asserted by an elementary proposition, which consists of names related to each other. Each name in the proposition represents an object in the fact, and the relation of the names represents the relation of the objects.

Against this view Mrs Daitz objected that

> . . . converting sentences into facts creates a difficulty: in conversion, an n-termed sentence becomes an n + 1-termed fact. Consider 'Sophia hates Amos'. This becomes the fact *'Hates' is between 'Sophia' and 'Amos'*, which has the consequences that it is impossible to gear the form of a sentence to form of the fact. The sentence 'Sophia hates Amos' is not identical in form with, i.e. has not the same number of elements as, the fact *Sophia hates Amos*. For the sentence is the fact *'Hates' is between 'Sophia' and 'Amos'*, i.e. it has four elements while *Sophia hates Amos* has only three. This view brings with it the consequence that all ordinary sentences have, for fact-stating purposes, one word too many! (p. 189 [pp. 119–20], see also p. 196 [p. 126]).

In his defence of Wittgenstein from this criticism Mr Evans agrees with Mrs Daitz on the number of elements in the sentence, writing: "Now the four elements into which Wittgenstein converts *'aRb'* are evidently the three signs and their order" (p. 259 [p. 133]). But he nevertheless defends the view that a sentence and the fact asserted by it have the same multiplicity, arguing that the fact as well as the sentence contains an extra element. Mrs Daitz asserted that the fact *Sophia hates Amos* contains only three elements. But Mr Evans counts it as containing four elements, writing: "Wittgenstein would have said, I think, that the fact that Sophia hates Amos contained four elements: the two people, the hating, and the structure of these . . ." (p. 260 [p. 134]).

Let us discuss this disagreement in terms of the fact *that aRb* rather than the fact *that Sophia hates Amos*, for the latter involves difficulties irrelevant to the present issue. Both Mrs Daitz and Mr Evans count four elements in the fact *'aRb'*, but they disagree on the number of elements in the fact *that aRb*. In the latter fact Mrs Daitz can count only three elements whereas Mr Evans can count four.

The four elements counted by Mr Evans in the fact *that aRb* are the two objects *a* and *b*, the relation *R*, and the structure of these. The fourth element cannot be the fact itself *that aRb*, since *elements of* that fact are being enumerated; it must be taken to mean a relation

175

whose relata are the first three elements enumerated: *a*, *b*, and *R*. But if *R* is not sufficiently related to *a* and *b* by relating *them*, so that a new (three-termed) relation is required, then that three-termed relation is not sufficiently related to *a* and *b* and *R* by relating *them*, and a new (four-termed) relation is required, which would constitute a *fifth* element in the now fast-growing fact *that aRb*. Clearly we are well into Bradley's regress. On the other hand, there may be some good reason for taking exactly one step into Bradley's regress. If so, there *would* be exactly four elements in the fact. But Mr Evans has neither presented any such reason nor given any hint as to what it might be.

Mrs Daitz and Mr Evans agree that there are four elements in the elementary proposition '*aRb*'. To find four elements in a sequence of three words or symbols one must count more than just words as elements. Mr Evans states explicitly that each sign is an element and that their order is an additional element (p. 259 [p. 133]). Mrs Daitz evidently shares this view, since she finds the same number of elements. But Wittgenstein's conception of a propositional element is quite different; "The propositional sign consists in the fact that its elements, the words, are combined in it in a definite way . . ." (3.14). Also, "These elements [of the propositional sign] I call 'simple signs' . . ." (3.201). "The simple signs employed in propositions are called names" (3.202). For Wittgenstein the elements of an elementary proposition are the words (names or simple signs) occurring in it; their order or arrangement is not regarded by him as an additional element. Hence for Wittgenstein the elementary proposition '*aRb*' contains *three* elements, not four.

It might be thought that the conclusion reached in the preceding paragraph would automatically settle the issue between Mrs Daitz and Mr Evans as to the number of elements in the fact *that aRb*. Atomic fact and elementary proposition "must both possess the same logical (mathematical) multiplicity" (4.04) and the elementary proposition '*aRb*' contains three elements, whence the atomic fact *that aRb* must also contain three elements. The issue, however, is not so easily resolved. Like the picture theory of meaning, the 'multiplicity' doctrine does not apply to ordinary language. Although the ordinary language proposition "ambulo" contains but a single word, it is nevertheless composite (4.032). In ordinary language, therefore, the number of elements contained in a proposition does not determine that proposition's multiplicity, hence the multiplicity of an ordinary sentence is not well defined. The 'multiplicity doctrine' (of 4.04) applies not to ordinary language but only to "a symbolism . . . which obeys the rules of *logical* grammar—of logical syntax". Before we can use the multiplicity doctrine to determine the number of elements in the atomic fact *that aRb* we must first discover how to express it in "logical symbolism" (3.325), "logical notation" (5.533), "correct logical notation" (5.534), or "an adequate notation" (6.122). The key to this problem is found in 3.1432:

> We must not say, "The complex sign '*aRb*' says '*a* stands in relation *R* to *b*' "; but we must say, "*That* '*a*' stands in a certain relation to '*b*' says *that aRb* ".

The negative injunction here expressed should not be taken simply to forbid use of the locution "The complex sign '*aRb*' . . ." *in* "an adequate notation", for that prohibition is enjoyed elsewhere. A propositional sign, being a fact, cannot be named (3.144, see also 3.24, 4.023). Hence putting quotation marks around a sentence does not form its name. Apart from truth operators, propositions contain only names (3.202, 4.22, 4.221, 5.55). Hence in no "symbolism . . . which obeys the rules of *logical* grammar" can we say "The complex sign '*aRb*'. . ."

Paragraph 3.1432 should rather be taken to forbid using the locution "The complex sign '*aRb*' says '*a* stands in relation *R* to *b*' " *of* "an adequate notation". In ordinary language and also in the not yet adequate notation of Frege and Russell (3.325) the fact *that aRb* is expressed in a sentence '*aRb*' containing the three words '*a*', '*b*', and '*R*'. But not in the "adequate notation" Wittgenstein recommends. If it were, he would have written ". . . we must say, '*That* "*a*" stands in a certain relation to "*b*" and to "*R*" says *that aRb*'." But he did not. He wrote instead ". . . we must say, '*That* "*a*" stands in a certain relation to "*b*" says *that aRb*'." The difference is crucial. In "an adequate notation" no propositional sign asserting *that aRb* contains the relation symbol '*R*'. Names for the relata *a* and *b* appear, but no name for the relation *R*. Here it must be remembered that the language *used* is not the "adequate notation" *mentioned*. Thus Wittgenstein can *use* '*aRb*' to say *that aRb* while insisting that it not be done (in "an adequate notation").

The fact *that aRb* is expressed in "an adequate notation" by a proposition containing only the two words '*a*' and '*b*'. Since only words count as elements, the proposition contains exactly two elements, and by the multiplicity doctrine, the fact *that aRb* contains exactly two elements. Those two elements are the objects *a* and *b* named by the proposition's elements '*a*' and '*b*' (3.203).

Since Wittgenstein conceives the fact *that aRb* to contain just two elements, Mrs Daitz's contention that there are three is closer than Mr Evans' contention that there are four, but neither is in agreement with Wittgenstein's count. Both Mrs Daitz and Mr Evans count four elements in an ordinary sentence such as '*aRb*'. Since Wittgenstein counts only words as elements, he would count only three elements in that sentence. Here too Mrs Daitz and Mr Evans are in disagreement with Wittgenstein.

Nevertheless, since the fact *that aRb* contains two elements and the ordinary sentence '*aRb*' contains three elements, Mrs Daitz is correct in her conclusion that "ordinary sentences have, for fact-stating purposes, one word too many" (p. 189 [p. 120]). The "one word too many" in ordinary sentences is in every case a relation word. But the extraordinary sentences of the "logical symbolism" recommended by Wittgenstein contain no relation words. Hence they do not contain "too many" words, and Mrs Daitz's criticism falls wide of the mark. We have here, incidentally, one reason why the sentence "Sophia hates Amos" cannot be an elementary proposition in an "adequate notation". That sentence contains the relation word "hates", whereas no relation word can occur in a "logical notation".

The question naturally arises: if propositional signs contain no words for relations, how can they express relational facts? Wittgenstein proposes to express a relation of objects by a relation of their names: "*That 'a' stands in a certain relation to 'b' says that aRb*" (3.1432, see also 3.1431). Against this proposal Mrs Daitz argues that relation words are necessary, and cannot be eliminated in favour of relations *of* words:

A sentence needs a mark where a picture does not: it cannot show that this adjoins that, but must *say* so. . . . Say we drop the word for *adjoins* and write 'This that' in place of 'This adjoins that'. How would we indicate that this adjoins as opposed to surpasses or divides into that? (p. 196 [p. 126]).

Mrs Daitz's present objection had been anticipated by Russell in *An Outline of Philosophy*:

Take, say, the fact that lightning precedes thunder. If we were to express this by a language closely reproducing the structure of the fact, we should have to say simply: "lightning, thunder", where the fact that the first word precedes the second means that what the first word means precedes what the second word means. But even if we adopted this method for temporal order, we should still need words for all other relations, because we could not without intolerable ambiguity symbolize them also by the order of our words (pp. 60, 275).

This objection presupposes that only one relation can significantly obtain between signs. (It is immaterial whether it is Mrs Daitz's *adjoining* or Russell's *preceding*.) Mrs Daitz seems to have considered just one kind of case: "A drawing of one thing adjoining another needs a mark for one thing and a mark for the other, but no mark for the relation of adjoining. This it shows by the spatial placing of the marks for the two things" (p. 196 [p. 126]).

178

In the case of adjacency, the pictured relation is represented by the same relation of parts of the picture. But not all relations among pictured objects are represented by placing the pictorial representations of those objects in identically the same relation that is to be represented. In painting, the relation *more distant than* is sometimes represented by the relation *bluer than*, sometimes by the relations *higher than* or *smaller than*. Although in pictorial representation relations are represented by relations, they are often represented by relations other than themselves.

Once it is understood that the picturing relation need not be the same as the relation pictured, it is easy to see how the picture theory of meaning can apply to relational propositions in general. Any relation of objects, spatial or non-spatial, can be represented by a spatial relation of the names of those objects. That a has relation R to b can be represented by writing 'a' some specified distance and direction from 'b', and that a has some different relation R' to b can be presented by writing 'a' some different distance and direction from 'b'. Wittgenstein described this method of representing relations explicitly: "The essential nature of the propositional sign becomes very clear when we imagine it made up of spatial objects (such as tables, chairs, books) instead of written signs. The mutual spatial position of these things then expresses the sense of the proposition" (3.1431).

A plurality of significant relations among signs is evident in elementary mathematics, where we use different spatial relations of the symbols for x and y to express their product, x raised to the yth power, y raised to the xth power, the xth y in a sequence of y's, and the yth x in a sequence of x's (xy, x^y, y^x, y_x, x_y). Since a relation can be represented by a relation other than itself, indefinitely many relations among objects can be represented by the indefinitely many spatial relations among the names of those objects, without any ambiguity in the symbolization. Once the error of its presupposition is revealed, the Russell-Daitz objection collapses, and Wittgenstein's proposal to eliminate relation words in favour of relations is seen to be entirely feasible.

To see how the *Tractatus* provides an answer to Bradley's argument against relations, it will be helpful to review Russell's discussion of the problem. His *Principles of Mathematics* states ". . . that the endless regress, though undeniable, is logically quite harmless" (p. 100). Later, however, Russell seemed no longer to be satisfied that the 'undeniable' regress was harmless, for he began to insist that the regress was deniable, or perhaps better, avoidable. His diagnosis of the original difficulty appears in *An Outline of Philosophy*:

A great deal of the confusion about relations which has prevailed in practically all philosophies comes from the fact that relations are indicated, not by relations, but by words which are as substantial as other words (p. 275).

Bradley's argument in particular was said to be grounded in that linguistic fact:

Bradley conceives a relation as something just as substantial as its terms, and not radically different in kind. . . . I think Bradley has been misled, unconsciously, by . . . the fact that the *word* for a relation is as substantial as the *words* for its terms (pp. 263–4).

We have already remarked on Russell's insistence that relation words cannot be eliminated in favour of relations, but that words for relations are necessary. Now if Russell is committed to the same linguistic practice as Bradley, how can he avoid the regress? On both their views, to assert a relational proposition requires using a word for the relation as well as words for the relata. These words must themselves be related, and we seem again to be launched upon a regress of the kind urged by Bradley. Russell noted this fact himself:

The first step in Bradley's regress does actually have to be taken in giving verbal expression to a relation, and the word for a relation does have to be related to the words for its terms. But this is a linguistic, not a metaphysical fact, and the regress does not have to go any further (p. 264).

Now how does this solution relate to the *Tractatus*?

There are no relation words in the "logical notation" recommended by Wittgenstein. Hence formulating a relational proposition in that language does *not* involve "the first step in Bradley's regress"; and the regress turns out not to be a fact at all, either linguistic or metaphysical. Wittgenstein's recommended "logical symbolism" would appear to provide a threefold answer to Bradley's argument against relations. First, as already explained, its adoption would prevent even the first step of Bradley's regress. Second, because it contains no relation words, its adoption would eliminate the circumstance that "relations are indicated, not by relations, but by words which are as substantial as other words" which Russell held to be "at the bottom of the hopeless muddle which has prevailed in *all* schools of philosophy as to the nature of relations". Third, Bradley's argument against the reality of relations could not even be formulated in the language recommended (one of Wittgenstein's avowed aims was to avoid errors by employing "a symbolism which excludes them" (3.325)).

Wittgenstein explicitly discusses ontological issues, even though these could not be discussed in the "correct logical notation" mentioned but not used by him. His pronouncement on relations is: "In the atomic fact objects hang one in another, like the [links] of a chain" (2.03). Here we have again the relation-link analogy drawn by Bradley. In a chain successive links are not "united by a link", nor are they well described as being united "by a spatial relation", as Russell would have it (p. 263). The linkage is not *between* links, but *of* them; it is not a relation between them, but the way they are related. As DeWitt H. Parker wrote in *Experience and Substance*: "Relations are modes of unification of elements, not further elements requiring unification" (p. 215). Every use of substantive terms to refer to relations is misleading. Russell was right to insist on this fact. But we should remember that it was earlier insisted on by Wittgenstein.

4. OBJECTS AND PROPERTIES

Traditional metaphysical categories are those of relation, property, and particular. Which of these traditional categories corresponds most closely to Wittgenstein's *objects*?

It should be clear from the extended discussion in Section 3 that his objects are not relations. The argument can be put very briefly as follows. All objects are represented by names (3.203, 3.22, 3.221), whereas relations are represented not by names, but by relations; therefore objects and relations are distinct.

It must be acknowledged that there is some evidence that properties *are* conceived as objects. Thus in a parenthetical remark ". . . (This blue colour and that stand in the internal relation of brighter and darker *eo ipso*. It is unthinkable that *these* two objects should not stand in this relation) . . ." (4.123), the term 'object' is applied to *this blue colour*. But this use of 'object' for a property is deprecated in the very next sentence of the paragraph cited: ". . . (Here to the shifting use of the words "property" and "relation" there corresponds the shifting use of the word "object") . . ." (4.123). Thus Wittgenstein acknowledges a certain looseness in his employment of these key terms, and seems to warn us against being misled by his atypical use of the term 'object' for a property in the passage cited.

Two other propositions are inviting premises for an argument designed to prove that properties are objects: "It is clear that however different from the real one an imagined world may be, it must have something—a form—in common with the real world" (2.022). "This fixed form consists of the objects" (2.023). The usual view, I think, is that the total number of particulars in the real world is contingent, and that different possible (imagined) worlds can contain different numbers of particulars, whence particulars cannot be common to all imagined worlds and the real one. So objects, being common to all such worlds, cannot be particulars. Therefore, since they are not relations either, objects must be properties.

The argument of the preceding paragraph is wholly unconvincing. There is no evidence Wittgenstein shared the "usual view" that different possible worlds can contain different particulars. But Wittgenstein definitely asserts that *different possible worlds can contain different properties*. The axiom of reducibility (*12.1 of *Principia Mathematica*) asserts the existence not of particulars but of first-order functions or properties. Hence when Wittgenstein writes that, "We can imagine a world in which the axiom of reducibility is not valid" (6.1233), his words surely imply that properties are not the same in all imagined worlds as in the real world. But since objects are the same in all imagined worlds, it follows that objects are not properties. Since objects are not relations either, it follows by elimination that objects must be particulars.

There is overwhelming evidence that objects are particulars rather than properties. I cite first what might be called *symbolic* evidence. "Thus a proposition '*fa*' shows that in its sense the object *a* occurs, two propositions '*fa*' and '*ga*' that they are both about the same object" (4.1211). Here the object *a* is represented by "*a*", which usually serves as an individual constant, not as a predicate or property symbol. Again, "So the variable name '*x*' is the proper sign of the pseudo-concept *object*. . . . For example in the proposition 'there are two objects which . . .', by '$(\exists x, y) \ldots$' . . ." (4.1272). Here the word "object" is symbolized by means of individual variables, not by means of predicate or property variables. Wittgenstein wrote further that "The names are the simple symbols, I indicate them by single letters (x, y, z). The elementary proposition I write as function of the names, in the form '*fx*', '$\phi (x, y)$', etc. . . ." (4.24). Here names (of objects) are symbolized by individual variables rather than predicate or property variables. These cited passages seem to me to provide a kind of "symbolic" evidence that objects are not properties.

Another kind of evidence for the distinctness of objects and properties is furnished by the paragraph: "The substance of the world *can* only determine a form and not any material properties. For these are first presented by the propositions—first formed by the configuration of the objects" (2.0231). The sharply contrasted terms "form" and "material properties" are not explicitly defined, but it is suggested that "formal" has the sense of "logical": "The fact that the propositions of logic are tautologies *shows* the formal—logical—properties of language, of the world" (6.12, see also 6.1224, 2.0141, 2.033, 4.126). The contrasted "material properties" can best be understood, therefore, as contingent or empirical properties. Now objects are not forms or formal properties, because objects can be represented (3.22, 3.221,

3.203, 4.0312) whereas formal properties can not be represented—
"To be able to represent the logical form, we should have to be able
to put ourselves with the propositions outside logic, that is outside
the world" (4.12, see also 4.121, 4.0312). But objects cannot be
material properties either. The second sentence of 2.0231 quoted at
the start of this paragraph asserts that material properties are "first
formed by the configuration of the objects". Now if objects *were*
material properties, that passage would assert material properties to
be first formed by the configuration of material properties, themselves first formed by the configuration of material properties, and
so on. Here, it seems to me, would be a regress more vicious than
any ever dreamed of by Bradley. The alternative to the vicious regress
is to deny that objects can be material properties. And from these
considerations it follows that objects cannot be properties, either
formal or material.

Perhaps more decisive evidence that objects are not properties can
be assembled as follows. In the first place, "The object is simple"
(2.02), "Objects . . . cannot be compound" (2.021). But *some* properties are definitely compound. The most that might be claimed,
therefore, is that *some* properties are objects, namely, the simple ones.
But symbols that appear to be names of the simplest properties
cannot occur in elementary propositions. Wittgenstein proclaimed a
radical pluralism, insisting that "Atomic facts are independent of
each other" (2.061), and that ". . . It is possible for all combinations
of atomic facts to exist, and the others not to exist" (4.27, see also
2.062). Since "The simplest proposition, the elementary proposition,
asserts the existence of an atomic fact" (4.21), it follows that "It is a
sign of an elementary proposition, that no elementary proposition
can contradict it" (4.211, see also 5.134). Now what shall we say of
two propositions, one asserting a given point in the visual field to be
red, the other asserting it to be blue? If *any* properties are simple,
specific colours ought to be counted among the simplest. If objects
are (simple) properties, and elementary propositions consist of names
of objects (4.22, 3.202, 3.203), then the two propositions mentioned
must be elementary propositions. But *can* they both be true? Wittgenstein's answer is unequivocal: "For two colours, e.g. to be at one
place in the visual field, is impossible, logically impossible, for it is
excluded by the logical structure of colour. . . . (It is clear that the
logical product of two elementary propositions can neither be a
tautology nor a contradiction. The assertion that a point in the visual
field has two different colours at the same time, is a contradiction)"
(6.3751). It follows that colour predications are *not* elementary propositions, and the implication seems clear that objects are *not*
properties.

Further evidence that his objects are particulars rather than properties is provided in Wittgenstein's later *Philosophical Investigations*, where after quoting the *Theaetetus* doctrine that "primary elements" can only be named, he adds "Both Russell's 'individuals' and my 'objects' (*Tractatus Logico-Philosophicus*) were such primary elements" (21*e*).

Since objects are neither relations nor properties, if they correspond to any of the traditional categories they must be particulars. Our earlier distinction between formal (logical) and material (contingent) properties permits three different kinds of particulars to be distinguished. First we note that possession of a material property implies possession of a formal property, but not conversely. If a particular possesses a material property it must also possess the formal property of being capable of possessing that material property. But it is logically possible for a particular to possess a formal property, say the capability of being (materially) related to other particulars, without possessing any material property at all. Now we define an *absolutely bare* particular as one possessing neither formal nor material properties, a *bare* particular as one possessing formal but no material properties, and a *qualitied* particular as one possessing both formal and material properties.

With the possible exception of Parmenides, I know of no historical philosopher who discussed absolutely bare particulars. In the *Timaeus* Plato's receptacle is bare but not absolutely bare: although "formless" or "devoid of any particular form" it has the capability of receiving form (50–51). Certainly Wittgenstein's objects are not absolutely bare; they have "internal" properties (2.01231) or "forms" (2.0141), where the form is a possibility (2.0141) and therefore logical. His objects are therefore either qualities or bare particulars.

It must be admitted that several of Wittgenstein's remarks suggest that objects have "external" properties as well as "internal" ones (2.01231, 2.0233, 4.023). Despite the difficulty of dealing with such passages, there seems to me to be overwhelming evidence that he regarded objects as bare particulars, having no material properties whatever.

In the first place, Wittgenstein explicitly denies that objects can have properties. His assertion that "objects are colourless" (2.0232) must be understood as synecdochical, for the context makes clear that he is not interested in denying colour qualities only, but all qualities or "material properties" (the term first appears in the immediately preceding paragraph (2.0231)).

Further evidence for the bare particularity of objects is furnished by Wittgenstein's assertions that states of affairs (complexes, facts) can be described (3.144, 3.24, 4.023) but that objects can only be named (3.221). For if an object *had* a property, that would be a fact whose assertion would constitute a *description* of that object. But objects can not be so described, whence it follows that objects have no properties.

A third argument for the bareness of particulars can be set forth as follows. Propositional signs are analysable (3.25), whereas names or simple signs are not (3.26), hence all propositional signs are composite (4.032), and every proposition must contain at least two elements. Since elementary propositions and the facts they assert must possess "the same logical (mathematical) multiplicity" (4.04), every fact must contain at least two elements. But the elements of an atomic fact are objects (2.01, 2.0272), and since objects are particulars, every fact must involve at least two particulars. Now if an object had a material property, *that* it had the property would be a fact involving only one particular. But no fact can involve just one particular, hence no object can have any material property, and all particulars are bare.

A fourth reason for taking the particulars to be bare is provided by Wittgenstein's remark in the *Philosophical Investigations* that his objects in the *Tractatus* were primary elements like those described in the *Theaetetus* (21*e*).

A consequence of Wittgenstein's doctrine that objects are bare particulars is that "Sophia hates Amos" cannot be an elementary proposition in an "adequate notation". Neither Sophia nor Amos are bare particulars, hence they are not objects and "Sophia" and "Amos" are not names, whence it follows that "Sophia hates Amos" does not have names as its elements and is therefore not an elementary proposition.

All atomic facts are relational, and no elementary proposition in a "logical notation" can predicate a property of any object. Hence Mrs Daitz is right in remarking: ". . . the notion that elements of the sign stand for elements in the signified . . ." starts us on ". . . the road that will end at the bare particular" (p. 187 [p. 118]). But since Wittgenstein accepts objects as bare particulars, Mrs Daitz's remark is scarcely a *reductio ad absurdum* of his picture theory of meaning—as it seemed intended to be. As bare particulars, objects can form the substance of the world (2.021), but not in the Aristotelian sense in which substances have material properties. Wittgenstein's objects are substantial in the later sense of substrata, and correspond more closely to Aristotle's prime matter than to his primary substances.

Material properties, then, are never properties of objects, but belong only to complexes. Russell's remark on this point in *An Outline of Philosophy* is extremely helpful:

. . . the sort of adjective we can know, such as "blue" and "round", will not be applicable to particulars. They are therefore analogous to the adjective "populous" applied to a town. To say "this town is populous" means "many people live in this town". A similar transformation would be demanded by logic in all the adjectives and relations we can know empirically (268).

In the same passage Russell asserts that "True adjectives . . . will require particulars for their terms . . ." but there he is definitely in disagreement with Wittgenstein, of whose particulars *no* adjectives can be truly predicated. For a logical form cannot be represented at all (4.12, 4.121), hence cannot be predicated of anything; and particulars have no material properties, hence no material properties can be truly predicated of them.

Although the present (partial) interpretation of the *Tractatus* runs counter to more usual interpretations, there seem to me to be strong arguments in its favour. They may not be decisive, but those arguments must be answered by proponents of alternative interpretations. I hope that this essay will stimulate those who disagree to re-examine the *Tractatus* from a new and different point of view.

Mr Copi on Objects, Properties, and Relations in the 'Tractatus'[1]

I AGREE with some of what Mr Copi says. But he has no justification for asserting that according to the *Tractatus* 'the fact that aRb contains exactly two elements'—namely the objects a and b. All that the *Tractatus* tells him is that the objects a and b occur 'in the sense' of the proposition 'aRb' (4.1211). 50 or 1000 or an infinity of other objects may occur in that sense as well.

Accepting what I think is Mr Copi's suggestion—which coincides with my own view—that Wittgenstein's theory demands that there shall be as many different possible expressive relations between 'a' and 'b' as there are different possible relations between a and b, the following arrangement of names might be one of them:

$$\text{`}\quad \begin{array}{ccc} & c & d \\ a & & b \\ & e & \end{array} \quad\text{,}$$

and this might be the fully analysed form of 'aRb'. There is no difficulty, as Mr Copi seems to think, about objects' having external properties. For example, a possible definite description of an object, e.g. 'R'b'—'the (thing that is) R to b' would give possible external properties of it (cf. 4.023); of course it would not define the object. Or again, if aRb, 'Rb' gives an external property of a.

G. E. M. ANSCOMBE

[1] From *Mind*, vol. 68, N.S., no. 271, July, 1959, p. 404. Reprinted by permission of the editor and the author.

'Tractatus' 6.3751[1]

EDWIN B. ALLAIRE

CONSIDER the sentence 'this is red and this is green'. Call it A. Assume that in A the two occurrences of 'this' refer to the same colour spot. In the *Tractatus* Wittgenstein claimed that A is contradictory. The claim has provoked varying reactions. Urmson argues[2] that the individuals of the *Tractatus* are rudimentary Aristotelian substances. Accordingly, though he acknowledges the rôle which the truth-table explication of logical truth plays in this work, he tends to minimize its importance. For this Bergmann takes him to task,[3] insisting, not unfairly, that he thus fails to appreciate a difficulty which the claim creates. Bergmann, himself, faces this difficulty head on by maintaining that the claim is inconsistent with what he calls the bulk of the *Tractatus*, which in this context I take to mean the truth-table explication of logical truth.

I propose to do three things. First, I shall show that as such the claim is not inconsistent with the truth-table explication of logical truth. Second, I shall show that the claim is not based on a substance doctrine. Third, I shall argue that Wittgenstein's determination to secure a privileged status for such sentences as A was a major motive for his eventual rejection of the *Tractatus*.

There are passages in the *Tractatus* that may be taken to advance a substance doctrine. Urmson is quick to exploit them. I shall ignore them. Not that they could be ignored in contesting other aspects of Urmson's analysis. They just happen to be irrelevant to my argument. For, I am not here arguing that the individuals of the *Tractatus* are

[1] I am obliged to Prof. Gustav Bergmann who has read the manuscript and made many helpful suggestions.

From *Analysis*, vol. 19, no. 5, N.S., no. 71, April, 1959, pp. 100–5. Reprinted by permission of the editor and the author.

[2] J. O. Urmson, *Philosophical Analysis*, London, 1956, pp. 57–9.

[3] Gustav Bergmann, "The Revolt Against Logical Atomism", *The Philosophical Quarterly*, vol. 7, 1957, pp. 323–39, and 8, 1958, pp. 1–14. Cf. pp. 338–9.

not rudimentary Aristotelian substances. I merely maintain that Wittgenstein's claim (i.e. that A is contradictory) is not based on a substance doctrine. If correct, this may detract from the plausibility of Urmson's contention that the *Tractatus*, even if only in a rudimentary and implicit fashion, does contain a substance doctrine. I, for one, do not believe that it does. But, again, this is a matter beyond the scope of this note.

What exactly is the difficulty of which Urmson makes too little and Bergmann too much? (*a*) The analytic-synthetic distinction must be explicated by means of the truth tables (cf. 5.525). (*b*) There are linguistic simples (cf. 3.144–3.262). Everyone agrees that both (*a*) and (*b*) are central to the argument of the *Tractatus*. But they are compatible with the claim that A is contradictory only if one denies that 'red' and 'green' are (linguistic) simples. For, if they were simples, 'this is red' and 'this is green' would be atomic. Hence, to maintain that A is contradictory one would have to maintain that a conjunction of two atomic sentences is contradictory, which is inconsistent with (*a*). Urmson has either not seen or not said this as clearly as one might wish. Bergmann, again, has either not seen or not told us about the way out that Wittgenstein proposed in the *Tractatus*:

6.375 As there is only a *logical* necessity, so there is only a *logical* impossibility.

6.3751 For two colours, e.g. to be at one place in the visual field, is impossible, logically impossible, for it is excluded by the logical structure of colour. Let us consider how this contradiction presents itself in physics. Somewhat as follows: that a particle cannot at the same time have two velocities, i.e. that at the same time it cannot be in two places, i.e. that particles in different places at the same time cannot be identical

(It is clear that the logical product of two elementary propositions can neither be a tautology nor a contradiction. The assertion that a point in the visual field has two different colours at the same time is a contradiction.)

6.3751 shows that Wittgenstein realizes the difficulty. It also contains the solution he then proposed. 'Red' and 'green' are not simples. Rather, they are defined. This I take to be the import of the phrase "the logical structure of colour". Two comments as to what does not matter for the argument might be helpful. Time is mentioned in the passage. Yet, we need not concern ourselves with the problems of time. The issue of coexemplification, if I may so express myself, arises already in a timeless universe. That is, even if 'this' in A referred to a momentary particular, the difficulty would persist. Visual fields are also mentioned. But, again, the phenomenalism-realism controversy, which some might wish to bring into the argument, can be safely ignored. For, the problem of coexemplification also confronts the phenomenalist. In sum, the problems of time and the realism-phenomenalism controversy are distinct from the problem at hand.

Wittgenstein, I conclude, was well aware of what he was committed to if he wanted to hold that A is contradictory. And committed he was. But he was not inconsistent. On the other hand, he created for himself a problem which, as we shall presently see and as he himself was soon to discover, is insoluble. But I have shown already, I think, that his claim is not at all based on a substance doctrine. It is made in the full light of both (*a*) and (*b*).[1] What Wittgenstein hoped to do was so to define 'red' and 'green' that not-A would become a deductive consequence of his definitions. Thus, since definitions are analytic, not-A would be shown to be analytic. Or, what amounts to the same thing, A would be contradictory.

In the *Tractatus*, though, all this remains a programme. Colour words are claimed to be definable, but their definitions are not given. Nor is this strange. The early Wittgenstein was greatly preoccupied with the syntactical features of his ideal language. Accordingly, epistemological considerations are scarce in the *Tractatus*. Nor is this a weakness. Considering the intent of the work it is rather a strength. But eventually the ideal language has to be interpreted. That is, the referents of the linguistic simples have to be chosen. In 1929 in the paper on logical form Wittgenstein finally turns to this task. What he there does he himself describes as a "logical analysis of phenomena".

Wittgenstein did not in 1929 abandon his commitment to the privileged status of A. As we shall see he never did. But another change has taken place. By now he rejects the solution proposed in 6.3751:

"If statements of degree were analysable—as I used to think—we could explain this contradiction (A) by saying that the colour R contains all degrees of R and none of B and that the colour B contains all degrees of B and none of R."[2] (pp. 168–9 [pp. 35–6]).

I need not for my purpose go into all the reasons that the Wittgenstein of 1929 adduces for the failure of his earlier programme. To see that it must fail it suffices to consider one which he himself does not mention. Assume, for the sake of the argument, that the (actually impossible) definitions are unexceptionable in all respects. Replace A by the sentence which predicates of the spot not that it is red and green but, rather, that it exemplifies two of the presumably simple shades from the spectrum of red and green, respectively. Call this

---

[1] A substance doctrine is not compatible with both (a) and (b). This, however, I have not undertaken to show in this note.

[2] L. Wittgenstein, "Some Remarks on Logical Form", *Aristotelian Society*, Supp. Vol. IX (1929), pp. 162–71 [present volume].

sentence A'. A moment's reflection shows that the difficulty which we first encounter in A now reappears in A'.

However good or bad some of the reasons may be which Wittgenstein himself gave in 1929 for the failure of his earlier programme, the conclusion he draws is correct. A cannot be shown to be contradictory in this way. But there are still two ways out. Either one modifies the syntax of the *Tractatus* (*a*), or one denies that there are simples (*b*). In 1929 Wittgenstein still opts for (*a*). In this he still clings to the idea of an ideal language. Later on, as we shall see, he chooses (*b*), which of course is incompatible with that idea. But he never wavers in his determination to preserve in some form the privileged status of A. As he himself puts it in 1929, "it will be clear to all of us in ordinary life, that . . . [A] . . . is some sort of contradiction (and not merely a false proposition)" (p. 168 [p. 35]).

Let us take a quick glance at the syntactical solution or, rather, the syntactical programme of 1929. For it too remained a programme. Its gist is contained in the following passage; more precisely in the sentence I italicize.[1]

"It is, of course, a *deficiency of our notation* that it does not prevent the formation of such nonsensical constructions [A] and a perfect notation will have to exclude such structures by definite rules of syntax. *These will have to tell us that in the case of certain kinds of atomic propositions described in terms of definite symbolic features certain combinations of T's and F's must be left out.* Such rules, however, cannot be laid down until we have actually reached the ultimate analysis of phenomena in question. This, as we all know, has not yet been achieved" (pp. 170–1 [p. 37]).

The gambit is natural enough. If, thinking in the syntactical vein, one cannot show A to be contradictory, one may try to show that it is ill-formed. This is the import of the italicized sentence. More specifically, since A is obviously well-formed, what is, or rather, what ought to be ill-formed is a certain line of its truth table. Whether or not this programme can be realized syntactically, it foreshadows the next and final stage by introducing a peculiar asymmetry between A and not-A. Not-A certainly makes sense and is meaningful. It is even true. A, according to the programme, is in some sense ill-formed. Use for the moment 'well-formed', 'making sense', and 'being meaningful' as if they were synonymous and you arrive at a state of affairs where of two sentences, one the negation of the other, one is meaningful while the other is not. That is the peculiarity. One possible way of making it palatable is to identify meaning with use. This, as we all know, is one of the key ideas of the final phase. If I am right, it follows that with respect to one very major issue, at least, the 1929 paper marks a

[1] The still persisting commitment to the syntactical approach appears in the italicized (my italics) phrase of the first sentence.

transitional stage between the thought of the *Tractatus* and that of the final stage.

To see this clearly one merely has to agree that the meaning of a term is determined by the "grammatical rules" for its use. If this is understood one can argue that the final stage is reached in *The Blue and the Brown Books* where one reads,[1]

" 'The colours green and blue can't be in the same place simultaneously'
... is a grammatical rule and states a logical impossibility."

Nor need one give up the earlier use of 'logical structure'. The old phrase can plausibly be explicated in the new manner by maintaining that the "logical structure" of colour must be explored by analysing the "grammar" of the use of colour words.

It may be worth mentioning in conclusion that as early as 1931 Schlick seems to have sensed the development which I have tried to make explicit. Consider the following passage from his essay, "Is There a Factual *a Priori*?".[2]

"Red and green are incompatible, not because I happen to have never observed such a joint appearance, but because the sentence 'This spot is both red and green' is a meaningless combination of words. The logical rules which underlie our employment of colour words forbid such usage ... *The meaning of a word is solely determined by the rules which hold for its use. Whatever follows from these rules, follows from the mere meaning of the word, and is therefore purely analytic, tautological, formal.* The error committed by the proponents of the factual *a priori* can be understood as arising from the fact that it was not clearly recognized that such concepts as those of colours have a formal structure. ... The first who, to my knowledge, has given the correct solution of the problem is Ludwig Wittgenstein (see his *Tractatus Logico-Philosophicus* and essay in the *Proceedings of the Aristotelian Society*, 1929. ... .''

The passage leaves no doubt that in 1931, at least, Schlick did not understand that the original as well as the 1929 defence of the synthetic *a priori* was doomed to failure. Nor, for that matter, did he see that the solution of the final phase is incompatible with those of the two earlier ones. Otherwise he would not have written the last sentence of the passage quoted. Yet, in the two sentences which I italicized he at least anticipated, however vaguely, what became in fact the crucial thought of the final phase. This is impressive.

[1] L. Wittgenstein, *The Blue and the Brown Books*, Oxford, 1958, p. 56.
[2] Moritz Schlick, "Is There a Factual *a Priori*?", *Readings in Philosophical Analysis*, New York, 1949, pp. 284–5. (My italics.)

About "*aRb*"[1]

ELLIS EVANS

IN the issue for April, 1958, there is an article by Mr Irving M. Copi on Wittgenstein's *Tractatus*. In the course of his argument he refers to my discussion note on paragraph 3.1432 of the *Tractatus*, which appeared in *Mind* for April, 1955. I had assumed in this note, as Mrs Daitz, to whom I was replying, had assumed in her article, and as Russell had assumed in his *Introduction* to the *Tractatus*, that 3.1432 was about the proper analysis of ordinary-language sentences of the form "*aRb*". Mr Copi, however, questions this assumption, as part of his general argument that the *Tractatus* is not about ordinary language. The paragraph is as follows:

3.1432 We must not say, "The complex sign '*aRb*' says '*a* stands in relation *R* to *b*' "; but we must say, "*That* '*a*' stands in a certain relation to '*b*' says *that aRb*".

Now Mr Copi maintains on page 155 [p. 177] that this should be taken as forbidding us to use the locution "The complex sign '*aRb*' says '*a* stands in relation *R* to *b*' " *of an adequate notation*. However, it follows from Wittgenstein's footnote to the first page of his exposition, that 3.1432 is intended as a comment on

3.143 That the propositional sign is a fact is concealed by the ordinary form of expression, written or printed.
(For in the printed proposition, for example, the sign of a proposition (*Satzzeichen*) does not appear essentially different from a word. Thus it was possible for Frege to call the proposition a compounded name.)

This, quite obviously, is about ordinary language, and makes the general point that printed propositions look like words or names, this resemblance concealing the true state of affairs, which is that

[1] From *Mind*, N.S., vol. 68, no. 272, October, 1959, pp. 535-8. Reprinted by permission of the editor and the author.

they are *facts*. What Wittgenstein means by calling them facts is explained in the paragraph on which 3.143 is itself a comment, i.e.

> 3.14 The propositional sign consists in the fact (*besteht darin*) that its elements, the words, are combined in it in a definite way. The propositional sign is a fact.

This definite way, moreover, expresses the sense of the proposition. (We learn this in 3.1431.) It seems to me, then, quite clear that Wittgenstein intends 3.1432 as a particular exemplification of the general point in 3.143. He has implied that the complete analysis of a propositional sign must show that it is not a mere word or name, but a fact, that is, a definite combination or ordering of terms. Thus we must not say of an "*aRb*" proposition for instance, that it says, that *a* stands in *R* to *b*, because this analysis merely repeats the sequence of terms in the analysed sentence. Such an analysis does not show what it is about "*aRb*" that expresses its sense. In order to show that, we must refer to the ordering of the terms in the sentence to be analysed. We must say "That '*a*' stands in a certain relation to '*b*' says that *aRb*". Then we have shown that an ordering of terms conveys the sense of the proposition.

This interpretation appears to me quite natural and coherent. No harm is done to the sequence of Wittgenstein's ideas. Mr Copi's interpretation, on the other hand, represents the paragraph as unnecessarily enigmatic, and also involves damage to the scheme of exposition in the *Tractatus*. The concept of an adequate notation is introduced at 3.325, some thirty paragraphs later, openly and in as many words. It would have been strange if Wittgenstein had introduced it at 3.1432, where he is still concerned with the question of how propositional signs *do* signify, and not yet with the idea that there ought to be a notation which would exclude confusions as to how they do so.

How *does* "*aRb*" signify? On page 154 [p. 176] Mr Copi wants to sentence me to Bradley's regress about relations of relations (*Appearance and Reality*, chapter iii). This is because I said in my note that to the order of the elements '*a*', '*R*' and '*b*' corresponds the structure of the elements *a*, *R* and *b*. However, I did not refer to *R* as a relation, and as for structure, I did not use only that expression, but kept on saying that the word-order showed *that aRb and not that bRa*, or *that aRb rather than that bRa*. Thus the word-order indicates that the fact *that aRb* is a kind of alternative. I'll try to explain what I mean by this.

"Telephone" is a word for a kind of object. Analogically, "*R*" could be a word for a kind of situation. For example: this book's being on this newspaper, this same book's being under this same newspaper, the kitten's being under the table, the dog's being under the table, the lamp's being above the table. These can be seen as situations of the same kind. There could be a word "*R*" for this kind of situation. Then "*R*" would be a sort of noun.

Though nouns are only words for *kinds* of object, we can use them to refer to *particular* objects. We may do so by accompanying them by other words that make the reference precise. These other words help to specify *which* object of that kind is meant. For example: the *new* telephone, the *black* telephone, the *Kruschev* proposal, the *goods* train. Notice that we have names and nouns here as well as adjectives.

Any familiar object has several features that could be mentioned in this specifying way. But, given its kind, there are typically just two features of a situation that are outstandingly important: the identity of the objects involved in it. A marriage has been solemnized, but who got married?

I interpret, then, "*aR*" as a reference, in which "*R*" shows the kind of situation, and "*a*" specifies. For example: in "Tom loves Mary", "loves" shows which kind of situation is meant: "Tom" specifies, so that the reference is to a love-situation involving Tom.

Possible features of an object may be asserted *of* it after it has been referred to. To assert such features, we mention them in a predicate. For example: the black telephone is *broken*: the broken telephone is *black*. Well then, if one such feature of a situation has been used to specify, why not any other such possible feature to assert? I use "Tom loves" to specify a love-situation involving Tom. The word-order shows that "Tom" is a specifier. I add "Mary" to say that the other member of the situation is Mary. So "Mary" is like a predicate. The word-order shows that it is.

So "Tom loves Mary" says at least this: a love-situation involving Tom, involves Mary. But this is a symmetrical assertion. I might just as well have specified with "Mary" and asserted with "Tom": I would have said the same. And all "*aRb*" sentences interpreted by this model become, in the first instance, symmetrical assertions. But consider the following analogy.

Sometimes we invert the subject-copula-predicate order for rhetorical effect, thus: calm is the sea. We can say, here are two syntactic patterns available for making assertions in English. Other patterns are available for other things: e.g. copula-subject-predicate gives a question: Is the sea calm?

Imagine a language that has, on the whole, the same patterns, parts of speech, and words as English, except for this: word-order also has a *semantic* function when it comes to colour-adjectives. These people perceive just the same colours as we do, but their language distinguishes each colour into a lighter and darker shade.

Their colour-words mean the lighter shade when they precede their nouns, and the darker shade when they follow them. Thus "red is the book" means that the book is light red, and "the book is red" means that the book is dark red. This is learned ostensively, from childhood. There is no question of colour-words signifying in any other way.

Then although the word "red" in isolation—e.g. in a dictionary, or chalked up on the wall—could be said to mean just what the English word "red" means, a speaker of this language could not just call something red. The order-convention would force him to assert the lighter or darker shade, since the adjective would have to precede or follow the noun by means of which he referred to what he wanted to characterize.

I see the kitten on the table. I put it under the table. I see that these situations are of the same kind. My seeing this is like a speaker of that language, who has watched the sunset turn from light to dark red, recognizing that it is still the same colour. Let there be a word "ϕ" for the kind of situation I recognize. Suppose I say "the kitten ϕ the table". By our previous analysis this says that kitten and table are in this kind of situation, and no more. We do not have such a word in English. If we had, it would be analysed as the name of a symmetrical relation—because it wouldn't matter whether the kitten was under the table or the table under the kitten: both these situations would be covered. It wouldn't matter whether I said "the kitten ϕ the table" or "the table ϕ the kitten".

We don't want to know just that the kitten ϕ the table. (Cf. a speaker of that language: we don't want to know just that something is red.) We want to know which of this pair of situations, covered by "ϕ", is the case. (We want to know whether it is light or dark red.)

Let there be another word, "ψ", which is also for the kind of situation here. So far, then, it is synonymous with "ϕ". But, unlike "ϕ", let it work with a semantic order-convention. The order of words is to say which of the pair of situations holds. Thus, let us say, the thing mentioned before "ψ" is to be the upper one. (This is ostensively learned.) And now if I say "the kitten ψ the table", I have said that the kitten is on the table, because by using "ψ" instead of "ϕ" I not only indicate the *kind* of situation of which the kitten is a member, but also *how* it is a member of that kind of situation: by putting "kitten" first rather than "table", I show that it is the kitten that is *on*. This is a theory of the word "on".

And if no word "ϕ" exists, but only "ψ" exists, I *cannot do otherwise* than express one of these paired situations. I *cannot say*, in this language, that kitten and table are in the kind of situation that "ψ" means, and leave it at that.

198

The suggestion is, then, that symmetrical relation-words are like "ϕ", and that non-symmetrical (including asymmetrical) relation-words are like "ψ". The semantic function of the word-order for each "ψ" is learned together with the meaning of each "ψ". The purely syntactic function of the "aRb" word-order is of course the same whether the "R" is like "ϕ" or like "ψ": it shows what word specifies, and what word asserts.

The so-called converse of an "R" now appears as the nearest available synonym for "R" that works with the reverse convention of order. E.g. "below" is more or less synonymous with "above" in that it is for the same kind of situation on the whole: but in "aRb" sentences the thing mentioned before "above" is the upper thing, and the thing mentioned before "below" is the lower. Thus "aRb" = "$b\ Rc\ a$". Of course, to have a "converse", the "R" must be a ψ-word, not a ϕ-word. Thus it is that the converse of a symmetrical relation is said to be identical with that relation.

If all this is right, talking about e.g. *the relation* "greater than" is like talking about The Telephone. Talk of the *sense* or *direction* of a relation is explicable in terms of a failure to distinguish between semantic and syntactic word-order. "Relation" itself vanishes as a term of the analysis, and the mode of assertion in "aRb" becomes comparable with the subject-predicate mode after all.

Scientific Laws and Scientific Objects in the 'Tractatus'[1]

GEORGE L. PROCTOR

IN a recent article[2] Copi voiced the need for further study of the *Tractatus*, particularly in reference to the concepts of objects, properties, and relations. Urmson's book[3] also voices this need and indicates that further study of the *Tractatus* is indeed helpful and essential to the understanding of the various doctrines associated with those philosophers who were generally grouped together under the name of Logical Positivism. There is one doctrine or theory, generally accepted by those positivists who wrote anything about the matter, which has not, to my knowledge, received sufficient attention and stands in need of a much more thorough analysis than it usually gets. I refer to the theory of scientific laws—and, presumably, the scientific objects whose names occur in such laws—as being logically constructed models, or schemata, which help us to organize and unify our statements about our experience, or which help 'the investigator to find his way about in reality'. That there is still some confusion concerning the theory is evidenced by Hutten's recent book[4] and Alexander's review of it.[5] I think that some of the difficulties of the theory may be cleared away by using the *Tractatus* as the basic foundation from which the theory is derived. The *Tractatus* offers the only basis upon which the theory, in any of its previously stated forms, can be made both intelligible and consistent. If scientific laws and scientific objects are to be conceived as logically constructed models, then it is not enough to explain analogically or

---

[1] From *The British Journal for the Philosophy of Science*, vol. 10, no. 39, November, 1959, pp. 177–93. Reprinted by permission of the editor and the author.
[2] Irving M. Copi, 'Objects, Properties, and Relations in the *Tractatus*', *Mind*, 1958, 67 [present volume]. [3] J. O. Urmson, *Philosophical Analysis*, Oxford, 1956.
[4] E. H. Hutten, *The Language of Modern Physics*, London, 1956.
[5] P. Alexander, *Mind*, 1957, 55.

metaphorically what is meant by calling them such. A derivation from more fundamental principles is also required. Otherwise the theory takes on something of an *ad hoc* character.

In this paper I shall give what seems to me to be the derivation of the 'model' theory from relevant propositions of the *Tractatus*, with a view to rendering the theory internally consistent. I shall not be concerned with the relative merits or demerits of the theory as *the* account of scientific laws and scientific objects. Problems concerning the theory as a whole and its conformity with the actual practices of scientists are not the topic of this paper. Consequently, any objection to the theory which is based on extraneous reasons lies outside the scope of this paper and will not be considered.

Assuming the division of statements found in the *Tractatus*, scientific laws, if statements at all, are either descriptive of reality, or are of a logical nature, or are nonsensical.[1] Any (empirical) proposition belongs to one or more of the sciences, and 'the totality of true propositions is the total natural science (or the totality of the natural sciences)' (4.11).[2] Since all molecular and general propositions are functions of atomic propositions, and since the truth-value of an atomic proposition is determined by its agreement or disagreement with the fact it pictures, all propositions have an ultimate factual reference and therefore belong to the realm of the natural sciences. It follows, then, that all the propositions of science are descriptive of reality, the descriptions being either true or false. For although the propositions may *exhibit* certain forms or structures, they cannot *say* anything about these forms and are thus descriptive only of possible states of affairs. If proposition 4.11 identifies science with the totality of true propositions, then scientific laws, if they are a part of science, must also be descriptive propositions. Since tautologies say nothing about the world, and therefore do not describe anything, tautologies are not a part of science proper. Consequently, scientific laws cannot be conceived as analytic statements. And if scientific laws say something about the world, as surely they must, then they are not nonsensical statements. Yet if all propositions are complexes of atomic propositions and if atomic propositions are logically independent of one another, then the only propositions that can be implied by a complex proposition are its own constituent propositions. Consequently, if scientific laws be taken as empirical

---

[1] The division is neither a strict one nor the only one. Strictly speaking, any statement is either sense or nonsense—yet both types may have uses other than descriptive and exhibitive. This, however, has no direct bearing on the present paper. As it is with complex propositions, it is *we* who make the divisions (as it were, for the sake of experiment) and uses of linguistic expressions.

[2] As is customary, all references to the *Tractatus* will be followed by its proposition number written in parentheses.

generalizations, then all that they could describe would be facts that have already occurred, and hence they would have no predictive power by means of which significant propositions about the future can be formulated and subsequently verified. Yet by means of scientific laws we can, and do, make predictions which are verified in the future. Moreover, the world is the totality of existing atomic facts, and since atomic facts are logically independent of one another, it makes no sense to speak of general facts as being what empirical generalizations describe. Consequently, it would seem that if scientific laws are general statements, they are not descriptive of the world and are genuine propositions. It follows that either they must be logical constructions from atomic propositions conceived analytically as rules for the formulation of genuine propositions, or else they are mere nonsense statements. If scientific laws be conceived as such rules, then they are prescriptive rather than descriptive and hence have nothing to do with the world that science is describing. If scientific laws be conceived as nonsense statements, then we are hard put to explain how sense can be derived from nonsense.

This, it seems to me, is fairly representative of the kind of confusion which prevails in most accounts of the theory of scientific laws as models, a confusion which results from the incompleteness of these accounts of the theory. On the other hand, it seems that scientific laws are neither empirical nor logical nor nonsensical, and yet, on the other hand, they seem to be empirical and logical and nonsensical. The trouble with the matter is that there are senses in which scientific laws can be understood in both ways. A review of the relevant propositions of the *Tractatus* will show this to be the case.

The sections of the *Tractatus* which deal explicitly with scientific theory and natural law are those which are numbered from 6.3 to 6.372. Generally speaking, there is an implicit distinction between a system and a law. A system is a way in which we can bring the descriptions of the universe into a unified form, and corresponding to the different mesh networks that could be used to bring the description of the white surface with the irregular black spots into a unified form are the different systems of describing the world (6.341). Laws are said to be possible forms of the propositions of science, and 'treat of the network and not of what the network describes' (6.35). We may take this distinction to be the same as the one that is generally made between theory and law. Thus, in some sense, both systems and laws are descriptive. A system, moreover, is said always to be a general description of the world (6.3432) and to be 'an attempt to construct according to a single plan all *true* propositions which we need for the description of the world' (6.343). It could seem, then, that if the true propositions of science are of various forms and if laws organize these propositions according to their logical forms, then systems are ways of organizing laws into a single unified whole. If this is so, then both laws and systems are, in some sense, generalized propositions.

The *Tractatus* admits of two forms of generality: essential (or logical) and accidental (or empirical). Since systems and laws are descriptive, they are not mere logical generalities. Logical propositions are tautologies and thus 'treat' of nothing, whereas systems and laws do 'treat' of something. But neither systems nor laws are, strictly speaking, empirical generalizations. For, since all non-elementary propositions are truth-functions of elementary propositions and can be constructed *a priori* according to successive applications of logical operations, and since what is the case is the existence of atomic facts, it makes no sense to speak of 'complex facts' or 'composite facts', and therefore no sense to speak of general facts which may be described by general propositions. In other words, there is no pictorial relation between an empirically general proposition *per se* and a fact; the pictorial relation holds only for elementary propositions and atomic facts. Indirectly, an empirically general proposition may describe the facts of the world in so far as the constituent elementary propositions that can be inferred from it picture possible atomic facts. But no generalization is, in itself, a possible description of what is the case. And since all generalizations can, theoretically at least, be constructed *a priori* by the successive application of the negation operation on the values of a variable, generalizations can be conceived as logical sums or logical products of the elementary propositions which are the values of the given variable. As the determination of the values of the variables, p, q, r, etc., is the description of the *propositions* for which these variables stand, so, in a general proposition, the inference of its constituent elementary propositions is the determination of those elementary propositions of the same logical form as the general proposition and the general proposition is a 'description' of the elementary propositions which are its 'values'. For example, the propositional form 'All x's are mortal' has as its values such general propositions as 'All cats are mortal', 'All men are mortal', 'All vertebrates are mortal', etc. The general proposition, 'All men are mortal', where 'men' is the variable sign, has for its values such propositions as 'This fat man is mortal', 'This tall man is mortal', 'This snub-nosed man is mortal', etc. So, in this sense, general propositions are descriptive of a certain class of propositions having a certain constant logical form, and in so far as they are descriptive of propositions as propositions, general propositions treat of the symbolism and not of what is symbolized. 'That which is peculiar to the "symbolism of generality" is firstly, that it refers to a logical prototype (*Urbild*, or model), and secondly, that it makes constants prominent' (5.522). A general proposition, then, is to be conceived as a logical prototype or model of a class of elementary propositions of a specific logical form.

Natural laws, then, being general propositions, will have the character of being logical models from which all propositions of certain logical forms can be derived or formulated, and as such are possible forms in which the propositions of science can be stated. As empirical generalizations based on past experience, they are logical sums or logical products of those propositions of certain forms that have been found to be true descriptions of actual states of affairs. But the scope of an empirical generalization is wider than the propositions describing past and present facts, since a general proposition is a description of *all* its values. 'All men are mortal' refers not only to descriptions of all past and all present individual men but also refers to the description of any man that can exist. Hence a general proposition refers to the descriptions of all possible facts of a certain form. Natural laws, then, have the character of being kinds of shorthand expressions of propositions of a certain logical form found to be true descriptions of facts of a given structure, as well as the character of being logical models in accordance with which we can formulate propositions descriptive of future facts of the same logical structure. But since no future event can be inferred from the past or present events, and since a proposition can imply only its own constituent propositions, a natural law, in its function as a possible form of the propositions of science, is an *a priori* rule in accordance with which we can make significant assertions about states of affairs that we have not experienced—or, as they have so often been characterized, natural laws are licences to make inferences where such inferences are not logically justifiable. We assume or postulate that the natural law—or, rather, any proposition formulated in accordance with the law—will be a true description of any fact having that particular logical structure. 'The process of induction is the process of assuming the *simplest* law that can be made to harmonize with our experience' (6.363). We bring the possible forms of the descriptions to the true descriptions of our experience and choose the simplest of these forms that we can find in those descriptions as our natural laws. The elementary propositions can be grouped together in various classes according to common forms and may thus be brought under a law, which is the model of the logical form of that class of proposition. The elementary propositions are the descriptions of the facts; the natural law says only how the facts are to be described.

Most accounts of the theory of scientific laws as logical models, if they come this far at all, stop at this point. The usual accounts draw an analogy between scientific laws and propositional functions, give a few illustrations or applications of this metaphor, and that is all. But the analogy should be extended further. Propositional functions not only contain symbols expressing a constant form, but contain symbols expressing variables as well. If scientific laws are to be conceived as being analogous to propositional functions, then the scientific objects that are mentioned in these laws must be conceived as being analogous to the variables of propositional functions. For the structure of a fact is nothing which can stand alone, apart from the form of the objects which combine to make that fact. As the *Tractatus* suggests, it is through the logical apparatus of natural laws that the laws themselves speak of the objects of the world (6.3431), and the 'logical apparatus' cannot be completely exhibited without some account of the variables of the functions. A theory of scientific objects is an essential ingredient in the theory of scientific laws, and such a theory can be worked out in terms of the treatment of formal properties and formal concepts found in the *Tractatus*. I shall attempt to outline such a theory in the next few paragraphs.

There seem to be three senses (not necessarily mutually exclusive) in which the *Tractatus* allows us to 'talk' about 'facts' and 'objects'. All these senses are, under the conditions laid down in the *Tractatus*, nonsensical rather than descriptive. Nonetheless, they do show or exhibit something about facts and objects. First, there is the elucidatory sense in which the *Tractatus* itself speaks of facts and objects. Secondly, there is the sense in which scientific laws, as analogous to propositional functions, say that true propositions, as descriptions of existential facts, may be grouped into classes according to their forms. Thus, for example, if there be a complete system of laws, this would say something about the structure of the facts so described by this system—i.e. it would at least say that the structure of the facts of the world stood to one another in internal relationships which allow them to be completely described by one general network of forms (which would be that of the system in question). This sense might also be expanded to include such activities as the devising and constructing of artificial language-systems. Thirdly, there is a sense in which formal concepts allow us to speak of 'facts'. It is in this sense that we may speak of scientific objects.

We can speak in a certain sense of formal properties of the objects and atomic facts, or of properties of the structure of facts, and in the same sense of formal relations and relations of structures. . . . An internal property of a fact we also call a feature of this fact. . . . A property is internal if it is unthinkable that its object does not possess it. . . . The existence of an internal property of a possible state of affairs is not expressed by a proposition, but it expresses itself in the proposition which

presents that state of affairs, by an internal property of this proposition.
... The existence of an internal relation between possible states of affairs
expresses itself in language by an internal relation between the proposition
presenting them (4.122–4.125).

Let *a*R*b* be any proposition, where *a* and *b* are names and **R** is the
way in which the names are combined. Every part of a proposition
which characterizes its sense (the possibility of the existence of the
atomic fact that it pictures) is called an expression, the '*a*', '**R**', and
'*b*' being arbitrary physical signs of the expressions. Expressions are
said to be that which propositions may have in common with one
another, and an expression is presented by a variable, the values of
which are the propositions which contain the expression. For example,
*x*R*b* determines the class of propositions which may contain the
expression for which the variable sign '*x*' stands: '*x* is darker than
pink' determines the class of propositions which may significantly
contain the names for which '*x*' stands. The values of a variable are
not determined either by a function or by a class, but rather the
variable is whatever values have the form of that expression—i.e.
have the formal property expressed therein. Also, the variable deals
only with the expressions, and has nothing to do with their meanings
—i.e. is a description of the symbols and not of what is symbolized.
In the above example, only 'colour names' would be the values of *x*,
and perhaps only 'colour names' of restricted kinds. Thus *x*R*y*
would exhibit the logical form of the class of propositions the variable
names of which are connected **R**-wise. Since objects have forms (i.e.
the possibility of their occurrence in facts), they also have formal
properties. The variable symbols in a propositional function are propositional variables standing for certain classes of names of objects
possessing a common form 'which may be conceived as a formal
property of these values' (4.1271). Objects have formal properties in
virtue of which they can combine with one another in order to make
facts—analogous to the sense in which physical atoms are said to
have valences. Wittgenstein gives space, time, and colour (colouredness) as examples of forms of objects (2.024). Since the ways in which
objects combine to make facts are nothing independent of the objects
themselves, and since the structure of the fact cannot be named (i.e.
is not itself an object) or described (i.e. is not itself a fact), internal
properties cannot be asserted by propositions and must be seen in the
expressions in which the names of the objects occur. The symbols
expressing objects are also said to express formal (internal) properties
of objects, an internal property being defined as any property of
which 'it is unthinkable that its object does not possess it' (4.123). 'If
things (objects) can occur in atomic facts, this possibility must already
lie in them' (2.0121). Given, for the sake of an example, that 'red' and

'pink' are objects, it is unthinkable that one does not stand in the internal relation of 'is darker than' to the other, just as it is unthinkable that '3' does not stand in the internal relation of 'is the successor of' to '2', and the symbols expressing these objects also express these internal properties and formal relations of objects, just as '2' and '3' also express internal properties and relations of numbers.

Formal concepts of classes of formal properties expressed by the symbols can now be formed, and although objects themselves cannot be ordered under formal concepts, their symbols will show that they (the objects) fall under formal concepts.

In the sense in which we speak of formal properties we can now speak also of formal concepts. . . . That anything falls under a formal concept as an object belonging to it, cannot be expressed by a proposition. But it is shown in the symbol for the object itself. (The name shows that it signifies an object, the numerical sign that it signifies a number, etc.) Formal concepts cannot, like proper concepts, be presented by a function. For their characteristics, the formal properties, are not expressed by the functions. The expression of a formal property is a feature of certain symbols. The sign that signifies the characteristics of a formal concept is, therefore, a characteristic feature of all symbols, whose meanings fall under the concept. The expression of the formal concept is therefore a propositional variable in which only this characteristic feature is constant (4.126).

Since the symbols expressing objects also express formal properties of objects, formal concepts of classes of formal properties expressed by symbols can be formed. For example, just as we can place any numerical sign under the concept of 'Number' and then assign it its place in the numerical series, because the numerical signs exhibit the formal property of being numbers and their internal relations to one another, so names exhibit formal properties in virtue of which they may be the values of a particular variable *and* in virtue of which formal concepts are formed. In the example, '*x* is darker than pink', only certain symbols—those presenting certain properties—'satisfy' the variable sign; thus '*x*', in this particular way, signifies a property —or a class of properties—and by doing so, 'shows' that the objects that its values name fall under this particular formal concept. Wittgenstein expressed this as follows:

The propositional variable signifies the formal concept, and its values signify the objects which fall under this concept. Every variable is the sign of a formal concept. For every variable presents a constant form, which all its values possess, and which can be conceived as a formal property of these values. So the variable name '*x*' is the proper sign of the pseudo-concept *object*. Wherever the word 'object' ('thing', 'entity', etc.) is rightly used, it is expressed in logical symbolism by the variable name. For example, in the proposition 'there are two objects which . . .', by (*Ex, y*) . . . '. Wherever

208

it is used otherwise, i.e. as a proper concept word, there arise senseless pseudo-propositions. So one cannot, e.g. say 'There are objects' as one says 'There are books'. . . . The same holds of the words 'Complex', 'Fact', 'Function', 'Number', etc. They all signify formal concepts and are presented in logical symbolism by variables, not by functions or classes (as Frege and Russell thought). . . . The formal concept is already given with an object, which falls under it (4.127–4.12721).

Thus, although objects themselves cannot be ordered by formal concepts and propositions cannot assert that such and such objects fall under a particular formal concept, their symbols will show that the objects may fall under certain formal concepts, in the same way that a numerical sign shows, as a feature of itself, that what it signifies will fall under the formal concept of 'Number'. We can in this sense talk of 'objects' ('number', 'fact', etc.) and of formal properties of objects. For we can take some aspect or property expressed by a class of names, form a concept of it and call it by a 'pseudo-name'. Although we are not actually saying anything about the world (since we are only describing the symbolic scaffolding and not what is symbolized), we are in a sense *showing* something about it—i.e. that its components are characterized by such and such features. It is easily seen from this that it makes no sense to speak of the existence or nonexistence of formal concepts.

The formal concepts of 'fact' and 'object' correspond analogically to the variables of the propositional functions which correspond to the scientific laws. Facts and objects may be brought into unity under formal concepts expressing some characteristic features of them. Most of the concepts used in the above 'elucidation' of concepts are formal concepts, and this is one of the chief activities of philosophy. To make propositions about the world—to determine how the world is to be described by determining which set or collection of functions is to serve as laws—is the activity of science. Thus, 'In the proposition a state of affairs is, as it were, put together for the sake of experiment' (4.031). To describe the world correctly, and to determine how this is best done, is the function of the scientist, not the philosopher. To the philosopher is left the task of elucidating the meanings of the concepts used in the description of facts and the elucidating of the sense of propositions by means of showing their syntactical relations to one another. Thus, two main tasks of philosophy are concerned with what subsequent analysts have called formation and transformation rules of language, particularly of the language of science.

Returning to scientific objects, if the description of facts may be brought into unity by scientific laws, and if scientific laws may be conceived as being analogous to propositional functions, the objects which combine to make facts may be brought into unity under formal concepts expressing some characteristic features of objects, and scientific objects may be conceived as being functionally analogous to the variables of propositional functions. If a natural law is to function as a schematic model in accordance with which propositions descriptive of facts can be formulated, then it is inadequate and misleading to say it is nothing more than a mere empty schema of the structure of the states of affairs that the propositions formulated in accordance with the schema picture. For the structure of a fact is nothing over and above the forms of the objects which combine to make that fact, and the forms of objects are to be conceived as formal properties of objects. Since the formal concept is expressed by the variable in the function, and since the formal concept is a class of formal properties, the variables in the schemata which are the laws of nature will be indirect expressions of the formal properties possessed by objects by means of which those objects can combine with one another. That the objects do so combine with one another as given in the schemata which are the laws of science is an empirical, and therefore contingent, matter. But in order to unify our true propositions by means of their logical forms into such schemata, it is necessary to order objects by means of their formal properties as signified by their expressions falling under formal concepts. A schema includes symbols for both the logical form of the propositions and the values which constitute the variables. It makes no sense at all to speak of propositional functions as bare empty schemata without explicit consideration of the variable. This is one reason why the *Tractatus* insists that it is through the *whole* logical apparatus of the natural laws that the laws speak of the objects of the world. For the objects are what the names that are the values of the variables stand for, and it is these symbols which have the formal properties that the variable signs express. Consequently, in assuming the simplest law that can be made to harmonize with our experience, we are at the same time assuming the simplest formal concepts that can be made to harmonize with the objects as ordering the names which can appear in the significant propositions formulated in accordance with the scientific law. If a scientific law is a structural model in accordance with which the particular propositions may be formulated, then the scientific objects about which such laws seemingly speak are those parts of such models (or, perhaps, component 'submodels') in accordance with which the values of the variables therein are limited to a particular class of names which the propositions so formulated can meaningfully contain. The natural law puts the facts—or rather, the descriptions of the facts— into the logical form by bringing the various descriptions of the facts into a unified form, but in order to do this it must in some sense determine the formal properties that the objects must possess in order that the propositions formulated in accordance with the law can describe these facts. As Copi suggests,[1] if a fact is an entity that can be described, then the objects that combine to make that fact must possess the formal property of being capable of combining in that particular way. And just as the structure of an atomic fact is the way in which the objects are combined, so the logical form of the schematic model is the way in which its scientific objects are combined. For example, the form of a law that 'says' that the observed motions of observed bodies traversing observed paths are to be described more accurately in terms of the unobserved motions of unobserved particles traversing unobserved paths will be determined by the formal properties of the particles used. Change the formal properties of the particles used in the description of the events and a change in the law will result. But in whatever way the particle be conceived, the 'particle' itself remains a conceptual model—a formal concept—of a group of properties possessed by that class of entities which is ordinarily called 'material' bodies, and the natural law holds only for those entities that possess those properties. An electron, for example, may be conceived as a model for all those entities, actual and possible, that possess a certain set of field properties, and whenever the name 'electron' occurs in a scientific law, propositions formulated in accordance with that law will be descriptive only of a corresponding set of facts (or set of material properties of facts, depending upon the way in which material properties are conceived), i.e. those facts which are the results of the interaction of the objects that possess the particular set of properties in question. And in the same way as scientific laws, scientific objects have the dual character of being logically constructed models and of being indirect expressions of properties of the objects of the world.

If the above represents an adequate outline of the foundations of the theory of scientific laws and scientific objects as logically constructed models, then it should throw some light upon the difficulties that Alexander finds with Hutten's version of the theory. Alexander's critical comments are restricted to Hutten's conclusions concerning the relations between theories, laws, and hypotheses, since the confusions that he notes result from the ambiguities of these relationships.

Alexander begins by noting a confusion in saying that a theory is at once a description of experiments and a formal calculus or language system. He notes that if a language system is *merely* 'a collection of syntactic and semantic rules', then it cannot be said to describe anything, rules being prescriptive rather than descriptive.[2] Yet, he continues, if a language system does in some sense describe experiments, then Hutten has confused the picture by saying that hypotheses—the quite specific existential statements, or empirical propositions—are

---

[1] Copi, op. cit., 163 [p. 184].   [2] Alexander, op. cit., 556.

both 'part of', or 'are contained within', the theory and are also 'derivable from' the theory. Since Hutten explicitly asserts that a theory consists of two parts—a formal calculus which deals with the purely formal properties of symbols and expressions, and a system of semantic rules which provides the empirical interpretation of the formal calculus—he is to be understood as clearly maintaining that a language system is not *merely* a collection of rules, but contains within its framework the descriptive hypotheses that can be formulated in accordance with these rules. He explicitly asserts that a purely formal calculus contains no assertions about experience, and that is why the semantic rules are necessary for its interpretation in terms of experience. But he also asserts that it is the scientific laws, rather than the theory, which function as the semantic rules, and that the hypotheses are derived from these laws. The confusion becomes all the more pronounced when Hutten speaks of hypotheses as being derived from a theory and as being sentences within a theory, without explaining just how this is to be conceived, or is even possible. Alexander seems to think that the source of the confusion lies in (i) the ambiguity of the expressions, 'contained within' and 'part of', as used in this context, and (ii) the fact that scientific laws may also function as premisses in a theory. In one sense, Alexander points out, any language system contains, as a part of that language system, all the statements that can be formed according to its rules. He calls this the 'weak' sense of specific hypotheses being contained by a language system. But Alexander maintains that, 'just because it contains them *all* it cannot say any one thing rather than another, which a description must do'.[1] According to him, the correct, or 'strong' sense in which a language system may be said to be descriptive of experience is the sense in which its descriptive statements are correct descriptions of certain *actual* states of affairs. As for himself, he thinks 'that it is normal to regard scientific theories as containing hypotheses in the strong sense and therefore correct to regard them as descriptive' and that it is incorrect to say that an hypothesis is derived from a theory 'but correct to say that it was derived from some of the higher-level statements of the theory'.[2] Thus, for Alexander, a theory, if it is descriptive at all, must be descriptive only of quite specific states of affairs that have happened or will happen, and any description of possible states of affairs that will not also be actualized must not be included in the scope of the theory. I do not think that Alexander has completely removed the confusion by distinguishing between these two senses in which a theory may be said to be descriptive or to contain descriptive statements. It would be closer to the truth to explain Hutten's comments concerning hypotheses as being both derived

[1] Alexander, op. cit., 556.   [2] Ibid., 557.

from and contained within a theory as unfortunate and inaccurate ways of expressing his main thesis regarding this matter. Alexander also suggests that this might be the case.

Hutten argues that a theory gives order to the symbols and expressions that we use to describe our experience and that it does this by showing the logical characteristics and interrelatedness of these symbols.[1] Theories are constructed by us and are attempts to systematize our descriptions of actual and possible experience. We might say that, for Hutten, theory construction begins with the descriptions of past experiences which have already been unified to some extent into the various unrelated scientific laws, and attempts to discover, in the possible logical relationships between these laws, a single system in terms of which all actual and possible states of affairs may be described. The scientific laws thus preserve the links that the theory has with the factual world in their function as models for the formulation of hypotheses (the descriptive statements). From this point of view, a theory is a system of laws from which the specific descriptions of the world may be derived or formulated. In so far as a law contains all the propositions that may be derived from it, a theory may be said to contain (in Alexander's weak sense) the specific hypotheses, and in so far as a theory *is* a system of laws, it is in this sense a general description of the world. But neither theories nor laws can be expected to give us the correct specific descriptions of a particular state of affairs at a given time. The conception of science as an instrument for the calculation of any and every event of this world died with the rigidly deterministic doctrine of scientific materialism. To expect a theory to contain (in the strong sense) the correct description of yesterday's weather at a given location would be like expecting a theological doctrine concerning the creation of individual souls to give the names and dates of each individual soul that ever was and ever will be created. As the *Tractatus* notes, a theory, or a law, is always quite general, there never being any mention of particular entities or particular events (6.3432). All that a law states is that if a given entity or event has such and such characteristics, then its description will take the form of that particular law. In other words, the theory or law only gives us directions concerning the form in which to describe the particular states of affairs of the world, and does not tell us that only such and such states of affairs can possibly occur. To quote the *Tractatus* again, 'At the basis of the whole modern view of the world lies the illusion that the so-called laws of nature are the explanations of natural phenomena' (6.371).

From the point of view of being a formal system alone, a theory asserts nothing about the world and therefore is not descriptive (in

[1] Hutten, op. cit., 32-3.

Alexander's strong sense). From this point of view, a theory is *merely* an uninterpreted symbolic system constructed according to certain formation and transformation rules, and the laws are in this sense analytic, functioning either as syntactical rules or as premises in the deduction of further symbolic expressions. To use Wittgenstein's example, the unapplied (or uninterpreted) mesh network is purely a geometrical design, and is not a picture of the white surface with the irregular black spots. Even after the network has been applied to the white surface, it does not assert anything about the surface.

Although the spots in our picture are geometrical figures, geometry can obviously say nothing about their actual form and position. But the network is *purely* geometrical, and all its properties can be given *a priori* (6.35).

The specific propositions that do describe the spots on the surface will have certain definite formal characteristics in virtue of which they may be brought together under specific laws—laws that specify that the spots may be 'described' by a particular kind of mesh of a definite fineness—and these laws may be further unified according to some formal characteristics that they have in common into a single plan (the mesh *network*, or theory). The laws become part of a single symbolic system and thus function both as syntactical rules or as premises *in the symbolic system* and as semantic rules for the formation of the specific propositions needed to describe the facts of the world. Thus, although in one sense it is true that specific propositions are put together for the sake of experiment, Alexander is correct in maintaining that it is misleading to say that they are derived from a theory, but not misleading if we say that they are derived 'from some of the higher-level statements of the theory'. Consequently, Hutten's specific hypotheses are contained within the theory only in Alexander's weak sense and can only improperly be said to be derived from the theory. The more accurate account is that the hypotheses are derived from the natural laws and are contained within the theory only in the weak sense since the theory itself does not determine the truth or falsity of the specific hypotheses that can be formed according to its laws.

The difficulty with Alexander's critical remarks regarding the sense in which a scientific theory may be said to be descriptive (or to contain descriptive statements) lies in his puzzling conception of what is required in order that a specific hypothesis (a proposition descriptive of a specific state of affairs) be descriptive and yet be 'contained within' the theory. His distinction between the weak and the strong senses of 'contained within' is essentially no more than the distinction between the logical possibility of a particular proposition being true and its actually being true. Any proposition that can be formed according to the rules of a language is contained within that language in the weak sense, but only those propositions that are formed according to the rules *and* are found to be a part of the description of actual states of affairs are said to be contained within that language in the strong sense. But, according to Alexander, a scientific theory must contain the specific hypotheses in the latter sense before it can properly be said to be descriptive. The difficulty of this requirement may be exhibited in the following manner. First, in demanding that scientific theories contain specific hypotheses in the strong sense, Alexander is demanding that theories be both generally and specifically descriptive at the same time. As he says, to be a specific description requires saying one thing rather than another about a specific state of affairs—e.g. 'It rained today', rather than 'It was a dry day today'. If a scientific theory be conceived as containing specific hypotheses in the strong sense, then the theory will—in part, at least—be descriptive of specific states of affairs. But the model theory demands that scientific theories and laws always be general descriptions, and to be a general description requires only that specific descriptions be generalized. Consequently, if scientific theories be conceived as general descriptions, they are descriptive only of the specific descriptions (of a certain logical form), and not descriptive of states of affairs. It follows that if a scientific theory be conceived as a general description, then it cannot also be a specific description as Alexander demands. But his requirement that scientific theories can in some sense 'say' certain things and do not say certain other things about, for example, the ways in which bodies move' can be retained if we do not also demand that they make statements about specific bodies and their specific motions. A scientific theory can 'say' that the descriptions of moving bodies may be better organized and unified in terms of this particular set of characteristic properties rather than in terms of that particular set of characteristic properties. In the case of different systems of science 'describing' the same states of affairs, each system only determines how the facts are to be described, and does not determine which specific descriptions will be true and which false, come what may. For the same 'true' descriptions of the observed astronomical 'facts' may be derived from both the Copernican and the Ptolemaic theories. The truth-values of the particular descriptive propositions can only be determined by a comparison with the facts of the world, and not by the fact that they can be derived from the theory. The theory is a way of *ordering* or *unifying* knowledge of facts, and is not a way of *determining* new knowledge of facts. According to Alexander's demand, however, a scientific theory should be able to perform both these functions, since the theory is not descriptive unless the descriptive statements derived from it are correct descriptions of actual states of affairs. If, in order for a scientific theory to be descriptive, it must contain the correct descriptions of actual states of affairs, then, in so far as it contains propositions asserting merely possible states of affairs, it cannot be said to be descriptive. According to Alexander, these latter propositions are not to be considered as part of the theory (in the strong sense). In short, for Alexander, a scientific theory, like Locke's particular idea of an abstract general triangle, should be at once general and specific.

It would seem that Alexander's critical comments add up to a possible objection to the entire conception of scientific theories and laws as being descriptive only in a general sense, on the grounds that scientific theories should give us specific descriptions—or even explanations—of the specific facts and events of the external world. But the question as to whether science does, or even should, perform such a function lies outside the intended scope of this paper. My only purpose has been to defend the particular theory under consideration against certain charges of being internally inconsistent.

Professor Stenius on the 'Tractatus'[1]

JUDITH JARVIS THOMSON

THE literature on the *Tractatus* is beginning to resemble the literature on the real meaning of the White Whale. Professor Stenius has contributed a book[2] which seems to me in some respects quite useful, in others misleading.

One of the central doctrines of the *Tractatus* is the picture theory of language, and Professor Stenius is concerned to present it clearly—while he does not everywhere agree with what he takes to be Wittgenstein's views on the matter, he believes that the picture theory can nonetheless be given a clear and consistent sense and that it is worth while examining it, not merely out of a purely historical interest, but more with a view to gaining an insight into the nature of language.

Professor Stenius introduces the concept of a picture in Chapter VI, but there is some important (and useful) preliminary material in Chapter IV, which is entitled "Logical Space". *Tractatus* 2.061 is: "Atomic facts are independent of each other", and 2.062 reads: "From the existence or non-existence of an atomic fact we cannot infer the existence or non-existence of another"; the question arises, what sorts of sentences can be elementary sentences[3] in view of the fact that for so many of the predicates of our language (e.g. "red", "long") there exists another predicate (e.g. "blue", "short") which is not the negation of the first, but which is nevertheless incompatible with it? By means of a simple artificial example, Professor Stenius introduces a concept "dimension", which he says can be generalized

[1] From *The Journal of Philosophy*, vol. 58, no. 20, September, 1961, pp. 584–96. Reprinted by permission of the editor and the author.

[2] *Wittgenstein's Tractatus; A Critical Exposition of Its Main Lines of Thought*, Erik Stenius. Ithaca, N.Y.: Cornell Univ. Press, 1960, xi, 241 pp.

[3] I use "sentence" rather than "proposition" throughout, following Professor Stenius. Numbers with decimal places refer to passages in the *Tractatus*.

as follows: "A world has as many dimensions as it has mutually independent components of description" (p. 40). The expression "component of description" is not defined, but what is meant may be put as follows. To say that a world has *n* dimensions is to say that of all the sentences true of that world, there is a set of at most *n* members $p_1 \ldots p_n$ such that no p_i is implied by any subset of the remaining members; if a sentence q_i is incompatible with p_i and is not incompatible with any subset of the members of the set other than p_i, then q_i reports a possible fact that is in the same dimension as the fact reported by p_i. Every conjunction of sentences that contains a description of one fact from each dimension determines, is a complete description of, a possible world; each of these possible worlds is a point in "logical space"—an *n*-dimensional logical space if the world has *n* dimensions. Now clearly facts, or states of affairs, of different dimensions are independent of one another, but possible facts of the same dimension are not. Any dimension in which there are only two possible facts is called a two-valued dimension, and any dimension in which there are more than two possible facts is called a many-valued dimension. As we said, most of the predicates of our language (e.g. "red") have contraries as well as contradictories in the language, and hence, for them, "That is *P*" will describe a fact that is in a many-valued dimension. A world all of whose dimensions are two-valued is said to fit into a "yes-and-no" space—i.e. if *P* is a predicate that has no contrary, but only a contradictory, say *Q*, then we can call one, say *P*, the yes-value for the dimension and the other, *Q*, the no-value for the dimension. Wittgenstein, then, is interpreted to be saying in the *Tractatus* that the logical space into which our world fits is a yes-and-no space: all the sentences of our language that have contraries in the language must be regarded as analysable into truth-functions of sentences that have only contradictories. Only the latter can be elementary sentences—and in fact, only the positive among them (e.g. "*x* is *P*" as opposed to "*x* is *Q*", which in a two-valued dimension means the same as "It is not the case that *x* is *P*"), in accordance with *Tractatus* 2, 2.06, and 4.211. Such sentences report atomic facts. And atomic facts are now clearly independent of one another.

Careful and clear interpretations are also given in Chapter IV of 1.11 to 1.13, and of 3.4 ("The sentence determines a position in logical space . . .") to 3.42.

So much seems quite correct as an interpretation of Wittgenstein's intentions with regard to elementary sentences and atomic facts. What is not made at all clear until much later is just why Wittgenstein should have developed such notions in the first place. *Why* atomic facts? In the concluding section of Chapter IV, certain passages from

218

the *Tractatus* are cited which suggest that Wittgenstein approved of what Professor Stenius calls "Hume's theses" to the effect that there is no necessary connection between states of affairs at one time and states of affairs at another, and this is said to be "closely connected with his [Wittgenstein's] conception of the world as constructed of mutually independent atomic states of affairs". But Hume, of course, had no such conception of the world as has been sketched above. Nor do we find any other clue to its sources in Chapters I to III. Chapter II is an attempt at an interpretation of *Tractatus* 1.1 ("The world is the totality of facts, not of things"), which appears to me entirely unsuccessful, even incoherent—e.g. the remarks of page 23 ("Since what we experience is always only *about* a thing and never the thing in itself, . . .") and the perceptual analogy of section 4 ("To sum up: The concept of a *field of perception* can be regarded as a concept within the category of *facts*. To organize it means that the field of perception *breaks up* into *simpler* facts. The particular objects are perceived because this breaking-up is combined with a *structuring* of the simpler facts into *things* and *predicates* of things . . ."). And Chapter III contains only a set of terminological distinctions ("Sachverhalt", "Tatsache", "Sachlage"). In Chapter VI (p. 107) and more fully in Chapter X (pp. 197 ff.) *one* route to this world picture is described, which Professor Stenius believes may not have been the only route, but which he believes contributed to a considerable degree. This route is the picture theory of language.

And I believe it is a relevant and important criticism to make of a book on the *Tractatus* that it first spells out the various doctrines, leaving the reader to wait for their sources later in the text. For the chief difficulty one faces in studying the *Tractatus* is just this question, what is the form of the argument? What does Wittgenstein take to be supporting what? One cannot see it rightly if one goes proposition by proposition, section by section, interpreting as one goes. Its elaborate numbering system leads the beginner to expect the ordering of a proof in mathematics: from the more to the less obvious. And this is of course just what we do not find in the *Tractatus*, which opens with some of the most obscure remarks in all of philosophy.

Chapter V is concerned with the concept "substance" in the *Tractatus* and contains some useful remarks on logical form, but for present purposes the important point made here is that Wittgenstein means by "objects" not only simple things but also properties (relational and nonrelational). This seems to me to be a mistake, but rather than cite passages in the *Tractatus* to make the point that it is,[1]

---

[1] Professor Irving M. Copi does so in "Objects, Properties, and Relations in the *Tractatus*", *Mind*, April, 1958 [pp. 167 ff.]. (Professor Copi also makes the point in this article that Wittgenstein did not regard truth-functions of elementary sentences as

I shall try to show why Wittgenstein cannot have meant this on pain of making the picture theory of language (the theory of pictures in general) incoherent.

"An articulate field *F* is called a picture (true or false) of the articulate field *G* if there is a key of interpretation (*C*) according to which the elements of *F* are considered to stand for the elements of *G*. The picture *F* is said to be true or false according as it is an isomorphic picture of *G* in respect of (*C*) or not" (Chapter VI, p. 96). Let us try this out. How might $a \to b$ be seen as picturing the fact that Smith hates Jones? For example, consider the letters "*a*" and "*b*" to stand for Smith and Jones respectively, and the arrow for— for what? the relation "hates"? But then the picture is not a fact, an articulate field; it is merely a collection of three objects. As Professor Stenius rightly insists (pp. 91 ff. and pp. 130 ff.) the arrow must not be taken to stand for a relation; it is rather that the relation in which "*a*" stands to "*b*"—namely "being at the tail end of an arrow which points to" (let us call this the "arrow-relation")—stands for the relation "hates". The arrow is not an element of the picture; it is what Professor Stenius calls a "characteristic of a predicate" (by "predicate" Professor Stenius means throughout not a verbal expression but a property, relational or nonrelational). The elements of the picture are the letters "*a*" and "*b*" and the arrow-relation; these stand for the objects Smith, Jones, and the relation "hates", respectively.

But this is very queer indeed.[1] Is the relational *property* "being at the tail end of . . ." an element of this picture? Though it is certainly exemplified in it, possessed by the objects "*a*" and "*b*". Well, why not say: in that this relation is here exemplified, we shall call it an element? The conclusive answer appears to me to be this. Suppose it is said that this, ⚡, is to be seen as picturing (from the rear) Smith standing to the left of Jones; the figures are considered to stand for Smith and Jones, and the relation "being to the left of" in the picture is considered to stand for the relation "being to the left

---

[1] But we cannot object, "And then what relates the elements?", for Professor Stenius has an answer: the elements are of different logical form, and nothing further is needed to relate them.

---

pictures. This will be discussed below.) Professor Stenius mentions this article in a footnote on page 137, but pronounces it a misinterpretation. It is of interest to note that both Professor Stenius and Professor Copi take the same passage in the *Philosophical Investigations* (#46) in which Wittgenstein refers to the "objects" of the *Tractatus*, to support their own views about the nature of "objects". Which it would do if all we were concerned with was the question, "What are the ultimate elements of the world?", because, as Wittgenstein points out in *Investigations* #48, it doesn't matter which we say. But we are not concerned here with this question, but rather with the question, "What can the ultimate elements be if a sentence is a picture of a fact?" And here it does matter which we say.

of" in the field pictured. But how is this? How do I take this relation as standing for itself? We should have to say that the picture and the fact pictured literally share an element (the relation "being to the left of")—and then what does the picturing or representing of what? Suppose, for example, I were to paint a picture of Smith's body, leaving a hole in the canvas where the head should be, and suppose I were to get Smith to put his head through the hole—and now call what is there a picture of Smith.

Moreover, things sound worse (though the point is the same) when we turn to sentences and consider Professor Stenius's struggles with 4.221 ("It is obvious that in the analysis of sentences we must come to elementary sentences which consist of names in immediate connection . . .", Stenius, p. 125) and 3.22 ("In the sentence the name deputizes for the thing", Stenius, p. 135). On page 136 we find Professor Stenius allowing that one relation (e.g. that which the word "Smith" has to the word "Jones" in the sentence "Smith is to the left of Jones") is the name of another (that of being to the left of). Even apart from the extreme peculiarity of regarding a relation as a name, this will rule out the possibility of sentences in which the relation between the names (of things) is the same as the relation between the things themselves—e.g. a sentence such as "ab", which is intended to say that Smith is to the left of Jones. But this would be an entirely arbitrary restriction. And in any event it seems directly opposed to Wittgenstein's own intentions—cf., for example, 3.1431 and 4.0311. (Professor Stenius cites these passages himself, but suggests that Wittgenstein sometimes misinterpreted Wittgenstein's picture theory.)

If properties, relational and nonrelational, are *not* regarded as elements of the picture and the fact pictured, then the fact that the relation between "a" and "b" in "ab" is the same as the relation Smith is being said to have to Jones constitutes no difficulty. We can say: that "a" is to the left of "b" says that Smith is to the left of Jones. (Cf. 3.1432.)

Nevertheless it is not for no reason that Professor Stenius so interprets "objects"—i.e. even apart from such textual evidence as he cites and from his account of facts in Chapter II. It seems to me that there are two reasons. First, if one takes "objects" as restricted to objects, it follows that elementary sentences and the facts they picture must be relational: there can be none of the sort "a is red", for sentences of the form "x is P" contain only one name of an object, and "An atomic fact is a combination of objects (entities, things)" (2.01). Well, one might ask, why not? Wittgenstein did, after all, explicitly tell us that sentences such as "a is red" are non-elementary (6.3751). The answer seems to be this: the picture theory becomes useless as an account of how an ordinary language has meaning, for we do not know what the analysis of such sentences could be. And Professor Stenius thinks to find something enlightening about language in the picture theory.

Second, if we accept Professor Stenius's interpretation, we can avoid a certain difficult problem. According to Professor Stenius, we see "Smith is to the left of Jones" (*S*) as a picture in that we are considering the elements "Smith", "Jones", and the relation between them to stand for Smith, Jones, and the relation "being to the left of"; one who is given this key of interpretation can then understand *S* as a picture of the fact that Smith is to the left of Jones. But if the relation between the words "Smith" and "Jones" in *S* is not element of *S*, and if I am thus not told what *it* stands for, am told only what the elements "Smith" and "Jones" stand for, how is it that I know (if I do) that the fact that these words stand in the relation they have to each other in *S* says that Smith is to the left of Jones? Perhaps there could be a language in which in every sentence the relation between the words is exactly that which is being ascribed to the objects named by the words, and perhaps it is some such language that Wittgenstein has in mind in the *Tractatus*; but even so the student of such a language would have to learn in some way that this was in general true of that language, and Wittgenstein does not tell us how this piece of information is to be understood. Miss G. E. M. Anscombe (*An Introduction to Wittgenstein's Tractatus*, Chapter 6) gives a very helpful account of *Tractatus* 5.542 ("But it is clear that 'A believes that *p*', 'A thinks *p*', 'A says *p*', are of the form ' "*p*" says *p*' . . .") in which she makes out that " '*p*' says that *p*" is a meaningful sentence in the system of the *Tractatus*, but it is not at all clear how such a sentence could be regarded as a picture or as a compound of sentences that are pictures. Obviously it cannot be that a relation (what? "says that"?) is being ascribed to the sentence-picture and the fact in the sentence " '*p*' says that *p*"—and indeed, it is not things, but facts to which such a supposed relation would have to be ascribed ("The picture is a fact", 2.14), and facts cannot be named (3.144).

But despite this, as we said above, it will not do to interpret "objects" so as to include properties as well as objects—on pain of making the picture theory incoherent. And this means that sentences such as "*a* is red" cannot be regarded as pictures—directly, that is, for they may be said indirectly to be pictures in that they are analysable into relational sentences which are themselves pictures.

In Chapter VIII Professor Stenius tries to make out that truth-functional compounds may also be regarded as pictures.[1] In sum,

---

[1] Once again, I do not here cite passages from the *Tractatus* that suggest that this is a mistake—for this, cf. Copi, op. cit. I try to show that the account given will not do, and this with only a minor concern for the question whether or not it is Wittgenstein's.

the account is as follows. Consider the compound sentence, "Alan loves Brian and Brian loves Alan"; this cannot be regarded as a picture in the sense of isomorphic representation, for the elements "Alan" and "Brian" of the sentence do not stand in a one-one correspondence with the objects they name—there are two "Alan"s to one Alan, and two "Brian"s to one Brian. Nevertheless rules can be given (p. 149) in accordance with which the sentence can be transformed into a picture—e.g. replace the tokens of the type "Alan" with one object, say "a", and the tokens of the type "Brian" with one object, say "b", and the relation "being to the left of the squiggle 'loves' to the left of" which holds between "Alan" and "Brian" and between "Brian" and "Alan" by the arrow-relation, and the result, which is a picture, is: $a \rightleftarrows b$.

But how does it come out that this is a picture of the fact that Alan loves Brian *and* Brian loves Alan? True, in the picture, "a" has the arrow-relation to "b" *and* "b" has it to "a", but how does it come out that the fact that both these relations hold between "a" and "b" says that both Alan loves Brian and Brian loves Alan?

I choose this example because it (mistakenly) seems most favourable for Professor Stenius's account, for things seem to get worse when we turn to the wedge and the horseshoe. How is "Alan loves Brian or Brian loves Alan" to be transformed into a picture? Of course alternations can be translated into conjunctions, but what is to be done with negation, then? Professor Stenius suggests that "It is not the case that Alan loves Brian" is to be transformed into a picture as follows: $a \quad b$. That is, the absence of the arrow-relation between "a" and "b" is to represent this fact. (Thus truth-functional contradictions clearly cannot be transformed into pictures.) But for one thing, this is not a picture at all for Wittgenstein, for whom a picture is a set of objects standing in a certain relation to each other. And Wittgenstein apart, it is quite absurd; because I do not show in my drawing of Alan and Brian every relation that I believe they have to each other, it by no means follows that I am representing them as *not* having these relations. If I want to represent the fact that Alan is not giving an apple to Brian, I do not draw Alan not giving an apple to Brian (what on earth should I draw if I were to try to draw this?); it seems rather that I draw Alan giving an apple to Brian and say that this is *not* the case. And this in fact seems to be Wittgenstein's own view of the matter.

In fact there is no way of regarding a compound sentence as a picture or transforming one into a picture. For the connectives cannot appear *in* the picture, either as deputizing elements (". . . My fundamental thought is that the 'logical constants' do not represent", 4.0312) or as the arrow in "$a \rightarrow b$" ("That $\lor$, $\supset$, etc., are not relations in the sense of right and left, etc., is obvious", 5.42). At best it can be the bases of the truth-functional compounds that are pictures. If the compounds were pictures they would be things whose sense you could understand independently, in which case the truth-functional calculus would be a sort of natural science of facts. Whereas it is not; and what we should say (according to Wittgenstein) is that the sense of a compound is a mere function of the sense of its bases (5.2341).

To return to the question, what is the source of the world-view sketched above: Professor Stenius's account is, in brief, as follows. (Cf. Chapter X, pp. 199, 200. I have altered the example used there because if "objects" are restricted to objects, then, as we said, "*a* is red" cannot be regarded as a picture.) The syntactical properties "preceding the expression 'is to the left of' which precedes" and "preceding the expression 'is to the right of' which precedes" are logically independent: it is possible to write "*a* is to the left of *b* and *a* is to the right of *b*". But if this is interpreted in the usual way, what it says could not be the case. But it looks as if it could be transformed into a picture. Hence it must be possible to analyse, translate "it into a sentence which shows that it *cannot* be transformed into a picture, i.e. a translation of it into a contradiction in the truth-functional sense". And this must be so also for every sentence "*p·q*" in which "*p*" and "*q*" are incompatible. Hence if "*p*" and "*q*" are contraries, they are not elementary sentences. And atomic facts are all independent of each other.

Professor Stenius brings out the mistake in this argument (cf. p. 201), thus stressing the independence of the (or at any rate *a*) picture theory and logical atomism. But what concerns us here is rather only this, the fact that, valid or not, it cannot have been Wittgenstein's argument. For it cannot be supposed that Wittgenstein regarded truth-functional compounds either as, or as transformable into, pictures.

It has often been said that Wittgenstein drew atomism somehow from the picture theory, but it has never in fact been successfully made out how he could have thought to do so. In fact I think we should regard them as having been related, in his mind, only in the following way. (1) All sentences must be analysable into truth-functions of independent elementary sentences if (2) the truth-functional calculus is to constitute a conclusive formal criterion for the distinction between sense and nonsense. Which it does. (3) The elementary sentences are little pictures of states of affairs. (4) And so thoughts are all pictures of states of affairs or functions of pictures of states of affairs; the rest is nonsense. 3 does not imply or even suggest 1, much less 2; it is rather like this, that 1, 2, and 3 together imply 4. It is 4 that he himself said was of prime importance to him, and it is only in 4 that the doctrines come together.

In Chapter IX, Professor Stenius has some interesting things to say about modality (the picture theory is to apply only to the phrastic, in Hare's terminology, and useful remarks are made about the modal neustic). Chapter X contains much that is very good indeed. It is primarily concerned with the similarity between the internal (formal) structure of language and the internal (formal) structure of Reality, and that the argument turns on the interpretation of the picture theory discussed above by no means detracts from its interest. An interpretation is given of what can be shown but not said, and among other things, the point is made that pseudo (non-depicting) statements ascribing formal properties are not translatable into respectable (depicting) statements about language. In Chapter XI a parallel is drawn between Wittgenstein and Kant.

* * *

In the end, the question always arises: was the trip worth while? From a historical point of view, a careful, detailed discussion of the *Tractatus* is certainly worth while in view of the obscurity of the work itself and the influence it had. But it seems to me that it has yet to be shown that a careful study of the *Tractatus* is of value from the point of view of one who is in search of a better understanding of the nature of language.

For a long time people ignored the *Tractatus*. After all, the *Tractatus* allows for only descriptive statements in the indicative mood, and, as Wittgenstein reminded us in the *Investigations*, there are countless many other uses of language—and besides, what is to be gained by doing analysis? But now people are studying the *Tractatus* again; they say we can separate out the good from the bad in it. Miss Anscombe (op. cit., p. 78) tells us that "Wittgenstein used to say [in his later years] that the *Tractatus* was not *all* wrong: it was not like a bag of junk professing to be a clock, but a clock that did not tell you the right time", and Professor Stenius tells us that there is nothing in the *Investigations* to suggest that Wittgenstein *rejected* the picture theory; "his remarks on the subject seem only to emphasize that the picture theory does not *explain* the essence of language to nearly so great an extent as he had believed in the *Tractatus*" (Stenius, p. 158).

But it seems to me that, if we consider only its most famous central doctrines, the *Tractatus* will harm rather than help us—and this even if we expect enlightenment with regard only to descriptive language in the indicative. For it encourages in general a too narrowly restricted conception of the nature of logical relations. Miss Anscombe (op. cit.) mentions the unfortunate remarks in the *Tractatus* about the will, which are consequences of this narrow conception of logical relations. Modality in general has no room in the *Tractatus*. And we can mention another unfortunate consequence, one which is, I think, also worth mentioning for its own sake.

As we all know by now, there are logical impossibilities that cannot be shown to be logical contradictions within formal logic— e.g. "*x* is red and blue", "*x* is to the left of *y* and *y* is to the left of *x*". We are told: ignore this; let us go along with Wittgenstein in supposing that such sentences are therefore analysable into truth-functional contradictions (or at any rate formal contradictions), with a view to understanding his main intention. But to ignore this is to ignore an important feature of language, which can be (very summarily) brought out as follows. S: For every pair of non-self-contradictory sentences "*x* is P_1" and "*x* is P_2" that are incompatible with each other, there is a third sentence "*x* is not Q" that is non-self-contradictory and is incompatible with both "*x* is P_1" and "*x* is P_2"— with only one class of exceptions. (a) This is obviously true if "*x* is P_1" (e.g. "*x* is red") and "*x* is P_2" (e.g. "*x* is blue") are mere contraries as opposed to contradictories. ("*x* is not not-yellow" is incompatible with both.) (b) But suppose that "*x* is P_1" and "*x* is P_2" are what certainly appear to be contradictories: i.e. suppose "P_2" is "not-P_1". Consider, for example, the pair "*x* is red", and "*x* is not red". But would one say of a sound or thought that it is not red? Of course it would not be incorrect to say this—for sounds and thoughts are indeed not red—but it would be misleading: the normal use of "It isn't red" is such as to imply that the thing is of some other colour, blue, green, purple, . . . If a man said of a thought he had just had that it was red, we should of course take him to be talking meta-phorically; and if it then came out that he was not, the situation would not call for "Thoughts are not red", but rather, perhaps, for "Thoughts are not the sorts of things that *can* have a colour, they aren't spatially extended objects", for he has not made a mistake as to the colour of a thing but as to the type of a thing—i.e. as to the meanings of the words he used. One can see this if one asks *how* it might come out that he was not talking metaphorically. To say of a thought that it is (literally) not red is like saying of "The King of France is bald" that it is not true: as Mr Strawson has reminded us, we do not say of a subject-predicate sentence whose subject fails to refer that it is just not true, for this in the normal use implies that it is false. And as Mr Strawson has pointed out, we seem to take the existence (we should add "in the relevant sense"—Mr Pickwick and Mr Strawson exist in different senses) of what the subject term pur-ports to refer to as a condition of the truth *or* falsity of a subject-predicate sentence. Hence while it is not incorrect to say that "The

226

King of France is bald" is not true—for it is indeed not true—it is misleading: it suggests that a certain condition is met which is in fact not met. Similarly, to say in the normal way of an object that it is not red is also to suggest that a certain condition is met, namely that the thing in question is spatially extended.

I shall call the pair "*x* is red" and "*x* is not-red" direct contradictories, and "*x* is not spatially extended" their radical[1] contrary. "*x* is P_1" and "*x* is P_2" are direct contradictories if "P_2" either is or is definable as "not-P_1"; and if there is a Q such that both direct contradictories suggest that *x* is Q, then "*x* is not Q" is their radical contrary. "Q" may then be said to be on a different (higher) level from that of P_1 and P_2. And S can be rewritten: with one class of exceptions, every pair of direct contradictories has a radical contrary.

And this seems true. For most P, "P or not-P" seems to mark a distinction only within a certain reference class, the class of Q's. "Coloured or colourless"—it is of bits of clear glass or cellophane that we in fact, in the normal way, say "They're colourless, they're not coloured". It would be as misleading to say of a thought that it is (literally) colourless as it would be to say of a thought that it is not red: it would suggest it was with that thought as with a bit of glass—untinted, clear. If a man said of a thought he had just had that it was coloured, we should of course take him to be talking metaphorically; and if it then came out that he was not, the situation would not call for "Thoughts are colourless", but rather, perhaps, for "Thoughts are not the sorts of things that can be coloured, they aren't spatially extended", for he has made a mistake as to the type of a thing—i.e. as to the meanings of the words he used. One can see this if one asks *how* it might come out that he was not talking metaphorically. Again "has more than five members or has not more than five members"—if I am forced to choose, I shall say that my left thumb has not got more than five members; but it is a mere joke to force a man to choose: my left thumb isn't a group, and so neither applies. "Is to the left of or is not to the left of"—my thoughts cannot be so ordered. In fact, the only pairs of direct contradictories that do exhaust the universe, that do not presuppose some reference class within which the distinction is being drawn, are those in which "P" is what might be called a type-characterization, expressions such as "is spatially extended", "is temporally extended", . . . The reference class for "is spatially extended or is not spatially extended" is the class of objects (individuals, subjects of predication). And hence it is only such pairs of direct contradictories that have no radical

---

[1] I borrow this latter term from Miss Anscombe's discussion (op. cit., pp. 48 ff.) of Wittgenstein on Russell's Theory of Descriptions; a subject-predicate sentence whose subject-term fails to refer, she called radically false.

contrary: the only Q such that "x is P" and "x is not-P" both suggest that x is Q, where "P" is a type-characterization, is: is an object (individual, subject of predication), and "x is (is not) an object (individual, subject of predication)" is plain nonsense.

The predicates of our actual language fall into different levels, and this is hidden from us by the systems of formal logic. "(x) (x is red or x is not red)" can of course be called a necessary truth if restrictions are made on the range of the variable x: this is just what is done in logic. And this, I think, is just what is done by Wittgenstein in the *Tractatus*. If elementary sentences must have no contraries, but only contradictories, then we might think that the predicates of elementary sentences would all have to be type-characterizations, in order that radical contraries be eliminated. And then it would follow that there could only be one elementary sentence, for "$a R_1 b$" and "$a R_2 b$" are incompatible if "R_1" and "R_2" are type-characterizations. Moreover, the elementary sentences would not be contingent in the way in which, say, "a is to the left of b" is contingent: if "a and b are spatially related" is true (false) of a pair of objects then it is necessarily true (false) of them, whereas although it is true that necessarily if a is to the left of b then a is to the left of b, it is not true that if a is to the left of b it is necessarily to the left of b. (It is worth stressing that, although something is gained when one reaches sentences whose predicates are type-characterizations, something else is lost. What is gained is the possibility of necessary truths of the form (x) (Fx or $-Fx$) where the range of the variable x is unlimited; but at the same time "Fx" has ceased to be contingent.) Wittgenstein, in fact, calls sentences whose predicates are type-characterizations formal (e.g. 2.0251: "Space, time and colour (colouredness) are forms of objects"—though I do not know what "colour" does in this list) and, therefore, attempts at saying what cannot be said, but can only be shown. Thus such sentences, far from being elementary, do not even have a sense. Their rôle is played by the prior restrictions on the types of objects whose names can appear in the various different elementary sentences. (Cf. 2.0121, ". . . If things can occur in atomic facts, this possibility must already lie in them . . .", and in general, 2.01 to 2.1.) But then where and under what label are we to examine these relationships amongst predicates which I have just now been pointing to?

Professor Stenius, of course, by no means overlooks the difficulties that would be involved in carrying out the programme of showing how our world really does fit into a yes-and-no space. He himself suggests that we disentangle the picture theory from this programme, the picture theory being stateable, and indeed useful, independently of it. And this brings me to my second general remark, namely that, divorced from this programme, the picture theory in the *Tractatus* seems very thin indeed. "A sentence is a picture, a model; understanding a sentence is like understanding a picture, a model." But what is understanding a picture? The only answer provided by the *Tractatus* is an answer that terminates in simple objects and atomic facts, and if this is eliminated, we are left with—aphorisms.

Perhaps the *Tractatus* should be studied, and not merely by those with an interest in the history of philosophy in this century. But it seems to me that its value lies not in what it says but in certain things that it hints at. Some of the aphorisms will bear much thinking on— 5.473 (". . . In a certain sense we cannot make mistakes in logic"), 5.4732 ("We cannot give a sign the wrong sense"), and 6.123 ("It is clear that the laws of logic cannot themselves obey further logical laws . . .") come to mind as of particular interest. I say "hints" rather than "suggests" for these *are* mere hints: the work remains to be done. And I think that one who sets out to do it will do better to begin on his own rather than hunt about for enlightenment in the *Tractatus*.

Wittgenstein's Three Languages[1]

RICHARD J. BERNSTEIN

IT seems a paradox that the author who wrote "What can be said at all can be said clearly", has bequeathed us an extremely obscure and perplexing work. Hailed as one of the most influential books in contemporary analytic philosophy, the *Tractatus* has been systematically misinterpreted. It is these misinterpretations that have exercised the most influence. The Vienna Circle read into it epistemological doctrines that were not there, and dismissed what was not compatible with positivist dogma as "metaphysical vagaries".[2] J. O. Urmson, in his semi-official history of philosophical analysis between the two World Wars, has argued that the *Tractatus* is primarily a variation on the logical atomism advocated by Russell in his famous lectures. Urmson presents strong arguments to show that logical positivism was not so much a reaction to classical metaphysics, but an answer to the metaphysics implicit in logical atomism.[3] But the assimilation of the *Tractatus* to Russell's logical atomism leads to grave confusions.

Perhaps we can say that the book has had a "negative" influence; the mistakes of the *Tractatus* have helped us to become clearer about the correct way of philosophizing. The difficulty with this view is that many of the criticisms of the *Tractatus* have been wide of the mark.[4] In denying the influence of the *Tractatus* (or rather affirming that it is the *Tractatus* misinterpreted that has been influential), I do not intend to slight its importance. On the contrary, we must distinguish

[1] From *The Review of Metaphysics*, vol. 15, no. 2, issue no. 58, December, 1961, pp. 278–98. Reprinted by permission of the editor and the author.
[2] Alexander Maslow, *A Study in Wittgenstein's Tractatus*, University of California Press, 1961, p. 19. For a criticism of positivist interpretations, see G. E. M. Anscombe, *An Introduction to Wittgenstein's Tractatus*, Hutchinson University Library, 1959, pp. 25 ff., pp. 150 ff.
[3] *Philosophical Analysis*, Oxford University Press, 1955, pp. 102 ff.
[4] For a penetrating criticism of misinterpretations, see I. M. Copi, "Objects, Properties, and Relations in the *Tractatus*", *Mind*, April, 1958, pp. 145–65 [present volume].

the *Tractatus* from both logical positivism and Russell's logical atomism, as well as from the subsequent criticisms of these positions, if we are to understand and appreciate it.

One might hope that with the recent publication of Wittgenstein's *Notebooks 1914–16*, three commentaries on the *Tractatus*, and several excellent articles, some of the confusion would be dispelled.[1] But if we had to reconstruct what the *Tractatus* said on the basis of these documents, we would be compelled to reconstruct several different books containing mutually exclusive propositions.

The *Notebooks* are intrinsically fascinating, for they show us how Wittgenstein worked. We will find here propositions that were extracted and reordered in the *Tractatus*, as well as propositions that approximate those in the *Tractatus*. These the editors have distinguished and noted. We see how Wittgenstein jots down an insight that he will develop later, or explores a suggestion that he may eventually reject. In general, the philosophic style of these notes reveals the incisive searching that is so evident in Wittgenstein's later writings. Philosophically, the notebooks are most helpful for appreciating the context of the *Tractatus*: they show that Wittgenstein was primarily concerned with the logical and meta-logical problems raised by Frege and Russell rather than with traditional epistemological issues. But if one hopes to find here the philosophic key to the *Tractatus*, he will be disappointed. Indeed, we must first decide what the *Tractatus* says before we can decide what weight is to be given to specific propositions in the *Notebooks*. We can see this in the crucial instance of deciphering what Wittgenstein means by "objects" (*Gegenstände*). If objects are particulars—an interpretation supported in varying degrees by Anscombe, Copi, and Sellars[2]—then we must reject the claim in the *Notebooks* that relations and properties are also objects. In this case, as in many others, what Wittgenstein says in the *Notebooks* is not sufficient to settle the issue.

Maslow's commentary has little value for understanding the *Tractatus*. Written in 1933, but published (without modification) in 1961, it has not benefited from the publication of the *Notebooks* or

[1] *Notebooks 1914–1916*, ed. by G. H. von Wright and G. E. M. Anscombe, Harper & Brothers, 1961. This book also includes notes given to Russell, notes dictated to G. E. Moore, and some of Wittgenstein's letters to Russell. The three commentaries are: Anscombe, op. cit.; Maslow, op. cit.; and Erik Stenius, *Wittgenstein's Tractatus*, Cornell University Press, 1960. In addition to Copi's article, W. Sellars has written a series of perceptive articles that deal with various aspects of the *Tractatus*. See "Being and Being Known", *Proceedings of the American Catholic Philosophical Association*, 1960, pp. 28–49; "Naming and Saying", forthcoming in *The Philosophy of Science* [present volume]; and "Truth and 'Correspondence'", forthcoming in *The Journal of Philosophy*. Sellars' papers, and discussions with him, have been extremely helpful in writing this study.

[2] See Anscombe, op. cit., pp. 109 ff.; Copi, op. cit., pp. 160 ff. [pp. 181 ff.]; Sellars, "Naming and Saying" [present volume].

any of the recent studies of the *Tractatus*. More important, it is written from the "point of view of logical positivism"—and even the positivism here is rather unsophisticated. There is no "attempt to separate sharply the strictly expository part of my work from the interpretational and even the commentatorial" (p. xii). Consequently there are unfounded or dubious statements on almost every page. It does show how the *Tractatus* was misread by the positivists and forced to take on an alien appearance.

Stenius' commentary is more promising. Written with great care and precision, the clarity of exposition enables the reader to get a firmer grasp of the *Tractatus*, even where one disagrees with Stenius. But I think that Stenius' interpretation is "off-centre". His claim that "Wittgenstein counts as 'things' [*Gegenstände*] not only individual objects but also predicates with different numbers of places" (p. 63) is a basic mistake—one that permeates his entire treatment of the picture theory. Stenius also overworks distinctions and concepts that are barely suggested in the *Tractatus*, as, for example, in his discussion of categories. Although his complicated heuristic devices are sometimes helpful, they also tend to mislead. One would think that there is a good deal about "articulate fields" and their interpretation in the *Tractatus* on the basis of the extensive use that Stenius makes of this concept.

Whereas the fundamental question for Stenius seems to be: How can we make sense of what the *Tractatus* says regardless of what Wittgenstein intended? the primary question for Anscombe is: What are the philosophic reasons that led Wittgenstein to say what he does in the *Tractatus*? This latter type of inquiry offers perhaps a more fruitful beginning, although there is certainly a need to answer both questions. As an *introduction*, Anscombe's book is a failure. There are passages that are at least as obscure as parts of the *Tractatus*. She attempts to supply the necessary background by paraphrasing doctrines of Frege, Russell, and Ramsey, but in order to understand what she says, the reader must have a better acquaintance with these philosophers than she provides. Nevertheless, Anscombe, better than anyone else, has grasped what Wittgenstein is saying and why. Her insights are genuine aids for understanding the *Tractatus*. Though not for the philosophic novice, her commentary is ultimately the best of the lot.

To appreciate better the virtues and shortcomings of the several commentaries, we must come to grips directly with the *Tractatus*. I intend to focus on the "picture theory", keeping in mind the questions: What is pictured? What pictures? and, What is involved in picturing? To answer these questions we must first destroy the myth of the "Two Wittgensteins".

Richard J. Bernstein

1. The myth, which has become part of the philosophic folklore of our time, usually follows this pattern: In the *Tractatus*, Wittgenstein is primarily concerned with the construction of a logically perfect language. Such an ideal language is truth-functional and contains only meaningful propositions. "Meaningless propositions" cannot occur in it. Ordinary language and philosophic language should be purged and brought into conformity with the logically perfect language. Only in so far as ordinary language conforms to this ideal, does it achieve its purpose of expressing meaningful propositions. The myth goes on to tell us that it was the great insight of the later Wittgenstein of the *Philosophical Investigations* to uncover the perversity of the quest for the ideal language. It was his supposed discovery that the quest for the logically perfect language is an error—indeed, the most fundamental error of past philosophy. The job of the philosopher is to elucidate the hidden structure of ordinary language, and the construction of ideal languages can only hinder and never aid this perpetual task of elucidation. There are two basic errors in this myth. It misdescribes the *Tractatus* and misconstrues the criticisms in the *Philosophical Investigations*.

There is no doubt that there are great differences between the style and content of the *Tractatus* and the *Philosophical Investigations*. But these differences have been exaggerated with a resulting misconception of both books. Over and over again, a careful reading will show that insights contained in the *Philosophical Investigations* were anticipated or suggested in the *Tractatus*.

Russell helped to start the myth when he wrote in his Introduction to the *Tractatus*:

Mr Wittgenstein is concerned with the conditions for a logically perfect language—not that any language is logically perfect, or that we believe ourselves capable, here and now, of constructing a logically perfect language, but that the whole function of language is to have meaning, and it only fulfils this function in proportion as it approaches to the ideal language which we postulate (p. 8).

At one time this was Russell's *own* view and there is an attack on such a position in the *Philosophical Investigations* (see § 81), but is this Wittgenstein's view in the *Tractatus*? Ramsey, in his critical notice of the *Tractatus*,[1] was the first to point out that Russell's characterization is "very doubtful" and cannot be easily reconciled with a proposition such as 4.002. "Colloquial language is part of the human organism and is not less complicated than it. . . . The [tacit conventions] to understand colloquial language are enormously com-

---

[1] Reprinted in *The Foundations of Mathematics*, Harcourt, Brace and Co., 1931, p. 270 [p. 9].

plicated."[1] There is also the striking remark in 5.5563, "All propositions of our colloquial language are actually, just as they are, logically completely in order." We cannot easily brush aside these remarks for there are many similar remarks in the *Notebooks*. At one point Wittgenstein declares, "I only want to justify the vagueness of ordinary sentences, for it *can* be justified" (p. 70).

Wittgenstein, to be sure, makes frequent references to an "adequate notation" (6.122), "a symbolism . . . which obeys the rules of *logical* grammar" (3.325). (See also 5.53 through 5.534.) We have here then an apparent inconsistency. Anscombe's hints, however, show us how to reconcile this inconsistency. In arguing that the view of the adequacy of ordinary language is essentially the same in the *Tractatus* and the *Philosophical Investigations*, she writes, "The sentences of ordinary language no more fail to express a sense than our Roman numeral fails to express a number. The one expresses a sense, the other a number, perfectly" (p. 92).

A language where there is a symbolism that obeys the rules of logical grammar is *not* conceived to be an ideal language that is to replace our other languages. The construction of such a language is a device by which we can become clearer about how any language works, not in all its complexity and tacit conventions, but primarily in the uses of sentences to make true and false statements. Following Sellars (see "Naming and Saying"), we shall call such a language the "perspicuous language", for the purpose of this language is to show perspicuously what is "hidden".

If we turn to the relevant passages in the *Philosophical Investigations*, we see that it is not the construction of such a language that is criticized, but rather the *misuse* or misunderstanding of an ideal language.

"But still, it isn't a game, if there is some vagueness *in the rules*."—But *does* this prevent its being a game?—"Perhaps you'll call it a game, but at any rate it certainly isn't a perfect game." This means: it has impurities, and what I am interested in at present is the pure article.—But I want to say: we misunderstand the role of the ideal in our language. That is to say: we too should call it a game, only we are dazzled by the ideal and therefore fail to see the actual use of the word "game" clearly. (§ 100)

The criticism here is directed more toward Russell's conception of the ideal language than toward the view expressed in the *Tractatus*. Wittgenstein was tempted by the view that he criticizes, though he

---

[1] It is well known that the Ogden translation of the *Tractatus* is inaccurate and at times misleading. A new translation is now being prepared. I have, however, adopted the convention of placing altered expressions in square brackets where my translation differs from Ogden's.

235

never fully *succumbed* to this temptation. (For other comments on the rôle of the ideal, see § 81 and § 131.)[1]

The language which we have labelled the "perspicuous language", and ordinary or colloquial language, are both mentioned in the *Tractatus*; but neither of these is the language that Wittgenstein *uses*. The language he uses, which may conveniently be called the "ladder language", is distinctive. (Cf. Sellars, "Naming and Saying".) The ladder language cannot satisfy the stringent truth-functional requirements of the perspicuous language. It is used, however, as a type of meta-language to describe the perspicuous language. Indeed, *within* the perspicuous language, the "propositions" of the ladder language could not occur. This is the point of Wittgenstein's remark, "My propositions are elucidatory in this way: he who understands me finally recognizes them as senseless, when he has climbed out through them, on them, over them. (He must so to speak throw away the ladder, after he has climbed up on it.)" (6.54).

Though the specific formulation of the distinction between "mention" and "use" is a contemporary one, the problem of distinguishing the languages or propositions spoken about, and the language used to speak about these propositions has always been one of the most central in philosophy. Wittgenstein's ladder language has affinities with Plato's dialectic, the language of Kant's *Critique*, and Carnap's meta-languages. The ladder language must be distinguished from all these in at least one important respect. Wittgenstein was keenly aware of the self-referential difficulties of a type-hierarchy or a series of meta-languages. It is for this reason that he stresses the differences in *how* the ladder language and the perspicuous language mean. The ladder language only elucidates or shows, while the perspicuous language describes or says. "What *can* be shown *cannot* be said" (4.1212). It is this radical distinction between showing and saying that lies at the heart of Wittgenstein's attempt to avoid the logical and philosophical confusions engendered by type-hierarchies.

To sum up: At least three languages are distinguished in the *Tractatus*: the perspicuous language, ordinary language, and the ladder language. The perspicuous language is an aid for understanding how language works when we use it to make true and false statements. It is not an ideal language which ordinary language must "approach" in order to fulfil its function. To describe this perspicuous language, we must use a language—the ladder language—which must not be confused with the object language that it des-

---

[1] Ordinary language philosophers have frequently criticized the construction of artificial languages by reconstructionists such as Carnap. In so far as these languages are used as heuristic devices to elucidate concepts, they serve the rôle that Wittgenstein delineates for "ideal" languages in both the *Tractatus* and the *Philosophical Investigations*.

cribes: the "propositions" in the ladder language cannot occur in the perspicuous language.

2. What is pictured? Elementary propositions (which occur only in the perspicuous language) picture atomic states of affairs,[1] and atomic states of affairs consist of "the configuration of the objects" (2.0272). What then are objects (*Gegenstände*)? What is it that names stand for? Are the objects that Wittgenstein refers to particulars, properties, relations? Or are these objects some other "type" of entity? None of the three commentaries agree on what is Wittgenstein's answer. Actually, the best discussions of this question are in Copi's "Objects, Properties, and Relations in the *Tractatus*" and Sellars' "Naming and Saying", though there are also difficulties in their interpretations.

Copi argues that neither relations nor properties are objects. All objects are particulars, and furthermore they are bare particulars, i.e. particulars having formal but no material properties. Although Copi presents strong arguments for this interpretation, he seems to drive himself and Wittgenstein into a *cul-de-sac*. We are told that we cannot predicate a property of any particular. "*No* adjectives can be truly predicated" of a particular (Copi, p. 165 [p. 186]). How are we to understand a fact which consists only of bare particulars in configuration? Wittgenstein tells us in the *Tractatus*, and Copi quotes him, that material properties are "first formed by the configuration of the objects" (Copi, p. 162 [p. 183]). But if objects are bare particulars, how can any configuration of them form a material property? Perhaps material properties are to be "constructed" from material relations, and Copi suggests this possibility, although he does not show how such a construction is to be made. Furthermore, if we follow Russell's lead (one implicit in Frege's analysis) that simple properties are monadic relations, then it certainly seems perverse to rule out *a priori* the possibility of monadic states of affairs—states of affairs where monadic relations are predicated of particulars. If we cannot "decide *a priori* whether, for example, I can get into a situation in which I need to symbolize with a sign of a 27-termed relation"

---

[1] I have followed Stenius' suggestion in translating "*Sachverhalt*" as "atomic state of affairs", instead of "atomic fact" as it appears in the Ogden translation. Anscombe objects to this and claims that Wittgenstein accepted the translation "atomic fact". Nevertheless, in her own translation of the *Notebooks*, she translates "*Sachverhalt*" as "situation". Underlying this verbal disagreement is an important philosophic point. For Wittgenstein, a *Sachverhalt* may be existing or non-existing. ("*Das Bestehen und Nichtbestehen von Sachverhalten. . . .*" 2.06; see also 2.062, 2.201.) A *nicht bestehender Sachverhalt* is still a *Sachverhalt*. Consequently, *in so far* as "atomic fact" suggests something that can only exist and "an existing atomic fact" is redundant, "atomic fact" is a misleading translation. "Atomic fact" is *here* used to mean "an existing atomic state of affairs".

Richard J. Bernstein

(5.5541), how can we decide *a priori* that I *cannot* get into a situation in which I need to symbolize with a sign of a 1-termed relation?

Fortunately, in the extremely subtle and illuminating "Naming and Saying" Sellars takes up the discussion just at this point. Agreeing with Copi that objects are particulars, he argues against the view that they are bare particulars. In effect he shows that properties can be treated in the same manner as relations. His conclusion is that just as a relation can be represented in a perspicuous language by a configuration rather than a name, so also a simple property can be represented without naming it. *"In a perspicuous . . . language . . . the predicate words . . . would appear as manners of being names, as, in a literal sense, internal features of the names."* He argues further that "objects are internally related to sets of 'external' properties", and consequently they are not bare particulars, at least not in the way that Copi thinks they are.

What is the purpose of this perspicuous language? How does a language in which there are only names of particulars, and where all predication is represented by configurations of names or manners of names, help us to understand how language works? The point is to *show* how radically different naming and saying really are; to elucidate the nature of predication. As Anscombe puts it:

> It should be apparent, however, that Wittgenstein's views are extremely Fregean. What, then, has become of Frege's 'concepts' in Wittgenstein's theory? They seem to have disappeared entirely; actually, however, instead of making concepts or universals into a kind of objects, as Ramsey wished to, Wittgenstein made the gulf between concepts and objects much greater than Frege ever made it. So far as concerns the content of a functional expression, that will consist in the objects covered by it. But in respect of having argument-places, concepts go over entirely into logical forms. In the 'completely analysed proposition', which is a 'logical network sprinkled with names', the Fregean 'concept', the thing with holes in it, has become simply the logical form. (pp. 108 ff.)

It is as if Wittgenstein were telling us that if we think of "concepts or universals" as objects or something like objects or things, then we are inevitably led to all the misleading analogies that plague the discussion of predication. And indeed this suspicion certainly has been vindicated by contemporary discussions of abstract entities. For the paradigm that lies behind many of these discussions is that if we can properly name something, refer to it, or talk about it, we are committed to its existence. And this is understood as meaning that we count it as part of our ontology along with other things such as concrete particulars. If "acceptance" of abstract entities or universals entails the acceptance of the view represented by this paradigm, it is little wonder that there has been so much objection to this caricature

238

of "platonism". It was Wittgenstein's insight (though he was not the first to make the point) that we can represent properties and relations without misconceiving them as another type of "particular"—a mistake that opens the door to some form of Bradley's infinite regress.

Wittgenstein's point can be seen from another perspective. We can ask bluntly whether he is a nominalist or a realist. If we use names as our guide, then, since within the perspicuous language the only names that occur are names of particulars, we would conclude that Wittgenstein is a nominalist. But Wittgenstein is not denying that there are properties and relations: he is denying that they are to be conceived on the model or analogy of objects as particulars. Indeed, if there were no properties and relations, there could be no atomic states of affairs. An atomic state of affairs is not a mixture of objects, but a *configuration* of objects. In the ladder language we can say that relations and properties are represented though not named. This can not be *said* in the perspicuous language, though it is *shown*.

Finally, we can bring this issue into sharper focus by comparing Wittgenstein with Peirce. In order to make his Scotistic realism clear, Peirce first showed how modern formulations of realism were little more than parodies. Richard Rorty has put it succinctly in an excellent article:

The parody consists in holding that realists believe in two independent sets of sharp-edged, fully determinate entities—particular universals and particular particulars. This reduplication of the world, like all parodies of philosophic theories, is easily refuted: in this case, the job is done by one variant or another of the "third man" argument. But for Peirce, this notion of what realism is could only have occurred to a mind so imbued with nominalism as to give a nominalistic twist to anything it encounters.[1]

Peirce, like Wittgenstein, saw the confusions that follow when we think of universals as quasi-objects or things. Nevertheless, he argued that an adequate analysis of signs compels us to recognize that universals or what he called "thirds" can be represented. And in a manner similar to Wittgenstein's treatment of relations and properties, he argued that unless they could be represented, there would be no propositions. However their positions differ, there is an important similarity in their insistence that properties and relations are not other types of individual things, together with their insistence

---

[1] "Pragmatism, Categories, and Language", *The Philosophical Review*, April, 1961, p. 208. Rorty shows fundamental similarities between the views of Peirce and the later Wittgenstein on the nature of language and reality. Some of these similarities can already be seen in the *Tractatus*. This is further evidence of the continuity between the *Tractatus* and the *Philosophical Investigations*.

that they can and must be represented if there is to be meaningful discourse.

Another striking feature of the perspicuous language can be seen by examining the stringent requirement for the independence of elementary propositions that Wittgenstein lays down in 6.3751:

> For two colours, e.g., to be at one place in the visual field, is impossible, logically impossible, for it is excluded by the logical structure of colour. . . . (It is clear that the logical product of two elementary propositions can neither be a tautology nor a contradiction. The assertion that a point in the visual field has two different colours at the same time, is a contradiction.)

If we take this passage literally, then Wittgenstein appears to exclude not only colour predications, but all empirical or observation propositions as candidates for elementary propositions. Even in the perspicuous language where there are no names for properties or relations, we still use expressions to predicate some property or relation of an object or objects. If our predications are not vacuous, then some other (atomic) state of affairs would seem to be logically excluded by it. And it is this line of reasoning that leads Anscombe to conclude that "whatever elementary propositions may be, they are not simple observation statements" (p. 27). Stenius attempts to construct a model of what a language would be like that did satisfy this requirement for independence (pp. 38 ff.). But his model only brings out more clearly that observation statements or more generally empirical statements which are used to describe *our* world do not satisfy this requirement. It is difficult to see how, even in theory, it is possible to translate any empirical statement into a language that satisfies this requirement. We must either (1) modify this strong independence requirement, or (2) admit that elementary propositions are not descriptions of our world. If we accept (2), then our conception of the function of the perspicuous language, and indeed our view of the *Tractatus*, will be radically altered.

One might argue for (1) as follows: Wittgenstein is overstating his point concerning the independence of elementary propositions. He wrote the *Tractatus* when he was under the influence of thinking that contradiction can be analysed "truth-functionally", and consequently neglected to account for the incompatibility which is an internal feature of propositions.[1] There are some grounds for this

---

[1] It might be argued that Wittgenstein's claim, "The assertion that a point in the visual field has two different colours at the same time is a contradiction", is true, but *elliptical*. It is true only when two propositions such as "*x* is red", and "*x* is green", are taken in conjunction with another (complex) proposition such as "Nothing can be red and green all over, etc." which is a statement about the "logical structure of colour". The propositions might thus be logically incompatible under the condition of a third complex proposition, although logically independent when considered as independent symbols. Of course this does not resolve the problem but only shifts it to the cognitive

position. In the only article that Wittgenstein published after the *Tractatus*, he deals with this problem and suggests a weakening of the independence requirement.[1]

But Wittgenstein did lay down this requirement in the *Tractatus* and an interpretation of this work must attempt to come to grips with the proposition as it appears. If this strong requirement for independence is to hold, and if we accept the premiss that the perspicuous language (which consists of elementary propositions and truth-functions of these) is intended to elucidate how we describe the world, then I think we are forced to the conclusion that *in some sense* there are no elementary propositions. The "existence" of elementary propositions is a logical requirement or presupposition for the possibility of meaningful discourse. Elementary propositions are not, however, a type of proposition for which we shall some day discover examples. They are conceived in thought, but not exhibited in actuality. It is not an accident, then, that we are not given any example of an elementary proposition, for it is impossible to isolate one.

The fact that we understand propositions (even in ordinary language), that we can reason correctly from both true and false propositions, presupposes that there are elementary propositions and atomic states of affairs corresponding to them. Wittgenstein does not start his investigation with noting what entities are in the world and then examining how they are to be represented, though this is the order of propositions in the *Tractatus*. The primary question is: How is it possible for propositions, even in ordinary language, to have meaning? In answering this question Wittgenstein argues that we must presuppose the "existence" of elementary propositions. In this way, and only in this way, can we determine the form and structure of atomic states of affairs.[2]

But how can we be sure that atomic states of affairs correspond to

---

[1] "Some Remarks on Logical Form", *Proceedings of the Aristotelian Society*, Supplementary Volume IX, 1929, pp. 162–71 [present volume]. In this paper, Wittgenstein does emend some of the doctrines of the *Tractatus*, but it is reported that he "was so dissatisfied with this paper . . . that he refused either to read or discuss it when the time came for its delivery". (John Passmore, *A Hundred Years of Philosophy*, p. 358.) The value of the paper lies in its indication of what problems were preoccupying Wittgenstein at this time. It also provides further evidence that we do not know what are to qualify as atomic states of affairs.

[2] I am not suggesting that Wittgenstein's "transcendental deduction" is valid, or even that Wittgenstein was fully aware of this strain in his thought; nevertheless it is present in the *Tractatus*. For the details of this argument, cf. Anscombe, pp. 31 ff.

---

status of the propositions required to state the "logical structure of colour". For a further discussion of this issue see E. B. Allaire, *"Tractatus 6.3751"*, *Analysis*, April, 1959, pp. 100–5 [present volume].

elementary propositions? "In order to discover whether the picture is true or false we must compare it with reality" (2.223). Wittgenstein seems to be in agreement with the naïve realists. But what are the criteria for correctly comparing propositions and states of affairs? The question highlights the importance of what Wittgenstein says about Occam's razor. "Occam's razor is, of course, not an arbitrary rule nor one justified by its practical success. It simply says that *unnecessary* elements in a symbolism mean nothing" (5.47321). (Cf. 3.328.) And we can add that if they mean nothing, then there is nothing in reality that corresponds to them. It is precisely this principle that informs Wittgenstein's discussion of the perspicuous language and his remarks about atomic states of affairs that correspond to elementary propositions. We cannot transcend our language or thought, but by the construction of the perspicuous language we lay bare the structure of reality. And we know how to construct this language by determining what elements are necessary for the symbolism to have *meaning*.[1]

3. What precisely is it that pictures? When Wittgenstein claims "The proposition is a picture of reality" (4.01, 4.021), and "The proposition only asserts something, in so far as it is a picture" (4.03), he is speaking about propositions in the perspicuous language—the propositions that describe reality. Sentences in ordinary language can be said to picture only in so far as they can be translated into this

---

[1] We can see now how standard descriptions of Wittgenstein's position are extremely confused. Consider Urmson's apparently straightforward statement: "Take an atomic fact pictured by 'This is red', then 'this' names the object" (op. cit., p. 58). There are at least eight mistakes or dubious points here. The elementary proposition which pictures an atomic fact consists of the concatenation of names, and names stand for particulars. Consequently, (1) neither is "is" a name (see 3.323), (2) nor is "red" the name of a particular, and thus they would not occur in an elementary proposition. (3) It is dubious whether "this" is a name (see 3.325). (4) In speaking of the atomic fact pictured by "This is red", Urmson writes as if we knew what were to qualify as atomic facts, but Wittgenstein never gives an example of an atomic fact and indicates that we do not know precisely what they are (see 4.2211, 6.3751). (5) In saying "this" names *the* object, Urmson suggests that the sentence is about *one* object, i.e. the object singled out by "this". But an elementary proposition is a concatenation of names (4.22) and represents a configuration of objects (3.21). If there were three simple signs in an elementary proposition, there would be three names (3.202), and consequently *three* objects would be named (3.203). (6) It is at least problematical whether an elementary proposition can be "about" a single object. In speaking of atomic facts Wittgenstein usually refers to objects (see 2.0231, 2.0272 ff.). (7) Urmson might agree that in the perspicuous language "This is red" would not occur, but nevertheless it can be properly translated into this language. But it is not clear how such a translation can be made. (See 6.3751, 4.211.) (8) Wittgenstein disqualifies colour predications of the type represented by "This is red" as elementary propositions (6.3751). In fairness to Urmson, it should be mentioned that he acknowledges that "in the light of later study, aided by posthumous publication of Wittgenstein's writings, many philosophers have come to doubt the accuracy of the sort of interpretation of Wittgenstein's *Tractatus Logico-philosophicus* that is given here" (p. ix). But all of the enumerated criticisms can be justified on the basis of internal evidence in the *Tractatus*.

language (though Wittgenstein does not explain how such translations can be made). There are also important sentences in ordinary language that cannot be so translated, e.g. normative sentences that use "ought" and "should", as well as conditional sentences that use "could" and "would". (See 6.42 ff.; 5.134 ff.) In a technical sense (where elementary propositions are our standard), sentences using these expressions are senseless. More accurately, and less paradoxically, sentences using such expressions are meaningful in some way other than the sentences used to picture reality.

The ladder language also makes use of expressions that cannot appear in the perspicuous language that pictures reality. "Object", and "atomic states of affairs", would not occur in this language; these expressions are not, properly speaking, names. Furthermore, "picturing", in so far as it signifies a "relation" that holds between a linguistic state of affairs and a non-linguistic state of affairs, is not a relation represented *within* the language that pictures reality. The proposition "a pictures b", where "a" stands for a linguistic fact (proposition) and "b" stands for a non-linguistic fact, would not satisfy the truth-functional requirements laid down for a language that contains only elementary propositions and truth-functions of these. Picturing, then, is something that we can elucidate only in the ladder language.

In short, only propositions in the perspicuous language picture reality, though to say this is to claim something *about* this language; the claim cannot be made *within* it. Furthermore, it is only propositions that picture, not the parts of propositions. Names do not picture, nor do the configurations that represent predicates. (See 3.203; *Notebooks*, p. 8.)

But there is still the problem of deciding whether only elementary propositions picture, or whether the truth-functions of these can also be said to picture. The issue is not trivial; it has important consequences for Wittgenstein's view of logic and logical operations. Copi presents the most forceful arguments for restricting picturing to elementary propositions. His main argument is that "non-elementary propositions contain elements which do not stand for objects, but all elements of pictures must stand for objects, therefore non-elementary propositions cannot be pictures" (p. 149 [p. 171]). The "extra" elements that non-elementary propositions contain are "truth-operations or logical constants" (p. 149 [p. 171]). I think that Copi is mistaken in his claim that non-elementary propositions *contain* truth-operations. A truth-operation is not something that is contained *in* any proposition; it is a *doing*, an operation performed upon elementary propositions. "The operation is that which must happen to a proposition in order to make another out of it" (5.23), and "The

243

truth-functions of elementary propositions are the results of operations which have elementary propositions as bases. (I call these operations, truth-operations)" (5.234). "Operation and function must not be confused with one another" (5.25). Wittgenstein's strategy here is similar to his strategy in handling predicates. Just as we saw that predicates are represented although not named (and the reason for this is that they function in atomic states of affairs in a way different from objects), so in the case of logical operations, Wittgenstein is telling us that they "work" in a way different from propositions that describe reality. The perspicuous language not only *shows* how predicates differ from objects, it *shows* how logical operations differ from functions.

A truth-operation is essentially a type of action. And the truth-functions which are the results of these operations are part of the *logical scaffolding of propositions rather than proper parts of these propositions*. Consequently, truth-operations are not contained in propositions, and the fact that elementary propositions are subject to truth-operations does not exclude the results of these operations from the picture theory.[1] (Cf. Anscombe, p. 81.)

4. But how do elementary propositions picture? A picture is not a mental image, and the images in our mind (if there are any) have nothing to do with the way in which elementary propositions picture atomic states of affairs. In this respect, Wittgenstein is closer to Frege than he is to Russell and the tradition of British empiricism. Frege sharply distinguishes ideas from both sense and reference. Ideas—which include mental images—are "wholly subjective", and logically irrelevant to the problem of how propositions represent reality.[2]

Even if we rid ourselves of misleading psychological associations, we may still think of Wittgenstein's picture theory as a variation of the correspondence theory of truth of the naïve realists. But we can come closer to understanding what Wittgenstein is saying by seeing how much his theory differs from traditional correspondence theories. The picture theory is not intended to explain how we *discover* the

[1] Discourse about logic and logical constants can lead us, and did lead Frege, Russell, and Wittgenstein in the *Notebooks* (p. 15), to think of "logical constants" as naming another type of object or entity. The position of the *Tractatus* is that logical operations and constants must not be thought of as entities; they are neither universals nor particulars. This is the point of the remark: "My fundamental thought is that 'logical constants' do not [stand for objects]" (4.0312). My disagreement with Copi is not over whether "logical constants" name anything. Indeed, it is essential to his argument that they are not names of objects. The issue is whether logical constants or truth-operations are contained in propositions. And my point is that Wittgenstein is suggesting that they are not, properly speaking, *contained* in the propositions of the perspicuous language.

[2] "On Sense and Reference", in *Philosophical Writings of Gottlob Frege*, p. 60.

truth or falsity of propositions; its purpose is to explain how propositions can have meaning. Both true and false propositions picture the same state of affairs.

Secondly, though Wittgenstein insists that "What *can* be shown *cannot* be said" (4.1212), this must not be interpreted as an appeal to obviousness or self-evidence. In so far as correspondence theories make an ultimate appeal to "seeing" or obviousness as a criterion for justifying the truth of a proposition, Wittgenstein rejects them. "If from the fact that a proposition is obvious to us, it does not *follow* that it is true, then obviousness is no justification for our belief in its truth" (5.1363). (For further evidence of Wittgenstein's suspicion of self-evidence, see 6.1271 and *Notebooks*, p. 4.)

Thirdly, it is clear from the examples that Wittgenstein gives that obviousness is irrelevant to picturing. "The gramophone record, the musical thought, the score, the waves of sound, all stand to one another in that pictorial internal relation, which holds between language and the world" (4.014).[1] If we restricted ourselves to observing the record and the score, we would never *see* any "internal similarity" between them. To assert that there is an internal similarity is not to claim that we see that the two are similar, but rather that there is a *rule* by which we can "construct" one from the other. "In the fact that there is a general rule by which the musician is able to read the symphony out of the score, and that there is a rule by which one could reconstruct the symphony from the line on a gramophone record and from this again—by means of the first rule—construct the score, herein lies the internal similarity between things which at first sight seem to be entirely different" (4.0141). The more one emphasizes the essential rôle of rules in determining the relation of language to reality, the more Wittgenstein's theory departs from that of the naïve realist. Little is said in the *Tractatus* about the character of these rules and rule-like behaviour in general. But these brief hints are taken up, expanded, and transformed in Wittgenstein's later work —one of the dominant themes woven into the texture of the *Philosophical Investigations* is the status and rôle of rules.

Fourthly, the differences between a picture and a proposition are as important as the similarities for understanding how a proposition functions. We have seen that we cannot explain picturing solely by reference to the proposition and the state of affairs that is pictured. A third "element" must be introduced, i.e. rules that relate one to the

---

[1] There is an extremely important ambiguity in 4.014 and 4.0141 that runs throughout the picture theory. Wittgenstein says that the gramophone record, the musical thought, etc., stand in that pictorial internal relation which holds between language and the *world*. Yet the correspondence that Wittgenstein sketches here is one that holds between two *languages*. For an exploration of these two types of correspondence, see Sellars' remarks on *signifying* and *picturing* in the three articles cited in note 1, p. 232.

other.[1] "[The picture must have in addition the depicting relation which makes it into a picture]" (2.1513).[2]

Furthermore, it is precisely Wittgenstein's point that a picture by itself does not say anything, whereas a proposition does: we "*use* the picture *in* saying how things are". (Anscombe, p. 65.) We ordinarily think of a picture as a thing or object, but it is essential for Wittgenstein's position that we view it as a fact having the same logical complexity as the atomic state of affairs that it pictures. Another way of bringing out the difference between a picture and a proposition is succinctly stated in the *Notebooks*.

Can one negate a *picture*? No. And in this lies the difference between picture and proposition. The picture can serve as a proposition. But in that case something gets added to it which brings it about that now it *says* something. In short: I can only deny that the picture is right, but the *picture* I cannot deny (p. 33).

Finally, Wittgenstein's position is the very antithesis of the pre-Kantian conception that we match our language to a reality which is independent of language or thought. We have no privileged position from which we can get "outside" of language and neutrally view language and reality. We cannot transcend language to *know* reality. This is not a practical difficulty, but a logical absurdity. Again we must remember that Wittgenstein argues from the fact that propositions have meaning to the necessity of presupposing that there are elementary propositions. *And from the necessity of there being elementary propositions he argues that there must be corresponding states of affairs that the propositions picture.*

Just as our discussion of atomic states of affairs and objects shows how Wittgenstein's analysis places the nominalist-realist issue in a new perspective, so here we see how he does something similar for the idealist-realist issue. If we cannot transcend language and thought, if we can never get beyond them to a reality that "underlies" them, then it would seem that Wittgenstein is squarely in the idealist camp. But Wittgenstein is not denying that there is a reality, independent of our language, to be described. Indeed, elementary propositions could not be *meaningful* unless there were corresponding states of affairs that they represent. And the totality of existing atomic states of affairs (atomic facts) is the world. Consequently

---

[1] It may seem that Wittgenstein conceives of picturing in a simple dyadic way, but he does insist on what Peirce would call the triadic character of representation. (See *Collected Papers*, 5.283.) An adequate account of picturing necessitates reference to the state of affairs pictured, the proposition that pictures, and the rules that relate the (parts of the) picture to the pictured. For a discussion of the triadic character of representation and its relation to the later writings of Wittgenstein, see R. Rorty, op. cit.

[2] This is Anscombe's translation. See her discussion of this proposition, p. 68.

(parodying what Wittgenstein says about solipsism in 5.64), idealism strictly carried out coincides with realism.[1]

5. Our discussion of Wittgenstein's three languages and the picture theory is intended to provide an orientation for the reading of the *Tractatus*. There is, however, a strong temptation to think that there is a key to the *Tractatus* which will reveal its mysteries and place everything in perfect order. Maslow expresses this when he says, "I feel that, if one could only, to use a metaphor, strike the right key from the beginning and give the proper meanings to Wittgenstein's essential terms, such as atomic fact, object, and form, one could go on without much trouble into the rest of this syncopated philosophical composition" (p. xiii). I do not believe that there is such a key. This way of looking at the *Tractatus* is misleading and misses what is of lasting value in it. What is fascinating and important about the *Tractatus* are its philosophic hints and insights, not its ultimate coherence or system. Wittgenstein had the rare ability (sometimes in spite of himself) to see the many complex facets of a problem, and to grapple with them. There is a parallel here between the *Tractatus* and a Platonic dialogue. Both exhibit a type of philosophic irony. They give us the illusion of having all their parts fit together, but after a more careful examination difficulties become evident and we are compelled to make new efforts to make the pieces "fit". If we do not succumb to over-simplified and distorted interpretations, or turn away because we cannot find the key, our struggles to reconcile opposites may nevertheless lead to better philosophic understanding. It is my opinion that the value of the *Tractatus* lies here. To understand it, we must go beyond it and struggle ourselves with the problems that it raises. "Philosophy is not a theory but an activity" (4.112). And one "must so to speak throw away the ladder, after he has climbed up on it".

[1] For a related discussion of Wittgenstein's solipsism and its relation to realism, see J. Hintikka, "On Wittgenstein's 'Solipsism'", *Mind*, January, 1958 [present volume].

Naming and Saying[1]

WILFRID SELLARS[2]

The essay adopts the Tractarian view that configurations of objects are expressed by configurations of names. Two alternatives are considered: The objects in atomic facts are (1) without exception *particulars*; (2) one or more particulars plus a *universal* (Gustav Bergmann). On (1) a mode of configuration is always an empirical relation: on (2) it is the logical nexus of 'exemplification'. It is argued that (1) is both Wittgenstein's view in the *Tractatus* and correct. It is also argued that exemplification is a 'quasi-semantical' relation, and that it (and universals) are "in the world" only in that broad sense in which the 'world' includes linguistic norms and rôles viewed (thus in translating) from the standpoint of a fellow participant.

THE topics I am about to discuss have their roots in Wittgenstein's *Tractatus*. My point of departure will be Professor Irving Copi's paper on "Objects, Properties, and Relations in the *Tractatus*"[3] in which, after a decisive critique of certain misinterpretations of Wittgenstein's so-called picture theory of meaning with particular reference to relational statements, he proceeds to attribute to Wittgenstein, on the basis of a by no means implausible interpretation of certain texts, a puzzling construction of Wittgenstein's objects as 'bare particulars'.[4]

I shall not waste time by formulating the misinterpretations in question and summarizing Copi's admirably lucid critique. For my concern is with the theory of relational statements as pictures which, in my opinion, he correctly attributes to Wittgenstein, and, specifically, with the power of this theory to illuminate traditional philosophical puzzles concerning predication generally.

The crucial passage, of course, is 3.1432, "We must not say: 'The

---

[1] From *Philosophy of Science*, vol. 29, no. 1, January, 1962, pp. 7–26. Reprinted by permission of the editor and the author.

[2] Presented as the opening paper in a symposium on Reference and Use at the May, 1961, meeting of the Western Division of the American Philosophical Association.

[3] *Mind*, 67, 1958 [present volume].   [4] Ibid., p. 163 [p. 184].

complex sign "aRb" says "*a* stands in the relation R to *b*" '; but we must say, '*That* "a" stands in a certain relation to "b" says *that* aRb.' " Part of Wittgenstein's point is that though names and statements are both complex in their empirical character as instances of sign designs, and hence, from his point of view, are equally *facts*, the fact that a name consists (in various ways) of related parts is not relevant to its character as name in the way in which the division of such a statement as (schematically)

$$aRb$$

into just the parts 'a', 'R' and 'b' is to its character as making the statement it does. The latter parts are themselves functioning (though not in the same way) as signs, whereas no part of a name is functioning as a sign. But the crucial point that Wittgenstein is making emerges when we ask 'What are the parts of the statement in question the relation of which to one another is essential to its character as statement?' For in spite of the fact that the obvious answer would seem to be 'the *three* expressions "a", "R" and "b" ', this answer is incorrect. 'R' is, indeed, functioning in a broad sense as a sign, and is certainly involved in the statement's saying what it does, but it is involved, according to Wittgenstein, in quite a different way than the signs 'a' and 'b'. To say that 'R' is functioning as a predicate, whereas 'a' and 'b' are functioning as names, is to *locate* the difference, but to remain open to perplexity. What Wittgenstein tells us is that while superficially regarded the statement is a concatenation of the three parts 'a', 'R' and 'b', viewed more profoundly it is a two-termed fact, with 'R' coming in to the statement as bringing it about that the expressions 'a' and 'b' are dyadically related in a certain way, i.e. as bringing it about that the expressions 'a' and 'b' are related as having an 'R' between them. And he is making the point that what is essential to any statement which will say that aRb is not that the names 'a' and 'b' have a relation word between them (or before them or in any other relation to them), but that these names be related (dyadically) *in some way or other* whether or not this involves the use of a third sign design. Indeed, he is telling us that it is philosophically clarifying to recognize that instead of expressing the proposition that a is next to b by writing 'is next to' between 'a' and 'b', we could write 'a' in some relation to 'b' using only these signs. In a perspicuous language this is what we would do. Suppose that the Jumblies have such a language. It contains no relation words, but has the same name expressions as our tidied up English. Then we could translate Jumblese into English by making such statements as

$$\begin{smallmatrix}\text{'a'}\\\text{b}\end{smallmatrix} \text{ (in Jumblese) means } a \text{ is next to } b$$

and be on our way to philosophical clarification. Of particular interest in this connection would be the Jumblese translation of *Appearance and Reality*.

It will be noticed that I have correlated the fact that in 'aRb' the 'R' plays the predicate rôle with the fact that in Jumblese the proposition expressed by 'aRb' would be expressed by relating the two names without the use of a predicate expression. Now in Frege's system, 'R' would be said to stand for (*bedeuten*) a concept, whereas 'a' and 'b' stand for objects. Thus what Wittgenstein puts by saying that configurations of objects are represented by configurations of names (3.21)—so that Jumblese 'ᵃᵇ' and PMese 'aRb' are equally configurations of two names, though the latter is not perspicuously so—could also be put by saying that to represent that certain objects satisfy an n-adic concept, one makes their names satisfy an n-adic concept.[1] Roughly, Wittgenstein's configurations are the counterparts of a sub-set of Frege's concepts, and Wittgenstein is taking issue with Frege by insisting that a perspicuous language would contain no concept words functioning predicatively, that is to say, as 'R' functions when we say that aRb. How a perspicuous language would do the job done by concept words in their non-predicative use is something on which Wittgenstein throws less light, though his sketchy treatment of the parallel problem of how a perspicuous language would handle belief statements in which, according to Frege, the *Bedeutung* of the subordinate clause is what would ordinarily be its sense, gives some clue to the answer.

Now the above remarks adumbrate many topics of importance for ontology and the philosophy of logic. Some of them I shall pick up at a later stage in the argument. For the moment, however, I shall concentrate on the question, 'What sort of thing are Wittgenstein's objects?' And the first thing I shall say is that in my opinion Copi is undoubtedly right in insisting that Wittgenstein's objects are particulars. To put the same point in a somewhat different way, Wittgenstein's names are names of particulars. This is not to say, of course, that expressions which function in unperspicuous languages in a superficially name-like way, but do not name particulars, are meaningless. It is simply to say that they would not translate into the names of a perspicuous language. Roughly, unperspicuous name-like expressions fall into two categories for Wittgenstein: (1) Those which would translate into a perspicuous language as, on Russell's theory of descriptions, statements involving descriptive phrases translate into unique existentials (compare Wittgenstein's treatment of complexes in 3.24); (2)—which is more interesting—those which would

---

[1] *Which* n-adic concept the names are made to satisfy is, of course, as philosophers use the term, a matter of convention.

not translate at all into that part of a perspicuous language which is used to make statements about what is or is not the case in the world. It is the latter which are in a special sense without meaning, though not in any ordinary sense meaningless. The 'objects' or 'individuals' or 'logical subjects' they mention are pseudo-objects in that to 'mention them' is to call attention to those features of discourse about what is or is not the case in the world which 'show themselves', i.e. are present in a perspicuous language not as words, but in the manner in which words are combined.[1] Thus it is perfectly legitimate to say that there are 'objects' other than particulars, and to make statements about them. These objects (complexes aside) are not in the world, however, nor do statements about them tell us how things stand in the world. In Wittgenstein's terminology no statements about such objects are 'pictures', and, therefore, in the sense in which 'pictures' have sense they are without sense.

Now one can conceive of a philosopher who agrees with Wittgenstein that in a perspicuous language the fact that two objects stand in a dyadic relation would be represented by making their names stand in a dyadic relation, but who rejects the idea that the only objects or individuals *in the world* are particulars. Such a philosopher might distinguish, for example, within the fact that a certain sensedatum (supposing there to be such entities) is green, between two objects, a *particular* of which the name might be 'a', and an item which, though equally an *object* or *individual*, is not a *particular*. Let us suppose that the name of this object is 'green'.[2] Let us say that green is a universal rather than a particular, and that among universals it is a quality rather than a relation. According to this philosopher,[3] the perspicuous way of saying that *a* is green (abstracting from problems pertaining to temporal reference) is by putting the two names 'a' and 'green' in some relation, the same relation in which we would put 'b' and 'red' if we wished to say that b is red. Let us suppose that we write 'Green a'.

Our previous discussion suggests the question: What would be the *unperspicuous* way of saying what is said by 'Green a', i.e. which would stand to 'Green a' as, on Wittgenstein's view, 'aRb' stands to, say, ^a_b? The philosopher I have in mind proposes the following answer:

a exemplifies green

[1] One is reminded of the peculiar objects which, according to Frege, one talks about when one attempts to talk about concepts.

[2] I shall subsequently discuss the dangers involved in the use of colour examples with particular reference to the interpretation of colour words as names.

[3] The philosopher I have in mind is Professor Gustav Bergmann and the views I am discussing are those to be found, I believe, in certain passages of his interesting paper on "Ineffability, Ontology and Method" which appeared in the January, 1960, number of the *Philosophical Review*.

And this is not unexpected, for where, as in this case, two objects are involved, what is needed for the purpose of *un*perspicuity is a two place predicate which is appropriately concatenated with the name of a particular on one side and the name of a universal on the other, and this is one of the jobs we philosophers pay "exemplifies" to do. Thus this philosopher would be saying that as on Wittgenstein's view the perspicuous way of saying that *a* is next to *b* is by writing 'a' in some relation to 'b', so the perspicuous way of saying that *a* exemplifies green is by writing 'a' in some relation to 'green'. Having thus made use of Wittgenstein's ladder, he would climb off on to his own pinnacle. For he must claim that Wittgenstein made a profound point with the wrong examples. He must, in short, deny that the perspicuous way of saying that *a* is next to *b* is by writing 'a' in some relation to 'b'. That this is so is readily seen from the following considerations.

Exemplification is not the sort of thing that philosophers would ordinarily call an empirical relation. This title is usually reserved for such relations as spatial juxtaposition and temporal succession. Yet exemplification might well be an—or perhaps *the*—empirical relation[1] in a more profound sense than is usually recognized, as would be the case if the simplest atomic facts in the world were of the kind *perspicuously* represented by 'Green a' and *unperspicuously* represented by 'a exemplifies green'.

For let us see what happens to what we ordinarily refer to as empirical relations if relational statements are approached in a manner consistent with the above treatment of 'a is green'. According to the latter, the fact that *a* is green is perspicuously represented by the juxtaposition of two names, 'a' and 'green', and unperspicuously represented by a sentence which contains three expressions, two of which are names, while the third, which might be taken by unperceptive philosophers to be a third *name*, actually serves the purpose of bringing it about that a distinctive dyadic relation obtains between the names. It is clear, then, that the parallel treatment of 'a is below b' would claim that it is perspicuously represented by a suitable juxtaposition of *three* names, 'a', 'b' and 'below', thus,

Below a b

and unperspicuously represented by a sentence which uses *four* expressions, thus, perhaps

Exempl[2] a b below

[1] Cf. Bergmann, op. cit., p. 23, n. 2.

[2] I use this way of putting the matter to make the point with minimum fuss and feathers. It is worth reflecting, however, that the grammatical parallel to 'a exemplifies green' would be either 'a exemplifies being below b' or 'a and b jointly exemplify below-ness (the relation of one thing being below another)'.

I will comment later on the interpretation of 'below' as a name, and on the fact that it is is *prima facie* less plausible than the similar move with respect to 'green'. I should, however, preface the following remarks by saying that I share with Professor Bergmann the sentiment which might be expressed by saying that ordinary grammar is the paper money of wise men but the gold of fools. For my immediate purpose is to contrast the Tractarian theory of predication with that of Professor Bergmann, who, though he decidedly prefers Saul to Paul, is by no means an orthodox exponent of the Old Testament; and I regard the point as of great philosophical significance.

According to the *Tractatus*, then, the fact that *a* is below *b* is *perspicuously* represented by an expression consisting of *two* names dyadically related, and *unperspicuously* represented by an expression containing, in addition to these two names, a two-place predicate expression. According to Professor Bergmann, if I understand him correctly, such facts as that *a* is below *b* are perspicuously represented by expressions consisting of *three* names triadically related, and unperspicuously represented by an expression containing, in addition to these three names (suitably punctuated), an expression having the force of 'exemplifies.' What exactly does this difference amount to? and which view is closer to the truth?

To take up the first question first, the difference can be reformulated in such a way as to bring out its kinship with the old issue between realists and nominalists. Wittgenstein is telling us that the only objects in the world are particulars, Bergmann is telling us that the world includes as objects both particulars and universals. Bergmann, of course, has his own razor and in his own way gives the world a close shave, but not quite as close as does Wittgenstein. Another way of putting the difference is by saying that whereas for Wittgenstein (Saul) it is *empirical* relations in the world that are perspicuously expressed by relating the names of their relata, for Bergmann empirical relations appear in discourse about the world as *nominata*, and it is *exemplification* and *only* exemplification which is perspicuously expressed by relating the names of its relata.

To clarify the latter way of putting the matter, some terminological remarks are in order. If we so use the term 'relation' that to say of something that it is a relation is to say that it is perspicuously represented in discourse by a configuration of expressions rather than by the use of a separate expression, then for Bergmann there is, refinements aside, only *one* relation, i.e. exemplification,[1] and what are ordinarily said to be relations, for example *below*, would occur in the world as *relata*. Thus if we were to continue to use the term

---

[1] Strictly speaking, there would be a relation of exemplification for each order of fact, and, on non-elementaristic views, a family of such relations for each type.

'relation' in such a way that *below* would be a relation, then exemplification, as construed by Bergmann, would not be a relation. For although, as he sees it, both *below* and exemplification are in the world, the former appears in discourse as a nominatum, whereas exemplification does not, indeed *can* not.

To keep matters straight, it will be useful to introduce the term 'nexus' in such a way that to say of something that it is a nexus is to say that it is perspicuously represented in discourse by a configuration of expressions rather than by a separate expression. If we do this, we can contrast Bergmann and Wittgenstein as follows:

Wittgenstein: There are many *nexūs* in the world. Simple relations of matter of fact are *nexūs*. All objects or individuals which form a nexus are particulars, i.e. individuals of type 0. There is no relation or nexus of exemplification in the world.

Bergmann: There is only one[1] nexus, exemplification. Every atomic state of affairs contains at least one (and, if the thesis of elementarism be true, at most one) individual which is not a particular.

If one so uses the term 'ineffable' that to eff something is to signify it by using a name, then Wittgenstein's view would be that what are ordinarily called relations are ineffable, for they are all nexūs and are expressed (whether perspicuously or not) by configurations of names. For Bergmann, on the other hand, what are ordinarily called relations are effed; it is exemplification which is ineffable.

Before attempting to evaluate these contrasting positions, let us beat about the neighbouring bushes. And for a start, let us notice that Wittgenstein tells us that atomic facts are configurations of objects, thus

2.0272 The configuration of the objects forms the atomic fact.

The question I wish to raise is how strictly we are to interpret the plural of the word 'object' in this context. Specifically, could there be a configuration of one object? It must be granted that an affirmative answer would sound odd. But, then, it sounds odd to speak of drawing a conclusion from a null class of premises. Philosophers of a 'reconstructionist' bent have often found it clarifying to treat one thing as a "limiting case" of another; and if Russell, for one, was willing to speak of a quality as a monadic relation, there is no great initial improbability to the idea that Wittgenstein might be willing to speak of a monadic configuration.

Would he be willing to do so? The question is an important one, and calls for a careful examination of the text. I do not think that

---

[1] See note 1, p. 254.

2.0272, taken by itself, throws much light on the matter. Yet when it is taken together with such passages as

2.031 In the atomic fact the objects are combined in a definite way.
2.03 In the atomic fact objects hang in one another like the members of a chain.

which are accompanied by no hint that there might be monadic 'combinations' or, so to speak, chains with a single link, the cumulative effect is to buttress the thesis that there is no provision in the *Tractatus* for monadic atomic facts.

Yet at first sight, at least, this would not seem to be inevitable. After all, one who says that the fact that *a* is below *b* would be perspicuously represented by an expression in which the name 'a' stands in a dyadic relation (to 'b') might be expected to say that the fact that *a* is green would be perspicuously represented by an expression in which the name 'a' stands in a monadic relation, i.e. in a more usual way of speaking, is of a certain quality. Thus one can imagine a philosopher who says that in a perspicuous language, monadic atomic facts would be represented by writing the name of the single object they contain in various colours or in various styles of type. The idea is a familiar one. Is there any reason to suppose that it was not available to Wittgenstein?

One line of thought might be that in such a symbolism we could not distinguish between a name and a statement. After all, a name has to be written in some style or other, and if so, wouldn't every occurrence of a name, in this hypothetical symbolism, have by virtue of its style the force of a statement, and therefore not be a name at all? This objection, however, overestimates the extent to which empirical similarities between expressions imply similarity of linguistic rôle. Obviously, writing 'a' alongside 'b' might be saying that *a* temporally precedes *b*, whereas an 'a' below a 'b' might have no meaning at all. Thus, to write 'a' in bold face might be to say that *a* is green, whereas an 'a' in ordinary type might function merely as a name. How this might be so will be discussed later on. My present point is simply that to understand expressions is to know which of the many facts about them (shape, size, colour, etc.) are relevant (and in what way) to their meaning. It could surely be the case that in a perspicuous language the fact that a heap of ink was a token of a certain name was a matter of its being an instance of a certain letter of the alphabet written in one or another of a certain number of manners. But one or more of these manners might be, so to speak, 'neutral' in that to write the name in such a manner would not be to make an assertion, but simply to write the name, whereas to write the name in other manners would be to make various assertions. Only, then, in the case of the non-'neutral' manners would the writing of the name be the assertion of a monadic fact.

Another line of thought would be to the effect that in a language in which monadic atomic facts (if such there be) were expressed by writing single names in various manners, there would be a difficulty about variables—not about variables ranging over particulars, for here the device of having special letters for variables could be used, but about variables such as would be the counterparts of the monadic predicate variables of *Principia* notation. Thus we could represent the sentential function 'x is green' by using the variable 'x' and writing it in bold face, thus

$$\mathbf{x}$$

But how would one say of *a* that it was of some quality or other? What would correspond to 'a is f' and '(Ef) a is f' as '**x**' to 'x is green' and '(Ex) **x**' to '(Ex) x is green'? Would we not have to introduce an expression to be the variable—after all, one can't write a manner by itself—and if one has separate variables to make possible the expression of what would be expressed in PMese by

$$(Ef) \ fa, \ (g) \ gb, \ \text{etc.}$$

i.e. variables other than those which range over *particulars*, would this not be, in effect, to treat the atomic propositions which are supposedly represented perspicuously by, for example,

$$a$$

as involving two *constants*, and hence two *names*? Must not its truly perspicuous representation be rather

Green a

as Bergmann claims?

Consider the following schema for translation from PMese into Jumblese:

PMese	*Jumblese*
I. *Names of particulars*	
a, b, c, . . .	The same letters written in a variety of neutral styles, the variety being a matter of height, the neutrality a matter of the use of the ordinary font: a, b, c, . . .; a, b, c, . . .; a, b, c, . . .

II. *Statements* (not including relational statements, which will be discussed shortly)

    Green a, red a, . . .   **a**, *a*, . . .

III. *Statement functions*

    (1) *Predicate constant, individual variable:*

    Green x, red y, . . .   **x**, *y*, . . .

    (2) *Predicate variable, individual constant:*

    fa, gb, . . .   Names in neutral styles (see I):
                                          a, . . .; a, . . .; a, . . .

    (3) *Predicate variable, individual variable:*

    fx, gy, . . .   Name variables in neutral styles:
                                          x, y, z, . . .; x, y, z, . . .; x, y, z, . . .

IV. *Quantification*

    (Ex) green x   (Ex) x
    (Ef) fa, (Eg) ga, . . .   (E() a, (E() a, ...
    (Ef) (Ex) fx, (Eg) (Ex) gx, . . .   (E() (Ex) x, (E() (Ex) x, ...

Notice that in the final samples of Jumblese, the (-shaped symbols serve to represent a neutral style; *which* depends on its size.

It is to be noted that in this form of Jumblese, the neutral styles by virtue of which an expression functions as a name without making a statement is also the neutral style which is illustrated by the expressions serving as the counterparts of the predicate variables of PMese. It is therefore an interesting feature of this form of Jumblese that expressions which function as names but not as statements *have the form of a statement*. It is often said with reference to PMese that the form of a predicate is, for example,

Red x

It is less frequently said that the form of a name is, for example,

f a

In the variety of Jumblese sketched above, the latter would be as true as the former. (Cf. *Tractatus* 3.311.) This point clearly should be expanded to take account of the forms of relational statements, but I shall not attempt to do this, save by implication, on the present occasion.

Now the difficulty, if there is one, pertaining to predicate variables is not limited to predicate variables pertaining to these putative monadic atomic statements. If there were a point to be made along the above line, it would pertain as well to dyadic and polyadic statements as Wittgenstein interprets them. Thus, to continue with our translation schema, we have

PMese	*Jumblese*
Larger (ab), Redder (ab)	^a_b, ^a_b
R(ab), S(ab), T(ab), . . .	ab, a b, a b, . . .
Larger (xy), Redder (xy), . . .	^x_y, ^x_y, . . .
R(xy), S(xy), . . .	xy, x y, x y, . . .
(Ex) (Ey) Larger (xy)	(Ex) (Ey) ^x_y
(ER) R(ab), (ES) S(ab), . . .	(E ..) ab, (E . .) a b, . . .
(ER) (Ex) (Ey) R(xy)	(E ..) (Ex) (Ey) xy

Here again we find the introduction of symbols to be the counterparts of the relation variables of PMese, i.e. symbols which illustrate the neutral manners which are used in

$$ab, a\ b, a\quad b, a\quad b, \text{etc.}$$

to express what is expressed in PMese by the statement functions

$$R(ab), S(ab), T(ab), \text{etc.}$$

Thus, in addition to the variables '(', '(', '(', . . . which correspond to the one place predicate variables of *Principia*, we have the variables '..', '. .', '. .', . . . to correspond to the dyadic predicate variables of *Principia*.

The topic of perspicuousness with respect to variables and quantification is an interesting and important one in its own right, and the above remarks have barely scratched the surface. The only point I have wanted to make is that if considerations pertaining to quantification or to distinguishing between names and statements support the idea that the atomic statements of a perspicuous language must contain at least two names, these considerations would do so *not* by supporting the idea that a minimal atomic statement would contain the names of two *particulars*, but by supporting the idea that it would contain the name of a universal. In other words, they would point to Bergmann's form of logical atomism as contrasted with that of Wittgenstein.

Now I side with Wittgenstein on this matter, that is to say I would argue that the atomic descriptive statements of an ideal language would contain names of particulars only. As I see it, therefore, it is of crucial importance to ontology not to confuse the contrast between *constant* and *variable* with that between *name* and *variable*. For to confuse these two contrasts is to move from the correct idea that

Green a

can be viewed against the doubly quantified statement

$$(Ef) (Ex) fx$$

to the incorrect idea that

Green a

is the juxtaposition of two *names*, and says perspicuously what would be unperspicuously said by

a exemplifies green.

To view the Jumblese statement

a

against the doubly quantified statement

$$(E() (x) x$$

is, indeed, to highlight two facts about the expression '**a**', the fact by virtue of which it is a writing in some style or other of a certain name and the fact by virtue of which, to speak metaphorically, green comes into the picture. But I see no reason to infer that because the expression's being a case of a certain name, and the expression's pertaining to green are each bound up with a monadic (though not, of course, atomic) fact about the expression, that both its being about *a* and its being about green come into the picture in the same way, i.e. that they are both *named*.

For the being about *a* and the being about green could each be true of the expression by virtue of monadic facts about it, and still not pertain to its meaning *in the same way* in any more important sense. The crucial thing about an expression is the rôle it plays in the language, and the fact that a certain expression is an '**a**' in some style or other, and the fact that it is in bold face, may both be monadic facts and yet play different rôles in the language. In which connection it is relevant to note that the monadic fact about the expression by virtue of which it pertains to green is not the monadic fact that it is thick, but the monadic fact that it is a thick instance of a name or name variable.

II

Before continuing with the substantive argument of this paper, I shall say something more to the historical question as to whether Wittgenstein himself 'countenanced' monadic atomic facts. I have argued that the passages in which he speaks of atomic facts as configurations of objects (in the plural) are not decisive, by pointing out that Russell might have spoken of atomic facts as related objects, but have so used the term 'relation' that one could speak of monadic relations. It seems to me that similar considerations prevent such passages as

2.15 That the elements of the picture are combined with one another in a definite way represents that the things are so combined with one another.

3.21 To the configuration of the single signs in the propositional sign corresponds the configuration of the objects in the state of affairs.

from deciding the issue against the idea that an atomic proposition could contain only one name.

On one occasion Wittgenstein seems to me to come as close to saying that there are monadic atomic propositions as he could have come without saying it in so many words. Thus consider

4.24 The names are the simple symbols. I indicate them by single letters ('x', 'y', 'z').
The elementary proposition I write as function of the names, in the form 'fx', '$\phi(x,y)$', etc.

This passage is the more striking in that it occurs very shortly after

4.22 The elementary proposition consists of names. It is a connection, a concatenation of names.

Now to interpret 4.24 it is important to note that although Wittgenstein tells us that atomic facts to the effect that two objects are dyadically related would be perspicuously represented by placing the names of these objects in dyadic relation without the use of any relation word, the *Tractatus* contains no *use* but only *mentions* (and indirect ones at that) of such perspicuous representations. Thus Wittgenstein does not *use* Jumblese, but always PMese, in illustrating the form of atomic propositions, thus always 'aRb' (cf. the '$\phi(x,y)$' of 4.24). What he does do is tell us that the symbol 'R' serves not as a name, but as a means of bringing it about that the names 'a' and 'b' are dyadically related.

This being so, Wittgenstein is telling us in 4.24 that when he uses an expression of the form 'fx' to write an elementary proposition, the function *word* represented by the 'f' is occurring not as a name, but as bringing it about that the name represented by 'x' occurs in a certain manner, i.e. that the name as occurring in a certain monadic configuration is a proposition.

Now if a philosopher combines the two theses, (1) there are no atomic facts involving only one particular, (2) all objects are particulars, it would be reasonable to say that he is committed to a doctrine of bare particulars. For, speaking informally, he holds that

261

though objects stand in empirical relations, they have no qualities. Notice that this would not be true of Bergmann's position, for while he holds that there are no atomic facts containing only one *object*, he insists that there are atomic facts which contain only one *particular*. Thus he can deny that there are bare particulars by insisting that every object exemplifies a quality.

Now in my opinion Copi is correct in attributing to Wittgenstein the second of the above two theses (all objects are particulars). If, therefore, he were correct in attributing to Wittgenstein the first thesis, his claim that Wittgenstein is committed to a doctrine of bare particulars would be sound. Conversely, if Wittgenstein did hold a doctrine of bare particulars, then he was committed to the thesis that there are no monadic atomic facts. It is not surprising, therefore, to find Copi arguing that his contention that Wittgenstein rejects monadic atomic facts is supported by what he (somewhat reluctantly) takes to be an affirmation of the doctrine of bare particulars. Thus after confessing that "It must be admitted that several of Wittgenstein's remarks suggest that objects have 'external' properties as well as 'internal' ones (2.01231, 2.0233, 4.023)", he writes (p. 163 [p. 184]):

> Despite the difficulty of dealing with such passages, there seems to me to be overwhelming evidence that he regarded objects as bare particulars, having no material properties whatever.
>
> In the first place, Wittgenstein explicitly denies that objects can have properties. His assertion that 'objects are colourless' (2.0232) must be understood as synechdochical, for the context makes it clear that he is not interested in denying colour qualities only, but all qualities of 'material properties' (the term first appears in the immediately preceding paragraph (2.0232)).

Now I think that this is simply a misunderstanding. The correct interpretation of the passage in question requires only a careful reading of the context. What Wittgenstein says is "Roughly speaking (*Beilauefig gesprochen*): objects are colourless", and this remark occurs as a comment on

2.0231 The substance of the world *can* only determine a form and not any material properties. For these are first presented by the propositions—first formed by the configuration of the objects.

What Wittgenstein is telling us here is that *objects* do not determine *facts*: thus even if a is green, the fact that a is green is not determined by a. It is interesting, in this connection, to reflect on

2.014 Objects contain the possibility of all states of affairs.

Thus, while a does not determine the fact that it is green, it does

262

determine the range of possible facts of which the fact that it is green is but one.

Names exist in a logical space which includes the predicates which combine with it to make statements. (*In a perspicuous language—Jumblese—the predicate words, as has been pointed out, would appear as manners of being names, as, in a literal sense, internal features of the names.*) And no atomic statement is analytic, hence,

2.01231 In order to know an object, I must know not its external but its internal properties.

When Wittgenstein says that

2.0123 If I know an object, then I also know all the possibilities of its occurrence in atomic facts.

this is as much as to say that if I understand a name, then I also know all the possibilities of its occurrence in atomic statements. When he says

2.013 Everything is, as it were, in a space of possible atomic facts.

this is as much as to say that every name is, as it were, in a space of possible atomic statements.[1] And when he says

2.0131 . . . A speck in a visual field need not be red, but it must have a colour.

he is making the point that objects are internally related to sets of "external" properties, but not to any *one* "external" property, i.e. that names are internally related to sets of primitive predicates[2] (configurations; cf. Jumblese).

Thus it is not surprising to us (though disturbing to Copi) to find Wittgenstein saying in the passage following that in which he says that (roughly speaking) objects are colourless,

2.0233 Two objects of the same logical form are—apart from their external properties—only differentiated from one another in that they are different.

For this means *not*, as it might seem, that objects are *bare*, but simply that two objects of the same logical form[3] determine the same range

---

[1] When he adds that "I can think of this space as empty, but not of the thing without the space", he suggests the intriguing possibility that we can make sense of the idea that the language we use might have had no application.

[2] Whether these sets constitute embracing sets of primitive predicates of different orders, or whether they fall into subsets (families of determinates), is a topic for separate investigation.

[3] I find here the implication that primitive one-place predicates (configurations)—if not all primitive predicates—come in families (determinates) and that objects are of different logical form if, for example, one exists in the logical space of colour, the other in the logical space of sound.

of possible facts, i.e. two names of the same logical form belong to the same range of configurations.

As far as I can see, Copi's second argument to show that Wittgenstein's objects are bare particulars is also a misunderstanding. He begins by correctly pointing out that according to Wittgenstein objects are named, whereas states of affairs are "described"—the word is Wittgenstein's. He then writes (p. 164 [p. 185]):

... if an object *had* a property, that would be a fact whose assertion would constitute a *description* of that object. But objects can not be so described, whence it follows that objects have no properties.

This argument overlooks the fact that Wittgenstein, under the influence of logistical jargon, uses the term 'describe' where one would expect 'assert' (cf. 3.221). Thus he is simply telling us that objects cannot be 'described', i.e. *asserted*; from which it by no means follows that they can't be described in the ordinary sense. Indeed, in 4.023, Wittgenstein writes "As the description of an object describes it by its external properties, so propositions describe reality by its internal properties".

The third argument has the form " . . . if an object had a material property, *that* it had the property would be a fact involving only one particular, hence no object can have any material property, and all particulars are bare" (p. 164 [p. 185]). The hypothetical is sound. The evidence adduced for denying the consequent is 4.032 which is interpreted as saying that all propositional signs are composite, and must consequently contain at least two elements, that is, at least two names. But 4.032 does not say that all propositional signs are *composite*, but that they are all "logically articulated", and I have attempted to explain how a propositional sign can consist of *one logically articulated name*. I grant that in a parenthetical remark which immediately follows Wittgenstein writes, "(Even the proposition 'ambulo' is composite for its stem gives a different sense with another termination, or its termination with another stem)", but I do not believe that this remark, which correctly points out that ordinary Latin is not perspicuous with respect to logical articulation, is decisive. (I am happy to acknowledge that my interpretation, like Copi's, has its difficulties.)

Copi's concluding argument is to the effect that Wittgenstein tells us in the *Investigations* that the objects of the *Tractatus* were primary elements like those described in the *Theaetetus* (21e). This would be cogent if we were given a reason for supposing either that the elements of *Theaetetus* 21e were bare particulars, or that Wittgenstein thought they were. I see no reason to think that either is the case.

The most telling argument in Copi's paper against the idea that the

Tractatus countenanced monadic atomic facts is not used by Copi directly to this end, but as part of his brief for the sound thesis that Wittgenstein's objects are not properties. Slightly redirected, it is to the effect that if there are any monadic atomic facts, surely they include such facts as that a certain point in a visual field is red. But, the argument proceeds, if 'a is red' is an elementary proposition, then 'a is blue' cannot contradict it. But, as is well known, Wittgenstein tells us (6.3751) that "For two colours, e.g., to be at one place in the visual field, is impossible, logically impossible, for it is excluded by the logical structure of colour. . . . (It is clear that the logical product of two elementary propositions can neither be a tautology nor a contradiction.)" Copi draws the conclusion (p. 162 [p. 183]) that "colour predications are *not* elementary predications".

Now, two points require to be made in this connection. The first is that one might be convinced that there *could* be monadic atomic facts (in that peculiar sense in which, for any n there could be n-adic atomic facts) without being able to give any examples. It is worth noting, in this connection, that in *Some Main Problems of Philosophy*, Moore, in effect, wonders whether there are any qualities (as opposed to relational properties), and specifically explores the logical space of colours to see if it provides us with examples of qualities. Moore was prepared to find that there are no qualities, i.e. that the simplest facts are already relational. True, Moore's qualitative facts would be Bergmanian rather than Wittgensteinian, that is, would each be a nexus of a particular *and a universal*, but the fact that Moore was prepared to suspend judgment with respect to the question "Are there qualities?" combined with the fact that he found the logical structure of colour to be very complex indeed, suggests that Wittgenstein might well have taken a similar attitude. After all, as Anscombe points out, Wittgenstein regards it as in some sense a matter of fact that the most complex *atomic* fact is n-adic rather than m-adic (m n)—cf. 4.2211. Could it not be in the same sense a matter of fact that the least complex is, say, dyadic rather than monadic?

Thus, perhaps the correct answer to the historical question is that Wittgenstein would have regarded the question 'Are particulars bare?' as, in a deep sense, a factual one, a question to which he did not claim to have the answer, and to which, as logician, he was not required to have the answer.

The second remark is that Wittgenstein may well have thought that there are monadic atomic facts, indeed that their existence is obvious, but that no statement in ordinary usage represented such a fact, so that no example could be given in the sense of written down. Although he thought that ordinary language contained elementary propositions, he emphasizes that they are contained in a way which is not perspicuous. There is no presupposition that any ordinary sentence as ordinarily used in the context of everyday life ever expresses an atomic proposition. Indeed, the presupposition is to the contrary.

III

It has been said by Broad, among others, that philosophers have been led into error in perception theory by concentrating their attention on visual examples. In my opinion they have been at least as frequently led into error in logical theory by a similar concentration on colour. The danger arises from the fact that such a word as 'red', for example, is really three words, an adjective, a common noun and a proper name, rolled into one. Thus we can say, with equal propriety,

> The book is red
> Scarlet is a colour
> Red is a colour

A moment ago I urged the importance of the distinction between descriptive *constants* and *names*. I suggested that while it would be correct to say that the statement

> Green a

consists of two *constants*, as is brought out by viewing it against the three quantified statements,

> (Ex) Green x
> (Ef) fa
> (Ef) (Ex) fx

it is most misleading to say that it consists of two names. And the reason, by now, should be clear. For if one does view the sentence 'Green a' as a juxtaposition of *names*, one will be bound, particularly if one has read the *Tractatus*, to think that by juxtaposing the names 'Green' and 'a' it affirms that the two objects or individuals or logical subjects *green* and *a* are 'united' or 'hang in each other' or are bound together by a 'characterizing tie' or whatever.

Now what makes this move all the more plausible is that there *is* an object *green* and that there *is* a relation which is often called exemplification, such that if a is green *then it is also true that a exemplifies green*. Thus it is tempting indeed to say that

> a exemplifies green

is simply an unperspicuous way of saying what is said perspicuously by

Green a

And the fascinating thing about it is that this claim would be absolutely correct *provided that 'green a' was not taken to say what is ordinarily said by 'a is green'*.

The point stands out like a sore thumb if one leave colours aside and uses a geometrical example. Thus consider the statement

a is triangular

or, for our purposes,

Triangular a

It would clearly be odd to say

a exemplifies triangular

although it is not odd to say

a exemplifies green.

The reason is that 'triangular' unlike 'green' does not function in ordinary usage as both an adjective and a singular term. What we must say is

a exemplifies triangularity.

Now in a perspicuous language, i.e. a language which had a built-in protection against Bradley's puzzle, we might say *that a exemplifies triangularity* by concatenating 'a' and 'triangularity' or *that Socrates exemplifies Wisdom* by writing

Socrates: Wisdom.

Our language is not such a perspicuous one, and to bring this out in this connection, we might write,

We must not say, "The complex sign 'a exemplifies triangularity' says 'a stands in the exemplification relation to triangularity': but we must say *'that "a" stands in a certain relation to "triangularity"'* says that a exemplifies triangularity."

Thus it is correct to say that

Green a

says perspicuously what is said by

a exemplifies green

only if 'green' is used in the sense of the singular term 'greenness'.
And when it is used in this sense, the statement

Green a

does not have the sense of the ordinary statement

a is green,

though it is logically equivalent to it.

Professor Bergmann thinks that

Green a

consists of two names, 'a', the name of a particular, and 'green', the
name of a universal, and, by being their juxtaposition, asserts that
the one exemplifies the other. On his view, philosophers who insist
that 'a is green' says that a exemplifies green but do not realize that
'a exemplifies green' is simply an unperspicuous way of juxtaposing
'a' with 'green' are attempting to eff the ineffable. He thinks, to use
the terminology I proposed earlier, that exemplification is the nexus,
the mode of configuration of objects which can only be expressed by
a configuration of names. Professor Bergmann sees configurations of
particulars and universals where Wittgenstein saw only configurations of particulars.

But what does

a exemplifies triangularity

say if it isn't an unperspicuous way of saying

Triangular a

Instead of giving an answer (as I have attempted to do on other
occasions) I shall attempt an analogy, and then claim that it is more
than a mere analogy. It seems to me that the necessary equivalence
but non-synonymy of

a exemplifies triangularity

with

a is triangular

is analogous to the necessary equivalence but non-synonymy of

That a is triangular is true

with

a is triangular

That the analogy is more than a mere analogy is suggested by the fact that instead of saying that a exemplifies triangularity, we might with equal propriety say that triangularity is true of a, or holds of a.

Now if

> a exemplifies triangularity
> triangularity is true of a
> triangularity holds of a

are to be elucidated in terms of

> That a is triangular is true

then exemplification is no more present in the world of fact in that narrow sense which Tractarians like Professor Bergmann and myself find illuminating, than is meaning, or truth, *and for the same reason*.

The crucial ineffability in the *Tractatus* concerns the relation between statements and facts. Is there such a relation? And is it ineffable? The answer seems to me to be the following. There is a meaning relation between statements and *facts*, but both terms are in the linguistic order. To say that a statement means a fact is to say, for example,

> 'Gruen a' (in German) means *Green a*, and it is a fact that Green a.

The first conjunct appears to assert a relation between a linguistic and a non-linguistic item, between a statement and an item in the real order. And the second conjunct to say of this item that it is a fact. As I see it, the first conjunct does assert a relation, but the relation obtains between a German expression and an English expression *as being an expression in our language*. It has the force of

> 'Gruen a' (in German) corresponds to 'Green a' in our language.

We could also put this by saying

> 'Gruen a' (in German) means *that green a*

for to put 'that' before a sentence has the force of quoting it with the implication that the sentence is in our language, and is being considered as such. The reason why we find it counter-intuitive to put it in this way is that since 'means' is the translation rubric, this would conflict with the usage according to which we say

> 'Dass gruen a' (in German) means *that green a*.

Suppose it is granted that meaning is the translatability relation between an expression which may or may not be in our language and one which is, and is being considered as such. What, then, does it mean to say

> That green a is a fact

Clearly this is equivalent to saying

That green is true

which calls to mind the equivalence

That green a is true ≡ green a

This, however, is not the most perspicuous way to represent matters, for while the equivalence obtains, indeed necessarily obtains, its truth depends on the principle of inference—and this is the crux—

From 'that green a is true' (in our language) to infer 'green a' (in our language).

And it is by virtue of the fact that we *draw* such inferences that meaning and truth talk gets its connection with the world. In this sense, the connection is *done* rather than *talked about*.

Viewed from this perspective, Wittgenstein's later conception of a language as a form of life is already foreshadowed by the ineffability thesis of the *Tractatus*. But to see this is to see that *no* ineffability is involved. For while to infer is neither to refer to that which can be referred to, nor to assert that which can be asserted, this does not mean that it is to fail to eff something which is, therefore, ineffable.

Wittgenstein's Picture-Theory of Language[1,2]

H. R. G. SCHWYZER

I argue that the current view (as held by, e.g. Warnock, Anscombe and Stenius) of Wittgenstein's theory of language in the *Tractatus* is mistaken. This view maintains that Wittgenstein's theory is one of 'isomorphism'; that, roughly, a sentence has meaning in virtue of its being a facsimile of a fact or possible fact. But a detailed study of significant passages in the *Tractatus* shows that Wittgenstein held no such view. His use of important terms, such as *Satz, Bild, Sachverhalt, Tatsache*, etc., has been crucially misunderstood. There is no isomorphism. The theory is not about *sentences* at all, but about *talking sense*.

IT is well known that Wittgenstein's *Tractatus* contains a 'picture-theory' of language.

In a picture of an object or scene, there is a kind of correspondence between the parts of or elements in the picture, and the parts of or elements in the object or scene. But these elements must not only be present; their structure, form, or arrangement must be the same—according of course to some system of projection, whether simple perspective or something more elaborate. Now 'an atomic fact is a combination of objects (entities, things) . . . The configuration of objects forms the atomic fact.' (*Tractatus* 2.01, 2.0272.) But the 'sentential sign' is itself also a fact; it too is a combination of elements, namely *words*. This sort of fact is therefore capable of 'picturing' those other, non-verbal facts; and it is thus that language can refer to the world, can *mean* something other than itself.

(G. J. Warnock: *English Philosophy since 1900*, p. 65)

[1] From *Inquiry*, vol. 5, no. 1, Spring, 1962, pp. 46-63. Reprinted by permission of the editor and the author.

[2] I am deeply indebted to Professor D. S. Shwayder, not only for the stimulation of many of the ideas expressed in this paper, but also for constant encouragement and invaluable criticism through its preparation.

271

I have quoted this passage because it seems to me to typify a common current interpretation of Wittgenstein's theory of language in the *Tractatus*; I think it is a mistaken interpretation, or, at best, misleadingly incomplete. For Warnock's account sets up a perfectly symmetrical relation between language and the world; it therefore tells us nothing about 'meaning'. Sentences, on this view, can 'mean' or 'picture' facts because sentence-signs are themselves facts and because their structure corresponds to that of non-verbal facts. But if this is true, then surely, and for precisely the same reasons, non-verbal facts can mean or picture sentences. Now there is a (trivial) sense in which we might accept such a view: that is to say, we could imagine a language in which we used *things* to talk about *words*—in which aRb stated that 'a' bears a certain relation to 'b', instead of the other way around. What we now call non-verbal facts would then mean or picture what we now call verbal facts. But in that language, of course, the picturing facts would again be the 'verbal', i.e. the linguistic ones. Whatever our language may be, in that language only the linguistic facts can do the meaning. But Warnock gives us no means of distinguishing between linguistic and non-linguistic facts, and so makes Wittgenstein's account of the nature of language appear quite unworthy of serious consideration.

Warnock is by no means alone in this characterization of the theory of picturing. Indeed, some philosophers have expressly attributed to Wittgenstein the view that the relation of the picture to what is pictured is simply reversible.

Professor Stenius, in his recent book,[1] seems initially to assume that only the 'true' pictures of the *Tractatus* are really pictures. These, he says, are isomorphic with facts, the prototypes of the pictures. And 'of two isomorphic fields F and G one, say F, *may always be considered as a picture of the other*' (my italics).

Miss Anscombe[2] reports Fr Colombo, the Italian translator of the *Tractatus*, as remarking that 'it was difficult to see why a described fact should not be regarded as itself a description of the proposition that would normally be said to describe it, rather than the other way round'. 'And', she continues, 'as far as concerns the internal features of proposition and fact, this is a strong point; for all the internal features are supposed to be identical in the proposition (or describing fact) and the described fact'. So Anscombe too holds that, for Wittgenstein, propositions (*Saetze*) are isomorphic with facts. But she is aware that isomorphism is not enough: it does not explain how it is that a *Satz* means something. She therefore finds it necessary to

---

[1] Erik Stenius, *Wittgenstein's 'Tractatus'*, Blackwell, 1960, pp. 95 f.

[2] G. E. M. Anscombe, *An Introduction to Wittgenstein's Tractatus*, Hutchinson, 1959, p. 67.

introduce an additional element, the speaker, as an 'external feature' of the *Satz* or picture.

So for Anscombe a *Satz* or picture does not in itself mean or describe anything at all, any more than does a fact mean or describe anything. It is *we* who mean and describe—by *using Saetze*, by *holding up* pictures and saying 'this is how things are'. There is, it would seem, nothing in the nature of the entities under consideration that could prevent our using facts to describe pictures or *Saetze*; it would merely be inconvenient. But Wittgenstein never speaks of our using *Saetze*, nor of our holding up pictures. Why not?

I believe that the views I have outlined misrepresent the theory of picturing entirely. To say that a *Satz* is a picture is *not*, I shall argue, to explain what sentences or propositions must be like if they are to be the kinds of things that *can be used* to make statements; it is to explain *what it is* to make statements, to mean something, to 'express a sense'. The 'relation', if you wish to call it a relation, between language and the world is asymmetrical—and this in virtue of the internal 'features' of the *Satz*, if you wish to call them features. For a *Satz* is an *assertion*; it is not the kind of thing that can be used, held up, in speaking, for it is itself an act of speaking.

In this paper I shall adhere very closely to the text of the *Tractatus* in an attempt to elucidate some important passages from the book which I believe to have been crucially misread. Wittgenstein's account of language may well be fundamentally incorrect. I hope to show that it is not a simple-minded theory of isomorphism between language and the world, as has commonly been supposed, but a profound and highly original examination of what it is to speak.

2.1   Wir machen uns Bilder der Tatsachen.[1]
2.11 Das Bild stellt die Sachlage im logischen Raume, das Bestehen und Nichtbestehen von Sachverhalten vor.
2.12 Das Bild ist ein Modell der Wirklichkeit.

From these remarks Stenius (op. cit., Ch. 6, i) concludes that pictures, for Wittgenstein, are 'representational': '. . . Wittgenstein always thinks of a picture as having a *real* prototype, which it represents'. Pictures, then, are facsimiles, replicas, reproductions of prototypes, of 'originals'; and these originals are held to be *facts* (*Tatsachen*). I shall argue that this apparently innocuous interpretation is unfounded and quite wrong. There are no prototype-facts in the *Tractatus*. If there were such entities, then we should expect Wittgenstein to mention them in those contexts in which, for example,

---

[1] Many passages from the *Tractatus* cannot be rendered into English without imposing a particular interpretation. I shall therefore frequently quote the German of the book.

reference is made to what corresponds to the elements of the picture. We should expect him to say, e.g., that the elements of the picture stand for the elements of the fact. But this is never said. Instead, we are told: 'The elements of the picture stand, in the picture, *for the objects*' (2.131, my italics; cf. 2.13, 2.15, 2.151, 2.1514, etc.). But perhaps this is purely accidental. After all, it will be argued, objects *are* elements of facts; and when Wittgenstein speaks of 'the objects' he really means 'the elements of a given fact'. But let us read this into the relevant passages. 2.151 says: 'The Form of Representation is the possibility that the things are combined with one another as are the elements of the picture'. And this must be understood to mean: 'The Form of Representation is the possibility that the elements of the fact (represented by the picture) are combined with one another as are the elements of the picture'. Now it is essential to pictures, for Wittgenstein, that they *can* be false (e.g. 2.225). But if in the present case the picture is false, then the elements of the prototype-fact will *not* be combined with one another as are the elements of the picture. And there is no sense in talking of the possibility of *their* being so combined; for if they *were* so combined, they would no longer be elements of the same fact, the prototype-fact, but of another fact. Clearly, *as elements of a given fact*, things cannot be combined in any way other than that in which they are combined. It follows that if 2.151 is to make sense at all then we must resist this interpretation. Wittgenstein is to be taken at his word: the elements of the picture correspond to objects, not to elements of a fact. There is, however, a very different way in which the word 'fact' might find a place in this statement: 'The Form of Representation is the possibility *that it is a fact that* the objects—which the elements stand for[1]—are combined with one another as are the elements of the picture'. There is no other fact 'represented' by the picture. The relation of fact to picture is not that of original to replica; a fact is not the kind of thing of which there *could* be a replica. So what is it?

1   Die Welt ist alles, was der Fall ist.
1.1   Die Welt ist die Gesamtheit der Tatsachen, nicht der Dinge.
2   Was der Fall ist, die Tatsache, ist das Bestehen von Sachverhalten.
2.01 Der Sachverhalt ist eine Verbindung von Gegenstaenden (Sachen, Dingen).

From 1 together with 1.1 it follows that 'fact', for Wittgenstein, means 'what is the case'. 2 is the explanation of this: what is the case, the fact, is the 'obtaining' of *Sachverhalte*. And this means: it is the

---

[1] Wittgenstein is not talking of objects in general—hence the definite article (which can be omitted in generalizations, in German as well as in English). So 'objects' must be qualified.

case that—the fact is that—*Sachverhalte* 'obtain'. *Sachverhalte*, therefore, cannot themselves be facts. The word '*Sachverhalt*' cannot be replaced by the clause 'it is the case that', for what is the case is precisely *das Bestehen von Sachverhalten*.[1] A *Sachverhalt* is simply a combination of objects (2.01). '*Das Bestehen von Sachverhalten*' is equivalent to a clause of indirect discourse. It is to be translated, 'that objects are combined in such and such a way'. We shall find a clear confirmation of this in the theory of picturing (see p. 51 [p. 276] of this paper). Take *red* and *square* as objects; then *red square* is a *Sachverhalt*, and *that the square is (is not) red* is a *Tatsache*.

Nearly all the commentators, perhaps following Russell, have rendered '*Sachverhalt*' as 'atomic fact', thus blurring the vital distinction between *Tatsache* and *Sachverhalt*. The relation between these has, I think, been misconstrued in the following way. It has generally been recognized that objects, for Wittgenstein, are simple and 'irreducible'; it has also been recognized that *Sachverhalte* are combinations of such objects. (This is, presumably, a reason for calling *Sachverhalte* 'atomic', as Wittgenstein was willing to do.) *Tatsachen* have then been taken to belong to the same category of things as *Sachverhalte*. Thus Russell[2] holds them to be *complex Sachverhalte*, non-atomic combinations of objects; and this view, as far as I can make out, is shared by Anscombe (op. cit., p. 30). Stenius, on the other hand, maintains that facts are *existing Sachverhalte*, 'real' combinations of objects (op. cit., pp. 30 ff.). On both of these views, facts are a species of *Sachverhalte*. Now Wittgenstein says that we make pictures of facts (2.1). But if facts are 'complex' or 'existing' combinations of things, then making a picture of one of these would have to be very much like producing a likeness, a facsimile. The 'reduction' of facts to combinations of things is therefore largely responsible for the theory of isomorphism between 'proposition' and fact.

But facts are not combinations of things, nor are they reducible to these. The world is the totality of facts, not of things—nor, we might add, of *Sachverhalte*. Once more: the relation between *Tatsache* and *Sachverhalt* is as follows. If a combination of things 'obtains', i.e. if things are combined in such-and-such a way—if the

---

[1] *Das Nichtbestehen von Sachverhalten*—that *Sachverhalte* do not obtain—is also a fact (see, e.g., 2.06). Of course Wittgenstein must leave room for the assertion of such facts, hence there must be a place in his system for the presentation of *das Nichtbestehen von Sachverhalten*. He must additionally allow for other varieties of truth-functional composition; and it is this which accounts for alternative formulations in terms of *das Bestehen und Nichtbestehen von Sachverhalten* (e.g. 2.11), and in terms of the agreement and disagreement with *das Bestehen und Nichtbestehen von Sachverhalten* (e.g. 4.2). It is not essential for the purposes of this paper that we consider the different varieties of *Satz*, and I shall therefore uniformly translate these passages.

[2] Introduction to the *Tractatus*, p. 9.

square is red, then it is a fact that it is; if the square is not red, then it is a fact that it is not. Wittgenstein's use of 'fact' is far closer to what we usually mean by the word than has been supposed.

But if 'fact' means 'that objects are combined in such-and-such a way', i.e. 'that such-and-such is the case', then how are we to understand 'we make ourselves pictures of facts'? For we have deprived ourselves of what might appear to be the obvious interpretation, viz. that we draw pictures of bundles of things in relation. If what I have said is right, then Wittgenstein must be saying that what we draw pictures of is *that* such-and-such is the case. And this doesn't seem to make sense. But we must find out what a Wittgensteinian picture is.

These are the opening statements of the theory of picturing.

2.1   Wir machen uns Bilder der Tatsachen.

2.11   Das Bild stellt die Sachlage im logischen Raume, das Bestehen und Nichtbestehen von Sachverhalten vor.

2.12   Das Bild ist ein Modell der Wirklichkeit.

2.13   Den Gegenstaenden entsprechen im Bilde die Elemente des Bildes.

2.131   Die Elemente des Bildes vertreten im Bild die Gegenstaende.

2.14   Das Bild besteht darin, dass sich seine Elemente in bestimmter Art und Weise zu einander verhalten.

2.141   Das Bild ist eine Tatsache.

2.15   Dass sich die Elemente des Bildes in bestimmter Art und Weise
(par. 1) zu einander verhalten stellt vor, dass sich die Sachen so zu einander verhalten.

We have already noted the necessity (in 2.13, 2.131 and 2.15) of speaking of objects, things—not elements of a fact—as the correlates of picture-elements. We should note also in passing that the picture is said to be a model of *reality* (2.12), not of any fact.[1]

What the picture does is to 'present' *das Bestehen und Nichtbestehen von Sachverhalten*. The picture is a *fact*, viz. that its elements are combined in a particular way. This fact *presents* that the objects are so combined.

Now it is important to note that 2.15 (par. 1) is a paraphrase, a restatement, of 2.11. 'That the elements of the picture are combined in a definite way' in 2.15, replaces *'das Bild'* in 2.11. 'That the objects are so combined' in 2.15, replaces *'das Bestehen und Nichtbestehen von Sachverhalten'* in 2.11. And this confirms what we said earlier, that *'das Bestehen von Sachverhalten'* is to be understood as equivalent to a clause of indirect discourse. It should be noted too that *'vorstellen'* ('present') introduces such a clause. What the picture does is to present that such-and-such is the case. But just how are we to

---

[1] What the picture *represents* (*abbildet*) is also not a fact; it is either reality (*Wirklichkeit*), or the world (*die Welt*). Cf. 2.17, 2.171, 2.18, 2.19, etc. 4.016 is an exception; so also is the entire passage in which it occurs. (See p. 62 [pp. 286–7] of this paper.)

understand 'present that'? The following translation of 2.15 (par. 1) will not do. 'That the elements of the picture are combined in a particular way *represents* [i.e. is a representation, copy, facsimile, of] the fact that the things are so combined'. If this were the case, then there could be no false pictures, every picture would be true *a priori*. For suppose the picture to be false. It would then clearly not be a representation of the fact that the things are combined as are the elements of the picture, for *ex hypothesi*, the things would not be so combined. So false pictures would not be models of reality, they would not be pictures at all. But Wittgenstein says that 'The picture presents what it presents independently of its truth or falsehood' (2.22). And this means that a picture's falsehood does not prevent it from being a picture.

Now if a picture presents that things are combined in a particular way *independently* of whether or not they are *in fact* combined in this way, then this means that it presents the things *as* being so combined. Just what it is to 'present' in this way cannot be more explicitly set out without anticipating what Wittgenstein goes on to say about thought and language. But it is already clear that 'presenting', with its peculiar connection with truth and falsity, is very much like *asserting* that something is the case.

Let us, in the meantime, ask this question: Shouldn't we understand Wittgenstein to be saying that the picture presents the *fact* that things are combined in a particular way? For we have seen that 'fact' means 'that-things-are-combined-in-such-and-such-a-way' (*das Bestehen von Sachverhalten*), and this is exactly what the picture presents. But to say that the picture presents a fact is again to beg the question of the truth of the picture, in just the way that we have seen. For if the picture is false, then there is no fact that the things are combined as presented. The *fact* is that they are *not* so combined, and this is *not* what is presented. To make a picture of the facts is to present not facts, but *that it is a fact* that things are combined in such-and-such a way. We might say that what the picture presents, it presents *as* a fact. Only because the picture bears *this* relation to the facts can it be said to be true or false.

In the passage we have been considering, Wittgenstein has spoken a) of *our making* pictures, b) of what pictures *are* (facts of a certain kind), and c) of what pictures *do* (present that). And all this is very puzzling. How, we might ask, are these three connected? How can pictures *do* anything anyway? Is the 'presenting that' an intrinsic feature of pictures, or are pictures that do not present still pictures? And what is the significance of calling them 'facts'? These are important questions, and I think they can be satisfactorily answered. Indeed we have already begun to answer some of them.

I shall suggest first of all that there is no difference between what we do when we make pictures, what the picture does when it presents that something is the case, and what the picture is. For the picture *is the presenting* (*das Vorstellen*) that something is the case, and it is of course we who do the presenting. The fact then that the picture-elements are combined in a particular way *is* the presenting that the objects are so combined. If this is true, then when Wittgenstein says, 'The picture presents that such-and-such is the case', he means, 'The picture is the presenting that such-and-such is the case'. We shall find that this peculiar use of a verb in the present indicative is very common in the *Tractatus*: pictures, picture-elements, thoughts, *Saetze*, names—these are clearly not *agents*; and when Wittgenstein says that they do things he is *explaining what they are*—he is saying that they are *acts*.

The suggestion that the picture is the act of presenting that something is the case will at the present point seem highly speculative. We shall, I think, see that it is borne out by the remarks that follow 2.15 in the *Tractatus*.

But how can *facts* be *acts*? How can the fact that the picture-elements are combined in a certain way be itself the act of presenting that the objects are so combined? The answer to this lies in the nature of the picture-elements. And we do not yet know what sort of thing a picture-element is.

2.15   Dierser Zusammenhang der Elemente des Bildes heisse seine
(par. 2) Struktur und ihre Moeglichkeit seine Form der Abbildung.

2.151   Die Form der Abbildung ist die Moeglichkeit, dass sich die Dinge so zu einander verhalten, wie die Elemente des Bildes.

2.1511   Das Bild ist *so* mit der Wirklichkeit verknuepft: es reicht bis zu ihr.

2.1512   Es ist wie ein Masstab an die Wirklichkeit angelegt.

2.1513   Nach dieser Auffassung gehoert also zum Bilde auch noch die abbildende Beziehung, die es zum Bild macht.

2.1514   Die abbildende Beziehung besteht aus den Zuordnungen der Elemente des Bildes und der Sachen.

2.1515   Diese Zuordnungen sind gleichsam die Fuehler der Bildelemente, mit denen das Bild die Wirklichkeit beruehrt.

Compare 2.15 (par. 2) with 2.151. It is clear that '*Moeglichkeit*' ('possibility') is being used in different ways in these passages. In 2.15 (par. 2) the Form of Representation is said to be the possibility of the connection of the picture-elements. This cannot mean that it is the possibility that the elements are connected in the picture, for they *are* connected in the picture. What Wittgenstein means is this: The Form of Representation is *what makes possible* the connection of elements in the picture. But (2.151) the Form of Representation is *at the same time* the possibility that the things are combined in the same way. Therefore the possibility that the things are connected in a particular way *is* what makes possible the same connection of picture-elements. But this is altogether incomprehensible unless the fact that the picture-elements are connected as they are *is itself the presenting that the things are so connected*. And Wittgenstein tells us how this can be so. What links the picture to reality is *that* it reaches up to it. And this means (*nach dieser Auffassung*) that what relates the picture to reality (i.e. the 'representing relation') is *in* the picture. This 'relation' consists of the co-ordinations of the elements of the picture with things. So these co-ordinations must equally 'belong to' the picture-elements, for the representing relation is what makes the picture into a picture. We have already observed that the elements of the picture 'stand for' things. We see now that this 'standing for' is not something over and above their being what they are: their being picture-elements *is* their standing-for-things. So a picture is this sort of fact. It is the fact that elements-standing-for-things are connected in a certain way, and this fact is the presenting-that the things which the elements stand for are combined in the same way. The Last Supper, regarding it *simply* as a 'picture of what happened', is not the fact that patches of colour are combined in a certain way. It is the fact that the figure standing for St John is related in a certain way to the figure standing for Christ, etc. And this is the presenting that the Beloved Apostle rested his head against the Master's shoulder, etc.

What I have said is to be contrasted with Anscombe's account (op. cit., p. 68) of the same passage from the *Tractatus*. She claims that there are two distinct features belonging to a picture: 'first, the relation between the elements of the picture; and second, the correlations of the elements in the picture with things outside the picture . . .' She then goes on to deny that this second feature 'belongs' to the picture at all: 'The correlating is not something that the picture does; it is something *we* do'. But Wittgenstein says that the representing relation, which consists of the correlations of the picture-elements with things, *is what makes the picture into a picture.* That is, if the elements do not already stand for things, if they are not already correlated with them, then there is no 'representing relation'; and this means that the picture is not a picture at all. That a picture-element stands for something *constitutes* its being a picture-element; that a picture presents that something is the case *constitutes* its being a picture. There are no 'distinct features' of the kind envisaged.

Readers of the *Tractatus* are often upset by the apparent unnaturalness or artificiality of speaking of 'true' and 'false' in connection with pictures. And indeed, if pictures were 'things', replicas of

Sachverhalte, then there would be no sense in ascribing truth-values to them; for, as we have observed, 'false' pictures would not be pictures at all. But Wittgenstein is quite clear on this point.

2.21 Das Bild stimmt mit der Wirklichkeit ueberein oder nicht; es ist richtig oder unrichtig, wahr oder falsch.

2.22 Das Bild stellt dar, was es darstellt, unabhaengig von seiner Wahr- oder Falschheit, durch die Form der Abbildung.

It is plain, then, that a Wittgensteinian picture *must* be either true or false. But some commentators have thought otherwise. Rather than abandon the theory of replicas-and-prototypes, they have been led to deny that pictures can be true or false at all. Thus Stenius (op. cit., p. 96), as we have seen, seems initially to hold that only 'true' pictures are really *pictures*, i.e. isomorphic representations of prototype-facts; a 'false' picture is merely an 'articulate field of which the question of its being or not being an isomorphic picture can be raised'. That is to say, false pictures are might-have-been-pictures— had they been true. For Anscombe, on the other hand, pictures are things that we use in making statements; they themselves are neither true nor false. We can 'hold them up' and ourselves say, 'This is how things are', and it is our assertion that is either true or false (op. cit., 64 ff.).

These comments are, to say the very least, wide of the mark. They rest upon the fallacy of the facsimile. If the picture is, as we have maintained, a presenting-that, then clearly it must be either true or false. For what is presented is that objects are combined in a particular way. If they are so combined then the picture is true; if not, then the picture is false.

2.182 Jedes Bild ist auch ein logisches.

3 Das logische Bild der Tatsachen ist der Gedanke.

3.02 Der Gedanke enthaelt die Moeglichkeit der Sachlage, die er (par. 1) denkt.

Compare this last with:

2.203 Das Bild enthaelt die Moeglichkeit der Sachlage, die es darstellt.[1]

Whatever else a picture may be, e.g. 'spatial', 'musical', it must

---

[1] In the *Tractatus*, '*darstellen*' and '*vorstellen*' are used synonymously. However, '*darstellen*' sometimes takes '*moegliche Sachlage*' instead of '*Sachlage*' as its accusative (see, e.g., 2.202). This does not mean that the picture presents the mere possibility of a state-of-affairs; but that what it presents *as* the case is nevertheless only a possible state-of-affairs—since no picture is true *a priori*. But Wittgenstein is sometimes careless. In 3.0321 and 4.0311, *Sachverhalt* is what is presented ('*dargestellt*', '*vorgestellt*', respectively). It is enough to point out that this is inconsistent with the vast majority of cases of the occurrence of '*darstellen*' and '*vorstellen*' in the *Tractatus*: cf. 2.11, 2.15, 2.201, 2.202, 2.203, 4.021, 4.031, 4.04, 4.1, etc.

also be a 'logical' picture. To be a logical picture is to be a thought; so all pictures are (at least) thoughts, and presenting is (at least) thinking. But what can be meant by saying, in 3.02, that the *thought thinks* the state-of-affairs? The only thing that this can mean is that the thought *is* the thinking-the-state-of-affairs. Now a state-of-affairs is *das Bestehen und Nichtbestehen von Sachverhalten* (2.11), i.e. that-things-are-combined-and-not-combined-in-such-and-such-a-way. So the picture is (at least) the thinking that such-and-such is the case. It may, in addition, be a 'spatial' thought, like the Last Supper; but this is not essential to its being a picture.

We now have a further confirmation of our thesis, that the picture is the presenting-that. There can be no picture without a presenting-that, any more than we can have thoughts without thinking. Wittgenstein's theory does not comprise pictures *and* thoughts *and* presenting *and* thinking. There is only *thinking*. Sometimes we think on canvas.

We saw at the beginning of this paper that Warnock's description of the *Tractatus* theory of language fails to isolate *meaning* as uniquely characteristic of language. Just what do pictures and thoughts—presenting and thinking—have to do with meaning? And where does language come in?

3.1 Im Satz drueckt sich der Gedanke sinnlich wahrnehmbar aus.
4 Der Gedanke ist der sinnvolle Satz.

Most philosophers of language distinguish a sentence from what it means or from what is meant by it. Thus Frege[1] held that the meaning (*Sinn*) of a sentence (*Satz*) was the thought (*Gedanke*) expressed by it. So, for Frege, 'aRb' expresses the thought that aRb, and this thought is the meaning or sense of 'aRb', specifiable independently of the sentence which expresses it. But this explanation of meaning did not satisfy Wittgenstein. He followed Frege in holding that the sense (*Sinn*) is what is expressed by the *Satz*. But for him a sense is not itself a thought, separable from the *Satz*: it is, as we shall see, necessarily *the* sense *of* a *Satz*. A thought, on the other hand, far from being a sense of a *Satz*, is itself a *Satz* (4);[2] thoughts, then, cannot *be* meanings, for they are precisely the kinds of things that *have* meaning, that *express* a sense. More strictly, a thought, for Wittgenstein, is an expression of sense—to think is to mean something. 'aRb' is the thought that aRb—out loud (on paper); to speak

---

[1] Geach and Black: *Translations from the Philosophical Writings of Gottlob Frege*, especially pp. 62 ff.

[2] Strictly speaking, '*sinnvoll*' is redundant in 4. There is no such thing as a '*sinnloser Satz*' (see, e.g., 4.064). The point of using '*sinnvoll*' here is to emphasize just this: that *every* Satz must have a meaning.

is to think perceptibly, and this is what is meant by 3.1. We shall see that the *sense* is *what* we think, or say.

Now if a thought is, as we have shown it to be, a thinking-that, and if a *Satz* is a thought-out-loud, it follows that a *Satz* is a saying-that-things-are-combined-in-such-and-such-a-way. It is therefore not a *sentence*, but a *language-act*. A sentence (*Satzzeichen*) is, as we shall see in a moment, a sign that we use in performing such an act.

But first a preliminary word about *Sinn* (sense). *Sinn* is first mentioned in the *Tractatus* in connection with pictures: 'Was das Bild darstellt ist sein Sinn' (2.221). But we have already seen that what the picture presents is a (possible) state-of-affairs, that things are combined in such-and-such-a-way. The sense, then, is the state-of-affairs presented by the picture. And the same must be true for *Gedanke* and *Satz*: *what* we think (or say) is the sense of our thought (or assertion). This is, incidentally, why Wittgenstein says that the sense is not 'contained' within the *Satz* (3.13); it is what the *Satz* presents.

3.11 Wir benuetzen das sinnlich wahrnehmbare Zeichen (Lautoder Schriftzeichen) des Satzes als Projektion der moeglichen Sachlage. Die Projektionsmethode ist das Denken des Satz-Sinnes.[1]

3.12 Das Zeichen, durch welches wir den Gedanken ausdruecken, nenne ich das Satzzeichen. Und der Satz ist das Satzzeichen in seiner projektiven Beziehung zur Welt.

3.5 Das angewandte, gedachte, Satzzeichen ist der Gedanke.

To use a *Satzzeichen* is to project a state-of-affairs into it. The way in which we project the state-of-affairs is by thinking that such-and-such is the case. The *Satz is* the use of the *Satzzeichen*; it is the *Satzzeichen* being used as a projection of the sense, the *Satzzeichen* with the sense thought into it. From this point on, when Wittgenstein speaks of the *Satzzeichen* he often means not just the sign, not just the written or spoken sentence, but the sign *in use*.

Like the picture, the sentence-in-use is a fact—it is *that* the words are combined in a certain way (3.14). These words are 'names' (3.202); names 'mean' (*bedeuten*) objects; they refer to them, name them (3.203). Like the picture-element, the name deputizes, stands for (*vertritt*) the object (3.22).

Now there is an important way in which this can be misunderstood. Wittgenstein is not saying that naming is a purpose (even *the* purpose) for which names can be used, any more than he is saying that thinking (presenting) is something that thoughts (pictures) are used to do. I repeat: thoughts (pictures) that do not think (present)

---

[1] '*das Denken des Satz-Sinnes*' is not the thinking *of* the sense—as if we thought *about* it. It is the thinking-the-sense; for the sense is *what* we think.

are not thoughts (pictures) at all. To say 'the thought thinks the *Sachlage*' is to explain not what thoughts do or can be used to do, but what they are. The case of names is exactly analogous. (Remember: the co-ordinations with things belong to the picture-elements.) To say that a name refers to a thing is to say that it *is* a referring-to-a-thing, a naming-a-thing, a meaning-a-thing. Names are words *in use*,[1] they are elements of the act of speaking.

We should think of words (in use) as steps in a dance, rather than as bricks in a house. The dance is composed entirely of steps in a definite sequence (*besteht darin, dass sich seine Elemente in bestimmter Art und Weise zu einander verhalten*, 2.14, 3.14). The dance is an act; each step an element of the act, a 'sub-act', if you wish. But a dance (or a figure of a dance) is not itself a step, say a larger one, a 'composite' one; it is a different kind of thing. And so it is with language. A *Satz* is not a name (3.143), a complex word-in-use, it is a sentence-in-use. And a sentence-in-use is the act of thinking out loud, of speaking. But it is not any kind of speaking you choose. A *Satz* is a saying-that-things-are-combined-in-such-and-such-a-way; it is an *assertion*. Assertions are, or can be, 'embodied' in sentences, and the referring elements of an assertion can be embodied in words. This is all that there is to the relation of *Satz* to *Satzzeichen*, and of name to word. An assertion is, for Wittgenstein, an arrangement of words in use, of 'referrings'. To arrange 'a' in a particular way to 'b' is to say that aRb; a particular arrangement of 'a' and 'b' *is* the assertion that aRb (see 3.1432). (To arrange these steps in this way is to dance this figure; this arrangement of these steps *is* this figure.) And this, I take it, is Wittgenstein's explanation of what it is to express a sense.

It is perhaps worth pointing out that the *signs* (words, sentences) that we use in speaking, need not, on the *Tractatus* theory, be restricted to vocal sounds or written inscriptions. We can, if we like, use pieces of furniture as words; indeed Wittgenstein suggests that it is illuminating to think of the sentence (*Satzzeichen*) as composed of such things (3.1431). This means that we could assert that aRb, not only by uttering or writing down the sentence 'aRb', but by, e.g., placing a chair next to a table. And this practice would presuppose the convention that a chair be used to refer to object *a*, and that a table be used to refer to object *b*. The possibility of such a language shows only that we could use whatever we wished as signs —given the necessary conventions of reference. It does *not* follow from this that non-linguistic entities can do the work of language, that something other than a *Satz* can express a sense. For our using the table and chair as words, our placing them next to each other—

---

[1] '*Name*' stands to '*Satz*' in the way that '*Wort*' stands to '*Satzzeichen*'. This is why Wittgenstein does not say, e.g., that the *word* means the object.

is our assertion (*Satz*), our thinking in furniture-language—that aRb.

Now if we are to understand one another when we speak, certain conditions must be fulfilled. We must, first of all, be acquainted with the conventions of reference. If I am to understand the assertion 'aRb', then I must *already* be acquainted with the 'meanings' (*Bedeutungen*) of 'a' and 'b'. If an unfamiliar name, 'c', occurs in an assertion, then I shall not understand what is being said until the meaning of 'c' has been explained to me (4.026). But, according to Wittgenstein, there are no conventions of sense corresponding to those of reference. This reflects a problem, which takes the form of puzzlement over how we can understand an assertion that we have never previously heard. If I know the *Bedeutungen* of 'a' and 'b' then, it seems, I will understand the assertion 'aRb' without further ado. It is in the nature of assertions that they can tell us something *new* (4.027). *What* they tell us need not, indeed cannot, be explained to us. When we speak, we *convey* (*mitteilen*) the sense of what we are saying to our audience. How is this possible?

Let us remind ourselves: To make a statement is to think aloud, i.e. to assert, that things are combined in such-and-such-a-way. And this is, as we have seen, to assert a sense, a meaning. But how does *asserting* a sense succeed in *conveying* a sense to our listeners? The answer is, of course, that a *Satz* is a picture (e.g. 4.021); asserting is presenting. Now 'presenting' ('*vorstellen*', '*darstellen*') has important overtones which mere 'asserting' ('*behaupten*') might not seem to have. When we *present* a state-of-affairs, we are at the same time *showing what* state-of-affairs it is that we are presenting. And it is only because saying in this way involves showing, that other people can immediately understand what we are saying—provided they know what objects we are referring to in our assertion (e.g. 4.024).

What I have said must not be taken to mean that 'presenting' is to be identified with 'showing'. For as we have seen, a picture presents what it presents independently of its truth or falsehood; and what it presents is that things are combined in such-and-such-a-way. This, we saw, is the explanation of what a picture is; it is what makes the picture into a picture. Now it is clear that the only circumstances under which we can say of a picture that it *shows* that such-and-such is the case are those in which we have prior knowledge of the picture's truth. We could not say this of pictures in general. Only if pictures were *a priori* true, could they be said, in general, to *show* that such-and-such is the case. But pictures must be true-or-false; 'presenting' is 'saying', not 'showing'.

Showing is linked to presenting (asserting) in the following way. When we present that something is the case, we thereby show not what *is* the case, but *what it is that we are presenting as the case*. In this way Wittgenstein can say, somewhat misleadingly, both that we assert, present, the sense (2.221, 4.064)—and that we show the sense (4.022). And in saying this he is not undermining his principle that 'what can be shown cannot be said' (4.1212). For when we say something we show what it is that we are saying, and *this* we cannot say; that is, we cannot say what it is that we are saying. We cannot even say *that* we are saying anything, for this too is shown. None of the 'internal properties' (*interne Eigenschaften*) of assertions, those properties which assertions must have in order that they should be the assertions that they are—none of these can be *said* to belong to assertions; all of them are shown *in* assertions. I cannot assert the conditions necessary for my asserting anything at all, nor can I assert those conditions necessary for my making the particular statement I am making. A picture can present neither what is presupposed in its being a picture, nor what is presupposed in its being the picture that it is; it cannot present that it has a sense, nor that it has the sense that it has (see, e.g., 2.172, 2.174, 4.121).

Showing, not saying, is the clue to understanding. To say that something is the case is to show what is the case when what we say is true (4.022). And to *understand* an assertion is to know what is the case when it is true (4.024). We, as it were, grasp what is shown, and thereby understand what is said.

Now I think we can see the relevance, for Wittgenstein, of the 'theory of picturing' to the theory of language. To say that a *Satz* is a picture may at first have seemed to add nothing to what we already knew. For the explanation that we gave of a picture, that it was a 'presenting-that', seemed to suggest that it was itself neither more nor less than a 'saying-that', an assertion. And if we already know that a *Bild* is a *Satz*, then to say that a *Satz* is a *Bild* is uninformative. But Wittgenstein appears to have felt that an account of assertion alone would not explain how it is that people can communicate. An assertion must show, must exhibit what its sense is, if we are to understand it. And the notion of 'showing' is derived from that of 'picturing', of 'presenting-that'.

Among the things that are presupposed, shown, by the act of assertion—and which cannot therefore be expressed through (*durch*) that act—are the existence and identity of the speaker. I cannot say 'I say p', for this is what must be shown by the assertion 'p'. Is this perhaps the reason why Wittgenstein so rarely mentions the speaker in his account of language? I think not. For if this were so, then the *Tractatus* could never have been written. Taken as a whole, the book is an avowedly futile attempt to express the inexpressible, to say what is presupposed in saying anything (6.54). Each of the remarks we have considered is 'senseless' in just this way. And if it is senseless to say 'the thought thinks', then clearly it is no *more* senseless to say 'I think'. That something cannot be said is, in the *Tractatus*, hardly an adequate ground for not saying it. If it is true that language bears a 'necessary' relation to the world, then it is equally true, surely, that *we* bear a necessary relation to language. The former is discussed at great length, the latter almost entirely ignored.

But the reason for this is by now quite clear. For on this theory of language, any mention of the speaker is simply redundant. Had Wittgenstein chosen 'sentence' or 'proposition' as the basic linguistic unit, he could not have avoided referring to those who use sentences, express propositions. But a *Satz* is not the kind of thing that can be used or expressed. For it is itself a use, for Wittgenstein *the* use, of a sentence, the expressing of a sense (*der Ausdruck, das Ausdruecken*, cf. 3.31). It is the act of making a statement.[1] And if language consists of acts, then there is no cause to look beyond its 'internal features' for whatever it is (the speaker) that makes it mean 'something other than itself'. This is why *Bild, Gedanke, Satz, Name* appear to have lives of their own. The remarks: 'The name means the object', 'The thought thinks the state-of-affairs', 'The picture presents a sense', are, as we have repeatedly seen, disguised explanations of the meanings of those terms.

This is all that I propose to say about the theory of picturing and its bearing upon the theory of language in the *Tractatus*. It is by no means all that could be said: and my interest has been limited entirely to what is fundamental in these theories. I have not, for example, concerned myself at all with what Wittgenstein says about negation or about *Elementarsaetze*. The passages I have selected for detailed consideration have, on the whole, been drawn from those early parts of the book where important terms are first introduced: *Tatsache, Sachverhalt, Bild, vorstellen, darstellen, Gedanke, Satz, Name, Sinn.* And I have shown how I believe these passages are to be understood. My purpose has been to elicit, in a general way, Wittgenstein's view of the nature of language. I do not believe, however, that this view was equally clearly and consistently held throughout the writing of the *Tractatus*. There are, for example, some important remarks (in the section 4.01–4.02) which seem to lend support to those accounts of Wittgenstein's theory that I have criticized. I shall consider two of the most striking of these remarks.

4.012 Offenbar ist, dass wir einen Satz von der Form 'aRb' als Bild

---

[1] 'But just as we use sentences and express propositions, so we *perform* language-acts.' And of coure this is true. But the performing is not distinguishable from the act: it is not what *relates* us to acts. To perform an act *is* to act.

empfinden. Hier ist das Zeichen offenbar ein Gleichnis des Bezeich-
neten.

Here Wittgenstein appears to have suddenly forgotten the important difference between the *Satz* and the *Satzzeichen*. It was never
claimed that the sentence, as it appears on paper, was to resemble
anything. And even if it were true—and it is certainly *not* 'obvious'
(*offenbar*)—that 'aRb' looks or sounds like what it is used to mean,
this would still not explain what is intended by saying that the *Satz*
'aRb' is a picture. I do not know what else to say about this statement. Perhaps it is some kind of concession to another, more
common, view: that pictures are things that hang on walls and that
look like other things. I do not want to suggest that we *cannot* regard
(some) Wittgensteinian pictures as likenesses; only *this* is not what
makes them into pictures. In 4.012 the notion of *vorstellen* has
disappeared.

> 4.014 Die Grammophonplatte, der musikalische Gedanke, die Noten-
> schrift, die Schallwellen, stehen alle in jener abbildenden internen
> Beziehung zu einander, die zwischen Sprache und Welt besteht.
> Ihnen allen ist der logische Bau gemeinsam. (See also 4.015.)

Again, the notion of *vorstellen* has dropped out. The score, the
symphony, the record-groove, all share the same logical structure;
they are isomorphic. Now Wittgenstein did say earlier (2.16–2.17)
that the picture, to be a picture, must have something in common
with what it represents (reality). But this common element was *not*
said to be the logical structure, but rather the Form of Representation. And, as we have seen, to say that the Form of Representation
is common to the picture and to reality is to say that what makes
possible the structure of the picture is the possibility that the things
are combined in the way in which the picture-elements are combined
(2.15, 2.151; see p. 54 [p. 279] of this paper). What makes it possible
to say 'aRb' is the possibility that aRb. The notion of Form of
Representation is thus geared into that of *vorstellen*, for there can
be no *possibility* that things are combined in a particular way unless
there is a *presenting-that* they are combined in such-and-such-a-way.
And thus the Form of Representation has to do with the possible
truth and falsehood of the picture (2.17). A picture may indeed be
said to have the same 'logical structure' as reality, but to say this is
not to say what makes it a picture.

But these passages are atypical of the *Tractatus*. This is fortunate,
for they suggest a view of language which is open to all the objections
we have raised against a theory of isomorphism between language
and the world.

By now it is clear that the predominant view of language expressed in the *Tractatus* is very different from this. A *Satz* has meaning not because it is isomorphic with anything else, but because it is itself the expression (*der Ausdruck*) of meaning, of sense; it is, as it were, the act of meaning that something is the case. There is no such thing as a 'relation' between language and the world; language is, if you wish, one of the ways in which *we* are related to the world. We speak, we assert that things are connected in particular ways, and that is all there is to it.

There are doubtless Nominalist tendencies in the *Tractatus*: Ockham's Razor has shorn off the 'proposition', Frege's *Gedanke*. But far more important than this is Wittgenstein's early realization that sentences (Frege's *Saetze*) are not the kinds of things that can express a meaning, and that meanings cannot be independent thoughts. What has meaning, what *means*, is necessarily an act of thinking.

Wittgenstein's Notion of an Object[1]

DAVID KEYT

The particular object is a very remarkable phenomenon.

Notebooks 11. 7. 16

1. *The ultimate constituents of the world.* In "The Philosophy of Logical Atomism",[2] which was influenced but not dominated by Wittgenstein's work before the First World War, Russell draws up an "inventory of the world" and offers the following as a complete list of the ultimate constituents of the world: particulars, qualities, relations, and facts (p. 270). One question that might arise concerning Russell's inventory is this: Why is it necessary to list facts in addition to particulars, qualities, and relations? So that I may contrast Russell's theory with the theory of the *Tractatus* I want to develop an answer to this question that is implicit in Russell's own theory. First of all, relations as well as particulars are counted as components of facts (PLA, p. 192). Secondly, one component may occur in several different facts (PLA, p. 193). It follows, then, as Russell himself allows ("On Propositions", p. 286), that two different facts might contain exactly the same components. This can be easily illustrated if we are allowed for the moment to think of human beings as particulars. The fact that Caesar loved Cleopatra is different from the fact that Cleopatra loved Caesar, but both contain the same components. This answers our original question, but now another arises: How do these two facts differ? The only answer that suggests itself is that the relation *is related to* the two particulars differently in

[1] From *The Philosophical Quarterly*, vol. 13, no. 50, January, 1963, pp. 3–15. Reprinted by permission of the editor and the author.
[2] Republished in *Logic and Knowledge* (ed. Marsh), to which all references to Russell refer.

the two cases. It is certain that Russell would object to this interpretation, for he says in a somewhat later essay that "if we mean—
as opponents of external relations suppose us to mean—that the
relation is a third term which comes between the other two terms and
is somehow hooked on to them, that is obviously absurd, for in that
case the relation has ceased to be a relation, and all that is truly relational is the hooking of the relation to the terms" ("Logical Atomism", p. 335). Nevertheless, it does seem that Russell's theory contains this absurdity.

Wittgenstein's theory in the *Tractatus* stands in elegant contrast to
Russell's. Wittgenstein's inventory of the world lists only two items
instead of four: objects and objects in configuration. And the puzzle
concerning relations disappears by the simple expedient of not counting relations as objects. For Russell an atomic fact consists of particulars and a relation (or a particular and a quality) in relation.
Thus relations occur twice, as a component of a fact and as joining
the components of a fact. (They need not occur more than twice,
however, if the way in which the components are joined is not itself
taken as a component of the fact.) For Wittgenstein an atomic fact
consists solely of objects, no one of which is either a quality or a
relation, in relation. Thus relations occur only once. Further, since
a configuration of objects must contain at least two objects, monadic
relations or qualities disappear altogether.

The interpretation of the *Tractatus* given in the last paragraph is
not universally accepted. Stenius, for example, holds that objects
form a genus of which particulars, qualities, and relations are
species.[1] What grounds are there for holding that objects are not of
different kinds? First, there is the chain simile—"In the atomic fact
objects hang one in another, like the links of a chain" (2.03)—which
suggests that objects are all fundamentally alike. Secondly, there is
the metaphor of logical space. In this metaphor an existent atomic
fact is the analogue of a material point; a possible atomic fact, of a
geometrical point; and an object, of the reference of a co-ordinate
of a point. In analytic geometry a point may be indicated by writing
three numerals in a certain relation, for example, by writing "(3, 2,
1)". Similarly an atomic fact may be indicated by writing names in a
certain relation. (See 3.032 and 3.4–3.411, and see in addition *Ntbk.*
29.10.14 and 21.6.15 para. 2.) Now if Wittgenstein held that in every
atomic fact one object must be a quality or a relation, then in the

[1] See *Wittgenstein's 'Tractatus'*, ch. V, sec. 1. On this point I follow Anscombe and
Copi. See Anscombe, *Introduction to Wittgenstein's Tractatus*, ch. 7, and Copi, "Objects,
Properties, and Relations in the *Tractatus*", *Mind*, April, 1958 [present volume].
Wittgenstein does say in the *Notebooks* that "relations and properties, etc., are *objects*
too" (16.6.15 para. 5); however, I can find no passage in the *Tractatus* that either says
or implies this.

metaphor a point should be indicated not by three co-ordinates but by two co-ordinates and the sign of a function, not by "(3, 2, 1)" but by "f(3, 2)" where "f(x, y)" is, say, "x—y". And, thirdly, there is Wittgenstein's notation in which small Latin letters from the beginning of the alphabet are used for names and from the end for name variables (4.24, 4.1211, 4.1272 para. 1), which is the Russellian way of denoting a particular (ambiguously in the case of a variable, unambiguously in the case of a name).

2. *The properties of objects.* Since qualities disappear altogether, it follows that *objects* have no qualities. And this is what we are told indirectly: "In passing: objects are colourless" (2.0232). This is the basis of the comparison that has been made between Wittgenstein's objects and Aristotle's prime matter.[1]

Although objects have no qualities, they do have properties, where "property" is used in a broad sense that covers relations.[2]

An object has both internal and external properties (2.01231, 2.0233, 4.023 para. 4). These are sometimes called *formal* and *material* properties (2.0231). It is a material property of an object that it *stands* in a certain relation to a second object. It is a formal property of an object that it is *possible* for it to stand in a certain relation to a second object. The basis for the former statement is Wittgenstein's comment that material properties are "first formed by the configuration of the objects" (2.0231). The basis for the latter is the proposition that "if I am acquainted with an object, then I am also acquainted with all the possibilities of its occurrence in atomic facts" (2.0123) taken together with the immediately following proposition that "in order to be acquainted with an object, I must be acquainted not with its external but all its internal properties" (2.01231).

Since there are no qualities, the properties mentioned above are the only properties an object has, with one very special exception: an object has the formal property of being an object. We shall return to this point presently.

3. *The objects as substance.* "The objects form the substance of the world" (2.021). In what sense are Wittgenstein's objects substance?

---

[1] See Copi's article, p. 164 [p. 185].

[2] Copi argued in his article that Wittgenstein's objects are "bare particulars, having no material properties whatever" (p. 163 [p. 184]). Copi himself noticed the passages that contradict this interpretation. Copi's mistake is that he failed to notice the broad sense in which 'property' is used in the *Tractatus*. His conclusion is sound if the word 'quality' is substituted for the word 'property'. See Anscombe, *IWT*, pp. 110–11, and "Mr. Copi on Objects, Properties and Relations in the *Tractatus*", *Mind*, July, 1959, p. 404 [p. 187].

Since Wittgenstein has so little to say in answer to this question, I propose to approach the question by way of Russell's discussion of the corresponding question about his own particulars.

Particulars "have the quality of self-subsistence that used to belong to substance, but not the quality of persistence through time" (PLA, p. 203). What does Russell mean here by self-subsistence? This he answers as follows: ". . . each particular that there is in the world does not in any way logically depend upon any other particular. Each one might happen to be the whole universe; it is a merely empirical fact that this is not the case. There is no reason why you should not have a universe consisting of one particular and nothing else" (PLA, p. 202). Russell's criterion of self-subsistence may be compared with Aristotle's criterion of separability (*Meta.* 1029^a27-8), which when strictly applied yields him the conclusion that the individual thing (Socrates, Bucephalus), which is a compound of form and matter, is substance. (Although the form of a thing is separable in definition, only the compound is absolutely separable (*Meta.* 1042^a30-31).) Wittgenstein's objects do not have this sort of self-subsistence; his objects *do* depend logically upon one another. "It is essential to a thing that it can be a constituent part of an atomic fact" (2.011). "An atomic fact is a combination of objects . . ." (2.01). Therefore, there could not for Wittgenstein be only one object in existence. There must be other objects with which it is at least possible for any given object to combine. Therefore, it would be false to say that objects do not depend in any way upon one another.

Although Wittgenstein's objects are not self-subsistent with respect to one another, they are self-subsistent with respect to the atomic facts. There can be no atomic facts unless there are objects, but there can be objects without there being any atomic facts. "Substance is what there is independently of what is the case" (2.024), and it is possible that nothing is the case. For with regard to the existence of n atomic facts there are 2^n possibilities. But one of these possibilities is that there are no existent atomic facts. (See the bottom row of each of the schemata of 4.31.) The self-subsistence of Wittgenstein's objects is similar not to the separate existence of Aristotle's concrete individuals one from another, but to the separate existence of Plato's Forms from his particulars. The Forms are internally related one to another, and thus one Form cannot exist separately from other Forms; but the world of Forms as a whole exists whether there are any particulars or not. On the other hand, there can be no particulars without there being Forms. Of course, Plato's particulars are not made out of Forms; the analogy breaks down at this point. Plato's Ideas provide the form but not the content of the world. Wittgenstein's objects, on the other hand, are both form and content

(2.025). In providing the content of the world the objects are similar to the atoms of Leucippus and Democritus.

The second criterion of substance mentioned by Russell was persistence through time. His particulars fail to fulfil this criterion. "A particular, as a rule, is apt to last for a very short time indeed, not an instant but a very short time. In that respect particulars differ from the old substances . . ." (PLA, pp. 203–4). Indestructibility, which entails being eternal, has often been taken as a necessary characteristic of substance; however, this has not been the case invariably. Aristotle's sublunary substances, for example, exist individually for only a finite time—although most exist for longer than one of Russell's particulars. But what about Wittgenstein's objects: Do they have the quality of persistence through time?

Anscombe refers to Wittgenstein's objects as "eternal and changeless simples" (*IWT*, p. 43), although she does not indicate the basis for this interpretation. Has she read Wittgenstein correctly? "An object is simple" (2.02). This much is certain. And from the fact that the objects are simple, it follows that they are changeless. Only a complex can change. For change requires something that remains the same *as well as* something that does not: the unmusical *man* becomes a musical *man*, to use Aristotle's example (*Phys.* I, 7). But from the fact that the objects are changeless, it does not follow that they are eternal. For passing into and out of existence completely cannot, on the above analysis, be counted as change. Wittgenstein himself at one point acknowledges this distinction: "As in death, too, the world does not change, but ceases" (6.431). Consequently, we must see if there are independent grounds for asserting the eternity of the objects.

Wittgenstein distinguishes two senses of 'eternity'. "If by eternity is understood not endless temporal duration but timelessness, then he lives eternally who lives in the present" (6.4311). What does it mean to say that the present is timeless? I take it to mean that such sentences as 'The present is past' and 'The present is yet to come' are meaningless. Thus to say that something is timeless is to say that temporal predicates do not apply to it. So the question is this: Are the objects timeless or are they of endless temporal duration or do they pass into and out of existence? I shall argue that they are timeless.

Wittgenstein makes only one direct comment on this problem: "So one cannot, e.g., say 'There are objects' as one says 'There are books' " (4.1272 para. 5). Why is this? Because the concept *object* is a formal concept, not a proper concept (ibid., para. 8). The distinction between formal and proper concepts is the same as that between formal and material properties.[1] Now, "formal concepts cannot, like

[1] Since there is nothing to indicate otherwise, I am assuming that as far as terminology goes Wittgenstein follows Frege in his use of 'property', 'concept', and 'mark'

proper concepts, be presented by a function" (4.126). So "*x* is an object" is not a sign of a genuine function. Why not? If it were, then the replacement of the variable by a name, "*a*", would yield an elementary proposition. And this elementary proposition would be about a single object. But an elementary proposition cannot be about a single object, for an elementary proposition always presents a configuration of objects (4.21 together with 2.01). Therefore, alleged propositions such as "*a* is an object" are nonsensical pseudo-propositions (4.1272 para. 4). But in this case "There are objects" is nonsensical; for this alleged proposition would be symbolized as "(∃*x*) (*x* is an object)", which is equivalent to "(*a* is an object v *b* is an object v . . .)" (5.52); and a disjunctive proposition every clause of which is nonsensical must itself be nonsensical.

According to the theory of the *Tractatus*, one can neither say "*a* exists" nor "Objects exist". Wittgenstein in his use of the word 'exists' in the *Tractatus* is guided by the use of the existential quantifier in logic. The existential quantifier never appears in front of an isolated name, so "*a* exists" cannot be said. And "Objects exist" cannot be said since "*x* is an object" is not a genuine function and, hence, not a function in front of which an existential quantifier may be placed. Therefore, existence cannot be predicated of objects either individually or collectively. And if 'exists' is not a predicate of objects, 'has existed' and 'will exist' are not predicates of objects either. This, however, is precisely what is meant by saying that the objects are timeless.

The argument stated very briefly is this. All that can be said of an object is that it enters or that it does not enter into particular configurations. Therefore, it cannot be said of an object either that it exists or that it does not exist. Therefore, it cannot be said of an object either that it will continue to exist or that it will not continue to exist. Wittgenstein expresses this point in the *Investigations* very succinctly: ". . . if everything that we call 'being' and 'non-being' consists in the existence and non-existence of connections between elements, it makes no sense to speak of an element's being (non-being); just as when everything that we call 'destruction' lies in the separation of elements, it makes no sense to speak of the destruction of an element" (I, 50).

('Merkmal'). (See 4.126 for all three words.) Frege's usage may be illustrated by considering the proposition that seven is a prime number. Seven falls under the concept *prime number*. The same thing would be expressed by saying that seven has the property of being a prime number. To be a number is a mark of the concept *prime number* and a property of seven. *Number* is related to *prime number* as genus to species; *number* is related to seven as genus to member. See *Foundations*, sec. 53, "On Concept and Object", pp. 201-2, and *Fundamental Laws*, I, p. xiv.

Once again Wittgenstein's objects turn out to resemble Plato's Forms more than Aristotle's concrete individuals: "We say indeed that it [i.e. being] was and is and will be, but in truth 'is' alone fits it" (*Tim.* 37 e 5–38 a 1).

We should also notice in passing the important proposition that "the object is the fixed, the existent; the configuration is the changing, the mutable" (2.0271), which suggests the fundamental dualism of being and becoming of Greek philosophy.

4. *The objects and possibility.* The objects determine the limits of logical possibility. "If all objects are given, then thereby are all *possible* atomic facts also given" (2.0124). "The objects contain the possibility of all states of affairs" (2.014). "Empirical reality is limited by the totality of objects" (5.5561). Since an atomic fact is a configuration of objects, when all objects are given, all possible configurations are also given. Once a deck of cards is given, all possible hands are also given. On the other hand, "substance is what there is independently of what is the case" (2.024). So when we know what objects there are, we know what is possible but not yet what is actual.

Wittgenstein goes on to say in 2.025 that the objects are form and content. Form and content of what? Of the world: "Only if there are objects can there be a fixed form of the world" (2.026). The form of the world consists, I take it, of the possible configurations of objects; the content, of the actual configurations.

5. *The status of the existence of objects.* "The whole question of what particulars you actually find in the real world is a purely empirical one which does not interest the logician as such." This statement is from Russell's "Philosophy of Logical Atomism" (p. 199). Could Wittgenstein make the same statement about his objects?

Is it an empirical matter what objects there are? Suppose that '*a*' is the name of an object. Is it an empirical matter that *a* exists? The denial of any empirical matter is conceivable. But what the sentence '*a* does not exist' attempts to state is inconceivable; for if it were true, it would be nonsensical since '*a*' would be referenceless. ("One would, however, like to say: existence cannot be attributed to an element, for if it did not exist, one could not even name it and so one could say nothing at all of it" (*Invest.* I, 50). The only empirical matters are which possible configuration of objects are actual, which not. Thus what objects there are is not an empirical matter.

But, oddly enough, it is not a logical matter either. For "the *application* of logic determines what elementary propositions there are"

(5.557). But what elementary propositions there are determines what names there are and, consequently, what objects there are. (Compare: "What the axiom of infinity is meant to say would be expressed in language by there being infinitely many names with different references" (5.535).) Therefore, the application of logic determines what objects there are. However, "what lies in its application, logic cannot anticipate" (5.557). Therefore, what objects there are, logic cannot anticipate. But this is to say that what objects there are is not a logical matter. Logic is used simply to uncover them.

Logic "is before the How, not before the What" (5.552). Wittgenstein has said earlier that "a proposition can only say *how* a thing is, not *what* it is" (3.221). That is, it can only show how a thing is related to other things. Thus the How is the existent atomic facts. (See also 6.432 and 6.44.) The What, on the other hand, is the objects. So logic comes after the objects but before the existent atomic facts. But what occupies this middle position? The possible atomic facts. Given the objects, logic determines what the possible atomic facts are.

What objects there are is a nonempirical, nonlogical matter. It is an empirical matter what configurations of objects are actual. It is a logical matter what configurations of objects are possible. But what objects there are to be configured is neither.

6. *The existence of objects and the existence of atomic facts.* ". . . outside logic all is accident" (6.3). Now, as we have just seen, there are two things that lie outside logic: the existence of objects and the existence of atomic facts. This suggests an interesting question: Is there any connection between the existence of objects and the existence of atomic facts? Suppose that I draw up a list of all possible atomic facts. That is, I write down all the elementary propositions. (These together with the propositions that can be formed from them (4.51) compose language (4.001).) Suppose also that I draw up a second list of all existent atomic facts. This time I write down all the true elementary propositions. (These together with all the propositions that follow from them compose the whole of natural science (4.11).) Now the question I want to ask is this: Can any name appear on the first list that does not appear on the second? One is inclined to reply immediately: Certainly it can; how the world is can in no way affect how it might be; but it would follow from a negative reply that if there were no existent atomic facts, there could be no possible atomic facts either; it would follow that if the second list were blank, the first would have to be blank also. (Of course, there is the problem that if there were no existent atomic facts, there could be no list of propositions, since a sentence (Satzzeichen) is a fact

(3.14).) To say that no name can appear on the first list that does not appear on the second certainly seems a paradox and, perhaps, even an unacceptable one. Nevertheless, it seems to me that this paradox is to be found in the *Tractatus*, although by no means close to the surface; and I shall now attempt to prove it.

"Two objects of the same logical form are—apart from their external properties—only distinct from one another in that they are different" (2.0233). Obviously. For an object only has internal and external properties; so if two objects have the same internal properties, then if one forgets their external properties, they have the same properties. This is as close to a truism as one can hope to get. Do two objects ever have the same form? "Space, time, and colour (colouredness) are forms of objects" (2.0251). I infer from this that all objects whose configurations yield colours, for example, have the same form. Thus all objects whose configurations yield colours are—apart from their configurations—identical.

"Either a thing has properties that no other has, in which case one can mark it out from the others through a description without more ado, and point to it; or on the other hand there are several things with all their properties in common, and then it is absolutely impossible to point to one of them. For if nothing marks a thing out, I cannot mark it out—if I did, it would be marked out" (2.02331). This is a comment on 2.0233; it is meant to explain or elaborate it. Thus Anscombe's fantastic interpretation must be rejected ("It is possible that he is here thinking of what is involved in e.g. distinguishing between and identifying particles of matter" (*IWT*, p. 111)); for Wittgenstein is clearly talking about his objects in 2.0233; and so he must still be talking about them and not about particles of matter in 2.02331. (Besides, would he have shifted from one subject to another without giving any indication that he is doing so?) If read carefully, this proposition is really not so obscure. Wittgenstein speaks of one thing being marked out from others by a *description*. How is an object described? ". . . the description of an object describes it by its external properties . . ." (4.023 para. 4). Thus what 2.02331 says is this: if an object has external properties that no other has, then it can be marked out; but if not, not. But what are the external properties of an object? The configurations into which it enters. So an object can be marked out only if it has external properties, only if it enters into configurations, only if it is a constituent of an existent atomic fact. But an object cannot be named unless it can be marked out. Therefore, an object that is not a constituent of an existent atomic fact cannot be named. So, to revert to our question about the two lists, no name can occur on one that does not occur on the other.

This interpretation is borne out by 5.526: "One can describe the world completely by completely generalized propositions, i.e. without from the outset co-ordinating any name with a definite object. In order then to arrive at the customary way of expression we need simply say after an expression 'There is one and only one x which . . .'; and this x is a." Now one can describe the world incorrectly. But can that part of one's description alongside of which names are introduced be incorrect? That is, can a proposition of the form "There is one and only one x, which . . ." alongside of which a name is introduced be false? Suppose that it is. It says that a particular external property belongs to one and only one object. So either no object has this property or more than one object has it. In the first case the alleged name that this proposition is used to introduce is referenceless; in the second, ambiguous. In neither case is it a genuine name. ("One name stands for one thing; another for another thing . . ." (4.0311).) Therefore, the proposition must be true in order for an object to be successfully named. So, again, no name can occur in *any* proposition without also occurring in a *true* proposition.

This interpretation might be thought to be inconsistent with Wittgenstein's denial of the principle of the identity of indiscernibles, but it is not. Wittgenstein says: "Russell's definition of '$=$' won't do; because according to it one cannot say that two objects have all their properties in common. (Even if this proposition is never true, it is still *significant*.)" (5.5302). What does it mean to say that two objects, a and b, have all their properties in common? Divide all the propositions that contain 'a' into two classes: those that also contain 'b' and those that do not. Let us suppose that a and b have the same logical form, that they have the same internal properties. In this case for every significant sentence that contains 'a' there is a corresponding significant sentence that contains 'b' in its stead. If a sentence contains 'a' and not 'b', then the corresponding sentence is gotten simply by replacing 'a' with 'b'. If a sentence contains both 'a' and 'b', then the corresponding sentence is gotten by switching their places. Thus for every proposition that asserts that a bears a certain relation to b there is a corresponding proposition that asserts that b bears the same relation to a. Since elementary propositions are logically independent of one another (4.211, 5.134), let us suppose any elementary proposition that contains 'a' is true if and only if the corresponding proposition that contains 'b' is true. In this case a and b have all of their properties in common. Therefore, it is *significant* to say that two objects have all their properties in common. On the other hand, if it were *true*, it would be impossible to give the two objects separate names, since they would be indistinguishable. So, only if it is false that two objects have all of their properties in common can one say that they *do* have them all in common. It will always be significant to

298

say of two objects of the same form that they have all of their properties in common, but it will never be true. Similarly one can say that every possible atomic fact that contains a particular object as a constituent is nonexistent; but if every such atomic fact *were* nonexistent, one could not say it since in this case no name could be attached to the object. This is, incidentally, the way Wittgenstein's proposition that "substance is what there is independently of what is the case" (2.024) is to be taken in the light of this interpretation.

There is also one passage that implies a proposition that might seem to be inconsistent with my interpretation: "If the world had no substance, then whether one proposition has sense would depend on whether another proposition was true" (2.0211). Since Wittgenstein wants to establish the falsity of the proposition that the world has no substance and since this can only be done by *modus tollens*, one may conclude that Wittgenstein holds that whether *one* proposition has sense cannot depend upon whether *another* proposition is true. As I have interpreted the *Tractatus*, every name must appear in at least one true proposition. Thus a proposition that contains a particular name has sense only if at least one proposition that contains the name is true. But the proposition itself contains the name. So whether it has sense or not does not depend upon the truth of *another* proposition: if it is true itself, that is sufficient. Therefore, my interpretation is consistent with the implication of 2.0211.

This discussion leads directly to the topic of solipsism.

7. *Solipsism.* ". . . what solipsism *intends*, is quite correct, only it cannot be *said*, but it shows itself" (5.62). This raises three questions. What does solipsism intend? Why can it not be said? How does it show itself?

What does solipsism intend? Wittgenstein tells us in the very next line: ". . . the world is *my* world . . ." What is *the* world, and what is *my* world?

The world is "everything that is the case" (1), "the totality of existent atomic facts" (2.04). It would be completely described by a list of all true elementary propositions (4.26). These true elementary propositions together with every proposition that follows from them compose the whole of natural science (4.11).

What is *my* world? My world, I shall argue, consists solely of the facts with which I am personally acquainted. What are the grounds for this interpretation? Since there are so few passages in the *Tractatus* bearing on this subject, I will buttress those that do occur with additional passages from the *Notebooks*. There is first of all the key proposition: "I am my world. (The microcosm.)" (5.63). Secondly, there is the comparison of my world to my visual field. "The world

299

and life are one" (5.621). Thus my world and my life are one. But "our life is endless in the way our visual field is without limit" (6.4311). So it can be inferred that my world is endless in the way my visual field is without limit. Therefore, if my interpretation is correct, we have here a comparison of my world to my visual field. (See also 5.633–5.6331.) And this interpretation is put beyond question by a passage from the *Notebooks*: "I know that this world exists. That I am placed in it like my eye in its visual field" (11.6.16 para. 2–3). Thirdly, there are Wittgenstein's comments on death. "As in death, too, the world does not change, but ceases" (6.431). "Death is not an event in life. Death is not lived through" (6.4311). This the equation of life and the world yields the proposition that death is not an event of the (and *a fortiori* of my) world. My interpretation is again borne out by the *Notebooks*: "Death is not an event in life. It is not a fact of the world" (8.7.16 para. 15). Fourthly, there are the two following passages in the *Notebooks*: "What has history to do with me? Mine is the first and only world!" (2.9.16 para. 3). And ". . . my idea is the world . . ." (17.10.16). We might in the fifth place throw into the hopper Wittgenstein's later interpretation of solipsism: "Only what *I* see (or: see now) is really seen" (*Blue Book*, p. 64). And, finally, where before Wittgenstein speaks of a list of all true elementary propositions (4.26), he now speaks of writing a book entitled *The World as I Found It* (5.631). (See also: "I want to report how *I* found the world" (*Ntbk*. 2.9.16 para. 4).)

What solipsism would say, if it could be said, is that *the* world and *my* world are identical, that the macrocosm and the microcosm are one, that the book entitled *The World I Found* and the one entitled simply *The World* differ only in title, not in contents.

Since there are no facts beyond those that I am personally acquainted with, and since each object must be a constituent of at least one existent atomic fact, it follows that the only objects there are are those that are contained in the facts that I am personally acquainted with.

Why can what solipsism intends not be said? The answer to this is quite simple. What solipsism attempts to say is: "I am the world". ("I am the vessel of life" (*Bl. Bk.*, p. 65).) However, the word "I" signifies neither a simple nor a complex. ("A composite soul would not be a soul any longer" (5.5421). "The I is not an object" (*Ntbk*. 7.8.16). "The thinking, presenting subject; there is no such thing" (5.631).) Therefore, the sentence "I am the world" is nonsensical since one of its constituents is referenceless. So, it seems, our two books *The World I Found* and *The World* cannot differ even in title. Thus "solipsism strictly thought out coincides with pure realism" (5.64).

Wittgenstein's Notion of an Object

How does solipsism show itself?[1]

Solipsism shows itself "in that the limits of *the* language [or, *language*] . . . mean the limits of *my* world" (5.62). But "*the limits of my language* mean the limits of my world" (5.6). The word 'mean' ('bedeuten') in these propositions indicates that two expressions are in each case being equated. So it may be inferred that the limits of language mean the limits of my language, that is to say, that the limits of language are no broader than the limits of my language. Now "language is the totality of propositions" (4.001); "propositions

[1] "Dass die Welt *meine* Welt ist, das zeigt sich darin, dass die Grenzen *der* Sprache (der Sprache, die allein ich verstehe) die Grenzen *meiner* Welt bedeuten" (5.62).

Anscombe translates this passage as follows: "That the world is my world shews in that the limits of *that* language (of the language that only I understand) mean the limits of *my* world". And she goes on to explain that " '*That* language' refers back to 'my language' [5.6], which is therefore my 'private' language" (*IWT*, p. 167). The translation of '*der* Sprache' as '*that* language' is rather implausible. For this means that by '*der* Sprache' Wittgenstein really means '*meiner* Sprache'. But this is unlikely in a passage where Wittgenstein indicates by italics that he is consciously playing upon the contract between 'der' and 'meiner'.

Anscombe's interpretation of this passage is likewise unacceptable. Wittgenstein holds, on the one hand, according to Anscombe that "there are . . . many 'languages', one of which I alone understand" (*IWT*, p. 167). This proposition says, first of all, that there are many languages; and it implies, secondly, that the objects that lie behind one language differ from those that lie behind another. So it follows, according to this line of interpretation, that there are other objects beyond those of my acquaintance. Wittgenstein holds, on the other hand, according to Anscombe that "the limits of my world and of the world are one and the same . . ." (*IWT*, p. 167). However, "empirical reality is limited by the totality of objects" (5.5561). Thus my world and the world contain the same objects. So, according to this second line of interpretation, there are no objects beyond those of my acquaintance. Therefore, if we accept Anscombe's interpretation, we must conclude that Wittgenstein's theory is blatantly inconsistent.

There is no need, however, to reach this conclusion; for Wittgenstein would certainly deny the first half of Anscombe's interpretation. That there are other objects beyond those of my acquaintance is something that can be neither said nor shown. It is the very paradigm of the nonsensical since it attempts to state something about the other side of the limit. As I interpret the *Tractatus* Wittgenstein's position is that there is only one language, my language.

Stenius in commenting on this passage says that "Wittgenstein ought to have used the word 'idealism' rather than 'solipsism' " (*Witt. 'Tract.'*, p. 221, footnote 3). This interpretation must also be rejected since we now know from a passage in the *Notebooks* that Wittgenstein distinguished idealism from solipsism: "Idealism singles men out from the world as unique, solipsism singles me alone out . . ." (15.10.16 para. 21).

The parenthetical remark in the passage above has been translated two ways. Stenius, as opposed to Anscombe, translates it as 'which is the only language I understand' (*Witt. 'Tract.'*, p. 221). There has been a long controversy over the proper translation, references to which can be found in both Anscombe and Stenius. Anscombe claims very reasonably that the proper translation is a matter for those whose native language is German to decide. It is thus a matter to be decided by authority. However, the authorities I have approached have not agreed with Anscombe's; they have preferred Stenius' translation. The most conservative conclusion that one can draw is that the parenthetical remark is genuinely ambiguous, in which case the proper translation could be settled only by a word from the master himself. Consequently, it seems to me that any interpretation that rests upon this parenthetical remark rests upon a sandy foundation. I choose, therefore, to base no part of my interpretation upon it.

are truth-functions of elementary propositions" (5); elementary propositions are concatenations of names (4.22); and names refer to objects (3.203). So, supposing that by the application of logic I have uncovered all the elementary propositions in my language, to say that the limits of language are no broader than the limits of my language is to say that there are no objects beyond those referred to in my language. It is to say that there are no objects beyond those I am acquainted with.

That there are no objects beyond those I am acquainted with shows itself as follows. Anything I say must be said in my language. But the names in all the elementary propositions in my language refer to objects of my acquaintance; and, on the other hand, any attempt to formulate an elementary proposition that has a constituent that does not refer to an object of my acquaintance leads simply to nonsense. ("The limit can . . . only be drawn in language and what lies on the other side of the limit will be simply nonsense" (preface).)

Solipsism, it will be recalled, attempts to say, however, not (1) that there are no *objects* beyond those of my acquaintance, but (2) that there are no *facts* beyond those I am personally acquainted with. Now we have seen that proposition (1) follows from proposition (2). But how is (2) to be inferred from (1)? (Anscombe fails completely to see that there is a problem here: ". . . the limits of my world and of the world are one and the same; therefore the world is my world" (*IWT*, p. 167).) If we were talking about ordinary objects, two persons, say, it would not follow from the fact that I was acquainted with both that I was also acquainted with every relation in which one stood to the other. The one might be the wife of the second, for example, without my knowing it. What happens in Wittgenstein's system that makes this impossible? I am not at all confident here, since there are no passages at all to go by. However, there are two relevant factors that separate Wittgenstein's objects from ordinary objects. First, his objects are simples; and, secondly, I am acquainted with *all* of them. Therefore, I would suggest that Wittgenstein intended us to infer (2) from (1) by using (2.02): "An object is simple". However, the notion of a simple is too obscure for me to be certain that this is a valid inference.

In conclusion I would like to note a parallel with Schopenhauer:

The world as representation . . . has . . . so to speak, two poles, namely the knowing subject plain and simple without the forms of its knowing, and crude matter without form and quality. . . . This subject is not in time, for time is only the more direct form of all its representing. Matter, standing in opposition to the subject, is accordingly eternal, imperishable, endures through all time. . . . Everything else is involved in a constant arising and passing away, whereas these two constitute the static poles of the world as representation. (*The World as Will and Representation*, Payne translation, vol. II, p. 15.)

Similarly, the world in the *Tractatus* floats between qualityless and eternal objects, on the one hand, and the metaphysical subject, which is an "extensionless point" (5.64), on the other. For Schopenhauer matter and the knowing subject turn out in the end to be the very same thing, the will. On this point he is not followed by Wittgenstein.[1]

[1] I am indebted for many of the translations of the *Tractatus* used in the course of this paper to Anscombe's *Introduction* and to a list of corrections of the Ogden-Ramsey translation prepared by Max Black for one of his seminars on the *Tractatus*. Others may also recognize a word of theirs here, a phrase there.

On the Picture Theory of Language: Excerpts from a Review[1]

DAVID S. SHWAYDER

IN his exertions to make sense of the picture theory, in a simple-minded understanding of "picture", Stenius fails to see that what Wittgenstein meant by "Bild" *had* to be something very special. A Wittgensteinian picture is not the kind of thing which is put into a frame and hung upon the wall. The picture, for Wittgenstein, is the *thought* which *may* be expressed by hanging the picture upon the wall. The effect of Wittgenstein's theory is not so much to assimilate the expression of thought to the production of pictures as the reverse; "Jedes Bild is *auch* ein logisches" (*Tractactus* 2.182). Wittgenstein is more to be criticized for his linguistic theory of pictures than for his picture theory of language. The implication, in Stenius' terms, is that every picture is adequate. While Stenius sees clearly that the picture theory was meant as an alternative to those other theories which hold that in expressing a proposition we refer to or name something or other, and that the picture theory enables Wittgenstein to resolve traditional problems that are generated by the Name Theory of propositional meaning—problems over falsehood and negation and the unity of the proposition and how we understand new senses without new conventions—, he still does not see that a picture for Wittgenstein can be nothing *at all* like a name; it is not the kind of thing we *use*.

I would summarize Wittgenstein's picture theory so: Every picture is a presentation (*Darstellung*) that such and such is the case; and

[1] From *Mind*, vol. 72, no. 286, April, 1963, pp. 275–88. Reprinted, with omissions, by permission of the editor and the author.

every presentation that such and such is the case is a picture; a presentation that such and such is the case is an act of thinking that such and such is the case; in a more fashionable idiom, it is an act, whether or not overt, of *asserting* that such and such is the case; a *Satz* is an overt picture, an overt act of asserting. A picture, at all events, is essentially assertional or propositional. Let us now look at the details.[1]

(*a*) A Wittgensteinian *Satz* is not a sentence, but a *thought* made manifest (3, 3.1). The *Satzzeichen* perhaps is a sentence, but surely not, as Stenius supposes, a sentence-token (3.203). The importance of this is that we can interpret neither the *Satz* nor the *Satzzeichen* as a material thing which embodies a sense, though perhaps we may speak of using or applying a *Satzzeichen* (3.11, 3.12, 3.262, 3.326, 3.327, 3.328, 3.5). Wittgenstein also speaks of the *Satzzeichen* with its constituents as having "*Zweck*" (3.341, 5.47321), viz. we write down or speak forth different instances of it.

(*b*) Thoughts are pictures, and every *Satz* is a thought (3, 3.5, 4, 4.01, 4.06, 4.463). All *Saetze* are equally pictorial. If *Elementarsaetze* are pictures, so too are truth-functions. Every *Satz* presents a *Sachlage*, or *moegliche Sachlage* (2.202, 2.203, 4.021, 4.031). Facts and states of affairs may be "elementary" or "molecular", "positive", "negative", "conjunctive", "conditional", "universal", or what have you (2.06, 5.5262).

(*c*) Every picture is a presentation that such and such; in presenting such and such it has a sense. Consequently, every picture must have a sense, and every picture must be "adequate", for we do not know what picture it is until we know its sense (4.032).

(*d*) We may analyse a presentation as a presenting that such and such truth-conditions are fulfilled (4.022, 4.063). We fix the identity of the picture by specifying the truth-conditions to be fulfilled. A presenting that such and such truth-conditions are fulfilled is a presentation *as* fact, *as* a state of affairs, *as* reality (4.01, 4.022, 4.031). If what a picture presents as fact is fact, the picture is true (2.222,

---

[1] This too is "interpretation", and there are passages of the *Tractatus*, chiefly at 3.001, 3.0321, 2.1, 4.011–4.016 and 4.0311, which would conflict with the tendency of my thoughts. But I am tolerably confident that those passages given key positions in the structure of the book would support what I shall say. I have not attempted to assemble complete references, usually supplying only a rather helter-skelter collection. (A more complete statement of this interpretation of the *Tractatus* will be found in Mr Schwyzer's contribution to this volume. Much of what I say here first came out in conversations with Schwyzer, to whom I am greatly indebted.) One proviso: In attempting to say what it means to picture or present that such and such, I shall advance to a higher level and say (e.g.) that the picture presents that such and such truth-conditions are fulfilled, or that the world is included in these possible worlds. That is a mistake, one which Wittgenstein was keenly alive to, the mistake of putting forward an analysis as a paraphrase. Wittgenstein of course did not allow that there was any sense in the idea of referring to truth-conditions.

4.05). To be a picture, i.e. to present as fact, is to represent the world as being so (2.201, 4.022).

(*e*) The picture theory therefore is a theory of presenting as the case, i.e. it is a theory of assertion and not a theory of "propositional content" (3.13, 4.062, 4.063, 4.064).

(*f*) If I introduce you to someone, what I *do* is to introduce you. But my act then must show that I mean to introduce you; and it must also show whom I mean to introduce you to. So too, the picture, as Wittgenstein sometimes but not always puts it, in being a presentation of sense, is an act of presenting sense, and not the sense itself; but it must show that it is a presentation of sense and what sense it is a presentation of (4.022). It presents what it shows, if it does, not because the showing and the presenting are the same (as some have interpreted Wittgenstein to be saying), but because it shows that it presents such and such; one does not in presentation, p, present that this is presentation, p, i.e. in asserting *p* one does not assert that he is asserting *p* (4.1212).

(*g*) A picture is a *thought* (*Gedanke*) (3), and a thought is a thinking that such and such (3.02). It is not, as with Frege, the *Sinn* thought. Nor is it what Moore calls a *proposition*, and even less is it a sentence. Wittgenstein, in a letter to Russell, made it entirely explicit that a thought was something psychological. A picture is a mental *act*, whether or not overt, of thinking that such and such is the case. A picture is a presentation of such and such by being a present*ing* of such and such. This is why I equate pictures with assertions, for these are acts of saying (outwardly thinking) that such and such is the case. *Saetze*, in the full sense, seem to be such overt presentations (3.1, 4). It follows, first, that pictures are not things which hang on a wall possibly *used* in asserting such and such, and, second, that acts of (e.g.) questioning are not pictures and do not include pictures, for picturing is the assertional mood.

(*h*) Pictures, interpreted as assertions, are special in one important respect. They are enacted, as it were, before the fact. The picture is not a replica or facsimile but a *model* of the world, against which the world is measured (2.12, 4.01, 4.031, 4.463). It is put forward to be verified or falsified, and is not therefore a report on the world as we find it to be; it is a model of the world as we suppose it to be. Picturing is not like taking a snap-shot, but more like projecting a film.

(*i*) I come now to a most difficult question: How are we to explain *sense* (*Sinn*). What is a *Sinn*? Unfortunately Wittgenstein is not constant in the way in which he formulates the relation between a picture and its *Sinn*. Sometimes he appears to equate the *Sinn* with what the picture presents, sometimes identified with a *Sachlage* or a *moegliche*

David S. Shwayder

Sachlage (2.221, 2.202, 2.203, 4.021, 4.031, 4.04). Elsewhere he says or suggests that a picture *has* a *Sinn*, or *expresses* a *Sinn*, or *thinks* a *Sinn* (3.02, 3.11, 3.3, 4.031, 4.061, 4.2, 4.431). Let us first consider a question, for which the answer is easily found, how we are to identify a *Sinn*, whatever it may be. Every picture has a single well-determined *Sinn* (3.23, 3.25). So, we could begin to identify the picture by specifying its *Sinn*. But we identify the picture by saying what it presents as the case, and thereby, I submit, we would also fix the *Sinn*. But a picture presents that such and such truth conditions are satisfied. So we fix the *Sinn*, say what the picture presents, by specifying the truth conditions (4.431). We do that by listing all the possible worlds in which the picture would be true. A possible world Wittgenstein calls a truth-possibility of *Elementarsaetze* (4.3), so we fix the *Sinn* by saying with what truth-possibilities the picture having that *Sinn* would agree and with what it would disagree (2.201, 4.2, 4.4, 4.41); we say what truth-possibilities would and would not be excluded as candidates for being the actual world by the picture's being true (4.024, 4.431). An assertion or picture presents that the actual world is included among *these* possibilities, with which it agrees. Wittgenstein also says that a picture presents "das Bestehen und Nichtbestehen der (von) Sachverhalte(n)" (2.11, 4.1), where the truth-possibilities with which the picture agrees are "possibilities of the Bestehen und Nichtbestehen der Sachverhalte" (2.201, 4.1, 4.3). I would reconcile these explanations by suggesting that the picture presents the truth-possibilities—possible worlds—with which it agrees, or, both more and less accurately, it presents that the world is included among *these* truth-possibilities (2.201, 4.463).

(*j*) Before returning to the question over the precise character of *Sinne*, we must consider how *Elementarsaetze* fit into the story. These, Wittgenstein says, assert ("behaupten"!) "das Bestehen eines Sachverhaltes" (4.21). Adjusting this according to the pattern cut above, we can say that an *Elementarsatz* presents precisely those truth-possibilities in which a particular *Sachverhalt besteht*, it agrees with just those truth-possibilities and no others. According to this an "*Elementarsatz* is a truth-function of itself" (5).

(*k*) "Das Bestehen eines (von, der) Sachverhaltes (en, 'e)" and "das Bestehen und Nichtbestehen von Sachverhalten" are not entirely transparent. What does it mean to say that a picture asserts "das Bestehen eines Sachverhaltes"? I propose to translate "Sachverhalt" as "relation between things" and "bestehen" as "obtain". We may then say that a picture presents the *obtaining of a relation between things*, which may be transformed to read that the picture presents that such and such relation obtains between such and such things, e.g. a picture pictures (asserts, presents as fact) that this object is to

308

the left of that. "Das Bestehen eines Sachverhaltes" is the equivalent of a clause in indirect discourse; and a great part of the impact of the "picture theory" comes from this way of converting such a propositional clause into an accusative. Now, if the relation between things obtains, then it is a fact that the relation between things obtains (2, 2.06). But the picture may present that such a relation between things obtains when the relation does not obtain. According to this, a picture does *not* present a *Sachverhalt*, nor does it present an obtaining (*bestehenden*) *Sachverhalt*; rather it presents *that the relation* (*Sachverhalt*) *obtains*. A *Sachverhalt*, whatever it is, is neither a fact nor a possible fact.

(*l*) But what of the *Sinn*, fixed as it is by specification of truth-conditions? It must be something external to the *Satz*, for "Im Satz ist also sein Sinn noch nicht enthalten. . . ." (3.13). Here it seems to me that there are two and only two strong candidates. First the *Sinn* may be what the picture presents (2.221), viz. that such and such is the case. Or, second, it may be the such and such which the picture presents as the case (4.2). Is it, then, that such and such truth conditions are satisfied, or is it the truth conditions which are or are not satisfied? It will be well to consider what both of these may be.

(*m*) What the picture presents is that such and such relation of things obtains. It presents something which might possibly be the case. We must of course see from the picture what possibility is meant and that this is indeed a possibility. So, while the *Sinn* is not contained in the picture, the picture must contain the possibility of that which is possibly the case, which possibility Wittgenstein calls the *Form* of the *Sinn*, otherwise the Form of Representation (2.15, 2.1513, 3.02, 3.13). If the picture happens to be true, then the *Sinn*, which is possibly the case, is actually the case. What is actually the case Wittgenstein calls a *fact* (1-2). According to this, then, the *Sinn* might be a fact or possibly a state of affairs (*Tatsache, Sachlage*, 1.1, 2.202, 2.203, 3.02, 4.031). But not all pictures are true; what a picture presents may not be the case. How then are we to describe the *Sinn*, if we identify it with what the picture presents? Only, I think, as a possible fact. A possible fact is what would be the case if any of such and such possible worlds were the actual world. My conclusion is that we might equate *Sinne* with what other philosophers have called possible facts, an interpretation strongly borne out by certain passages of the *Tractatus*. What counts against this is that in this instance the *Sinn* certainly may be stated, and is not necessarily *only* shown, though as we have seen there is a way round passages 4.022 and 4.1212.

(*n*) Suppose that we say that the *Sinn* is what the picture presents as the case: what is that? The truth-conditions themselves. But what are they? The only possible reply is that the truth-conditions are a configuration of possible worlds, precisely those with which a picture having the *Sinn* would agree. This too is something outside the picture. A configuration of possible worlds is moreover not to be found in any single possible world; hence it is neither fact nor possible fact and therefore cannot in any sense be stated or pictured; nor is it an object in the world.

(*o*) Wittgenstein holds that a picture and the signs in which it is embodied are facts (2.16, 3.142). If I am right, it is also an act of thinking. But what kind of fact can such an act be? The fact that such and such is thought to be the case. But what is that, for not all facts are of this kind? Take it that the picture is the fact that such and such relation obtains between such and such things. The things related must be the elements of a thought. That poses my final question: What kind of relation is this, and what are the elements related? Though there is some uncertainty on this, I suggest that the objects being in fact related as they are is the "abbildende Beziehung", which at once belongs to and constitutes the picture (2.1513). But what of the relation itself? Well, relations are not objects in the world, but more in the nature of "forms". This then would be the natural place to discuss Wittgenstein's three Forms, the *Form der Abbildung* (2.15, 2.151, 2.16–2.172), the *Form der Darstellung* (2.173, 2.174) and the *Form der Wirklichkeit* (also, *logische Form der Abbildung*, 2.18, 2.19, 2.2), which are at once what makes the picture possible and the possibility of that which the picture presents as the case (2.15, 2.151). I cannot go farther into these difficult matters. But something more must be said about the pictorial elements (2.13–2.1515). These elements when embodied in signs stand for (*vertreten*, 2.131, 3.22, 3.221), or refer to (*bedeuten*, 3.203), or signify (*bezeichnen*, 3.3411), simple objects in the world which correspond to (*entsprechen*, 2.13, 3.21) the pictorial elements or simple signs (3.201–3.21) or names (3.202, 3.203, 3.22, 3.26, 3.3, 3.3411) in which they are embodied. The associated object we may call the referent (*Bedeutung*, 3.203, 3.3). The object determines the "*eigentliche Name*" (3.3411), which I take to imply that if you change the referent you change the pictorial elements, whatever the signs in which embodied. How can that be so if the pictorial element is an element of thought and the referent is something outside the picture? Only if the pictorial element is essentially connected with the referent. Wittgenstein gives his sense here in a highly figurative manner, declaring that the picture reaches to and touches the objects (2.1511, 2.15121). Return now to the "*abbildende Beziehung*". It both belongs to and constitutes the picture and may be read as the fact that the pictorial elements are related as they are. But Wittgenstein also says that it consists out of

310

the co-ordinations of the elements of the picture with the things (2.1514). It is not clear that this is coherent, but I am inclined to think that it may be, if only we can correctly identify the pictorial elements. Here I must reach for an answer, one to be sure strongly suggested by the above discussion and by my view that the picture is an assertion. A pictorial element is a *reference to* a simple object, A, realized only in an act of asserting or thinking that A is related to other objects. Such references are the ultimately simple elements of acts of thought, the *eigentlichen Namen*. A picture is a fact that such and such relation obtains between the constitutive references, by token of which the picture presents that the referents are related in such and such a way.

(*p*) Taking seriously Wittgenstein's analogue of projection (3.13) and following the passages from 2.15 to 2.1515, a picture of Wittgenstein's picture theory, at least as it holds for so-called *Elementarsaetze*, would be drawn like this. A picture is a set of pictorial elements or references, shown as the rays α, β, γ to simple objects A, B, C, and a centre of projection, O. We may think of (O, α, β, γ) as cut by lines,

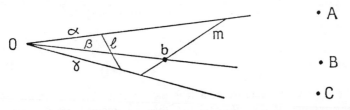

1, m, representing different *Satzzeichen*, used to express the same sense; the intersection points (e.g. b) represent words to name the objects (e.g. B).

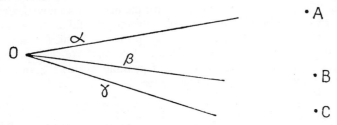

Be clear that (O, α, β, γ) is the "essential picture", not 1 or m. The system (O, α, β, γ) presents that objects A, B, C have a certain relation. (O, α, β, γ) is not a projection *from* A, B, C; it is not a report, a record of observed fact. It is a representation *as* fact. The image again is that of a projector not of a camera. (O, α, β, γ) is a "*Masstab*" against which the world is measured (2.1512), only in this case want of concordance incriminates the measure and not the world. We measure the world by taking (O, α, β, γ) to see whether the references, the "feelers" (2.1515) can be made to coincide with the referents. That presumes, of course, that the referents are there to be found: α cannot occur as element of any picture unless there exists A. So either

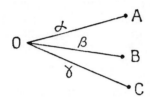

or something like

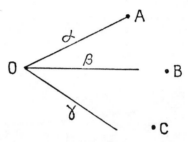

The former is a picture of a true picture; the latter a picture of a false picture. If the rays and the objects coincide, then the picture presents the fact that A, B, C are related as they are. Regardless of whether (O, α, β, γ) is true, it is required that α, β, γ all have *Bedeutungen*, which may be presumed to stand in some one or several relations. That is indeed a presumption for picturing as we now describe it, for we must be able to know what objects are held to stand in the presented relation. Perhaps this is the "prototype" which, according to Stenius, a Wittgensteinian picture *represents*. We may put this otherwise by saying that to speak of possible worlds requires that one of these is the one actual world (see 1).

Wittgenstein's Picture-Theory[1]

A Reply to Mr H. R. G. Schwyzer

ERIK STENIUS

In a paper published in this journal, vol. 5, no. 1, 1962, pp. 46–64 [pp. 271–88], Mr H. R. G. Schwyzer has argued that 'the current view (as held by, e.g., Warnock, Anscombe and Stenius) of Wittgenstein's theory of language in the *Tractatus* is mistaken'. The editor of the journal has asked me for a reply. My reply concerns only my own book, and it amounts to the statement that Mr Schwyzer's attack on the book has very little to do with what is said in it.

MR SCHWYZER claims (p. 46 [p. 271]) that his opinion of the interpretation of the *Tractatus* is founded on 'a detailed study of significant passages' in it. Though I think a still more detailed study of all significant passages in the *Tractatus* might have improved his interpretation, I should be happy if his discussion of my book[2] were founded on anything like an equally detailed study of significant passages in it. Why this is so I shall explain by a comparison between Mr Schwyzer's statements of what I have said and the passages to which these statements refer.

1. On p. 47 [p. 272] of Mr Schwyzer's paper we read:

(a) . . . Indeed, some philosophers have expressly attributed to Wittgenstein the view that the relation of the picture to what is pictured is simply reversible.

(b) Professor Stenius, in his recent book, seem initially to assume that only the 'true' pictures of the *Tractatus* are really pictures. These, he

(c) says, are isomorphic with facts, the prototypes of the pictures. And

---

[1] From *Inquiry*, vol. 6, no. 2, Summer, 1963, pp. 184–95. Reprinted by permission of the editor and the author.
[2] Erik Stenius, *Wittgenstein's 'Tractatus'*, Blackwell, Oxford, 1960.

(d) 'of two isomorphic fields F and G one, say F, *may always be considered as a picture of the other*'.

I have marked the different statements occurring in this quotation by letters (a)–(d). For the statements (b)–(d) Mr Schwyzer refers to my book, pp. 95 f.

Now the quotation (d) is—except for the italics, which Mr Schwyzer points out as being his own—from p. 95. But in order to see its relevance for the statement (a) the context of this quotation ought to be taken into consideration. On p. 91 I say:

Wittgenstein's use of the notion of 'representation' (*Abbildung*) and related concepts is not free from a certain amount of ambiguity, and I do not think it possible to grasp exactly what idea he connects with them. I shall therefore adopt the following method of analysis. First I shall define an exact concept of 'representation' called 'isomorphic representation'. Then I shall interpret Wittgenstein's statements about pictures with reference to this sort of depicting. In this way we obtain a model that satisfies many of Wittgenstein's statements on the subject. This model can be used as a system of reference for the analysis of Wittgenstein's application of the concept of a picture in his theory of language.

In accordance with this programme, which is stated in the beginning of Ch. VI, § 3, I introduce the concept of 'isomorphism' in this section and define the concept of 'isomorphic representation' in § 4. In § 5 I proceed to the concept of a picture in the *Tractatus*. This section starts on p. 96. Thus it seems to be clearly indicated that *what I state on p. 95* refers to the concept of 'isomorphic pictures' as *defined by myself* and cannot be taken as '*attributing*' *any kind of views to Wittgenstein*. Least of all can it be taken as doing so 'expressly'. This I think ought to have been clear to a reader even if the explanation on p. 91 quoted above had escaped him, since the section starting on p. 96 is expressly contrasted to the preceding section by being called THE CONCEPT OF A PICTURE IN THE TRACTATUS.

2. But even as a statement about the concept of an 'isomorphic picture' *as defined by me* in Ch. VI, § 4, the quotation (d) cannot be interpreted as stating that the 'relation of the picture to what is pictured is simply reversible'. The passage from which (d) is taken reads in full like this:

Of two isomorphic fields *F* and *G* one, say *F*, may always be considered as a picture of the other. If so, we call *F* an *isomorphic picture* of *G*, the relation between *F* and *G* one of *isomorphic representation* and the key of isomorphism the *key of interpretation*.

Now I thought the use of the expression 'considered as a picture' rather than 'considered a picture' or 'regarded as a picture' ought to hint at the fact that according to my view the mere isomorphism of *F* and *G* does not *make F* a picture of *G*. And, as we see from the context, for *F* to be 'considered as' a picture of *G* it is required that the *key of isomorphism* be conceived of as a *'key of interpretation'*, which, as is shown by the examples preceding the passage in question, means that the elements of *F* must be interpreted as *standing for* the corresponding elements of *G*. But now we cannot at one and the same time take the elements of *F* as 'standing for' the elements of *G*, and the elements of *G* as 'standing for' the elements of *F*. Therefore the relation of 'being an ismorphic picture of' is *not* symmetrical in any other sense than this: If *F* can be interpreted as an isomorphic picture of *G*, then, by reversing the key of interpretation, *G* could be interpreted as a picture of *F*. But that this is so Mr Schwyzer admits as 'trivially true', as seems to be clear from the following quotation. Speaking of Warnock he says (p. 47 [p. 272]):

Sentences, on this view, can 'mean' or 'picture' facts because sentence-signs are themselves facts and because their structure corresponds to that of non-verbal facts. But if this is true, then surely, and for precisely the same reasons, non-verbal facts can mean or picture sentences. Now there is a (trivial) sense in which we might accept such a view: that is to say, we could imagine a language in which we used *things* to talk about *words*—in which aRb stated that 'a' bears a certain relation to 'b', instead of the other way around.

What Mr Schwyzer here takes as 'trivially' true goes even a bit further than I would be prepared to accept.

3. I come to statement (b). What could be meant by the phrase 'seems initially to assume . . .'? Statement (b) is repeated on p. 55, where we read:

(e) Readers of the *Tractatus* are often upset by the apparent unnaturalness or artificiality of speaking of 'true' and 'false' in connection with
(f) pictures. And indeed, if pictures were 'things', replicas of *Sachverhalte*, then there would be no sense in ascribing truth-values to them, for, as we have observed, 'false' pictures would not then be pictures at all.
(g) But Wittgenstein is quite clear on this point.
    2.21 Das Bild stimmt mit der Wirklichkeit ueberein oder nicht; es ist richtig oder unrichtig, wahr oder falsch.
    2.22 Das Bild stellt dar, was es darstellt, unabhaengig von seiner Wahr- oder Falschheit, durch die Form der Abbildung.
(h) It is plain, then, that a Wittgensteinian picture *must* be either true
(i) or false. But some commentators have thought otherwise. Rather than
(j) abandon the theory of replicas-and-prototypes, they have been led to deny that pictures can be true or false at all. Thus Stenius (op. cit.,

(k) p. 96), as we have seen, seems initially to hold that only 'true' pictures are really *pictures*, i.e. isomorphic representations of prototype-facts;
(l) a 'false' picture is merely an 'articulate field of which the question of its being or not being an isomorphic picture can be raised'. That is to
(m) say, false pictures are might-have-been-pictures—had they been true.

'Thus Stenius . . .,' Mr Schwyzer says in (k). This cannot mean anything else than that I am one of the 'commentators' mentioned in (i) against which the whole of this passage is directed. Being upset as described in (e) and thus being misled as stated in (f), I have not noticed the obvious facts mentioned in (g) and (h), neglecting what Wittgenstein says in 2.21 and 2.22. My way of interpreting Wittgenstein's concept of a picture can thus be characterized as in (j), as is shown by (k) and confirmed by the quotation (l), the meaning of which can be paraphrased as in (m).

The basis for this description of my views is, according to Mr Schwyzer's reference, what I say on p. 96 of my book. This reference is really to my section on Wittgenstein's concept of a picture. Let us, therefore, have a look at what I say in this section. The beginning of it reads thus:

Many of the statements in the *Tractatus* can be given a good interpretation if the words 'picture' (*Bild*) and 'representation' (*Abbildung*) are taken as referring to isomorphic pictures and representations. But there are some easily noticeable differences, too, between the concept of a picture in the *Tractatus* and our concept of an isomorphic picture.

One we have already touched upon. As stated above (p. 89) a picture, according to Wittgenstein's terminology, may be called either 'true' or 'false': 'The picture agrees with reality or not; it is right or wrong, true or false' (2.21), 'In the agreement or disagreement of its sense with reality, its truth or falsity consists' (2.222). But the words 'true' and 'false' cannot be used in this way in connection with the expression 'isomorphic picture'. (On the whole I think it is unnatural to speak about 'false' pictures.) Either a field F does represent the field G isomorphically according to a key (C)—or it does not. In the first case F is, in the second it is *not* an isomorphic picture of G. Thus to talk about 'false' isomorphic pictures is meaningless.

It follows that the concept of an isomorphic picture does not correspond logically to Wittgenstein's concept of a 'picture' but rather conforms to his concept of a 'true picture'. To bring our terminology in accordance with that of the *Tractatus* we must therefore think of a picture not as an isomorphic picture but as an articulate field of which the question of its being or not being an isomorphic picture can be *raised*. We obtain such a concept if we adopt the following definition:

(VI. 1) *An articulate field F is called a picture (true or false) of the articulate field G if there is a key of interpretation (C) according to which the elements of F are considered to stand for the elements of G. The* *picture F is said to be true or false according as it is an isomorphic picture of G in respect of (C) or not.*

Does this passage give any evidence for my being a commentator of the kind mentioned in (i)? I think it gives full evidence to the contrary. Far from being misled by any kind of argument like (f), I myself stress the difference between a concept of a picture according to which a 'false' picture would not be any picture at all and Wittgenstein's concept of a picture, stating the same thing about the latter as Mr Schwyzer states in (g) and (h), and like Mr Schwyzer, quoting statement (2.21) as evidence for this view.[1]

What is true in statement (k) is only that the definition of an 'isomorphic representation' and 'isomorphic picture' *precedes* the passage just quoted and that I state that only 'true' pictures in Wittgenstein's sense could be thought of as being isomorphic with their prototypes. What in (l) stands between the quotation marks is correctly rendered; however, it does not refer to 'false' pictures only, but to Wittgenstein's concept of a picture in general. The paraphrase (m) is entirely Mr Schwyzer's own invention.

4. In addition to being in obvious disagreement with what I say on the page to which it refers, statement (k) also reveals a misapprehension of my terminology in other places of my book as well as a confusion about the consequences of what is said in the *Tractatus*, that require further comment. In some way Mr Schwyzer seems himself to be a victim of being too 'upset by the apparent unnaturalness or artificiality of speaking of "true" or "false" pictures' to see the significance of this terminology. With reference to § 1 of my Ch. VI, Mr Schwyzer argues (p. 48 [p. 273]) that I conclude from 2.1, 2.11 and 2.12 'that pictures, for Wittgenstein, are "representational": ". . . Wittgenstein always thinks of a picture as having a *real* prototype, which it represents" '.

Now I do not use the word 'representational' as a characteristic of Wittgenstein's concept of a picture; I only say that it does not include 'nonrepresentational' pictures. In my original typescript I had 'nonfigurative' instead of 'nonrepresentational' but I was told that 'nonfigurative' was called 'nonrepresentational' in English. Thus my statement that a picture in Wittgenstein's sense cannot be 'nonrepresentational' does not—as seems to me to be clear from the context—in·itself imply that a picture in the *Tractatus* always is thought of as having a *real prototype*.

This is a minor point, since I really *say* that Wittgenstein always

---

[1] As further evidence for this view I quote 2.222, whereas Mr Schwyzer quotes 2.22. The fact that Mr Schwyzer does not mention 2.222 is significant, since 2.222 gives strong evidence for the adequacy of my argument in section 5 below.

thinks of a picture *as* having a *real* prototype. But it is quite important to note that as evidence for this contention I take statements 2.1 and 2.12 only, not 2.11, where, indeed, Wittgenstein does not talk about prototypes at all.

The argument for my opinion reads like this (p. 89):

> From 2.12 ['The picture is a model of reality'] it seems to follow that Wittgenstein always thinks of a picture as having a *real* prototype, which it represents. I shall therefore call a picture a genuine *representation* (*Abbildung*) only if it represents a real prototype; otherwise I shall call it 'fictitious'.
>
> What we form pictures of is *facts*, according to 2.1. Since by 'reality' Wittgenstein means a 'real state of affairs', what a picture is a model of according to 2.12 is also a fact. I think Wittgenstein must be understood literally here: that a picture has a real prototype means in his terminology that it is either a 'true' or a 'false' representation of a fact. (Cf. 2.0212, 2.17, 2.21 ff.) But what are we then to mean by a representation of a fact?

Now Mr Schwyzer seems to be so taken up with the idea that 'having a prototype' means being a *true* picture of that prototype, that, contrary to what I expressly and immediately add to my statement that Wittgenstein always thinks of a picture as having a *real* prototype, he comments on it like this (p. 48 [p. 273]): 'Pictures, then, are facsimiles, replicas, reproductions of prototypes, of "originals"; and these originals are held to be *facts* (*Tatsachen*). I shall argue that this apparently innocuous interpretation is unfounded and quite wrong. There are no prototype-facts in the *Tractatus*.'

As can be seen from my text the 'apparently innocuous interpretation' does not occur in it, and I agree that such an interpretation is wrong, because if it were right then there would be no room for false pictures.

5. But I think Mr Schwyzer's inference from this to the conclusion 'There are no prototype-facts in the *Tractatus*' is obviously mistaken. Among other reasons why it must be mistaken, there is one that Mr Schwyzer ought to have noticed, since he so emphatically insists on his observation that Wittgensteinian pictures are thought of as either 'true' or 'false'. This reason is that there is *no sense* in saying that a picture is 'true', or that it is 'false', *unless there is a prototype to compare it with*. Far from showing that 'there are no prototype-facts in the *Tractatus*', Wittgenstein's employment of the terms 'true' and 'false' in connection with pictures *implies* that there *are* 'prototype-facts in the *Tractatus*'.

6. What Mr Schwyzer has in mind, when he states that there are no prototype-facts in the *Tractatus*, seems to be a quite different

thing. This is that for a fact *F* to be a picture there need not, according to the *Tractatus*, be any kind of prototypes of which *F* is a *true* picture. Thus he (p. 51 [p. 276]) quotes the first paragraph of 2.15:

2.15 Dass sich die Elemente des Bildes in bestimmter Art und Weise (Par. 1) zu einander verhalten stellt vor, dass sich die Sachen so zu einander verhalten.

and adds the following comment:

The following translation of 2.15 (par. 1) will not do. 'That the elements of the picture are combined in a particular way *represents* [i.e. is a representation, copy, facsimile, of] the fact that things are so combined.'

I think Mr Schwyzer is right in this comment, but I do not know of anybody who has made such a translation. For my part I have made the first paragraph of 2.15 the main topic of a whole section called WHAT A PICTURE REPRESENTS AND WHAT IT DEPICTS OR PRESENTS. (Ch. VI, § 6, pp. 98 f.) In this section I contrast the term 'represent' (*abbilden*) to the two terms 'depict' (*vorstellen*) and 'present' (*darstellen*). I stress that a picture 'depicts' or 'presents' what it 'depicts' or 'presents' independently of its truth or falsehood (referring to 2.22) and point out that this is not to be understood as implying the existence of some 'imaginary fact' acting as a prototype of a false picture. The argument is summed up like this:

(VI. 2) *A picture is an interpreted fact that 'represents' a real prototype (truly or falsely). Its elements deputize for the elements of the prototype and it*
(a) *'presents' ('depicts') these elements as combined in the way shown by its external structure, and thus*
(b) *shows the possibility of their being combined in such a way.*

Mr Schwyzer, on the other hand, quotes (p. 52 [p. 277]) 2.22 in the same wording as I do and adds: 'Now if a picture presents that things are combined in a particular way *independently* of whether they are *in fact* combined in this way, then this means that it presents things *as* being so combined.'

There seems to be a considerable agreement between Mr Schwyzer's statement of his view on this point and mine. Why does not Mr Schwyzer pay any attention to this fact?

7. One reason might be that Mr Schwyzer thinks that from observations of the kind mentioned above can be made certain inferences which can be given striking and sensational formulations and which are, certainly, in disagreement with what I have said in my book. His arguments for these conclusions I find, I am sorry to say, very

vague. In so far as I can make out Mr Schwyzer's line of thought, it amounts to something like this:

Since a picture need not be true, it is not *essential* to a picture to be in any sense 'isomorphic' with a prototype. Therefore pictures in the *Tractatus* are not 'isomorphic' with any prototypes. This applies also to Wittgenstein's theory of a *Satz* as a picture. There is no 'isomorphism' (p. 46 [p. 271]). And 'there are no prototype-facts in the *Tractatus*' (p. 48 [p. 273]).

The fallacy leading to the latter conclusion I have already pointed out. The fallacy leading to the former one is this: The fact that 'false' pictures are not 'isomorphic' with their prototypes does not show that *true* pictures or *true* sentences are not in some sense 'isomorphic' with their prototypes, or that it is not essential to Wittgenstein's theory of language that this is so. On the contrary: 'The sentence *shows* how things stand, *if* it is true' (4.022).

What would be the idea of employing the term 'picture' in the theory of sentence meaning, if even *true* sentences had not any similarity with the facts they describe?

Now Mr Schwyzer must of course admit that there are numerous statements in the *Tractatus* where 'similarity in structure' is indicated as an essential concept in Wittgenstein's theory of language. But he dismisses them as 'atypical' (p. 63 [p. 287]). I am afraid that in order to be consistent in his terminology Mr Schwyzer would have to dismiss almost all of what is said on the subject in the *Tractatus* as 'atypical'.

8. This leads me to the impression that such exclamations of Mr Schwyzer's as 'There is no isomorphism' are not intended to be taken literally but have the function of giving his contentions a more provocative ring. This impression is increased by the fact that he adds (p. 46 [p. 271]): 'The theory is not about sentences at all, but about *talking sense.*' Nobody would deny that Wittgenstein's theory of language is, among other things, about talking sense. But most interpreters have believed that his investigation of what is the criterion of 'talking sense' is founded on a theory about the way in which sentences have sense. How can Mr Schwyzer have arrived at an opposite conclusion?

The method is simple. When on page 46 [p. 271] he says that Wittgenstein's theory is not about sentences, he lets the reader remain in the belief that the word 'sentence' stands for the German word *Satz*, and that he thus adopts my translation of this German word. But his argument for his sensational thesis is based on the fact that he does not take 'sentence' as a translation of *Satz* but of *Satzzeichen*. So what lies behind his alleged sensational disagreement with other interpreters on this point is a rather less sensational thesis, which in *my* vocabulary would be rendered, 'The theory is not about sentence-tokens at all but about talking sense'.

Even if formulated like this, however, the thesis is an exaggeration of what Mr Schwyzer's argument really contains. So, for instance, he says on p. 57 [p. 282]: 'The *Satz* is the use of the *Satzzeichen*; it is the *Satzzeichen* being used as a projection of the sense, the *Satzzeichen* with the sense thought in it.' But if this is so, is not Wittgenstein's theory, among other things, precisely about what Mr Schwyzer calls 'sentences', i.e. about how 'sentence-tokens', in my terminology, get their sense?

9. By the way, I think that Mr Schwyzer is right in saying that 'the *Satz* is the *Satzzeichen* with its sense thought in it', in so far as the *interpretation* of a *Satzzeichen* is a necessary condition for making it into a *Satz*. In my terminology this means that a (semantical) 'sentence' is an interpreted sentence-token (cf. my book pp. 129 and 135 f.). But otherwise his formulation is misleading—as a consequence of the incorporation into the *Tractatus* of the key-term 'use' from the writings of the later Wittgenstein. It is connected with one of two really original[1] features in Mr Schwyzer's interpretation of the *Tractatus*. These are the following:

(a) A picture in the *Tractatus* is to be understood as an *act*, and, in particular, a *Satz* is to be understood as a *language-act* (p. 57 [p. 282]). This is the essential difference between a *Satz* and a *Satzzeichen*.

(b) *Sachverhalte* cannot themselves be facts, since 'a *Sachverhalt* is simply a combination of objects (2.01)' (p. 50 par. 1 [p. 275 par. 1]), 'but facts are not combinations of things, nor are they reducible to these' (p. 50 par. 3 [p. 275 par. 3]). In order to make a fact out of a *Sachverhalt* we must add the word 'obtain' (*bestehen*)—or 'does not obtain'. 'Take *red* and *square* as objects; then *red square* is a *Sachverhalt*, and *that the square is* (*is not*) *red* is a *Tatsache*' (p. 50 par. 1 [p. 275 par. 1]).

10. Mr Schwyzer seems to arrive at the interpretation (a) in the following way (pp. 52 f. [pp. 277 f.]): (1) According to the *Tractatus* a picture 'presents' a (possible) state of affairs (cf. p. 57 [p. 282]). (2) According to the *Tractatus* it is an essential feature in thinking or speaking that *we* form pictures. (3) A picture cannot *do* anything. (4) The state of affairs 'presented' by the picture or sentence is thus

---

[1] (Added in proof) After having read Professor Shwayder's critical notice on my book in *Mind* (April, 1963) [present volume] I have realized that Mr Schwyzer is not so original as I believed.

presented by *us*, by our making a picture. (5) Therefore, a picture or a sentence is the *act* of presenting a state of affairs.

One could believe one was reading Heidegger. First 'present' is taken in the meaning of 'depict' or something like this—as the words *vorstellen* and *darstellen* are used in the *Tractatus*. Then 'present' is taken as an *activity* which requires an *agent* 'doing' something. Finally the product of this activity, i.e. the picture, is identified with the activity of making this picture. (By the way Mr Schwyzer seems to find a support for this identification in the fact that some words, and in particular the word 'thought', can be used as referring both to an activity [the activity of thinking] and to the product of this activity.) Therefore pictures are *acts*, Q.E.D.

11. The argument for the interpretation (b) is this (pp. 49 f. [pp. 274 f.]): In the *Tractatus* it is said that '*die Tatsache ist das Bestehen von Sachverhalten*'. This means that 'the fact is that . . . *Sachverhalte* "obtain". *Sachverhalte*, therefore, cannot themselves be facts.'

This argument is like saying, that since '*p* is true' is a sentence, '*p*' cannot be a sentence.

Otherwise the interpretation is too absurd to require comment. The most remarkable thing about it, however, is that Mr Schwyzer does not seem to realize that his interpretation is original at all. Thus (p. 50 [p. 275])—referring to Russell, Miss Anscombe and me—he presents an argument of the following kind: Since all of us have taken the view that 'facts are species of *Sachverhalte*' (which, strictly speaking, is true of none of us) we have thought of facts as 'combinations of things' or as 'reducible to combinations of things'. This ' "reduction" of facts to combinations of things is . . . largely responsible for the theory of isomorphism between "proposition" and fact'. The result of the argument is summed up like this:

But facts are not combinations of things, nor are they reducible to these. The world is the totality of facts, not of things—nor, we might add, of *Sachverhalte*. Once more: the relation between *Tatsache* and *Sachverhalt* is as follows. If a combination of things 'obtains', i.e. if things are combined in such-and-such a way—if the square is red, then it is a fact that it is; if the square is not red then it is a fact that it is not. Wittgenstein's use of 'fact' is far closer to what we usually mean by the word than has been supposed.

'Than has been supposed . . .' This cannot mean anything else than that Russell, Anscombe and I have taken a fact 'as a combination of things' in a sense in which 'red square' is a 'combination of things', thus thinking that it cannot be a fact that the square is red even if the square is red. How Mr Schwyzer has arrived at that interpretation is beyond my imagination. By the way, I have not even used the word 'combination' occurring in the Ogden translation of 2.01 as a rendering of the German *Verbindung*, but have rejected it as misleading (see my book, p. 61).

12. To sum up: There are indeed many points in which I cannot agree with Mr Schwyzer's interpretation of the *Tractatus*. But there are also important points on which it is in accordance with the view presented in my book, though Mr Schwyzer claims this not to be so. As for his renderings of what I have said in my book, I have found one statement, which, if favourably interpreted, is correct. This is the statement (c) in the passage quoted above on p. 1 [p. 313].

The 'Tractatus': Nominalistic or Realistic?[1]

EDWIN B. ALLAIRE

THE *Tractatus* is nominalistic. This claim, designed by Anscombe and Copi,[2] is now the fashion. It does not deserve to be: the *Tractatus* looks foolish in it. In this paper I want to try a realistic interpretation on the work.[3] Since this interpretation itself is not wholly fitting, much of my concern will be with how and why it fails to fit exactly.

If the *Tractatus* were neatly realistic, it would exhibit these lines: (1) properties as well as particulars are constituents of atomic facts; (2) properties are different in kind from particulars. In other words, if the early Wittgenstein had not been somewhat inhibited by deep and reasonable concerns, he would have *explicitly* analysed 'this is red', asserted truly of a speck in the visual field, as follows: both 'this' and 'red' refer not only to different entities but to different kinds of entities.

According to Anscombe and Copi, the *Tractatus* denies that properties are constituents of atomic facts. In other words, they claim that it denies both (1) and (2). As indicated above, I shall argue that it affirms both (1) and (2). I stress the difference in order to remark on what one might think is another possibility; viz. that it denies (2) but

---

[1] From Edwin B. Allaire *et al.*, *Essays in Ontology*, Iowa Publications in Philosophy, vol. i, Hague: Nijhoff, 1963, pp. 148–65. Reprinted by permission of the publisher and the author.

[2] Anscombe, G. E. M., *An Introduction to Wittgenstein's Tractatus*, London, 1959. Cf. ch. 7. I. M. Copi, "Objects, Properties and Relations in the *Tractatus*", *Mind*, 67, 1959, 145–65 [present volume]. Two reviewers of Stenius' *Wittgenstein's 'Tractatus'* (Oxford, 1960) rely heavily and uncritically on the arguments of Anscombe and Copi. Cf. Richard J. Bernstein, "Wittgenstein's Three Languages", *The Review of Metaphysics*, 15, 1961, 278–98 [present volume] and Judith Jarvis, "Professor Stenius on the *Tractatus*", *The Journal of Philosophy*, 63, 1961, 584–96 [present volume].

[3] Though several philosophers, e.g. Bergmann, Stenius, and Ramsey, have stated that the *Tractatus* is realistic, none have argued that it is.

affirms (1). In the case of the *Tractatus*, and perhaps in general, the possibility is illusory. One can argue that Wittgenstein affirms (1) only by showing that he affirms (2). That is so because he provides no examples of properties.

The point of the preceding paragraph can be better expressed by noticing an ambiguity of 'property'. Consider, again, 'this is red'. One might argue that 'this' and 'red' refer to distinct and unanalysable entities and yet deny that they are different in kind. By using 'property' *in an ordinary or grammatical sense*, one might then say that particulars and properties *exist*, even though they are not different in kind. Since Wittgenstein gives no example of a property in the ordinary sense one can show that he accepts (1) only by showing that he believes that there are properties *in an extraordinary or ontological sense*. In other words, one can show that he is a realist only by showing that he believes that the ontological assay of an atomic fact will reveal different kinds of existents. If one can show that, as I hope to do, one must then explain, as I also hope to do, why he provides no examples of properties.

I want to begin my argument by offering three nontextual reasons for disbelieving that the *Tractatus* is nominalistic. Being nontextual they are perhaps inconclusive. They are nonetheless impressive. First, shortly before and shortly after the *Tractatus* Wittgenstein holds a realistic position. Second, when speaking in the later works about the *Tractatus*, he suggests that it is realistic. Third, the nominalistic position imputed to the *Tractatus* by Anscombe and Copi is sheer nonsense.

In the recently published *Notebooks 1914–16*, many passages enforce realism. The two that follow are typical.

> Could one manage without names? Surely not. Names are necessary for an assertion that *this* thing possesses *that* property.[1]

> Relations and properties . . . are objects.[2]

In the 1929 paper, "Some Remarks on Logical Form", Wittgenstein is bizarrely realistic.

> I only wish to point out the direction in which, I believe, the analysis of visual phenomena is to be looked for and that in this analysis we meet with logical forms quite different from those which ordinary language leads us to expect. The occurrence of numbers in the forms of atomic propositions is . . . an . . . unavoidable feature of the representation. . . . Numbers will have to enter these forms when—as we should say in ordinary language—we are dealing with properties which admit of gradation, i.e. properties

---

[1] Wittgenstein, L., *Notebooks 1914–16*, Oxford, 1961, p. 53e.
[2] Ibid., p. 61e.

such as the length of an interval, the pitch of a tone, the brightness or redness of a shade of colour, etc. It is characteristic of these properties that one degree of them excludes any other. One shade of colour cannot simultaneously have two different degrees of brightness.[1]

For the purpose at hand, these passages need no comment, only emphasis: both before and after the *Tractatus* Wittgenstein advocates a bold realism.

Speaking in the 1929 paper about—I presume—the *Tractatus*, Wittgenstein says:

One might think—and I thought so not so long ago—that a statement expressing the degree of a quality could be analysed into a product of single statements of quantity and a completing supplementary statement. I maintain that the statement which attributes a degree to a quality cannot further be analysed.[2]

Without exploring the subtleties and peculiarities of this passage, one can say unreservedly that Wittgenstein once held, presumably at the time of the *Tractatus*, that some properties, those referred to by certain quantity words, are constituents of atomic facts.

In the *Blue Book* he says:

Talking of a fact as a "complex of objects" springs from this confusion (cf. *Tractatus Logico-philosophicus*). Supposing we asked: "How can one *imagine* what does not exist?" The answer seems to be: "If we do, we imagine the nonexistent combinations of existing elements." A centaur doesn't exist, but a man's head and torso and arms and a horse's legs do exist. "But can't we imagine an object utterly different from any one which exists?" We should be inclined to answer: "No, the elements, the individuals, must exist. If redness, roundness, and sweetness did not exist, we could not imagine them."[3]

This passage, though perhaps less trustworthy than the preceding one, also suggests that at least some of the constituents of atomic facts are properties. Whether or not the passages just quoted bear faithful witness to what Wittgenstein held in the *Tractatus* is not worth arguing. They are at least typical of the way in which he speaks of the earlier work in the later ones. He never speaks of it, at least with respect to the nominalism-realism issue, as Copi and Anscombe do. According to them, the only entities that enter into atomic facts are bare particulars, the sorts of entities Russell claimed to be the referents of logically proper names. Whatever such entities be, and they are elusive at best, they are neither qualities nor qualitied particulars. That is, bare particulars are neither colours nor coloured

[1] Wittgenstein, L., "Some Remarks on Logical Form", *Aristotelian Society*, Supp. vol. 9 (1929), pp. 162–71 [present volume]; pp. 166–7 [p. 34].
[2] Ibid., p. 167 [p. 35].
[3] Wittgenstein, L., *The Blue and Brown Books*, Oxford, 1958, p. 31.

things; they are the entities having or exemplifying the colours. The strangeness of bare particulars aside, the question is: What, upon the Anscombe-Copi interpretation of the *Tractatus*, are properties? They are "configurations of bare particulars". Consider these statements by Anscombe.

Wittgenstein does not speak of 'concepts' or 'universals' as a kind of thing to be found in the world; it is quite clear that for him there is nothing but objects in configuration.[1]

Red is a material property, and therefore formed by a configuration of objects.[2]

This position, i.e. the one attributed to the early Wittgenstein, is nonsense, though not in the sense in which, according to some, all ontological positions are, nor in the less damaging and admittedly queer sense that it is unique, without historical roots or parallels, not even in seventeenth-century atomism. The position is nonsense— sheer nonsense I said—in that, unlike the traditional ontological positions, it has no rationale whatsoever. To lean on the later Wittgenstein, there are no grammatical analogies that can show how the early Wittgenstein got into such a bottle. At least there are none that I can discover. The position is, I submit, pathetically verbal, being words about mere marks on paper. Nor does Anscombe try to make it more than that. She tries to make it neither intelligible—she does not think it is—nor worthy of sympathy.

The above reasons for disbelieving that the *Tractatus* is nominalistic (at least in the sense that it denies that property words refer to unanalysable entities) are impressive even if inconclusive. Wittgenstein may have been fickle, chasing now nominalism now realism; he may have been a poor guide to his past; he may have been an advocate of sheer nonsense. However, to claim that he was all three demands *very* convincing textual evidence. What is offered by Anscombe and Copi does not convince.

I cannot hope to examine all the textual arguments offered by Anscombe and Copi. Nor would that be worthwhile: the *Tractatus* would be lost in the effort. Accordingly, I shall examine only three of their arguments. Two are formidable; one is not. My reason for examining the latter—it is advanced by Anscombe—is that it is illuminating and will aid me in speaking to the point about the realism of the *Tractatus*.

Consider the following passage from Anscombe.[3]

. . . at 2.0231 we learn that the substance of the world—i.e., the objects— *can* only determine a form, not any material properties. For it needs

---

[1] Anscombe, G. E. M., op. cit., p. 99.　　　　[2] Ibid., p. 111.
[3] Ibid., p. 111.

propositions (as opposed to names) to represent material properties; such properties are only formed by 'the configuration of objects.' Red is a material property, and therefore formed by a configuration of objects.

Anscombe's argument is a paraphrase of 2.0231, a stern test for any realistic interpretation.

The substance of the world *can* only determine a form and not any material properties. For these are first presented by the propositions—first formed by the configuration of objects.

As the context (roughly 2.011–2.025) makes clear, the main point of 2.0231 is that there is no logical connection between an entity and the facts in which it actually occurs. 2.0231 is therefore a variant of the thesis of logical atomism. It declares that the constituents of atomic facts are simple. Just as there is no logical connection between two atomic facts, so too there is no logical connection between an entity and the facts in which it actually occurs. There is, however, some "logical" connection between entities and facts. It is this: the *kind* an entity is determines the facts in which it *can* occur. That is what is meant by "the substance of the world can only determine a form". That it can *only* determine the facts in which an entity can occur and not any material properties means, to repeat, that there is no logical connection between the kind an entity is and the specific properties it has.

Wittgenstein himself expresses a similar thought in 2.01231: "In order to know an object, I must know not its external qualities, but its internal qualities." Another expression to this end is 2.0131: "A speck in the visual field need not be red, but it must have a colour." The difference stressed in these passages as well as in 2.0231 may be explained in several ways. For example, the determination that a string is well formed is different from the determination that it is true or false. The former determination is logically prior to, and independent of, the latter one. A person can know what a sentence means without knowing whether it is true or false. Another way of explaining the difference is by saying that it strives to capture the difference between knowing what a word means (what it refers to and the syntactical rules governing its use) and knowing true sentences in which it occurs. Still another way, perhaps the most satisfactory one, is as follows. To represent the formal properties of an object one needs to exhibit only the formation rules governing the sign referring to it; to represent the material properties of an object one needs to exhibit the true sentences in which the sign for it occurs.

In the light of this last expression of the difference between material and formal properties, the first part of the second sentence (of 2.0231) becomes clear. In saying that material properties are first presented by the propositions, Wittgenstein simply means that in order to represent that (e.g.) a speck in the visual field is red one must make a sentence, i.e. put words in combination. It is not enough to give the rules for the word referring to the speck. Now consider the last part of the second sentence, "material properties are first formed by configurations of objects", recalling that it is there to echo the first part. If the last part were expressed linguistically, and mark that Wittgenstein's initial effort is linguistic, there would be no difficulty. It would say just what the first part does. Unhappily it is not expressed linguistically. Nevertheless its meaning ought by now to be clear. The material properties an entity has depends on the entities with which it is combined. The formal properties do not so depend and are, indeed, "internal" to the entity.

In 2.0231 Wittgenstein is enforcing a difference between formal and material properties. In so doing, he first says that the substance (in the sense of unanalysable entities) of the world determines a form. This means that entities have formal properties which do not depend on their being in configurations but which determine the configurations in which they can occur. He also says that material properties are not so determined, meaning that the specific property an entity has is not determined by its formal property. Attempting to illuminate this difference, he further says that material properties are first presented by the propositions—first formed by the configurations. This means that, unlike the formal properties, the material properties are determined by the configurations in the sense that the material properties are accidental and appear only in configurations. Stated briefly, 2.0231 strives to secure the difference between the fact that a speck must be coloured and the fact that a speck is red. The former is logical and depends on the kind the entity is; the latter is not logical and depends on the other entities (e.g. red) with which the speck is combined. (That Wittgenstein speaks of formal properties as internal and material ones as external is merely more of the same.)

2.0231, then, has nothing to do with the question of whether or not properties are constituents of atomic facts. In its obscure way it insists on a difference between the formation rules of a language and true sentences of it. The former show the kinds of entities that can be combined in facts; the latter the entities that are combined. Therefore, the former depend on the formal or internal properties of the entities; the latter on the material or external properties of them. Since 2.0231 is neutral regarding the nominalism-realism issue, the nominalistic interpretation is without one of its most prominent pillars.[1]

---

[1] Sellars has recently attacked the nominalistic interpretation on this same point. 'Naming and Saying", *Philosophy of Science*, 29, 1962, 7–26 [present volume].

The 'Tractatus': Nominalistic or Realistic?

I want now to examine another of Anscombe's arguments, the one I said was illuminating though not formidable.

> ... if [the elementary proposition] is just a concatenation of names—then it is not reproduced by a formula consisting of some letters for names and some letters for functions. And this is borne out by many passages. Notably for example 3.1431: The nature of the propositional sign becomes very clear, if we imagine it as composed of three-dimensional objects ... instead of written signs.[1]

Anscombe is arguing that function signs do not occur in the atomic sentences of Wittgenstein's picture language. That needs no argument, and even if it did 3.1431 would not bear it out. The entire effort of that passage is to convince one that sentences are not, as Frege believed (cf. 3.143), names. Whether or not they are is quite distinct from whether or not function signs occur in sentences. That lapse aside, Anscombe's point needs, to repeat, no argument. 4.22 expresses it openly: elementary propositions are concatenations of names. That Anscombe argues for what needs no argument reveals how significant she believes the point to be. For her, its significance is due to a comparison between Frege and Wittgenstein on which she bases much of her interpretation of the *Tractatus*.

Her comparison emerges in the following passage.[2]

> What has become of Frege's concepts in Wittgenstein's theory? They seem to have disappeared; actually, however, instead of making concepts or universals into a kind of objects. ... Wittgenstein made the gulf between concepts and objects much greater than Frege ever made it. ... In respect of having argument places, concepts go over entirely into logical forms. In the 'completely analysed' proposition ... the Fregean concept, the thing with the holes in it, has become simply the logical form.

Anscombe's comparison and the argument she bases on it may be stated this way. Frege holds that there are concepts as well as objects. He also holds that the former are represented by functions, the latter by names. For Frege, an atomic sentence would thus consist of a function and a name. In contrast, Wittgenstein holds that an atomic sentence consists only of names. That is her comparison. Her argument is that since Wittgenstein denies that functions occur in atomic sentences, he also denies that the sorts of entities Frege calls concepts occur in atomic facts. In other words, since Wittgenstein admits only names into atomic sentences, he grants existence only to the sorts of entities Frege calls objects. (According to Anscombe, these are bare particulars.)

The comparison is shallow; the argument, naive. The comparison

---

[1] Anscombe, G. E. M., op. cit., p. 100.   [2] Ibid., p. 108.

331

is shallow because it fails to explore Wittgenstein's own deep commitment to the propositional-function notation. Exploring that, one finds the true nature of Wittgenstein's disagreement with Frege. The argument is naive because the claim that only names occur in atomic sentences does not entail that properties are not constituents of atomic facts. Nothing whatsoever recommends her silent premiss that Wittgenstein could not have thought that names represent properties.

Let me first explore Wittgenstein's use of the propositional-function notation. Consider 4.126.

Formal concepts cannot, like proper concepts, be presented by a function. For their characteristics, the formal properties, are not expressed by functions. The expression of a formal property is a feature of certain symbols. The mark that signifies the characteristics of a formal concept is . . . a characteristic of all symbols whose meanings fall under the concept.

The propositional-function notation is sometimes used as follows. Assume that red is a concept and that '$f_1(x)$', a propositional function, represents it. The objects falling under the concept red are those referred to by the substitution instances of 'x' resulting in true sentences. In 4.126 the notation is not used in that way. 4.126 distinguishes between formal and proper concepts, speaking of the latter as falling under the former which cannot themselves be represented by functions. Wittgenstein's meaning may be illustrated as follows. Consider again '$f_1(x)$'. It is a function representing the proper concept red. It falls under the formal concept, property, in virtue of having the characteristic mark 'f' which, since it represents no entity, is not a function. It is a variable. 4.126 makes clear therefore that not only does Wittgenstein rely heavily upon the function notation but that he thinks of proper concepts as entities, i.e. as constituents of atomic facts.

In 4.1272 one hears:

. . . the variable name 'x' is the proper sign of the pseudo concept object. Whenever it is used otherwise, i.e. as a proper concept word, there arise senseless pseudo propositions. So one cannot, e.g., say 'There are objects' as one says 'There are books'.

Again, Wittgenstein's point is that some concepts, the formal ones, are not represented by signs. Instead, they are represented by variables, i.e. the characteristic marks of the substitution instances of them. For example, red, a proper concept, falls under the formal concept property. Therefore, red is represented by a sign which is an instance of the variable representing the pseudo concept property.

Further and stronger evidence for Wittgenstein's adherence to the propositional-function notation is contained in the following passages.

3.3   Only the proposition has a sense; only in the context of a proposition has a name meaning.

3.31   Every part of a proposition which characterizes its sense I call an expression.

3.311   An expression . . . is the common characteristic of a class of propositions.

3.312   It is therefore represented by the general form of the propositions which it characterizes, and in this expression is *constant* and everything else *variable*.

3.313   An expression is thus presented by a variable, whose values are the propositions which contain the expression.

Besides leaving no doubt that Wittgenstein makes full use of the function notation, these passages emphasize two of his most significant ideas: first, that no sign can meaningfully occur alone and, second, that *all* signs, those for particulars as well as those for properties, are in one sense functions. The first point is the linguistic counterpart of 2.0122: the thing is independent in so far as it can occur in all *possible* circumstances, but this form of independence is a form of connection with the atomic fact, a form of dependence. Wittgenstein might have expressed the point this way: that entities occur only as constituents of facts is shown by the fact that single signs cannot occur meaningfully in the picture language. The second point, viz. that all signs are in some sense functions, is a little more difficult to expose for it incorporates several themes. Recall that in 2.0131 Wittgenstein says: "a speck in the visual field must have a colour, a tone a pitch, the object of touch a hardness, etc." In other words, he distinguishes amongst kinds of particulars. His purpose is to stress that some particulars *must* have certain properties. He would also, I suppose, argue that a speck in the visual field cannot have a tone. The implication is that particulars, being of various kinds, are limited as to the other entities (i.e. properties) with which they can combine to make facts. Wittgenstein might have expressed the point this way: that particulars as well as properties are limited as to the combinations in which they can enter is shown by the fact that *all* entities must be represented by functions. For, functions are implicit formation rules and thus reflect the limitations of the entities they represent.

Even though Wittgenstein argues that all entities must be represented by functions he does not deny the distinction between names and functions. However, for him the distinction does not have the same import that it has for Frege. Frege holds that the distinction between functions and names reflects the distinction between two kinds of entities; Wittgenstein holds that it reflects the distinction between two features of entities; more accurately, the name represents the entity; the function, its formal properties. Perhaps I can get Wittgenstein's point across by recalling the distinction between formal and proper concepts.

Formal concepts cannot be represented by functions because they are not entities. Proper concepts can be so represented because they are entities. However, when representing an entity by means of a function one is representing the formal properties of the entity, one is representing the sorts of facts in which the entity can occur. One is not representing the material properties of the entity, one is not representing the other entities with which it is combined. If one wished to do the latter, one would have to make a true sentence, combining the signs referring to the entities combined. And in the sentence no functions, only names (i.e. words) occur. A sentence represents the entity combination with other entities. A sentence does not represent the formal properties of an entity.

At this point a slight digression is necessary in order to attend to a possible confusion between an entity's form and its formal properties. The form of an entity is its ontological kind, e.g. being a particular or being a property. The form is *shown* by the sign for an entity being a substitution instance of a certain variable. The formal properties of an entity are the kinds with which it can combine in a fact. For example, properties can combine with either particulars or properties of properties. Thus, formal properties are *represented* by functions which are implicit formation rules.

The same distinction can be stated as follows. On the one hand there is the type distinction; on the other, the type rules. In other words, one can distinguish signs according to shapes and then specify which shapes can combine to make sentences. Such a procedure enables one to show, first, what kinds of entities there are, and, second, what kinds can combine in facts. Wittgenstein himself does not state the distinction in this way because he uses functions rather than rules in order to express the rules. One of his deepest reasons for so doing is that he denies logic any ontological status. To express the point differently, he grounds the formation rules on the entities rather than on a logical relation or nexus. (3.334: The rules of logical syntax must follow of themselves, if we only know how every single sign signifies.) The consequence is that every entity must be represented by a function, at least in the metalanguage.

Notice that even though an entity's form can show itself in the object language its formal properties cannot. That is because one cannot show in the object language all the sentences in which a sign can occur. On the other hand, one can show by a single occurrence, the form or kind of an object; that is shown by the shape of the sign.

The distinction between form and formal property has another root. Wittgenstein implies that particulars as well as properties are of different kinds. For example, there are visual and auditory particulars; colour and tone properties. That is, he implies that being a property is a form (2.0131) whereas being a colour is a formal property (4.122–4.125). Though he is not very clear about the distinction, its import is not hard to divine. By taking colour and visual as formal properties, the function representing red shows that it can combine only with visual particulars. The reason for making formal properties so narrow is to cope with the issues of elementarism and the synthetic *a priori*. For what I am about neither is relevant. Here I only want to state that the distinction between form and formal properties is compatible with holding that both properties and particulars are constituents of atomic facts. So much for the digression.

Wittgenstein is struggling with the difference between a sign and its rules. More accurately perhaps, he is struggling with the significance of that distinction. The sign occurs in (object-language) sentences; the rules do not. The latter depend on the form and formal properties of the entity and are thus represented by functions (in the metalanguage) which Wittgenstein sees for what they are, implicit formation rules. Nor should it be overlooked that Wittgenstein correctly sees both that functions do not literally occur in sentences and that signs for particulars as well as for properties are governed by rules. In brief, Wittgenstein sees that Frege's distinction between names and functions is muddled.

Before examining Anscombe's argument, I want to stress that Wittgenstein's denial that functions occur in sentences does not constitute a denial that properties are constituents of atomic facts. Indeed, the foregoing examination of his use of the function notation reveals that he affirms that the constituents of atomic facts are not all of the same kind. What he denies is the Fregean distinction between properties (concepts) and particulars.

The gist of Anscombe's argument can be gleaned from the following passage.[1]

the problem of 'universals' can . . . be given this form: was Frege right to introduce two wholly different kinds of 'reference' for words, namely objects and concepts. A concept was the reference of a predicate; now the characteristic mark of a predicate is its possession of an argument-place or -places, which could be filled with names of now one, now another object, hence a 'concept' is a universal. In Wittgenstein's fully analysed propositions, we have nothing but a set of argument places filled with the names of objects; there remains no expression that could be regarded as standing for a concept.

Anscombe's movement of thought is straightforward. First, she

[1] Anscombe, G. E. M., op. cit., p. 110.

states the problem of universals: are there two kinds of objects? Second, she offers a specific syntactical explication of the problem: Are there both names and functions in the language? Third, she claims that since the atomic sentences of Wittgenstein's language do not contain function signs, the atomic facts represented by those sentences do not contain concepts in the sense that they do not contain the entities Frege calls concepts, e.g. the colours.

The argument is astonishingly naive. For example, even if it were the case—and it is not—that Frege's syntactical distinction between names and functions is the only way to explicate the distinction between objects and concepts, it still would not follow that Wittgenstein by denying Frege's distinction denies that the entities called concepts are constituents of atomic facts. Wittgenstein could have thought they were nameable. Of deeper significance is the fact that Frege's distinction is far from sacred. Indeed, Wittgenstein shows it to be mistaken.

Wittgenstein's denial of the Fregean difference between names and functions is of great significance, even if Anscombe fails to reveal it. The significance is this: Wittgenstein denies that Frege is right concerning the difference between particulars and properties; he is affirming that they are more nearly alike than Frege realized. Not only are both kinds of entities limited in their possibilities for combining with other entities, both are unsaturated or incomplete. Let me explain this last. Frege's distinction fosters the terminology that particulars are complete or saturated whereas properties are incomplete or unsaturated. That terminology fosters in turn, whatever the intention be, the claim that particulars are independent, capable of existing alone, whereas properties are dependent. For example, Russell once said that "there is no reason why you should not have a universe consisting of one particular and nothing else. That is the peculiarity of particulars." Wittgenstein himself vigorously rejects that idea and thus has further grounds for rejecting Frege's distinction between names and functions. At 2.0121 he puts forth his own thesis: "Just as we cannot think of spatial objects at all apart from space, or temporal objects apart from time, so we cannot think of *any* object apart from the possibility of its connection with other things." That theme recurs throughout the *Tractatus*. In 2.0122 it is explicated in this way: it is impossible for words to occur in two different ways, alone and in the proposition.

Though Wittgenstein more often than not emphasizes his rejection of the Fregean difference between particulars and properties, thereby suggesting that particulars and properties are the same in kind, he does at times imply that there is a difference. For example, his discussion of formal concepts rests on just such a difference. (To speak about the form of an object is without point unless there are different forms.) In 5.5261 the implication is perhaps clearest.

> A completely generalized proposition is like every other proposition composite. (This is shown by the fact that in '(Ex, ϕ) (ϕ, x)' we must mention 'x' and 'ϕ' separately. Both stand independently in signifying relations to the world as in the ungeneralized proposition.)

By distinguishing between 'x' and 'ϕ' and by emphasizing that even in ungeneralized propositions both stand independently in signifying relations to the world, Wittgenstein gives voice to a type distinction, implying thereby that the referents of the different types are different in kind. For Wittgenstein of course, the type distinction is between functions.[1] Nevertheless, in so far as functions fall under different formal concepts, the consequence is the same.

Wittgenstein's disagreement with Frege concerns the difference between the referents of subjects and the referents of predicates. Whereas Frege holds them to be radically different, Wittgenstein holds them to be more nearly alike. In the *Tractatus*, he sets himself the task of establishing that. Thus, even though he occasionally suggests that there is some difference between properties and particulars, the difference does not preoccupy him. What does preoccupy him is the sameness of the kinds. It is therefore not surprising that in the *Tractatus*, just as in the *Notebooks*, 'object' is used broadly to cover both particulars and properties. In this connection, I want to call attention to a passage from Moore's notes on Wittgenstein's lectures of 1930–3.

> [Wittgenstein] went on to say that if we are talking about 'individuals' in Russell's sense (and he actually here mentioned atoms as well as colours, as if they were 'individuals' in this sense).[2]

Moore's parenthetical remark expresses astonishment that Wittgenstein should ignore or take lightly the difference between particulars and properties. If I am right regarding the *Tractatus*, Wittgenstein's lack of concern should not astonish us.

Wittgenstein's failure to dwell on the difference between particulars and properties is not the only reason why the *Tractatus* looks slightly odd in the realistic interpretation. A perhaps deeper reason is that Wittgenstein can provide no example of a simple property. This reason can be uncovered by examining one of Copi's arguments for the nominalistic interpretation.[3]

---

[1] Cf. "Types and Formation Rules: A Note on *Tractatus* 3.334", *Analysis*, 21, 1960, 14–16.

[2] Moore, G. E., "Wittgenstein's Lectures in 1930–33", *Mind*, 63, 1954, 1–15; 64, 1955, 1–28 and 289–315. Cf. 64, 2–3.

[3] Copi, I. M., op. cit., p. 162 [p. 183].

If *any* properties are simple, specific colours ought to be counted among the simplest. If objects are properties and elementary propositions consist of names of objects . . . then the propositions ['this is red' and 'this is blue'] must be elementary propositions. But can they both be true? Wittgenstein's answer is unequivocal: "For two colours, e.g., to be at one place in the visual field, is impossible, logically impossible, for it is excluded by the logical structure of colour. . . . (It is clear that the logical product of two elementary propositions can neither be a tautology nor a contradiction. The assertion that two different colours are at the same place at the same time, is a contradiction.)" (6.3751) It follows that colour predications are not elementary propositions, and the implication seems clear that objects are not properties.

Copi's argument is imposing. Thus, I want, first, to try to get clear on what 6.3751 says and, second, to distinguish carefully between the two conclusions Copi believes are implied by it. In 6.3751 Wittgenstein begins by asserting that it is logically impossible for two colours to be, simultaneously, at one place in the visual field. What makes it impossible is "the logical structure of colour". After comparing this impossibility with an apparently similar one regarding particulars at the same time at the same place, he further asserts, *parenthetically*, that the logical product of two elementary propositions can be neither a tautology nor a contradiction as well as repeating that the assertion that two colours are at the same place at the same time, is a contradiction.

Now Copi says that "it follows that colour predications are not elementary, and the implication seems clear that objects are not properties". With the former there can be no quarrel. That colour predications are not elementary does indeed follow from 6.3751. With the latter there can be a quarrel. That objects are not properties does not follow from 6.3751, but rather from that passage *together with* what Copi himself asserts in the first sentence of the quoted passage, viz. that "if *any* properties are simple, specific colours ought to be". For what I am about it is crucial to realize that Copi's first conclusion follows from 6.3751 whereas his second conclusion follows from it only together with a further premiss. I want to contend that Wittgenstein does not accept that premiss. In other words, Wittgenstein does not believe, at least at the time of the *Tractatus*, that if a specific colour is not a property, nothing is. He in fact believes that words like 'red' and 'green' can be defined. Before trying to substantiate what I have just said, it might help to get clear on what problem Wittgenstein is struggling with in 6.3751.

The specific problem is: in what sense is 'this is red and this is blue' (where 'this' refers to a speck presently in the visual field) a contradiction? The general problem is: Given the truth-table explication of 'necessary' and 'contradictory', how can one show, as Wittgenstein hopes to, that what the tradition called synthetic-*a-priori* sentences express contradictions or necessities? No solution is offered in 6.3751. We are told only that the components of conjunctions like 'this is red and this is blue' cannot be elementary. Though "the logical structure of colour" is said to preclude such possibilities, that is no solution. It is merely a vague phrase.

Now it is not idle to remark that the nominalistic interpretation does not, in its simple form at least, provide a solution. If 'this is red' is transcribed as an elementary sentence, then the problem has not been solved, regardless of whether properties are or are not constituents of atomic facts. The solution to the problem requires that the transcription of 'this is red' be a molecular sentence which either contains the negation of 'this is blue' or logically entails it. In other words, if I am right regarding the problem raised, but not solved, in 6.3751, colours cannot be mere configurations of particulars.

Of course, that the nominalistic interpretation does not even approach solving the problem raised in 6.3751 does not make it incorrect. However, in so far as the nominalistic interpretation is based on 6.3751, it is dubious. Certainly, it would be better if one could find an interpretation of the *Tractatus* which provides an at least apparent solution to the problem of 6.3751. I suggest that the realistic interpretation does. In particular, I suggest that the denial that 'this is red' is atomic implies that 'red' is not indefinable, i.e. red is not simple, in the sense, not of being a configuration of particulars, but of being analysable into other simpler properties. To this end let me comment again on 6.3751, in particular, on the parenthetical remark contained in it.

In the parenthetical remark Wittgenstein seems to be saying something like this: "and colour predications are *not*, as one might think, elementary. They cannot be; if 'contradiction' is explicated by means of the truth tables and 'this is red and this is blue' is a 'formal' truth, as all will agree." Now since Wittgenstein does not pursue the matter, does not make an attempt to solve the problem, the parenthetical remark stands as a challenge or, perhaps better, as an admission of a difficulty. The implication, then, is not that properties are configurations of particulars. It is that there are difficulties here which are not yet solved. There is however a hint regarding the direction in which Wittgenstein thinks the solution may be found. The hint is that since red and blue are not simple, 'red' and 'blue' can be defined. This is what is intended by the phrase 'the logical structure of colour'. What evidence is there for my claim? The 1929 paper provides excellent evidence. Furthermore, it leads us to a plausible Wittgenstein.

In the confused and, even to its author, disappointing 1929 paper,

339

Wittgenstein makes clear that he once believed colour words to be definable.

> If statements of degree were analysable—as I used to think—then we could explain this contradiction ['this is red and this is blue'] by saying that the colour R contains all degrees of R and none of B and the colour B contains all degrees of B and none of R.[1]

This passage leaves no doubt that Wittgenstein once hoped to make 'this is red and this is blue' a contradiction by defining the colour words in terms of the words referring to the, say, unanalysable shades of them and the addition of the dubious phrase 'and none of . . .' Regardless of the feasibility of the programme, at the time of the *Tractatus* he had hopes for it. But he did not know how to carry it out and may even have been dimly aware that it could not be carried out. Be that as it may, 6.3751 hints at the programme, even if its main task is to acknowledge the difficulty.

The difficulty is a profound one, one that played a decisive rôle in Wittgenstein's eventual rejection of the *Tractatus*.[2] Wittgenstein, hoping to secure the formal character of synthetic-*a-priori* sentences while explicating 'necessary' and 'contradictory' by means of the truth tables, is forced to suggest that all the apparently indefinable property words are really definable. The suggestion remains just that: he knows neither how to define them nor what the indefinable ones are. Thus, in the *Tractatus* we are offered no examples of simple properties; we are offered no more than a vague programme.

Of course, in the 1929 paper Wittgenstein reveals that he sees what Copi sees, viz. that if specific colours are not simple, no properties are. In other words, he sees that the programme hinted at in 6.3751 can not be managed. His response is, first, to accept colours as simple, and, second, to argue that the truth-table explication of 'necessary' and 'contradictory' is not quite accurate and needs some modification, if one is to accommodate the *formal* character of synthetic-*a-priori* sentences. The 1929 paper thus marks the onset of his rejection of the *Tractatus*. But he did not see in 1915 what he saw in 1929. If he had, the *Tractatus* would be other than it is.

I have argued that the *Tractatus* is realistic, i.e. that it affirms that the constituents of atomic facts are of at least two kinds. Nevertheless, the realism is subdued; at times disguised. On the one hand, Wittgenstein's assault on the Fregean difference between particulars and properties prompts him to emphasize their sameness at the expense of their difference; on the other, his commitment to the formal character of synthetic-*a-priori* sentences prohibits him from

---

[1] Wittgenstein, L., "Remarks on Logical Form", pp. 168–9 [pp. 35–6].
[2] Cf. "*Tractatus* 6.3751", *Analysis*, 19, 1959, 100–5 [present volume].

providing examples of unanalysable properties. The realism is further subdued because it is not crucial to the major theses of the *Tractatus*. First, the truth-table explication of 'necessary' and 'contradictory' (5.525), insisting as it does only on a specific analysis of the connectives, is independent of the ontological analysis of atomic facts. Second, the picture theory in its limited and apparently superficial form insists only that a sentence and the fact it expresses share a structure (2.032, 4.0311). Again, the specific structure of the fact makes no difference.

The picture theory has, however, a deeper and far more significant core which does require realism (in the sense of there being different kinds of entities). In so far as the picture theory insists that there is an isomorphism between language and the world a type distinction is demanded. The isomorphism is such that "to a definite logical combination of signs corresponds a definite logical combination of their meanings [i.e. the objects the signs stand for (3.203)]". The picture theory thus asserts that what is possible (well-formed) in the atomic-sentence language is possible in the world.[1] Linguistic possibility is a matter of formation rules which Wittgenstein grounds on the entities (3.334). In so far as the formation rules depend on a type distinction (and in a PM-like language there is nothing else for them to depend on) a difference of kind is clearly implied.

That Wittgenstein is fully aware of what he holds in the *Tractatus* becomes painfully clear when one examines both the 1929 paper and his later efforts. He had to accept realism in order to feel the destructive tension among it, the truth-table explication of necessity, and the formal character of synthetic-*a-priori* sentences. His coping with that tension helps to explain his later philosophy. Wittgenstein certainly meant what he said in the Preface to the *Investigations*: "Four years ago I had occasion to re-read my first book. . . . It suddenly seemed to me that I should publish those old thoughts and the new ones together: that the latter could be seen in the right light only by contrast with and against the background of my old way of thinking."

[1] For an incisive discussion of the picture theory and the several meanings of 'possible' see Gustav Bergmann, "Stenius on the *Tractatus*", *Theoria*, 29, 1963.

The Glory and the Misery of Ludwig Wittgenstein[1]

GUSTAV BERGMANN

THE *Tractatus Logico-Philosophicus* appeared in 1921; the *Philosophical Investigations*, posthumously, in 1953. Wittgenstein will live through these two books. The contrast between them is striking. In the author's view, and not in his alone, the second repudiates the first. As his epigones see it, his glory is the second. The first they consider, however tenderly and reverently, a relative failure. As I see it, Wittgenstein's glory is the *Tractatus*; his misery, the *Investigations*. The disagreement could not be more complete. Yet I agree with the epigones that the connection between the two books is very close indeed. I see in the second the reaction, dictated by the council of despair, to the relative failure of the first.

The *Tractatus*, then, if I am right, is a glorious failure. It is also, I am deeply convinced, an achievement of the first rank. Nor is that paradoxical. None of our predecessors achieved more. No one among us and our successors will do better. The fundamental metaphysical problems are too difficult for this to be otherwise. Fortunately, their number is small. Even the secondary ones, though quite a few, are not too many. Good philosophers therefore do not pursue many questions. Rather, they are pursued by a few which they articulate ever more richly and explore ever more deeply, down toward the fundamental ones. The few great among the good can

[1] This is the English original of a lecture delivered in the universities of Turin, Milan, and Rome during December 1961. It appeared first in Italian translation under the title "La gloria e la miseria di Ludwig Wittgenstein" in *Rivista di Filosofia*, 52 (1961), pp. 387–406. Some of the many points on which it touches, often rather briefly, have been elaborated in "Stenius on the *Tractatus*", *Theoria*, 29 (1963), pp. 176–204, reprinted in *Logic and Reality*, Madison: University of Wisconsin Press, 1964. The present essay is reprinted from *Logic and Reality*, pp. 225–41, with permission of the copyright owners, the Regents of the University of Wisconsin, the editor of *Rivista di Filosofia*, and the author.

rethink a fundamental problem on their own. Such a problem always consists of a group of dialectically connected questions. To rethink it is either to discover a new dialectical connection within the group or, at the very highest, to affect these connections even more radically by discovering a new question to be added to the group. The new question permits and requires new answers. The glorious failures are those who knew how to ask the new question but did not find the new answer.

Wittgenstein all through his philosophical life was obsessed by two fundamental problems. What is the nature of logical truth? Call this the first. What is the nature of mind? Call this the second. Both have shaped both books. The first dominates the *Tractatus*; the second, the *Investigations*. On the first, he asked the decisive new question, led a part of the way toward the new answer. On the second, he merely misled, lending specious plausibility to a stale old answer.

(1) There are no philosophical propositions. Those passing for such are neither true nor false but, literally, nonsense. (2) The illusion that keeps us from seeing through this sort of nonsense is linguistic. (3) To destroy the illusion, or, in a phrase that has become famous, to show the fly the way out of the bottle, is to direct attention to the ineffable, which language shows but cannot say. That is Wittgenstein's conception of the philosophical enterprise. (1) states his nihilism; (2) is the root of the linguistic turn; (3), that of the therapeutic approach. I reject (1) and (3). There are philosophical propositions. Nor is there anything ineffable. Wittgenstein's insistence on the linguistic turn, more radical and more profound than Russell's, is the other half of his glory. But he executed it wrongly, herostratically. That makes (2) his other glorious failure, which, since our questions as well as our answers depend on our conception of the philosophical enterprise, made the other two, the glorious as well as the miserable one, inevitable. So I shall next execute the right linguistic turn.

(1) Words are used either *commonsensically* or *philosophically*. A proposition in which at least one word is used philosophically is a philosophical proposition. As such, philosophical uses are un-intelligible. But they can and must be made intelligible by explicating them, i.e. by talking commonsensically about them. Thus explicated a philosophical proposition says something about the world, which, as the case may be, is either true or false. (2) Every systematically constructed language *shows* some things which cannot without futility be *expressed* in it. These things, though, far from being ineffable, can, and for certain purposes must, be expressed by talking about the language and what it talks about. Jointly, (1) and (2) are the gist of the right linguistic turn. Technically, they are equally fun-

344

damental. Nontechnically, (1) is the heart of the matter. So I leave (2) until later, comment next on (1).

"Bodies don't exist, only minds do" is a classical philosophical proposition. "Minds don't exist, only bodies do" is another. "Characters don't exist, only individuals do" is a third. If the words are all taken commonsensically, such propositions are not at all nonsensical. Rather, they are patently and blatantly false; so patently and blatantly indeed that only a madman could assert any of them. Yet each has been asserted by some philosophers. According to Wittgenstein, these men either futilely tried to express the ineffable, or, confusingly and themselves confused, presented as an assertion about the world what is at best one about the way we use language. I believe that these men often succeeded very well in directing attention to certain pervasive, or, as one says, categorial features of the world. Only, I also insist that these features can and must be talked about commonsensically.

Classical ontology is dominated by the several ontological uses of 'exist' and 'existence'. Since the core of all fundamental problems is ontological, I shall next indicate the explications of two such uses.

(a) *If something is presented to me, so is its existence.* The formula explicates the use. To have "existence" in this sense and to have "ontological status" is one thing and not two. The idea is commonsensical. Yet some comments will be helpful. *One.* Something may exist without being presented. If converted, the formula is no longer commonsensical. *Two.* Perception is one kind of presentation. Direct awareness is another. Do both kinds make the formula the truism it must be if it is to serve its purpose? By this question hangs a huge body of dialectic. For my purpose tonight the answer does not matter. *Third.* In such sentences as 'There is a coffee house around the corner' existence is represented by the phrase 'there is'. Existence (a) or ontological status can always be so expressed. But we also say, commonsensically, that there is a prime number between 4 and 6. Are we then prepared to grant some ontological status to such "entities" as numbers? Wittgenstein, we shall see, is not. I am. The way I just used 'entity' is ontologically neutral. It will be convenient to have this neutral word available.

(b) *What exists is simple.* The formula explicates another philosophical use of 'exist', provided only we understand this very special, though commensensical use of 'simple'. An entity is thus simple if the only way of directly referring to it, in any language, is by naming it. A *name*, in this very special sense, is also called a label. That conveys the idea that a name can only be attached to what is or has been presented. There is also the idea that a label as such does not tell us anything about what it labels except, of course, that it exists (a). This, though, we shall see, is not quite correct in the case of linguistic labels or names. In a systematically constructed language a name is, of course, a primitive descriptive sign. Notice that an equivalent formula has become available: An entity exists (b) if and only if, provided it is presented, it can be named. Notice, too, that an entity which could not be named, or, more precisely, as we shall presently see, an entity which could not be named without futility, may yet be presented and even be represented in the language by something which is not a name. Such an entity would exist (a) without existing (b).

The sentential tautologies so-called are familiar instances of logical truth. What is the structure of such truths? We are ready for Wittgenstein's first fundamental problem. Rethinking it, he discovered the new question which is his glory. How does any sentence, whether or not it expresses a logical truth, manage to express what it does? In appearance the new question is unduly linguistic, in an obvious bad sense of 'linguistic'. In substance, it points to the ontological core of the problem. Even better than that, the right answer provides an invaluable lesson, teaching us how to do ontology after the linguistic turn. That is why the glory of the one who first asked the question is great, even though his answer went wrong. Here is what we are told. Take the (written) sentence itself as a fact. This (linguistic) fact shares with the fact it expresses a "logical form". That is how the former manages to express the latter. 'Logical form' is used philosophically and, unhappily, remains unexplicated. So we are not surprised when we are also told that "logical form" is ineffable, merely shows itself. There is an easy transition, noticed, or, more likely, unnoticed, from being ineffable to being nothing, or, what amounts to the same, not having any ontological status, not existing (a). This sort of transition I call a verbal bridge. The original question Wittgenstein answered as follows. A truth is logical if and only if the sentence expressing it is true by virtue of its "logical form" alone. But, then, we are also told that a sentence expressing a tautology (logical truth) really says nothing and is therefore not really a sentence. This supports my belief that, unwittingly, Wittgenstein walked that bridge. Whether or not he did, his answer does not recognize the ontological status of what, speaking philosophically, he calls "logical form". That is the fatal flaw. The right answer, conversely, crucially recognizes the ontological status (existence (a)) of what I call the world's *form*. And, of course, it provides an explication for this use of 'form'. Notice, for later reference, that I suppress the adjective, 'logical', speak of the world's form instead.

These are the bare bones of my thesis. Putting some flesh on them, I shall first state the right answer. But, of course, if that needs to be said at all, without Wittgenstein's glorious failure, there would be no right answer today.

Suppose that, being presented with a green spot, I say, truly, 'This is green'. Limiting ourselves to true sentences merely avoids problems which, though most weighty in themselves, can at this point be avoided. What an (indicative) sentence expresses is a fact. The fact in the example is the spot's being green. Call it F; the sentence, S. S and F, each in its way, is as simple as a fact or a sentence can be, though of course neither is simple (b). Now if S is true, there must be something that makes it true. Or, as one says, the truth of S must be grounded ontologically. On this first move idealists and realists agree. The only difference between them is that for the realist the ground is independent of the mind to which F is presented, while for the idealist F depends on, or even more strongly, is the activity of this mind. But, then, do not in the idealist's world minds and their activities have ontological status?

S thus is true because it expresses F and F exists (a). If, therefore, we want to know how S manages to express F, we must first find out what there is to be expressed. In other words, we must begin with an ontological assay of F.

I hold that there are individuals and characters, all of the former and some of the latter being simple (b). Calling them both *things*, I also hold that, when presented with F, I am presented with two things, an individual named 'This' and a simple character named 'green'. Hence, my assay of F yields *at least* two simples. That raises two questions. (1) Is this assay complete? More strongly, could it possibly be complete or must it yield something else? (2) Is it correct as far as it goes? (2) may be controversial; (1), to my mind, is not. As it happens, my main point hangs on (1).

Simples enter into complexes. F, for instance, on any assay I can think of, is a complex. Take now two spots, one green and square, the other blue and round. If my assay is correct as far as it goes, there are thus six things "tied" into two complexes. You see already the deeper point. There must be "something" which ties anyone's simples (or, for that matter, things, if there should be no simples) into complexes. Also, this "something" must be presented. For, if it were not, how could I know that in the example, say, green goes with square but not with either blue or round. It follows that there must be ties, having ontological status, which tie the simples into complexes. What then, one may ask, ties the ties to the simples? There are only two possibilities. One is, paradoxically, an infinite regress, which is the way Bradley took to monism. The other is my solution. There are *fundamental ties*, I also call them *nexus*, which tie without themselves being tied to what they tie.

The nexus which ties an individual and a character into a fact I call *exemplification*. It follows that the ontological assay of *F* yields at least three constituents, two simples and exemplification. Notice, too, that a fundamental tie is not a relation. In the complex 'This is louder than that', for instance, there are three simples, this, that, and the relational character louder-than, held together by (relational) exemplification.

Further analysis, which I cannot tonight reproduce, shows that the complete assay of *F* yields two further nonthings, individuality and universality. When I am presented with an individual, I am also presented with its individuality. For, if I were not, how would I know that it is one? As for individuals, so for characters. As I use 'form', these three nonthings, exemplification, individuality, universality, are constituents of the world's form. As I use 'subsist', their peculiar ontological status is *subsistence*.

Does Wittgenstein agree with what has been said so far? There are very, very many passages in the *Tractatus* which seem to make it crystal clear that he, too, so assays *F* that 'This' and 'green' in *S* name two simples in *F*. I say seems because there are also many passages, such as 3.1432, which have been much written about recently, that cannot be reconciled with those very, very many others. On the nominalism-realism issue—for that is, of course, what the matter amounts to—the *Tractatus* is confused. Historically, I believe, that has something to do with the great impact Frege's views had on its author. Concerning exemplification, turn to 2.03: *Im Sachverhalt haengen die Gegenstaende ineinander wie die Glieder einer Kette*. That is exactly what they don't do.[1] If they did, there would be no need for a nexus. The image, admirably clear, leaves no doubt that Wittgenstein is radically wrong, making exemplification a part of that "logical form" which is "nothing".

How does *S* manage to express *F*? In a systematically constructed language *S* becomes '*Ga*', i.e. in essence, the juxtaposition of two marks of different shape (capital and lower case). '*a*' names or labels the individual; its shape represents, without naming it, the individuality of the thing named. As for '*a*', so for '*G*'. Names are thus not pure labels. Their shapes, which are geometrical characters, represent, without naming them, ontological categories. Exemplification, finally, is represented, though, again, not named, by the relational geometrical character of juxtaposition. *S* is a geometrical fact. Between certain geometrical features of *S* on the one hand and

---

[1] Or, if you care to put it this way, things are *independent*. The philosophical uses of 'independent' are crucial. The formula "Only what is independent exists" controls indeed several philosophical uses of 'exist'. E. B. Allaire (*Philosophical Review*, 6, 1960, 485–96) has very ingeniously distinguished four relevant commonsensical uses of 'independent'. If I am not mistaken, I just identified a fifth.

the constituents of *F* there is a one-one coordination of the kind called isomorphism. To understand a language is to know the rules of this ismorphism. Or to say the same thing differently, *S* manages to express *F* by virtue of this isomorphism. This is my answer. Let us confront it with Wittgenstein's.

S manages to express *F* by virtue of a shared "logical form", which is ineffable. That is his answer. The isomorphism mentioned in mine is anything but ineffable. I just stated it by speaking commonsensically *about F* and *S*. Now this isomorphism is also the only explication I can think of for Wittgenstein's philosophical use of 'logical form'. The explication makes his answer intelligible. Rather strikingly, it also makes it false. Nor is that difficult to show. Assume for the sake of the argument that the two marks in *S* are individuals. Then the geometrical fact *S* has five constituents which are things, namely, the two marks, the two geometrical characters which are the shapes, the relational geometrical character of juxtaposition; and, in addition, individuality twice, universality thrice, exemplification thrice. That makes 13. *F*, we remember, has all together 5 constituents. And there is of course no one-to-one coordination between 5 and 13. Such are the bitter fruits of using words philosophically, without explication.

The ontological distance between, say, an individual and individuality is tremendous. Wittgenstein safeguards it without effort. For him, the individual exists; individuality, being part of "logical form", is nothing. For me the two are alike in both having ontological status (just as they are both presented). The difference so far is merely that in the language I constructed the individual is named while its individuality is otherwise represented, namely, by the shape of its name. That is not yet enough to secure that tremendous distance. I secure it by showing that the subsistents could *not without futility* be named. Take individuality. Let us try to name it. If it is a thing, then it is of course a (simple) character. Name this alleged character by '*I*'. That makes '*Ia*' the crucial sentence. The point is that it says what it says, namely, that *a* is an individual, only because the shapes of *a* and *I* and their juxtaposition represent, without naming them, individuality, universality, and exemplification, respectively. That shows what I mean when I say that the introduction of '*I*' is futile.

If one wishes, one may put the last point as follows. *a*'s being an individual is *shown* in the language by the shape of its name; but one cannot without futility *say* in this language that it is one. Remember now the second part of the right linguistic turn: Every systematically constructed language shows some things which cannot without futility be expressed in it. When first stating this part, I postponed comment. Now, without further comment, we understand. We have recovered all that is recoverable from Wittgenstein's famous ineffability thesis. The rest is nonsense, not because it is metaphysics, but because it is bad metaphysics.

There is of course much more to the world's form than is represented in *S*, just as there are many more facts than can be expressed by sentences as simple as *S*. We have had no more than a glimpse. And, of course, we cannot pursue. So I must venture to state the idea. Philosophy is a dialectical structure that rests on a phenomenological base. What is presented to us is a matter of phenomenology. If certain entities were not presented to us, we could not know what commonsensically we do know, e.g. that this is red, that green, this to the left of that, and so on. That is the dialectical twist. What must be presented to us must also be represented in our language, otherwise it could not express what it does. That is how language may be brought in. Then we are ready for the linguistic turn. 'Ontological status' has been used philosophically. I explicate this use by the formula: What must be represented has ontological status. That, though, is only the beginning. The furniture of the world is not all of one kind. The different kinds, even the glimpse we had taught us that, are represented very differently, i.e. in the written case, by very different geometrical features of the language. Or, rather, that is how I explicate the traditional ontological vocabulary. Enough has been said to support a claim made earlier. The right answer to Wittgenstein's new question is the key to the new ontology.

We are ready for the original question. What is logical truth? It is nothing. Nor is the sentence expressing it really a sentence. That, succinctly, is Wittgenstein's answer. I answer that it is a fact of (in) the world's form and that the sentence expressing it is a sentence like any other, except, of course, that its truth depends only on those of its geometrical features which represent constituents of the world's form. Lest the difference between the two answers seem slight, let me point out two consequences which loom large.

1. The connection between the philosophical uses of 'logical' and of 'necessary' is very close. "A logical truth is a necessary truth, and conversely." We all know this classical proposition. Partly because of it, I avoid 'logical' wherever I can, speak instead of formal truth (instead of: logical truth) and of the world's form (instead of: logical form). And I explicate the philosophical use of 'necessary' in that classical proposition so that a truth is necessary if and only if it is formal. That turns the proposition into a tautology. Wittgenstein disagrees. According to him, the formal truths of our world are also the formal truths of all possible worlds. Replace 'formal truth' by 'logical form' and you will see the verbal bridge. "Logical form" is nought; and nought, as it were, is the same in all possible worlds.

But, then, what shall we make of that phrase, 'all possible worlds'? Clearly, it is used philosophically. So it must be explicated. I can think of two explications. One turns the proposition into a tautology: Every world which has the same form as ours has the same form as ours. With the other explication, the proposition says that any world *must* have the same form as ours. I simply do not understand this *must*. If the logical is to be identified with the necessary, in some unexplicated and inexplicable sense of 'necessary', then, if you permit me an aphorism, there is nothing logical about logic. Technically, upon the explication which does not trivialize it, Wittgenstein's thesis, that the logic of our world is that of all possible ones, is simply false. I must not be technical tonight. But I can identify for you another bridge he walked on this as well as on many other occasions, all through his work. It leads from 'possible' to 'conceivable'. That is his psychologism. For it puts into the act what, if it is what it is supposed to be, must be a feature of the act's intention. Historically, Wittgenstein inherited this fateful mistake from Kant.

2. There is a class of truths, Kant calls them synthetic *a priori*, which are clearly not formal. "Nothing is (at the same time all over) both red and green" is a familiar example. Many philosophers tried to secure for these truths a special status, in the same boat with formal truths. In Wittgenstein, throughout his philosophical life, the urge was very strong. (In this, too, he shows the influence of Kant.) In the *Tractatus* he satisfies it by the claim that the sentences expressing those truths are, like tautologies, true by virtue of their "logical form" alone. That clashes with the very numerous passages according to which only tautologies can be true by their "logical form" alone. There is in the *Tractatus* one lonely passage (6.3751) which shows unmistakably that Wittgenstein himself was not wholly at ease. In the short paper of 1929, the only other publication during his lifetime, he returned to the attack; but again, alas, to no avail. This dissatisfaction may well have been one of the major intellectual motives for his eventual repudiation of the *Tractatus*.[1]

This chair's being brown is a physical fact. That water if heated boils is another. Your perceiving that the chair is brown is a mental fact. So is my wondering whether this speech is too long, his remembering something, and so on. That there are both physical and mental facts, or, for short, both minds and bodies, is common sense. Perceiving something, remembering something, thinking of something, are mental facts of the kind called *acts*. There are also others, but we

---

[1] E. B. Allaire has argued this point very convincingly in the first of two short but very weighty papers he has already published on Wittgenstein (*Analysis*, 19, 1959, 100–5 [present volume], and 21, 1960, 14–16). Frequent discussion with him during the last years has been invaluable to me.

can safely ignore them. The fundamental task is the ontological assay of the act. In this task Wittgenstein failed. His way out was to reject it. There is nothing to be assayed; there are no minds. The failure is foreshadowed in the *Tractatus*. The *Investigations* are virtually materialistic. Materialism is absurd. That makes the failure so miserable. We shall understand it better if I first tackle the task.

What one perceives when perceiving something, what one knows when knowing something, and so on, is the act's *intention*. To perceive something, to know this thing, to remember it, are different acts with the same intention. What they differ in I call the act's *species*. Acts thus may differ in species and intention. Acts are mental, of course; intentions, either physical or mental. What we perceive is physical; that is part of what perceiving means. No thing is both physical and mental. In perceiving, therefore, the act and its intention have no thing in common. (I say no thing, rather than nothing because the world's form is pervasive and neither physical nor mental.) This, by the way, is true for all acts. But we can tonight stay with perception, where the distinctness of act and intention is, if anything, even more obvious.

The perceptual complex has three constituents, (1) the act, (2) the intention, (3) the body, i.e. the relevant physical facts about the perceiver's body. 'Complex' I use advisedly, to remind you that if there is to be a complex, its constituents must be tied together. Now for three constituents to make a complex there must be at least two and there may be three ties. (2) and (3) are both physical. (2) causes (3). This is the tie the scientists investigate. The tie between (1) and (3) is that between a mind and its body. This tie I take to be parallelistic. The third tie, call it the *intentional tie*, connects (1) and (2), the act and its intention. Its nature is the heart of the problem.

Do not confuse the intentional tie with the mind-body tie. When I perceive a landscape I perceive a landscape, not the relevant facts it causes in my body. Since the landscape is causally tied to the body and the body in turn parallelistically to the mind, there would still be a complex even if there were no intentional tie. To say the same thing differently, one may try to replace the direct intentional tie by a chain with two links, one causal, one parallelistic. For two weighty reasons that will not do. (a) I perceive the square tower to be round. More dramatically, I have a hallucination. In the first case, the physical fact invoked differs from the intention. In the second, there is none. (b) Some sentences are compounded of others. A language is called truth-functional or extensional if and only if the truth value of a compound depends only on the truth values of its components. Consider now the compound 'Smith believes that Caesar was murdered'. Assume it to be true. Replacing the true component 'Caesar was murdered' by the equally true 'The husband of Calpurnia was murdered' one obtains 'Smith believes that Calpurnia's husband was murdered'. Unless Smith knows that Caesar was Calpurnia's husband the new compound will be false. As for believing, so for all species. Statements expressing the intentional tie are not extensional. The causal tie, on the other hand, as well as the parallelistic one can be expressed in an extensional language. So, therefore, can the two-link chain. It follows that the intentional tie is a direct tie between the act and its intention. What, then, is its nature? Before I answer, one more idea must be introduced. But notice first that the author of the *Tractatus* was profoundly committed to the thesis that everything can be expressed in an extensional language.

None of the three constituents of the perceptual complex is a simple. Thus they, too, must be ontologically assayed. Crucial, of course, is the assay of the act. The tradition is dominated by one idea. Its formula is: A mind can only know what is *in* it. Everything depends on what the 'in' stands for. The tradition thinks of the mind as an individual of a very special kind, called a substance, and of its properties and only its properties being in it. What the mind knows is in it as its colour or its shape are in the flower. That makes what I call the species a case of exemplification, or of whatever comes closest to it in these ontologies. The trouble is that in all of them, except perhaps the Aristotelian-Thomistic one, the intentional tie cannot be accounted for. In the perceptual case, for instance, the intention is itself a substance with properties. *And how can a substance be a property of another substance?* Dialectically, this is the deepest root, much deeper than the relatively shallow skeptical one, of the development from Descartes to idealism. Be that as it may, I am now ready for the answer.

An act is an individual exemplifying two simple characters. This individual is not at all a substance—there are none in my ontology—but momentary and bare, a bare particular so-called. One of the two properties is the species. The other I shall here call a *thought*. The intentional tie is between the thought and the intention. When we say, for instance, that the thought that Peter is tall *means* that Peter is tall, 'means' represents this tie. I say represents rather than names and also speak of the *meaning tie* because it is a nexus and, as such, belongs to the world's form. So, by the way, do the causal and the parallelistic tie. Only, they also belong to the form of a world otherwise like ours but without mind. In this sense, intentionality is the essence of mind.

How does this assay account for those cases, false belief, imagination, and so on, in which the fact S intended by the thought $[S]$ does not exist (a)? Or, synonymously, if 'S' is false, how can '$[S]$ means S'

be true? If the meaning nexus were a relation, it couldn't. Since it is a part of the world's form, there is no difficulty. To get a glimpse of the idea, consider '*S* or not-*S*', where the nexus is "or." Either *S* or not-*S* does not exist (a).[1] Yet, '*S* or not-*S*' expresses a truth in the world's form. So does '[*S*] means *S*'.

Turn now to *Tractatus* 5.542. '*A* believes that *p*', '*A* thinks that *p*', and so on, all mean no more nor less than 'The sentence '*p*' means *p*'. That is the gist of this passage. The sentence, here as always, is for Wittgenstein a physical fact. Substituting the sentence for the thought, he thus substitutes a physical fact for one that is mental. That is the decisive step toward materialism. Abstract thought is indeed, as one says, largely verbal. Properly understood, though, that means merely that such thought consists largely of awarenesses of words and sentences! Wittgenstein's 'says', if it means anything at all, stands for my 'means'. If so, then, even with the substitution of the sentence for the thought, ' '*p*' says *p*' is no longer extensional. Nor is that all. The sentence '*p*' "says" *p* only by virtue of a shared "logical form", which is ineffable. Hence, ' '*p*' says *p*' is not really a sentence. The only thing that makes sense to me in all this is that the intentional nexus is indeed part of the world's form. For Wittgenstein, being part of "logical form", it is nothing. Once more, therefore, the act and its intention have fallen apart. The two ways out are idealism and materialism. Husserl took the first; Wittgenstein, the second.

This is the place to call attention to an ambiguity in the use of 'express'. A sentence as such does not "express" anything. We express a thought by means of it. This can be done because of the isomorphism between certain geometrical features of the sentence and what it "expresses". The ambiguity, if unnoticed, leads to disaster in the philosophy of mind. Outside of it, no harm is done. That is why I let it pass until now.

Materialists replace philosophy by science. Or they mistake the latter for the former. The later Wittgenstein is no exception. Not surprisingly in one as preoccupied with language as he was throughout his career, the key science is the psychology and sociology of language, or, if you please, of communication. Not that the *Investigations* is a conventional scientific book. It is merely a medley of comments. Some are very keen; some others, more or less obvious; the rest, standard armchair psychology in the standard behaviouristic style. Underneath, and not just underneath, there is always the effort to convince us—or should I perhaps say to convince himself?—

---

[1] More precisely, one of the two exists merely in the mode of possibility. This point, though of the greatest importance in some other contexts, may be safely ignored in this essay.

that philosophy is all a mistake. The author was nevertheless a profound philosopher. So one comes every now and then upon a profound philosophical insight. The buzzing of the fly intrigues.

Assume that one tries to teach his language to one with whom he cannot talk at all. To teach the colour words, he may use colour charts, will do a good deal of pointing, and so on. As for the colour words, so, with two differences, for the words referring to mental things. For one, the physical aspects of behaviour will be much more prominent among the cues given by the teacher and taken by the pupil. (I put it this way because pointing is also behaviour.) For another, the pupil could not learn unless he knew, from his own mind and body, which states of the two typically go with each other. The important truism that basically language must be learned and taught this way is characteristic of methodological behaviourism. Metaphysical behaviourism is materialism. The former makes sense, the latter doesn't. The transition from the one to the other is fallacious. The Wittgenstein of the *Investigations* makes it. Or he nearly makes it. Here and there a tortured qualification betrays the uneasy conscience and the inner struggle.

How does the teacher know that the lesson has been learned? When the pupil comes to use the words correctly, thus showing by his behaviour that he knows what they mean. That is the root of the formula before which the epigones prostrate themselves: (1) meaning is use. 'Meaning' itself, of course, has many uses. Its use in the *Tractatus* may be epitomized by two formulae: (2) meaning is reference, and (3) the meaning of a sentence is the method of its verification. Each of the two transitions, from (2) and (3) to (1), relates to a philosophical problem. Had Wittgenstein been able to solve these problems, or, what amounts virtually to the same, had he been able to make the required dialectical distinctions, he would not have made the transitions.

Take an individual and its name. By (2) the former is the meaning of the latter. Imagine that you are with only two persons in a room; one is your friend; the other you have never seen before. In this "context" your friend says, with or without pointing, "This is Peter." Because of the context you understand what he says. The next time you meet Peter you will recognize him. But you will recognize him only by the combination of characters he exemplifies. We do not recognize individuals as such, whether you use 'individual' as I just did or so narrowly that only sensa and their like are individuals. Thereby hangs an important philosophical point. Much less importantly, it follows that, first, communication depends on context, and, second, since a design of marks or noises not relying on context would have to contain names of individuals, we could not by means of it communicate. (That is the heart of the overblown quarrel about "ideal languages".) The epigones, convinced that there are no names, are in danger of convincing themselves that there are no things to be named. There is only language. Hence, in spite of the materialistic substitution of words for thoughts, the idealistic structure so clearly discernible in so much of what they say.

One knows what a sentence means if and only if one knows what to look for in order to decide whether it is true or false. If one can look, he must inspect what he finds. Then he can actually decide. Negatively, sentence is meaningless, not really a sentence, unless it can in this sense be "reduced" to what can be inspected. Much detail apart, this is the gist of (3). 'Inspect', which I use advisedly, has two connotations. By one of these hangs a fundamental philosophical problem. 'Inspection' may connote public inspection, i.e. not only by myself but also by others. With this connotation, since obviously we cannot inspect each other's minds, (3) obviously entails philosophical behaviourism. Statements about minds, to be meaningful, must be construed as statements about bodies. With the other connotation, one can inspect only what can be checked and rechecked. But one can only check and recheck what persists more or less unchanged. In this sense, mental individuals cannot literally be inspected, not because they are private, but because they are momentary. Yet there is a substitute. The mind within one specious present often shifts back and forth between an awareness and the awareness of this awareness. Assume three such shifts to have occurred. Then there are six awarenesses, two groups of three, the members of each group of the same kind. This is the substitute. Dialectically pursued, it leads to the fundamental problem of time and identity. For all other problems, the substitute will do. Wittgenstein, I believe, did not start out a materialist. But it seems that in the fashion of the phenomenalists he always thought of mental facts as sense data, or something like sense data, always completely missed the act. Sense data are awarenesses, of course. But the awareness of an awareness is always an act. Hence, if there were no acts, there would not even be the substitute for the inspection of mental things. This, I suggest, is the structural root of that underground affinity between phenomenalism which causes some to seesaw between the two. One cannot but think of Russell.

Remember, finally, that festering dissatisfaction about the synthetic *a priori*. The formula that meaning is use offers a specious way out. One who knows the rules for the use of language knows that 'this is both red and green' violates these rules. Or, as it is now put, nothing being both red and green is part of the meaning of the words 'red' and 'green'. Still differently, 'nothing is both red and green' is true not because the world is what it is but because we use language as we do. I merely ask two questions. Is every true (general) sentence true by virtue of the meanings of the words that occur in it? If not, where and how do you draw the line? The second question has no answer. One may try to answer the first by admitting, or even insisting, that the meaning of a word changes as we discover what is true and false about what it represents. There is of course *a* meaning of 'meaning' for which this is true. If, however, this were *the* meaning of 'meaning' in which we must first know what a sentence means before we can even ask whether it is true or false, then we could never know whether any single proposition containing a word is true without first knowing the totality of propositions which contain the word and are true. The holistic and idealistic structure of the doctrine is unmistakable. The ultimate subject of all predications is the Absolute. John Dewey, another structural idealist, propounds substantially the same doctrine of meaning. His Absolute is the sociopsychological process of inquiry. The epigones' Absolute is language.

Wittgenstein is a philosopher of the first rank. So we must study his work for its own sake. But we also may and should relate it to that of his peers, particularly if they are his contemporaries. So far, this century has seen four philosophers of the first rank. The other three are Husserl, G. E. Moore, and Russell. Moore, for whom I have a very special affection, was an *éminence grise*. Either one says very much about his contribution or one better says nothing. Tonight I shall say nothing. Russell's lasting achievements are easily identified. Tremendous as they are, they lie all in the area of logic, in the narrower sense of 'logic'. If asked to list four, I would mention his analysis of relations, the theory of types, his analysis of definite descriptions, and the logization of arithmetic. If asked to select among these four the one of greatest philosophical import, I would without hesitation point at the first. No one before Russell really understood relations. Wittgenstein has learned much from Russell and Moore. The most interesting confrontation is none the less with Husserl.

The world of my ontology, or, for short, my world is structured. The entities structuring it all have ontological status. Otherwise there would be no structure. No structure and no world is perhaps not quite the same. But the difference, if any, is not great. Among the entities which provide the structure there is one major division. Some are relations. Some belong to the world's form. Relations are things, share the ontological status of nonrelational characters. That is Russell's epochal insight. The Husserl of the *Untersuchungen*, who was still a realist of sorts, did see that the world's form has ontological status. Unfortunately, he located it, together with all characters, in a realm of Platonic essences. That is one seed of his later tragedy.

Most of my world is physical. Some of it is mental. Through the intentional tie, minds may know the world. In this sense, minds may also know themselves. In another sense, they don't. The awareness of an awareness is always a second awareness, never a part of the first. From this one point, which he took from Husserl, Sartre spun his philosophical fable.

The minds or my world do not create its structure. Nor do they impose it on what is without structure presented to them. Rather, it is presented to them. Our minds are of course active and even creative in many commonsensical ways. Or, alas, some minds are at some times. But, just as there are in my world no substances, there is nothing in it which, in this philosophical sense, is either creative or even active. Nor is that a coincidence.

The minds or Selves of the great tradition are not bare individuals. They are individual substances. If an image will help, think of such a Self as the inner of a sphere; of its properties, which you remember are the only things it can know, as coatings of the surface. The inner either actively creates these everchanging coats; or, at least, it actively imposes a structure upon what is, without one, impressed on the surface from without. Just think of Kant's synthetic unity of apperception! One who sets his feet into this path and walks it steadily will arrive at idealism.

Husserl's incomparable glory is the ontological assay of the act in the *Untersuchungen*. Yet, he understood neither relations, nor the need for fundamental ties, nor the difference between them. That is the other seed of the tragedy. Had he understood these things, he would not have said that the constituent of the act which I call the thought is "intrinsically relational". Nothing is intrinsically relational. The very phrase is a contradiction in terms. In particular, act and intention remain unconnected. Eventually, therefore, one or the other will be lost. That makes even the *Untersuchungen* a glorious failure. Eventually, deeply rooted in the Leibniz-Kant tradition as he was, the master dialectician of the *Untersuchungen* became the idealist of the *Ideen*.

Wittgenstein came as close to the correct ontological assay of the extensional part of the world's form as Husserl came to that of the act. Yet he shrank away from giving ontological status to what he was the first to see so clearly. Nor did he countenance active minds which might have provided that status. The possibility of minds which can know the world without being active in that certain philosophical sense he did not see. Thus mind was lost, the world left without form. Such a world is not much of a world. Thus, eventually, the world was lost. The epigones talk about language.

Wittgenstein's Philosophy of the Mystical[1]

EDDY ZEMACH

THE present essay is an attempt to develop a systematic exposition of that part of Wittgenstein's philosophy (in his "Tractarian" period, 1913–1919) which is commonly known as his account of "the mystical". Not that I believe that this part of the Tractarian philosophy is to any extent "mystical", or that it can be separated from the main part of the philosophy of the *Tractatus*. As a matter of fact I shall try to prove that this is not the case: the philosophy of "the mystical" is an integral part of the *Tractatus*, and thus it presupposes a detailed and thorough understanding of the preceding parts of the work. I shall try to show, in the following pages, that what Wittgenstein says about "the mystical" depends heavily on what he says about facts, objects, logic and language; that any interpretation which brings in "mystical", alien doctrines and concepts to clarify Wittgenstein's intentions totally misses the mark.

But this is not all. Just as the later part of the *Tractatus* presupposes the earlier, the earlier finds its natural and necessary completion in the later. The metaphysics, ethics and aesthetics developed in the last sections of the *Tractatus* are not an appendix to a body of thought already completed, a group of scattered remarks concerning various disconnected topics, or remainders that might as well be ignored. They are rather a culmination of the work reflecting back on everything that went before. The philosophy of the *Tractatus* is a complete philosophy and must be considered as such. Its unity and complete congruity are perhaps its most remarkable features. I believe it might be highly significant, not only to a Wittgenstein scholar but to everyone who is interested in the kind of questions asked in philosophy, to follow Wittgenstein's reasoning and see what conclusions it leads to—in all the areas of philosophy.

[1] From *The Review of Metaphysics*. Reprinted by permission of the publisher and the author.

Two preliminary remarks must be made. The first is about my use of the *Notebooks*.[1] As the editors say in their preface to the *Notebooks*, "it does shew clearly . . . what problems formed the context of Wittgenstein's remarks in the *Tractatus*". If used with care, the *Notebooks* can serve as the best commentary on the *Tractatus*. Sometimes (though not always) they are much clearer than the *Tractatus*, more detailed, the style more conversational and explicative. No doubt there are propositions in the *Notebooks* to which the author of the *Tractatus* would not agree. But the importance of these few places (mainly concerned with the question of common-sense objects) should not be exaggerated. I shall quote the *Notebooks* only when the ideas expressed there seem to be the natural continuation of those expressed in the *Tractatus*. I believe, however, that there is not one passage in the *Notebooks* (nor, of course, any in the *Tractatus*) that conflicts with the conclusions I arrive at.

The second remark is about the use of the *Tractatus* itself. As I said, I believe that concepts like "form", "logical space", "generalized (quantified) propositions", etc., have an immense bearing on Wittgenstein's thinking about the nature of art and ethics. Since my reading of the *Tractatus* and my interpretation of the above concepts are often quite different from those of most Wittgenstein commentators, I shall have to return often to the earlier sections of the book and explicate these "merely logical" notions. If my thesis is right, these excursions will prove to be not casual digressions, but the very heart of the matter.

I. GOD

"The world is the totality of facts" (1.1). There is nothing in the world, according to the Tractarian philosophy, except facts. A fact is what is the case. It is, so to speak, "objective". It does not depend upon my will or wishes. Hence "the world is independent of my will" (6.373). Moreover, "even if all that we wish for, were to happen, still this would be a favour granted by fate, so to speak: for there is no *logical* connection between my will and the world" (6.374). This is one of Wittgenstein's most deep-rooted convictions: the world of fact is what it is. What is the case is a matter of factual contingency. Man is not an agent: whatever happens, including psychological phenomena, happens according to the laws of the natural sciences.

---

[1] Wittgenstein, L., *Notebooks 1914–1916*, ed. by G. H. von Wright and G. E. M. Anscombe and translated by G. E. M. Anscombe (Oxford, 1961). All references to the *Notebooks* in the text will be by date; those to the *Tractatus* will be by proposition numbers. In general I have used the Pears and McGuinness translation of the *Tractatus*. In some instances, where the older Ogden translation better reflects the original German, I have used it.

There can be no exceptions. This is provided for *a priori*.[1] Psychical events are also just facts.[2] *A fortiori*, there cannot be any necessary connection between what I want (a fact) and what actually happens (another fact). There is no such necessary connection between facts in the world. Facts are entirely independent of each other (1.21). The belief that inductive reasoning can establish a necessary connection is a superstition (6.3631–6.37, 5.1361). The facts of the world cannot obey my will. Factuality is what makes the world a world. Factuality lies at the basis of the whole *Tractatus*, and it is, if I am not greatly mistaken, what Wittgenstein names "God".

One may see how this idea emerges in the *Notebooks*: "The world is *given* me, i.e. my will enters into the world completely from outside as into something that is already there. . . . That is why we have the feeling of being dependent on an alien will. *However this may be*, at any rate we *are* in a certain sense dependent, and what we are dependent on we call God. In this sense God would simply be fate, or, what is the same thing: The world—which is independent of our will" (8.7.16). The words are simple enough and need no explanation. So is the Schopenhauerian use of the term *fate*. The "alien will" is just what is independent of my will, the factual character of reality. God, Fate, and World (*qua* the totality of facts) are synonyms.

Wittgenstein's famous concept of *das Mystische* appears in propositions 6.522, 6.44 and 6.45 of the *Tractatus*, which, read together with 6.432, give us a definition of this concept. "There is indeed the inexpressible. This *shows* itself; it is the Mystical" (6.522). "How the world is, is completely indifferent for what is higher. God does not reveal himself *in* the world" (6.432). "Not *how* the world is, is the mystical, but *that* it is" (6.44). One can learn from these propositions (1) that the mystical is *that* there is a world (and not *how* it is), (2) that this "fact", i.e. that there is a world, is not itself *in* the world, and (3) that this "fact" cannot be *pictured* by facts, but it can be *shown* by them.

The first of these propositions (6.44) obviously echoes F. H. Bradley's famous definition of ultimate reality.[3] But Wittgenstein, as he likes to do quite often, adopts the foreign formula and gives it an utterly different interpretation. For Wittgenstein, *that* things stand in a certain way, "*daß es sich so verhält*", is a fact.[4] Language and thought (3) can represent everything which is or can be a fact.[5] However, the factuality of facts, e.g. *that* that-*p* is a fact, is not a

---

[1] See *Tractatus* 6.32–6.361, *et passim*.
[2] See *Notebooks*, letter to Russell dated 19.8.19 pars. 2 and 4. Also *Tractatus* 4.1121, 5.542, 5.5421.
[3] Cf. F. H. Bradley, *Appearance and Reality*, second edition, London, 1897, pp. 162 ff.
[4] Cf. *Tractatus* 3.1432, 4.022.
[5] Cf. *Tractatus* 2.222–2.224, 3.03–3.05, 4.016–4.0311.

fact but a formal feature of a fact (4.1272, 4.221, 4.124). Similarly the "fact" that these, and no others, are all the facts of the world, is a *formal property* of facts and thus is not a fact itself. But language can describe only facts or possible facts, and not formal features of facts. Since the form of all facts, i.e. factuality, is not a fact, it is not *in* the world. It is the *limit* of the world of facts. Thus it can be named "Fate" or "Alien Will", because there can be no reason *why* these are the facts. God is exactly this essence of the facts, their factuality. He is not, therefore, *in* the world. He is "the meaning of the world" (11.6.16).

Immediately this raises a question. "To have a meaning" is a very precise term for Wittgenstein. A fact has a meaning (*Sinn*) if and only if it *shows* a certain state of affairs (*Sachlage*) and *says*, i.e. states, another fact (*Tatsache*). (See 4.031, 4.022, etc.) However, one fact (e.g. *that 'a'* stands in a certain relation to *'b'*) says another fact (e.g. *that aRb*) only if we have a certain method of projection (3.11–2) which relates the elements of these two facts with each other (e.g. establishing *'a'* as the name of *a*). But if we turn to the totality of facts, or the world, the situation is essentially different. The world, unlike any of its parts, cannot be regarded as a propositional sign. Since the world is *all* the facts, if it refers to something, it can refer only to itself and thus contain its own referent, which is impossible (3.332–3). Hence if God is the meaning of the world, i.e. what the world represents, God must be a fact which is neither in nor outside the world. But this again is impossible.

Before attempting to remove this difficulty, let me introduce a notational device. Let us refer to formal features of facts, which Wittgenstein calls "formal" or "internal" properties of facts (4.1211, 4.122, 4.124, etc.), as ' "facts" ', in double quotation marks. Such a "fact" is not a fact at all but that which makes facts possible (2.033, 3.315, 4.126). E.g. the "fact" that the proposition '*Fa*' has a subject-predicate form, that the object *a* occurs in its sense, are all "facts", i.e. formal properties of facts. I shall also refer to such "facts" as formal "facts". The factual character of the world is a formal property of the world. We can say that it is a formal "fact". Now formal "facts" cannot be expressed in language. Facts can only say facts. A formal "fact", e.g. the subject-predicate structure of *Fx*, is *shown* by the picture '*Fx*' as its form (4.1211, 4.124, 4.1274). "What *can* be shown, *cannot* be said" (4.1212).

Now formal "facts" are *shown* by their respective facts even when no "method of projection" (key of translation) is given, whereas having such a method is absolutely essential when one fact *says* another fact. The factuality of facts is not something facts say, but rather something they show. A fact cannot express its factuality, only exhibit it. Thus the factuality of the universe is not effable, though it is exhibited by the facts. It shows itself not by the specific way in which the fact *"sich verhält"*, but by the "fact" *that* the fact is a fact. God, the inexpressible, the mystical, is a formal "fact". The formal "fact" *that* the world is, namely, *that* there is the totality of facts, is God.

One must pause here to make explicit an important distinction. Though *both* the sense of a fact *and* its formal features are *shown* by that fact, the two things shown are by no means identical. The difference between *form* and *sense* is absolutely essential to the understanding of the *Tractatus*.[1] However, in this special case, dealing with the function of God in the *Tractatus*, one can see that the two elements "shown", form and sense, become identical. The reason is simple. Sense is what is displayed by the arrangement of the elements of a fact (3.142, 3.1431, 4.025–7, etc.). When a certain method of projection is given, the fact becomes a logical picture and its sense is a certain *Sachlage*. The logical picture shows what it would be like, the state of affairs which would obtain, if the picture (the proposition) is true (4.063). But if no "key of the symbolism" is given, the sense will be identical with the form, namely, with what is mirrored in the fact (5.512, 4.121) even when no method of projection is given. In this case one may say either that this fact has no sense, or that the only sense it has is provided by its form.

The form of the world is thus also the sense of the world, or the meaning of life (world = life; 5.621). "The problem of life" (6.521) or *"the riddle"* (6.5) is the question, Why is the world thus and not otherwise? What does it mean that these are the facts and no others? This question is answered by showing that life cannot have any sense beyond life. (Cf. 6.4312.) Because life (= the world) is the *totality* of facts, life can refer to no fact beyond itself. Therefore "the solution of the problem of life is seen in the vanishing of the problem" (6.521). To say that the only *sense* that the world can have is its *form* is to answer the problem of life by the "fact" that the world is precisely the realm of facts, i.e. that which does not admit of such questions. The form of the world is the factuality of facts (not *how* they are but *that* they are as they are). It is the mystical: it shows itself, but, being a formal "fact", is ineffable (6.522).

By "the factuality of facts" I mean the feature of facts which is not revealed by the specific way in which a fact presents itself, but by the "fact" *that* it is a fact. This formal "fact" *shows* itself. Now, one of the central ideas of the *Tractatus* is the essential difference between

---

[1] Anyone who collapses this distinction will not be able to reconcile 2.221 ("What a picture represents is its sense") and 4.022 ("A proposition *shows* its sense") with 4.121 ("What finds its reflection in language, language cannot represent").

"to contain" ("*enthalten*") and "to have" ("*haben*"). A proposition, for example, *has* a sense: it *presents* (*stellt dar*) it. But it does not *contain* it (2.203, 3.13). A sense (a *Sachlage*) is expressed by a proposition, but it is not itself incorporated in the proposition. What the proposition does contain is only the *form* of the sense, namely the possibility of presenting it (2.17–2.173, 3.13). What is pictured, the sense, is *outside* the proposition that expresses it. The sense of a proposition (a proposition is a fact plus a method of projection) is just *shown* by it (4.022), but it is never *contained* in it (3.13). A logical picture (= a proposition) contains the possibility of the *Sachlage* (= sense) which it pictures (2.203) but not this *Sachlage* itself (3.02, 3.13).

Thus, the sense of the world is not contained *in* the world. It is, so to speak, "*higher*" (6.432). "Propositions can express nothing of what is higher" (6.42). Every *Sinn* is "higher" than the fact that represents it. But the "*Sinn des Lebens*", i.e. the "*Sinn der Welt*", is "higher" than the totality of facts. For this reason God is said to be "higher" and to never reveal himself *in* the world (6.432). "The meaning of life, i.e. the meaning of the world, we can call God" (11.6.16). God is the meaning of the world, the "fact" that the world is what it is, a totality of facts. Thus also "to pray is to think about the meaning of life" (11.6.16).

We are now at the heart of the matter. If what we have said is true, if God is the essence of the world, the world's meaning and form, then we know much more about God than we thought we knew. For the essence of the world, its form, etc., is nothing but *the general form of the proposition*. Let us consider the following propositions: "The general propositional form is the essence of a proposition" (5.471); "To give the essence of a proposition means to give the essence of all description and thus *the essence of the world*" (5.4711). "*The general form of the proposition is: This is how things stand*" (4.5). "*How things stand, is God. God is, how things stand*" (1.8.16).[1]

Why, in giving the general form of the proposition, is the essence of the world given? To be a world is to be something whose parts can be represented by propositions. The general form of the proposition is the general condition that everything in the world must be a fact, that it must be of the form "the so-and-so is such-and-such" (objects configured). This status, shared by everything in the world, is the general form of the proposition: "This is how things stand" (4.5).

The concepts "form", "essence" and "nature" are strictly identical in the *Tractatus*. (Cf. 2.011 and 2.0141; or 3.342 and 3.3421; or 5.471 and 5.4711 and 22.1.15.) The essence of the world, "*das Wesen allen*

---

[1] My italics.

Seins", is exactly what is first expressed in 2.0231 and 2.18, and given a final form in 6: the general form of the proposition. The common form of every world, the general form of the proposition, is that which is *wesentlich* for any world to be a world, that there are facts (no matter which). Facts are combinations of objects. The general form of the proposition shows how all possible facts can be constructed from objects. In this way the picturing relation between language and reality is possible *a priori* (2.18). This relation is the essence of language and the essence of the world. Only that which can be expressed can exist (3.02–3.0321), and the general form of the proposition is the form (the possibility) of every fact that can be expressed in language. The existence of facts, i.e. logical places (3.411), is the determination of it through stipulation of values. It follows that the general form of the proposition is precisely *logical space*, within which (and only within it!) every possible fact can be (5.501, 5.511, 3.41). It is thus the general precondition of being (7.11.14) and the common denominator (form) of all facts (5.47, 4.5). The general form of the proposition and God are one.

The entire problem of generality-propositions (quantified propositions) is highly relevant to our inquiry. On this point Wittgenstein was again misinterpreted by his followers. (Although Wittgenstein criticizes Frege and Russell for introducing quantification "in association with logical product or logical sum" (5.521) and explicitly says: "I dissociate the concept *all* from truth-functions", his own theory of quantification is "explained" by some commentators precisely in these terms!)[1] For Wittgenstein, a generalized proposition is the *logical form* or prototype ("*Urbild*") of a group of propositions (3.24, 5.522 and 5.524; or 20.1.15 and 25.10.14; or 1.11.14 and 5.47). As a function is the prototype of a class of arguments (3.333), so a generalized proposition is the prototype of a class of functions (5.526, 5.5262). A completely generalized proposition does not *have* a form but *is* a form (25.10.14). Hence it "is not actually a proposition" (12.11.14). Though the prototype '$(x)Fx$' is *shown* by the logical product of Fa, Fb, Fc, etc., it is not identical with this row of propositions (1.11.14). No form *is* the content that *has* this form. The form is given simultaneously with the content ("If elementary propositions are given then at the same time *all* elementary propositions are given." 5.524), but, in the general case,[2] it is not identical with the

---

[1] Cf. Erik Stenius, *Wittgenstein's Tractatus*, Ithaca, 1960, p. 153. Section 4 ("Quantification") opens with the following sentence: "Obviously Wittgenstein thinks that sentences containing quantifiers should be treated according to his truth-functional scheme."

[2] The general case is described in 3.31 (cf. also 3.311–3.315; 4.52). The only exceptions are the *objects*. For objects, form and content are *identical* (2.025; 2.014 and 2.0141). "Objects are simple" (2.02).

content. The general form is the possibility of the specific cases, and is presupposed by them (2.033, 2.18, 2.2).

Now the concept *form* is identical, for Wittgenstein, with the concept *limit*. A generalized proposition is the form of a certain domain and its limit (5.5262, 4.12721, 5.522). The generalized proposition '$(x)Fx$' leaves Gx outside the boundaries of the domain whose general form it is. But how can we give the form of the all-inclusive domain, the world? Wittgenstein suggests three ways: (1) By enumerating all existing states of affairs, the general form will show itself (5.524, 4.51). But this is impossible for men: we just do not know everything that is the case. (2) By enumerating all the functions that there are. But this also becomes an infinite task. (3) By giving a formal law that governs the construction of all possible propositions (5.501). This can be done and Wittgenstein shows us exactly how he does it. This law is the general form of the proposition. In 5.52 Wittgenstein shows us how the general form of the proposition is the form of all propositions—both generalized and non-generalized. "The subject matter of general propositions is really the world; which makes its appearance in them by means of a logical description. And that is why the world does not really occur in them, just as the subject of the description does not occur in it" (29.10.14). Though the world does not appear in a completely generalized proposition (it has no name-thing connection with the world), the completely generalized proposition, as a prototype of all propositions, does "mean" the world. It may also be said to be the world's "meaning".

A completely generalized proposition gives us a description of a certain domain as a limited whole (5.5262). Thus "the mystical" is "the feeling of the world as a limited whole" (6.45). "The mystical", or God, is not *how* the world is but *that* it is (6.44). Since the world is the totality of facts, its most general characteristic held in common by all facts, viz. factuality, is revealed to be nothing but the general form of the proposition. The form *world*, or *God*, is the "fact" that there are facts, and that these are all the facts (positive and negative). But such a "fact" about facts is obviously a formal concept, which cannot be named or described (4.126–4.1273). Wittgenstein shows us how we can get rid of such concepts: when we use a variable, the formal traits that are shared by all possible assignments of values to this variable show themselves. Thus "the variable name 'x' is the proper sign for the pseudo-concept *object*" (4.1272). The general propositional form "$[\bar{p}, \bar{\xi}, N(\bar{\xi})]$" is a variable name (4.53) which is the proper sign for the pseudo-concept *God*.

Let us summarize. We began, following some passages in the *Notebooks*, with a simple identification of God and World. We have seen that this formula, as it stands, will not do, since Wittgenstein conceives of God as transcendental. God does not reveal himself in the world. Thus we continued to analyse other propositions dealing with God and the Mystical, and we found out that not to be revealed *in* the world may mean to be manifested as the limit of the world. We have found several passages that supported this interpretation. To be a limit of a domain means to be the general *form*, i.e. the possibility of this domain. With respect to the total domain, to be a form is to be its sense. Since form and essence are identical, God is the sense and the essence of the world. The essence of the world, i.e. the totality of facts, is the general form of the proposition. Thus the general form of the proposition is identical with the concept *God*.

II. THE SECOND GODHEAD

We have seen that no "form of representation" ("method of projection") can be given for the world as a whole. We saw that, if there were such a method, some fact would have been pictured by the world. This fact must be located outside the world (2.173), but this is impossible since the world is the *totality* of facts. Hence no method of representation can be given, and the question about the meaning of life cannot be answered. The sense of the world is identical with its form (= God).

One way, however, may still be open. What will happen if something which is not factual is projected through the form of representation? But can we conceive of something which is not factual? To ask this question is to answer it: values are not facts. Facts may have value, but, so it seems, value is what is other than fact. *That* a fact has value is not a formal "fact" about this fact, since a value cannot be a given feature of a fact. If whatever is in the world is a fact, values cannot be in the world.

The sense of the world must lie outside the world. In the world everything is as it is and everything happens as it does happen: *in* it no value exists—and if it did, it would have no value.

If there is any value that does have value, it must lie outside the whole sphere of what happens and is the case. . . .

It must lie outside the world (6.41).

So another possibility for the sense of the world can after all be conceived. We may take, as a basis for a possible "key", *not* the actual traits of the facts in the world but their values. If the world is to be conceived in this way, as a sign whose "key of interpretation" is its value, i.e. its ethical "attributes", it will have a sense independent of its form. The world *qua* representing duties, values, obligations and tasks projects "the will, in so far as it is the subject of ethical attributes" (6.423). Obviously, "it is impossible to speak about the will"

(6.423) since language is a set of pictures of *facts*, and the subject *qua* will is not a fact.

We have seen that Wittgenstein names God "the alien will". Now we have found another will: my will, the ethical subject. In this way Wittgenstein arrives at his *"double Godhead"* theory. "There are two godheads: the world and my independent I" (8.7.16). The world is, as we saw, the first God. The willing I is the second. Unlike the world-God, the I-God makes its appearance when we believe that "the facts of the world are not the end of the matter" (8.7.16). From the ethical point of view, facts constitute an *"Aufgabe"* for us: a duty and a task (6.4321). We shall later see in what sense this task is possible.

This theory of the willing subject should be distinguished from Wittgenstein's theory of the thinking subject. The subject *qua* the experiencer of facts in the world is identical with the world as a totality. "I am my world" (5.63). "The I makes its appearance in philosophy through the world's being *my* world" (12.8.16, 5.641). Wittgenstein's comments on solipsism make it clear that the I as a metaphysical subject is the entire world. It limits it (5.632). Solipsism is shown to coincide with pure realism (5.64), since it deals with the *thinking* subject. There is no such thing as the subject that thinks (5.631). "The thinking subject is surely mere illusion. But the willing subject exists" (4.8.16).

The limit of the world which from one point of view can be named God, can from another point of view be named the thinking I. The thinking I gives the world a form. The willing I gives it a sense—a significance. Both Godheads are transcendental, i.e. world-constituting. My spirit is the world-spirit, the one spirit common to the whole world, to animals and lifeless things (15.10.16). "Things acquire 'significance' only through their relation to my will" (15.10.16), therefore my will is what is projected by the world through the ethical attributes. "And in this sense I can also speak of a will that is common to the whole world. But this will is in a higher sense *my* will" (17.10.16). The double-Godhead theory is, perhaps, best expressed in the following proposition: "As my idea is the world, in the same way my will is the world-will" (17.10.16).

The willing I, the value-endower, cannot exist *in* the world which is nothing but the totality of facts. "My will enters into the world completely from outside as into something that is already there" (8.7.16). "My will penetrates the world" (11.6.16). "The will is an attitude of the subject to the world" when "the subject is the willing subject" (4.11.16). "Good and evil only enter through the *subject*. And the subject is not part of the world, but a boundary of the world" (2.8.16). To occupy the ethical standpoint is, consequently, to place oneself outside the world, so to speak, at a place where no facts may hold. Hence Wittgenstein's expression in his paper on ethics (as reported by Anscombe[1] and Malcolm[2]), that when he fixes his mind on ethical value, he wonders at the existence of the world.

Since the value-endowing will is outside the world of facts, an endowment of a fact with value, the bestowal of importance upon a hitherto unimportant fact, cannot be said to "change" the fact. Nothing in the fact is really changed. Wittgenstein rejects the inherence of the "third-order" qualities, for the subjective "colouring" of a fact can not be another trait of this fact, alongside its other qualities.

If good or bad acts of will do alter the world, it can only be the limits of the world that they alter, not the facts, not what can be expressed by means of language.
In short their effect must be that it becomes an altogether different world. It must, so to speak, wax and wane as a whole (6.43).

In the parallel passage in the *Notebooks* we find an important addition to this: "As if by accession or loss of meaning" (5.7.16). A change of value seems to make the world wax or wane as a whole. "The world of the happy is quite another than that of the unhappy" (6.43). The ethical experience, thus, creates a wonder at the independent existence of the world of facts.

Wittgenstein recognizes two transcendental theories: logic and ethics (6.421, 6.13). Neither treat of the world, but are the transcendental conditions of the world (24.7.16). Logic and ethics provide two possible "methods of projection" for finding the world's sense. For logic, the sense of the world is its inalterable form: God. For ethics, it is the willing subject.

III. ETHICS

Since goodness or badness cannot be qualities of the world, they must be qualities of the willing subject. The ethics which follows is rather simple: "What is good and evil is essentially the I, not the world" (5.8.16). "As the subject is not a part of the world but a presupposition of its existence, so good and evil are predicates of the subject, not properties in the world" (2.8.16). "My will is good or evil" (11.6.16). But what do good and evil mean? Wittgenstein tells us in the *Notebooks*: "Simply the happy life is good, the unhappy bad" (30.7.16). Or "I am either happy or unhappy, that is all. It can

---

[1] G. E. M. Anscombe, *An Introduction to Wittgenstein's 'Tractatus'*, London, 1959, p. 173.
[2] Norman Malcolm, *Ludwig Wittgenstein, a Memoir*, London, 1958, p. 70.

be said: good or evil do not exist" (8.7.16). Thus there is only one
categorical imperative: "Live happily!" (8.7.16, 29.7.16).

Now comes the application of the distinctions previously made to
this kind of hedonism (which, as we shall later see, is more Schopenhauerian than hedonistic): "The world of the happy is a different
world from that of the unhappy. The world of the happy is *a happy
world*" (29.7.16). On this basis Wittgenstein develops a *"tautological"*
theory of reward and punishment as the first law of his ethical
theory.

> The first thought in setting up an ethical law of the form "thou shalt . . ."
> is: And what if I do not do it? But it is clear that ethics has nothing to do
> with punishment and reward in the ordinary sense. This question as to the
> *consequences* of an action must therefore be irrelevant (6.422).

Certainly, if a consequence must be a fact, and facts as such have
nothing to do with value. The solution is given in the disguise of the
old formula: "There must indeed be some kind of ethical reward and
ethical punishment, but they must reside in the action itself" (6.422).
The next sentence almost lets the secret out: "And it is also clear that
the reward must be something pleasant and the punishment something unpleasant" (6.422). The sinners, i.e. the unhappy, live in an
unhappy world, and the world of the happy is a happy world. Sin is
its own punishment and likewise merit is its own reward. Since the
only sin is to be unhappy, the sinner is punished by his sin.

Only one more step is now needed. Wittgenstein can conclude his
argument by saying that a happy life is "justified of itself". It is an
ethical tautology. "And if I *now* ask myself: But *why* should I live
happily, then this of itself seems to me to be a tautological question; the happy life seems to be justified, of itself" (30.7.16). A *logical*
proposition is self-justifying if it can show itself to be a tautology. It
seems that Wittgenstein applies the same criterion to decide in what
ethical justification consists.

IV. THE GOOD LIFE

The Good is happiness. But what is happiness? To this Wittgenstein
has a Schopenhauerian-Spinozistic answer: "In order to live happily
I must be in agreement with the world. And that is what 'being happy'
means" (8.7.16). This definition of happiness provides us with a
unique solution to a baffling problem: how can the independence of
the "second Godhead" be reconciled with the absoluteness of the
"first Godhead"? Wittgenstein answers that indeed there is only one
way to be free, independent and happy: to accept fully, without any
reservations, the brute factuality of the world. The previous passage

continues thus: "*I am* then, so to speak, *in agreement with that alien will* on which I appear dependent. That is to say: '*I am doing the will of God*'" (my italics). God is the inevitable, fate, the factuality of facts. By desiring facts to be other than they are, by wishing some events to happen rather than other events, man breaks his harmony with the universe, i.e. with God. No desire *can* be fulfilled. Thus to wish is always to wish the impossible, i.e. to be unhappy. Even if my desire is fulfilled, it is by "a favour of fate and not through the exercise of actual agency" (6.374). Therefore, the good will is precisely the will that wishes nothing, giving its consent to whatever happens as it happens. This is the only way to bring the "world of the willing I" into harmony with the "world of God", and by infinite submission to the "will of God" to acquire happiness. So Wittgenstein can say: "Certainly it is correct to say: *Conscience is the voice of God*" (my italics) (8.7.16). The religious mask appears very thin, behind which the Schopenhauerian pessimism is clearly visible. This ideal of ataraxia can assume also a non-religious, e.g. existentialist, complexion: "In this sense Dostoievsky is right when he says that the man who is happy is fulfilling the purpose of existence" (6.7.16). Given the cash-value meaning of "the voice of God", "the purpose of existence", "happiness", etc., one finds what Wittgenstein considered to be the bitter truth behind this fanciful phraseology.[1]

It is important to note in this context how Wittgenstein distinguishes between "to will" and "to wish". Wittgenstein does not say, with Schopenhauer, that the will is bad in itself. Not because their opinions on the matter differ, but because Wittgenstein defines "will" differently, and distinguishes between "will" and "wish". "The wish precedes the event, the will accompanies it" (4.11.16). The will does not involve any expectation, desire or hope. It does not try to make things different from what they are. Rather, it goes along with the fact, or the action, when it occurs. This somewhat peculiar account of the nature of willing is clarified in the following passage:

This is clear: it is impossible to will without already performing the act of the will.

The act of the will is not the cause of the action but is the action itself. One cannot will without acting.

If the will has to have an object in the world, the object can be the intended action itself (4.11.16).

The will, one may say, is the shadow, not the forerunner, of facts.

[1] I cannot see on what basis Anscombe decides that "Wittgenstein thought that the world is good" and that "the goodness of the world, however, is not anything in *how* it is, but in its being at all" (op. cit., p. 172). For Wittgenstein, rather, the world just is what it is, and that is the end of the matter, as far as the world is concerned. "The world in itself is neither good nor evil. . . . It is not the world of Idea that is either good or evil; but the willing subject . . . good and evil are predicates of the subject, not properties in the world" (2.8.16).

The fact that I will an action consists in my performing the action, not in my doing something else which causes the action. . . .
Can I try to will something? (4.11.16).

The wish, on the other hand, "relates, e.g. to the movement of the chair" (4.11.16); I do not *accompany* the movements of the chair by *willing*, but *wish* the chair—in vain—to "behave" thus or thus. "Wishing is not acting. But willing is acting" (4.11.16). To wish, therefore, is to will in a futile way, to will to change the world. This is entirely impossible: "I cannot bend the happenings of the world to my will: I am completely powerless" (11.6.16). But I am capable of willing the good, that is, doing exactly what Schopenhauer called *not* willing. 'I can only make myself independent of the world—and so in a certain sense master it—by renouncing any influence on happenings" (11.6.16). By a conscious submission to fate I acquire freedom.

"How can man be happy at all, since he cannot ward off the misery of the world? Through the life of knowledge. The good conscience is the happiness that the life of knowledge preserves" (13.8.16). Nothing can be done about the world; facts are facts. But "good conscience" can still be acquired by clearly seeing what the meaning of life (i.e. the meaning of the world) consists of; that is, by "praying to God". Or, to put it in the language of 6.54, by climbing up the Tractarian ladder and then "seeing the world rightly". This theory which states that our only pleasure is understanding, can illuminate the sentence in the preface where Wittgenstein describes the *"Zweck"* of his book: "Its object would be attained if it afforded pleasure to one who read it with understanding." Knowing the eternal truth about himself and the world, acknowledging his absolute dependency upon the inevitable facts, man still can make himself independent of fate (8.7.16) by living a life of knowledge and willing the necessary.

To attain his freedom, the subject must be freed from time and the fear of death. Again, one must warn the reader against a theistic or an existentialist interpretation of this thesis. One must rather inspect Wittgenstein's own thought, follow his definitions, and find the meaning he assigns to formulae that are also used by others. For Wittgenstein, to live in time is to live in the sphere of wishes. A wish has an essentially temporal character: it is directed toward the future. (While the will, as we saw, is always a thing of the present, since it is simultaneous with its object.) The orientation toward the future may take two forms: the wish can appear as a fear or as a hope. Goethe referred to fear and hope as man's two greatest enemies. Wittgenstein wholeheartedly agrees. "Whoever lives in the present lives without fear and hope" (14.7.16), and "Only a man who lives not in time but in the present is happy" (8.7.16). To live in time means to have fears and hopes, to expect something, positively or negatively,

from the world. But the world of facts cannot possibly—logically—satisfy those hopes or fears. In the world of facts, time is not basically different from the other three dimensions. Logic has no use for time. Tautologies are given "at once". The world of facts is a static world. To live in time means not to be in agreement with the world. Therefore to live in time is to be unhappy, i.e. to live in sin. On the other hand, "eternal life belongs to those who live in the present" (6.4311). The only way to evade the temporal character of human existence is *not* to wish, to be content (6.7.16), not to hope and not to have anticipations. Those who lead this kind of life live in an eternal present. Thus those who "do the will of God", "live forever".

A further analysis shows that "Death is not an event of life. Death is not lived through" (6.4311). To acknowledge death will be to take over something that has significance, i.e. something from the world of the willing I, and regard it as an event of life, i.e. of the world of facts. No willing subject exists as a fact. Thus no subject, *qua* willing, can die. The significance-endower cannot create a significance which would deny him as a significance-endower. Thus, the fear of death is the sign of the "moral vice" of mixing facts with the willing I, and wishing them to happen or not to happen. And so Wittgenstein can say, resuming his "moralistic" tone: "Fear in the face of death is the best sign of a false, i.e. a bad, life" (8.7.16).

V. Aesthetics

In proposition 6.421 of the *Tractatus* we read: "Ethics and aesthetics are one." No other mention of aesthetics is made in the *Tractatus*, though in the *Notebooks* the reasons for this identification are given quite clearly. The author of the *Tractatus* presumably relied on the fact that "those who have themselves already thought the thoughts which are expressed" in the *Tractatus* (preface) are, no doubt, familiar also with the writings of Schopenhauer, and thus will understand the reference to the latter's theory of art. For Schopenhauer, art, like philosophy, can bring man to see the "ideas", the eternal forms, the observation of which is the only non-frustrating occupation man can engage in. This theory of aesthetics is very close to what Wittgenstein thought to be the basic truth of ethics. Wittgenstein proceeds thus to show that aesthetics and ethics are really one and the same thing.

Ethics is the theory of how man's life (= the world) should be conducted, that is, how one should look at the world (since the world cannot be *changed*), if he is to be happy. But this is exactly the rôle of art: "Is it the essence of the artistic way of looking at things, that it looks at the world with a happy eye?" (20.10.16); and we know that

to regard the world with a happy eye means to live in a happy world
(6.43). "For there is certainly something in the conception that the
end of art is the beautiful. And the beautiful *is* what makes happy"
(21.10.16). Now since what makes man live happily is ethics, ethics
and aesthetics are one.

The identity of ethics and aesthetics can also be established by
scrutinizing the nature of the aesthetic object. A beautiful object is
something existing in and of itself, an autotelic being which is not
regarded instrumentally nor judged by its relations to other happenings at other times. It is isolated, as if plucked out of space and time
and regarded as constituting a space and time of its own. Any thing,
when regarded aesthetically, ceases to be just "one among the many
things in the world", and becomes itself a whole world (8.10.16).
"For it is equally possible to take the bare present image as the worthless momentary picture in the whole temporal world, and as the
true world among shadows" (8.10.16). The last phrase of this sentence reminds one of the way Rilke described the rôle of the poet on
earth.[1]

We may sum up what we have found by saying that the aesthetic
attitude regards facts not *in* time but *sub specie aeternitatis*. Now, is
this not exactly what Wittgenstein's doctrine of the *eternal present*
advocates in ethics? To live morally, i.e. in a happy world, one must
live in the present, renouncing every wish, voluntarily accepting the
inevitable, the given facts. Both ethics and aesthetics are, thus, the
theories of the eternal present. "The work of art is the object seen *sub
specie aeternitatis*; and the good life is the world seen *sub specie
aeternitatis*. This is the connection between art and ethics" (7.10.16).

But what does it mean to see the world *sub specie aeternitatis*?
The answer to this question will finally combine Wittgenstein's
teachings on the mystical, the ethical and the aesthetic. To begin, let
us remind ourselves what the good life is. We saw that "the only life
that is happy is the life that can renounce the amenities of the world"
(13.8.16), and that this life is the life of knowledge, since "the life of
knowledge is . . . happy in spite of the misery of the world" (13.8.16).
Good conscience, i.e. happiness, is thus achieved only through the
life of knowledge, "Good conscience is the happiness that the life of
knowledge preserves" (13.8.16). Now conscience, we remember, is
the voice of God, and the life of knowledge is knowing the essence of
the world, the theory of facts. This theory is the theory about the
limits of the world, or the presentation of the world as a limited
whole. To see the world as a limited whole, i.e. as everything that can
be expressed by the general form of the proposition, is the mystical
(6.45). And this is what it means, "to view the world *sub specie*

[1] *Die Sonette an Orpheus*, I.9.

aeterni" (6.45). To regard something from this point of view is to know it *as a fact within the logical framework.* "The thing seen *sub specie aeternitatis* is the thing seen together with the whole logical space" (7.10.16). The art object is thus self-sufficient because it is seen as an expression of the ultimate status of being a fact. It is beautiful because it is an expression of factuality, i.e. of the will of God. Wittgenstein can thus use another theory, the theory of art as expression, to clothe his own ideas: "Art is a kind of expression. Good art is complete expression" (19.9.16). The aesthetic is the expression of the mystical, i.e. the factuality of facts. Ethics and aesthetics are the same. They are man's expressions of wonder as he, the willing I, encounters the mystical: the existence of the world. "Aesthetically, the miracle is that the world exists. That what exists does exist" (20.10.16).[1] Ethics and aesthetics are the way by which the second Godhead brings itself into harmony with the first Godhead, the mystical. They are the infinite acceptance of that which is, as it is.

---

[1] "Das künstlerische Wunder ist, daß es die Welt gibt. Daß es das gibt, was es gibt."

Wittgenstein's Picture Theory
of Language[1]

DAVID KEYT

"My *whole* task consists in explaining the nature of
the proposition."

—*Notebooks* 22.1.15

WITTGENSTEIN'S version of the picture theory of language[2] in the
Tractatus is sharply outlined, but many of the details are indistinct.
It is hard to see, in particular, how Wittgenstein meets the traditional objections to the picture theory. Thus it is difficult to assess the
merits of Wittgenstein's version of the picture theory and, consequently, of the philosophy of the *Tractatus* as a whole.

In this paper I begin by presenting the main features of Wittgenstein's theory—the sharp outline. Then the traditional objections to
the picture theory are set forth: these may be collected together and a
paradox of the picture theory formulated. With this paradox in mind
I turn to the details of Wittgenstein's theory. One needs here to consider the various interpretations offered by different commentators
on the *Tractatus*. These interpretations are considered from two
points of view: as interpretations of the *Tractatus* and as solutions of
the paradox. The conclusion I reach is that none of the interpretations
so far offered resolve the paradox and that probably none are correct
interpretations of the *Tractatus*. Finally, I present what I believe is a
good interpretation of the *Tractatus* and also what I think is a satisfactory solution of the paradox, but these two turn out to be distinct.

[1] From *The Philosophical Review*, 73 (1964), pp. 493-511. Reprinted by permission of the publisher and the author.
[2] The new Pears-McGuinness translation of the *Tractatus* (London, 1961) is used
throughout. The few changes of terminology that I have made are enclosed within
brackets. I have used the *Notebooks 1914–1916* (Oxford, 1961) extensively and have
made whatever use I could of the backward-looking parts of *The Blue and Brown
Books* (Oxford, 1958) and the *Philosophical Investigations* (Oxford, 1953). The propositions of the *Tractatus* are referred to by number alone; the titles of the other works
are given, some in abbreviated form.

David Keyt

THE THEORY

I shall be concerned in this paper with a single but basic facet of the picture theory of the *Tractatus*: the elementary proposition and how it portrays. There are other facets. One of these is the idea that the sole function of language is to picture reality (4.001 together with 4.01). Another is the problem of how propositions of ordinary language picture reality. Wittgenstein's solution very briefly is that this is revealed by logical analysis, that the vehicle of logical analysis is a perspicuous notation along the lines of that of *Principia Mathematica*, and that upon analysis a proposition of ordinary language is resolved into a number of elementary propositions plus some logical constants. A final evaluation of the picture theory of the *Tractatus* must take both of these other facets into account, but neither will be discussed in this paper.

Elementary propositions, as they are defined in the *Tractatus*, have the following features. They contain no logical constants, no words such as "not" or "and" or "all". They are logically independent of each other (4.211, 5.134). They are made up entirely of names (4.22), and each name stands for a simple object (3.203, 3.22, 2.02). Finally, an elementary proposition "asserts the existence of [an atomic] state of affairs" (4.21).

Many things that Wittgenstein and his commentators say about elementary propositions apply also to simple propositions of ordinary language such as "Mercury is smaller than Venus". Whenever this is so, I speak simply of propositions instead of elementary propositions and of states of affairs instead of atomic states of affairs. But even when I speak of propositions in this general way, I still intend to refer only to propositions of the form $R(x_1, x_2, \ldots x_n)$, that is, to propositions that contain a single verb and no logical constants.[1]

How does an elementary proposition portray reality? First, the negative side. Although a name stands for an object, it is not a picture of an object: "The *name* is *not* a picture of the thing named!" (*Notebooks*, 3.10.14; cf. 3.221). The pictorial aspect of an elementary proposition is the *arrangement* of names: how names are arranged (combined, configured, related, structured) pictures how objects are allegedly arranged (3.21). I say *allegedly* since, although every elementary proposition pictures a possible arrangement of objects, not every one (apparently) pictures an actual arrangement: every elementary proposition has a sense (cf. 4.031; *Notebooks*, 26.10.14, par. 3)

---

[1] By a proposition with two verbs I mean one like "I *know* that Mercury *is* smaller than Venus".

but not every one is true. I say *apparently* since it is, of course, logically possible for every elementary proposition to be true.

The problems toward which this theory is directed are two: the problem of the new proposition[1] and the problem of the false proposition.[2]

The problem of the new proposition is to explain a striking difference between names and propositions. "The [references] of simple signs (words) must be explained to us if we are to understand them" (4.026); but, on the other hand, "we understand the sense of a propositional sign without its having been explained to us" (4.02). Wittgenstein sums it up this way: "A proposition must use old expressions to communicate a new sense" (4.03; cf. 4.025). How on the picture theory is this difference explained? Why must the reference of a new name be explained to us but not the sense of a new proposition? The answer, quite simply, is this. A name is not a picture of the thing named. Name and object are connected by arbitrary convention. But a proposition *is* a picture of its sense. "A proposition *shows* its sense" (4.022; cf. *Investigations*, 523). Thus a proposition is *essentially* connected with the state of affairs it expresses (4.03). So the one connection needs to be explained, the other not. For example, if we wished, we might let "*s*" stand for Seattle and "*k*" for Spokane and lay it down further that one name to the left of a second depicts one thing west of another. We may adopt these as conventions or not as we please. But if we adopt them, then necessarily "*sk*" depicts Seattle as west of Spokane and "*ks*" the reverse (cf. 3.342).

The problem of the false proposition springs from a second difference between names and propositions. A name, if there is no object that it signifies, is meaningless: it is not a name at all (3.203; cf. *Investigations*, 40). But a proposition, if there is no fact that it signifies, is not meaningless but simply false. Thus what a name signifies must exist, but what a proposition signifies need not. So the question is: how can a proposition be false without being meaningless? (Cf. *Notebooks*, 15.11.14, *Blue and Brown Books*, p. 31, ll. 8–15, *Investigations*, 518.) The answer given by the picture theory is this. A proposition is composite (3.141, par. 2; 4.032). And what each part signifies exists even if what the whole signifies does not. What a false proposition signifies is simply a nonexistent *arrangement* of existent objects (*Blue and Brown Books*, p. 31, ll. 16–24). How does it do even this? Well, the names themselves, given the method of projection, are arranged as the objects would be arranged if the proposition were

---

[1] "It belongs to the essence of a proposition that it should be able to communicate a *new* sense to us" (4.027).

[2] "It must not be overlooked that a proposition has a sense that is independent of the facts" (4.061).

true (4.0311; *Notebooks*, 4.11.14). So it turns out that even the arrangement itself exists, though it exists as an arrangement of names, not of what the names stand for.

THE PARADOX

The picture theory of language is faced with an interesting puzzle. Consider the proposition "Seattle is west of Spokane". This is not an elementary proposition—it will be well to bear this in mind—but let us suppose for the moment that an elementary proposition is at least like this. This proposition is composed of three parts (giving a logical rather than a grammatical analysis): two proper names and the predicate "is west of". Now the first bit of the puzzle is this. The fact pictured by the proposition is an arrangement of *two* cities but the proposition itself is an arrangement of *three* parts. Thus the fact and the proposition do not appear to have the same number of parts. But Wittgenstein holds that they must: "In a proposition there must be exactly as many distinguishable parts as in the situation that it represents. The two must possess the same logical (mathematical) multiplicity" (4.04). Suppose we preserve the one-to-one correspondence between the fact and the proposition by dropping the predicate and writing the proposition simply as "Seattle Spokane". But if this arrangement of names pictures the fact that Seattle *is west of* Spokane, how will we picture the fact that Seattle *is north of* Portland? Well, we can do this by writing "Seattle" over "Portland":

Seattle
Portland

This gives us the second part of the puzzle. For this is no longer a proposition but a map. Surely one important difference between a proposition and a map is that a proposition is a linear or one-dimensional structure.[1] So either the picture theory is able to explain only a poverty-stricken language (one in which, say, the relation of being west of can be expressed, but not the relation of being north of) or else it ignores a striking difference between propositions and maps.

The problem facing the picture theory is that it seems to embrace three propositions that appear to be irreconcilable:

1. There is a one-to-one correspondence between the parts of a

---

[1] Strictly speaking, written propositions of English are two-dimensional. But, as Morse Code shows, this second dimension is not essential. Notice also that the words of a proposition are not strung out but are bunched together with at most a single space between one word and the next. Thus the problem cannot be solved by reminding ourselves that the points of a plane can be mapped onto the points of a line.

proposition and the objects of the state of affairs pictured by the proposition (4.04).
2. Propositions are linear structures.[1]
3. Every possible state of affairs can be expressed in language.[2]

PROPOSED SOLUTIONS

The simplest way to resolve the paradox would seem to be to take the fact pictured by "Seattle is west of Spokane" to be an arrangement of three parts, not two: Seattle, Spokane, and the relation of being west of. The two proper names stand for the two cities and the predicate for the relation, so there is a one-to-one correspondence between the parts of the proposition and the parts of the fact. This sort of interpretation is given by Ellis Evans. Evans in fact goes one step further and counts four elements in both fact and proposition, the fourth element of the proposition being the *order* of the words and the fourth element of the fact being the *structure* of the relation and its two terms:

Wittgenstein would have said, I think, that the fact that Sophia hates Amos contained four elements: the two people, the hating, and the structure of these, i.e. that it is Sophia and not Amos that is doing the hating and Amos and not Sophia that is receiving it. The individual words correspond to those first three elements, and the order of the words to the fourth.[3]

There are two points to be made against this interpretation. The first is that it would be better not to call order an *element* of a proposition and structure an *element* of a fact. For if one does, Wittgenstein's solution of the problem of the false proposition loses its point. A false proposition has sense even though there is no fact that it pictures because each of its elements, even when it is false, still stands for an object. (On Evans' interpretation one of these objects will be a relation.) But what does the order of words of a false proposition stand for? Nothing. Thus if one calls the order of words an element of a proposition, this element must be treated differently from the other elements. The second point to be made against this interpretation is more serious. Evans, in correlating the elements of the proposition "Sophia hates Amos" with the elements of the fact

---

[1] Whether or not Wittgenstein subscribes to this proposition in the *Tractatus* is discussed below.

[2] "Man possesses the ability to construct languages capable of expressing every sense" (4.002).

"Propositions can represent the whole of reality" (4.12; cf. 4.26).

"We can indeed say: everything that is (or is not) the case can be pictured by means of a proposition" (*Notebooks*, 26.5.15).

[3] "Tractatus 3.1432", *Mind*, 64, 1955, 260 [present volume].

that Sophia hates Amos, has overlooked one of the elements of the proposition. For if the fact has four elements—Sophia, Amos, the relation of hating, and the structure of the first three—then the proposition has five—the three words "Sophia", "hates", and "Amos", the triadic relation of one word being between two others, and the structure of the relation and its three terms. So it turns out that Evans' suggestion does not really resolve the paradox since, upon following it up, it turns out that again a proposition has one element more than the state of affairs that it pictures.

The second solution I want to examine, given by Erik Stenius, starts at the point at which Evans' solution breaks down.[1] First of all, Stenius does not count the structure of a state of affairs as one of its elements. Secondly, he gets rid of the extra element with which Evans is left by combining two of Evans' elements into one. He allows the verb in such a proposition as "Sophia hates Amos" to be absorbed by the relation of betweenness. Thus Stenius takes the predicate of the proposition to be not the *word* "hates", but the *relation* of one word being to the left and a second to the right of "hates". This predicate is a dyadic relation that is formed from the triadic relation of one word being to the left and a second to the right of a third, by filling the third place with the word "hates". Stenius calls the word "hates" a *characteristic* of the predicate. The predicate, Stenius says, "is always derived from a relation between the logical subjects and one or more symbols which appear as 'characteristics' of the predicate" (p. 134). Finally, Stenius explicitly distinguishes propositions from diagrams on the grounds that the former unlike the latter are one-dimensional structures (p. 147).

My objection to this solution is a metaphysical one. Suppose that Amos and Sophia hate *each other*. Then there are two facts: the fact that Sophia hates Amos and the fact that Amos hates Sophia. Both of these facts contain the same three elements and differ only in structure. Now what is structure on this analysis? It is the way the relation is linked to its terms. But this means that this linking relation is the only real relation, the only relation that does any work. The relational element of each fact, the hating, is reduced to a mere term of the linking relation. Structure on Stenius' analysis is, in short, the relation that relates the relational element of a fact to its terms. This sort of analysis is objectionable since it interposes a second relation between a relation and its terms. It is, nevertheless, a tempting analysis. For by covertly replacing the multitude of relations by a single relation, the linking relation, it provides neat solutions to two problems faced by the picture theory of language.[2] One problem is

---

[1] *Wittgenstein's "Tractatus"*, Oxford, 1960, especially ch. vii.

[2] One must distinguish an *arrangement itself* from a *kind of arrangement*. Being

how to picture in one dimension more than a single relation between objects. If there *is* only a single relation, this problem is easily solved. A second problem is to explain the identity of structure that obtains between a true proposition and the fact that it pictures. Again, if there is only a single relation, then the elements of a true proposition are related in exactly the same way as the objects they go proxy for; and this problem also finds a neat solution.

As a solution of the paradox the type of theory offered by Evans and worked out consistently by Stenius is unsatisfactory. But how does it stand as an interpretation of Wittgenstein? It is clear from the *Notebooks* that Wittgenstein at one time in his life held the sort of theory Stenius outlines. During the pre-*Tractatus* period Wittgenstein held the two basic propositions upon which Stenius' theory rests: that relations and properties as well as individuals are objects (*Notebooks*, 16.6.15, par. 5) and that the predicate of a proposition is not a word or an expression but a relation of one or more places. This last point is made again and again in the early "Notes on Logic" and "Notes Dictated to G. E. Moore in Norway" (*Notebooks*, pp. 93–118). Wittgenstein says, for example, that "in 'aRb', 'R' is *not* a symbol, but *that* 'R' is between one name and another symbolizes" (*Notebooks*, p. 108; cf. p. 121, ll. 14–21). There are strong reasons, however, for holding that when Wittgenstein wrote the *Tractatus*, he had changed his mind on the first matter.[1] The key passage in the *Tractatus*—one, incidentally, for which there is no parallel in the *Notebooks*—is 2.03: "In a state of affairs objects [hang in] one another like the links of a chain." This simile, if taken seriously, cannot be reconciled with the notion that one of the objects of a state of affairs is a relation. First of all, to suppose that a relation is to its terms as one link of a chain is to other links is to violate the theory of types, since links of a chain are all of the same type whereas a relation is one type higher than its terms. Secondly, in an *atomic* state of affairs, which is what Wittgenstein is discussing in this passage, there

[1] See especially Irving M. Copi's review of Stenius' book in the *Philosophical Review*, 72, 1963, p. 382.

---

north of is one kind of spatial arrangement. That Seattle is north of Portland is a particular arrangement of this kind. That Portland is north of Seattle is a possible but not an actual arrangement of the same kind. Now the word "relation" sometimes means "kind of arrangement"; at other times it means simply "arrangement". Thus we say that being north of is one relation, being west of, another. But we also speak of the relation of Seattle to Portland, namely, that Seattle is north of Portland. This double use of the word "relation" may be partially responsible for the philosophical puzzle of how the terms of a relation are related to the relation itself. In this paper, to avoid prolixity, I use "relation" in both senses; but I think it will always be clear from the context in which sense the word is being used. In counting relations one will, naturally, get different answers depending upon the sense of "relation". In speaking in the text of a single relation I mean obviously a kind of arrangement.

is only one relation. Consider now a state of affairs in which there is a triadic relation. Such a relation is not at all like a link of a chain, for a link of a chain joins at most two other links whereas a triadic relation ties together three terms. A triadic relation is more like a key ring that holds three keys than a link of a chain. Thus if we suppose that relations are objects, the simile collapses completely.

Is the world of the *Tractatus*, then, a world without relations? No. Wittgenstein simply conceives relations differently from the way they have usually been conceived. In the chain metaphor the relation is that of hanging together, and this is what Wittgenstein calls structure: "The determinate way in which objects [hang together] in a state of affairs is the structure of the state of affairs" (2.032). So relations go over into structure. Monadic relations or qualities, however, do seem to disappear since the relation of hanging together is a polyadic relation. Thus while Stenius and the early Wittgenstein distinguish three kinds of thing within a state of affairs—one or more individuals, a relation of one or more places, and a structure—the Wittgenstein of the *Tractatus* distinguishes only two—two or more individuals and a structure. How does this affect Wittgenstein's analysis of predicates in the *Tractatus*? One would expect the predicate of a proposition to disappear completely, its rôle being taken by the arrangement of names. And this is, indeed, the interpretation adopted by two commentators on the *Tractatus*: Irving M. Copi and G. E. M. Anscombe.[1]

The interpretations of Anscombe and Copi, which differ slightly but significantly, rest upon the premiss that in the *Tractatus* qualities and relations are not kinds of objects. Since a fully analysed elementary proposition consists entirely of names (4.22, 5.55) and names are proxies for objects (3.203, 3.22), they conclude that no word or expression in a fully analysed elementary proposition refers to a quality or a relation. A relation of objects is expressed by a relation of their names. But how can the many different relations of objects be pictured by the single relation of names, that of concatenation? Both solve this problem by simply denying that this is the only relation of names. Copi says, for example:

Any relation of objects, spatial or non-spatial, can be represented by a spatial relation of the names of those objects. That a has relation R to b can be represented by writing "a" some specified distance and direction from "b", and that a has some different relation R' to b can be presented by writing "a" some different distance and direction from "b".[2]

[1] Copi, "Objects, Properties, and Relations in the *Tractatus*", *Mind*, 67, 1958; Anscombe, *An Introduction to Wittgenstein's Tractatus*, London, 1959, ch. 7; "Mr Copi on Objects, Properties and Relations in the *Tractatus*", *Mind*, 68, 1959 [present volume].
[2] *Mind*, 67, 1958, 157-8 [p. 179].

And Anscombe even produces an illustration of what a completely analysed elementary proposition might look like:

$$\begin{array}{ccc} & c & d \\ a & & b \\ & e & \end{array} \quad {}_1$$

On this reading a fully analysed elementary proposition does not differ in any respect from a diagram or a map.

Anscombe's interpretation differs in one respect from Copi's. Copi supposes that when the elementary proposition "*aRb*" is fully analysed and set out diagrammatically, the diagram will contain only the two names "*a*" and "*b*". Anscombe correctly points out that the predicate "*R*" may conceal further names which will emerge on analysis. Anscombe's diagram above might, for example, be the analysis of "*aRb*". This point is an inference from two passages in the *Tractatus* taken in conjunction. Wittgenstein makes the comment that every atomic state of affairs might consist of infinitely many objects (4.2211), and then only a few lines later he says that he writes elementary propositions as functions of names, for example, "*fx*", "*ϕ(x,y)*", and so forth (4.24). The implication is that the predicate of the elementary proposition "*fa*" may conceal infinitely many names.[2] This is a good point the significance of which Anscombe does not see.

The sort of solution given by Anscombe and Copi resolves the paradox of the picture theory by denying one of the propositions composing it. According to it the only propositions that are completely and directly pictorial are not linear. This is an unsatisfactory solution for it, in effect, concedes that the picture theory is inconsistent with a characteristic feature of language. There may indeed be this inconsistency, but if so, this means that the picture theory is untenable.[3]

Have Anscombe and Copi interpreted the *Tractatus* correctly? There is very little direct evidence either for or against their theory as an interpretation. The main passage cited by both Copi and Anscombe in support of their interpretation is 3.1431: "The essence of a propositional sign is very clearly seen if we imagine one composed of spatial objects (such as tables, chairs, and books) instead of written signs. Then the spatial arrangement of these things will express the sense of the proposition." But this passage is not decisive. The point Wittgenstein is making in the entire passage 3.14–3.144 is that a

---

[1] *Mind*, 68 (1959), 404 [p. 187].

[2] Ibid. See also *An Introduction to Wittgenstein's Tractatus*, pp. 99–102.

[3] Incidentally, by this solution what would a spoken proposition be like? Would pitch be essential?

propositional sign is a fact and not a name or a jumble of names.[1] A propositional sign formed by putting a number of spatial objects all in a line (say, a book on a chair and the chair on a table) illustrates this point perfectly. So this passage is consistent with the view that in the *Tractatus* propositions are linear structures.

Perhaps Wittgenstein attached no importance to the linear character of propositions. There is an interesting comment on this matter in *The Brown Book*: "Though from certain points of view we should call the linear character of the sentence merely external and inessential, this character and similar ones play a great rôle in what as logicians we are inclined to say about sentences and propositions" (I, 41). When Wittgenstein wrote the *Tractatus* did he consider this linear character external and inessential or, writing as a logician, did he allow it to play a great rôle? There is one passage in the *Notebooks* that suggests that Wittgenstein distinguished propositions from pictures on the basis of the linear character of the former: "It can be said that, while we are not certain of being able to turn all situations into pictures on paper, still we are certain that we can portray all *logical* properties of situations in a two-dimensional script" (29.9.14). Since Wittgenstein speaks of a two-dimensional script, this appears to say the very opposite of what I say it says; but this is mere appearance. For, first, Wittgenstein is contrasting pictures on paper with portrayals in a two-dimensional script; but if a proposition were itself exactly like a diagram or map, there would be no contrast. Secondly, Wittgenstein in a passage written three days earlier asks: "What is the ground of our—certainly well founded—confidence that we shall be able to express any sense we like in our two-dimensional script?" (26.9.14). Now if the two-dimensional script Wittgenstein is talking about is *our* script, he must be referring to the familiar linear script of ordinary language and logical symbolism. Why, then, does he call it a two-dimensional script? Probably because *letters* and *words* are two-dimensional. Finally, in support of my reading of these passages, we need to recall that the theory of the *Notebooks* easily allows for the linear nature of propositions. Notice, incidentally, that Wittgenstein says a bit later: "It all depends on settling what distinguishes the proposition from the mere picture" (2.12.14). Jumping now from the *Notebooks* to the *Investigations*, we may note one passage that indicates rather strongly that in the *Tractatus* propositions are thought of as linear structures. Wittgenstein in the course of his discussion of logical atomism, a discussion which is meant naturally to embrace the *Tractatus*, devises a language game for which the account of language given by logical atomists is valid (48). He sets the stage by introducing two things:

---

[1] That is, not a *thing*.

first, names for coloured squares and, second, the arrangement of squares described by an arrangement of names. Now the interesting point is that matters are worked out in such a way that a linear arrangement of names describes a two-dimensional arrangement of squares. The sample proposition Wittgenstein writes out is a linear structure consisting entirely of names.

The considerations adduced in the last paragraph do not really count for very much. They are merely skirmishing points. The solid argument against the Anscombe-Copi interpretation is this. Anscombe and Copi hold that fully analysed elementary propositions *must* be two-dimensional diagrams: this is an essential and not an accidental feature of them. Now what I want to argue is that, even if it be allowed that an elementary proposition might be expressed by such a diagram, it cannot be an *essential* feature of an elementary proposition that it be two-dimensional. We need, first of all, to recall Wittgenstein's distinction between the essential and accidental features of a proposition:

3.34 A proposition possesses essential and accidental features. Accidental features are those that result from the particular way in which the propositional sign is produced. Essential features are those without which the proposition could not express its sense.

3.341 So what is essential in a proposition is what all propositions that can express the same sense have in common.
And similarly, in general, what is essential in a symbol is what all symbols that can serve the same purpose have in common.

3.3411 So one could say that the real name of an object was what all symbols that signified it had in common. Thus one by one, all kinds of composition would prove to be unessential to a name.

By an argument parallel to that by which it is shown that composition is unessential to a name it can be shown that the possession of two dimensions is unessential to an elementary proposition. Suppose that

$$b$$
$$a$$

is an elementary proposition written as Anscombe and Copi would have us write it. Now there are two relations in this diagram that are symbolic: that "*b*" is at a certain distance from "*a*" and that "*b*" is in a certain direction from "*a*". The state of affairs depicted by this diagram, on the other hand, being an *atomic* state of affairs, contains but a single relation. That is to say, what we have here is an atomic state of affairs pictured by a molecular state of affairs: a *Sachverhalt* pictured by a *Tatsache*. But just as it must be at least possible, no matter how impractical, for one simple object to serve as the name of another, so it must be possible for one atomic state of affairs to serve as the propositional sign that pictures a second. Consequently, the complexity endemic to a two-dimensional diagram cannot be an essential feature of an elementary proposition.

THE PARADOX RESOLVED

A satisfactory interpretation of the picture theory of the *Tractatus*—if I am correct so far—must embrace six propositions: that an elementary proposition consists solely of names, that a name stands for an object, that qualities and relations are not objects, that an elementary proposition is a linear structure, that it is also a picture in which a relation between objects is shown by a relation between names, and finally that a complete list of elementary propositions would express every possible relation between objects. The picture theory of the *Tractatus* is not limited to these six propositions—I have not, for example, mentioned the doctrines of analysis, of the logical independence of elementary propositions, or of the absolute simplicity of objects—but it is these six that seem especially difficult to reconcile with each other.

These six propositions, although difficult to reconcile, are not perhaps completely irreconcilable; for they are inconsistent, not among themselves, but only together with a seventh proposition. The seventh proposition is that the number of possible relations between objects is greater than the number of possible concatenations of their names. This proposition is obviously true for ordinary objects. For example: "Hitler Stalin" and "Stalin Hitler" exhaust the possible concatenations of the two names "Hitler" and "Stalin"; so if the first concatenation symbolizes, say, that Hitler hates Stalin and the second, consequently, that Stalin in turn hates Hitler, there will be no concatenation left to symbolize, say, that Hitler fears Stalin. But what is true for ordinary objects may or may not be true for Wittgenstein's simple objects. So the question needs to be raised whether this seventh proposition holds for Wittgenstein's simple objects. A rather satisfactory interpretation of the *Tractatus* can, in fact, be built upon the supposition that it does not hold.

Such an interpretation is not as simple-minded and as absurd as it may sound initially. For from the fact that there are many dyadic relations between two bodies such as the sun and the moon or between two cities, one cannot infer that there must also be many dyadic relations between two simple objects. Relational expressions of everyday language such as "north of" occur only in nonelementary propositions. The elementary propositions into which such a proposition will be resolved upon analysis may, for all we know, be quite complex. And, further, this interpretation is consistent even with there being a multitude of elementary propositions "aR_1b", "aR_2b", "aR_3b", and so forth. For here we need only recall Anscombe's point that the relational expressions in these propositions indicate that the proposition is not yet fully analysed. Upon analysis these propositions will on this interpretation turn out to be, say, "*acb*", "*abc*", "*acdbfg*", and so forth. So to suppose that the number of possible relations between Wittgenstein's simple objects is not greater than the number of possible concatenations of their names is at least not absurd.

Is there any support for such an interpretation? To begin with, this interpretation avoids the difficulties faced by the rival interpretations. This gives it some initial plausibility. Further, Wittgenstein's metaphor of logical space strongly suggests such an interpretation. Wittgenstein speaks of "a space of possible [atomic] states of affairs" (2.013). I take this to mean that a possible atomic state of affairs is the analogue of a point in space. An atomic state of affairs that is actual and not merely possible (an atomic *fact*) is the analogue of a material point (cf. *Notebooks*, 29.10.14, par. 6). Thus Wittgenstein likens a world of positive and negative facts to black spots on white paper (4.063, 6.341): a point represents a possible atomic state of affairs, a black point an existent atomic state of affairs, a white point a nonexistent atomic state of affairs. The co-ordinates of a geometrical point are numerals; those of a point in logical space are names. An elementary proposition asserts that a particular point in logical space is occupied; its denial is that it is empty. The logical product of a number of elementary propositions is like an equation of physics giving the exact location of all the matter in a particular area. The logical sum, on the other hand, is like an equation giving the size, shape, and location of the orbit of a planet: the planet occupies one point of the orbit at any one moment, but such an equation does not tell us which point. Now this metaphor supports my interpretation in this way. The number of points in space with the co-ordinates "*a*", "*b*", and "*c*" is the number of ordered triples of these three numerals. There are six such triples and six points. Thus the number of points with these co-ordinates does not exceed the number of linear arrangements of the co-ordinates. But this is precisely my supposition for the points in logical space, that the number of possible configurations of objects does not exceed the number of linear arrangements of the names of these objects. Thus this interpretation of Wittgenstein's picture theory fits his metaphor of logical space very neatly.[1]

[1] Stenius takes Wittgenstein's metaphor in a radically different way. See *Wittgenstein's "Tractatus"*, ch. iv. On Stenius' reading each point of logical space is a possible

The considerations of the last two paragraphs are far from conclusive. But they do establish, I believe, that this interpretation of the *Tractatus* is at least not an unreasonable one.

The idea that the number of possible atomic states of affairs is limited to the number that can be pictured linearly resolves the paradox within the framework of the *Tractatus*. But such a solution is not likely to rejuvenate the picture theory of language. For the paradox has only been resolved by shaping the world to fit our linguistic theory: we have cut the man to fit the bed. This is Wittgenstein's general strategy in the *Tractatus*, but it is none the better for that.

Three solutions of the paradox have been considered. The Evans-Stenius solution reinterprets the first proposition of the triad, the one about one-to-one correspondence. The Anscombe-Copi solution denies the second, that propositions are necessarily linear structures. And my interpretation of the *Tractatus* finds a way out through the third by imposing an unexpected limitation on the number of atomic states of affairs of any one form. The first two are unsatisfactory both as solutions of the paradox and as interpretations of the *Tractatus*. The third seems to me to be a good interpretation of the *Tractatus* but a bad solution of the paradox. In conclusion I want to present what I think is a good solution of the paradox. My solution, like the Evans-Stenius solution, looks for a way out through the first proposition of the triad; and also, like theirs, mine applies to any proposition of the form $R(x_1, x_2, \ldots x_n)$ and not simply to the very special elementary propositions of the *Tractatus*. My solution, unlike theirs, however, works only for n greater than one.

The dilemma facing the picture theory is this. Either a proposition contains a predicate or else it does not. (It is like "Seattle is west of Spokane" or like "Seattle Spokane".) If it does, there is no one-to-one correspondence between the parts of the proposition and the parts of the state of affairs expressed by the proposition. If it does not, then of the many possible relations between the things named by the names in the proposition, only a single one can be symbolized. This might be called the problem of the predicate.

If the proposition "Seattle is west of Spokane" contains one part too many for there to be a one-to-one correspondence between proposition and state of affairs, why not simply not count the

world, not a possible atomic state of affairs; and its logical co-ordinates are propositional signs, not names (see especially pp. 54–8). The co-ordinates of each point are thus the factors of a logical product that embraces each elementary proposition or its denial. An elementary proposition, however, resembles the set of co-ordinates of a geometrical point much more closely than a logical product does. A logical product is not affected by rearranging its factors; but an elementary proposition, like the set of co-ordinates of a geometrical point, *is* affected by rearrangement.

predicate? Would this be cheating? This is the question I want to consider.

Take maps. Here, surely, is the ideal case of a one-to-one correspondence between symbols and state of affairs symbolized. Is the case, however, so ideal? If we think so, we are ignoring certain symbols customarily found on maps: the arrow and the scale. But both of these, we want to reply, are written in the margin: this is why they can be ignored. Why, however, do we feel that they are, so to speak, written in the margin? The reason, I think, is that the arrow does not enter into a triadic relation with the symbols for, say, Seattle and Spokane. The arrow, rather, indicates how the dyadic relation between these two symbols is to be taken: if the one symbol is left of the other, the arrow indicates (perhaps) that this relation pictures the one city as west of the other.

The predicate of a proposition, I want to argue, functions very much like the arrow on a map. The following discussion makes the best sense if we think of propositions written in logical notation. Let us take as our sample proposition "sWk" ("Seattle is west of Spokane"). One point that has been often repeated in this paper is that the order of symbols in a proposition is itself symbolic: "sWk" and "kWs" are different propositions. A second point, which has not been made, is that we get different propositions only if we rearrange names; if we change the position of the predicate, we get either a different notation ("Wsk") or nonsense ("skW"). The position of the names in a proposition symbolizes something; the position of the predicate does not. This suggests that the predicate of the proposition "sWk", like the arrow of a map, does not enter into a triadic relation with the two names. It would make sense to write the predicate first followed by a colon: "$W: sk$". The predicate indicates, as this notation suggests, how the relation between the two names is to be taken: that "s" is left of "k" shows Seattle as west of Spokane, and that it shows this is indicated by "$W:$". Every proposition of the form $R(x_1, x_2, \ldots x_n)$, where n is greater than one, is literally a minimum map. Thus there is as much of a one-to-one correspondence between a proposition and the corresponding state of affairs as there is between a map and its corresponding state of affairs. Surely, this is as much as one can demand of the picture theory of language.

I once thought that this sort of theory could be found in the *Tractatus*, but it does not seem possible to reconcile the notion that a fully analysed elementary proposition contains a predicate with Wittgenstein's statement that "an elementary proposition consists of names. It is a nexus, a concatenation, of names" (4.22). This passage strongly implies that elementary propositions consist of names *alone*. Wittgenstein at one place does discuss two symbols that are a bit like

391

David Keyt

the arrow on a map, the sharp and flat symbols in musical notation (4.013).[1] But he does not appear to have any special theory regarding them.

[1] Cf. G. E. Moore, "Wittgenstein's Lectures in 1930-33", *Mind*, 63 1954, p. 12; reprinted in *Philosophical Papers*, London, 1959, p. 264.

Bibliography

I. *Wittgenstein's Works:*

W1 "Extracts from Letters to Russell", in W4, Appendix III.

W2 "Notes on Logic", *Journal of Philosophy*, 54 (1957), pp. 231–45. Repr. with corrections in W4, Appendix I.

W3 "Notes Dictated to G. E. Moore in Norway", in W4, Appendix II.

W4 *Notebooks, 1914–1916*, ed. by G. H. von Wright and G. E. M. Anscombe, trans. by G. E. M. Anscombe, Oxford: Blackwell, 1961.

W5 *Tractatus Logico-Philosophicus (Logisch-Philosophische Abhandlung).* German version appeared in *Annalen der Naturphilosophie* (Leipzig), 44 (1921), pp. 185–262.

(*a*) Trans. into English by C. K. Ogden and F. P. Ramsey, London: Kegan Paul, 1922.

(*b*) Trans. into Chinese, *Ming Li Lun*, by Chang Shên-Fu, in Che-hsüeh p'ing-lun (*The Philosophical Review*), Peking, vol. 1, no. 5 (1927), pp. 53–98, and vol. 1, no. 6 (1928), pp. 31–80.

(*c*) Trans. into Italian with critical introduction and notes by G. C. M. Colombo, Archivum Philosophicum Aloisianum, Serie III, vol. I, Milano-Roma: Bocca, 1954.

(*d*) Trans. into Spanish by T. Galván, Madrid: Revista de Occidente, 1957.

(*e*) Trans. into Yugoslavian by G. Petrović, Sarajevo: Veselin Masleša, 1960.

(*f*) Trans. into French (together with *Philosophical Investigations*) by P. Klossowoski, Paris: Gallimard, 1961.

(*g*) Trans. into English by D. F. Pears and B. F. McGuinness, London: Routledge and Kegan Paul, 1961.

(*h*) Trans. into Swedish by Anders Wedberg, Stockholm: Orion/Bonniers, 1962.

(*i*) Trans. into Danish by David Favrholdt, Copenhagen: Gyldendal, 1963.

W6 "Some Remarks on Logical Form", *Knowledge, Experience and Realism, Proceedings of the Aristotelian Society*, sup. vol. 9 (1929), pp. 162–71. Repr. in present volume.

W7 Letter to the Editor, *Mind*, 42 (1933), pp. 415–16.

W8 *The Blue and Brown Books*, Oxford: Blackwell, 1958.

Bibliography

W9 *Philosophical Investigations*, ed. by G. E. M. Anscombe and R. Rhees, trans. by G. E. M. Anscombe, Oxford: Blackwell, 1953; 2nd ed., 1958.

   (*a*) Trans. into French (together with *Tractatus*). See W5 (*f*).

W10 *Remarks on the Foundations of Mathematics*, ed. by G. H. von Wright, R. Rhees, and G. E. M. Anscombe, trans. by G. E. M. Anscombe, Oxford: Blackwell, 1956.

W11 *Schriften: Tractatus logico-philosophicus, Tagebücher 1914–1916, Philosophische Untersuchungen*, Frankfurt/Main: Suhrkamp-Verlag, 1960.

W12 "A Lecture on Ethics" (1929), *Philosophical Review*, 74 (1965), pp. 3–12.

II. *Books and Articles:*

Aldrich, V. C., "Pictorial Meaning, Picture-Thinking, and Wittgenstein's Theory of Aspects", *Mind*, 67 (1958), pp. 70–9.

Allaire, Edwin B., (1) "Tractatus 6.3751", *Analysis*, 19 (1958–9), pp. 100–5. Repr. in present volume.

—— (2) *A Critical Examination of Wittgenstein's 'Tractatus'*, Ann Arbor, Michigan: Univ. Microfilms, 1960.

—— (3) "Types and Formation Rules: A Note on *Tractatus* 3.334", *Analysis*, 21 (1960), pp. 14–16.

—— (4) "Existence, Independence, and Universals", *Philosophical Review*, 69 (1960), pp. 485–96. Repr. in (Allaire *et al.*).

—— (5) "The Tractatus: Nominalistic or Realistic?" in (Allaire *et al.*), pp. 148–65. Repr. in present volume.

Allaire, Edwin B., *et al.*, *Essays in Ontology*, Iowa Publications in Philosophy, vol. i, Hague: Nijhoff, 1963.

Anscombe, G. E. M., (1) "Note on the English Version of Wittgenstein's *Philosophische Untersuchungen*", *Mind*, 62 (1953), pp. 521–2

—— (2) "Misinformation: What Wittgenstein Really Said", *Tablet* (London), Apr. 17, 1954, p. 373.

—— (3) Letter, *Tablet* (London), May 15, 1954, pp. 478–9.

—— (4) "Mr. Copi on Objects, Properties and Relations in the *Tractatus*", *Mind*, 68 (1959), p. 404. Repr. in present volume.

—— (5) *An Introduction to Wittgenstein's Tractatus*, London: Hutchinson, 1959. 2nd ed., 1963.

—— (6) Letter, *Times Literary Supplement*, May 29, 1959, p. 321.

Ayer, Alfred J., (1) "Atomic Propositions", *Analysis*, 1 (1933), pp. 2–6.

—— (2) ed., *Logical Positivism*, Glencoe, Illinois: Free Press, 1959.

Ayer, Alfred J., *et al.*, *The Revolution in Philosophy*, London: Macmillan, 1956.

Bachmann, I., *et al.*, *Ludwig Wittgenstein, Schriften: Beiheft*, contributions by I. Bachmann, M. Cranston, J. Mora, P. Feyerabend, E. Heller, B. Russell, G. von Wright, Frankfurt/Main: Suhrkamp-Verlag, 1960.

Barone, Francesco, (1) "Il solipsismo linguistico di Ludwig Wittgenstein", *Filosofia*, Rivista trimestrale, 2 (1951), pp. 543–70.

—— (2) *Il neopositivismo logico*, Torino: Edizioni di 'Filosofia', 1953.

Bibliography

Barone, Francesco, (3) "Ludwig Wittgenstein", *Enciclopedia filosofia*, Venezia: Instituto per la callaborazione culturale, 1957.

Beard, Robert W., "*Tractatus* 4.24", *Southern Journal of Philosophy*, 2 (1964), pp. 14–17.

Bell, Julian, "An Epistle on the Subject of the Ethical and Aesthetic Beliefs of Herr Ludwig Wittgenstein", in (Vines). Repr. in present volume.

Bell, Richard H., "Names and the Picture Theory in Use", *Graduate Review of Philosophy* (University of Minnesota), 4 (1962), pp. 20–8.

Bennett, Jonathan, Reviews of (Copi (1)), (Anscombe (4)), (Evans (2)), and (Copi (2)), *Journal of Symbolic Logic*, 27 (1962), pp. 118–20.

Bergmann, Gustav, (1) "Logical Positivism, Language, and the Reconstruction of Metaphysics", *Rivista Critica di Storia della Filosofia*, 8 (1953), pp. 453–84. Repr. in (Bergmann (2)).

—— (2) *The Metaphysics of Logical Positivism*, New York: Longmans, Green and Co., 1954.

—— (3) "Intentionality", *Semantica, Archivio di Filosofia*, Roma: Bocca, 1955, pp. 177–216. Repr. in (Bergmann (5)).

—— (4) "The Revolt against Logical Atomism", *Philosophical Quarterly*, 7 (1957), pp. 323–39, and 8 (1958), pp. 1–13. Repr. in (Bergmann (5)).

—— (5) *Meaning and Existence*, Madison: Univ. of Wisconsin Press, 1960.

—— (6) "The Glory and the Misery of Ludwig Wittgenstein", in (Bergmann (8)), pp. 225–41. Repr. in present volume. Italian trans., "La Gloria e la Miseria di Ludwig Wittgenstein", *Revista di Filosofia*, 52 (1961), pp. 387–406.

—— (7) "Stenius on the Tractatus: A Special Review", *Theoria*, 29 (1963), pp. 176–204. Repr. in (Bergmann (8)).

—— (8) *Logic and Reality*, Madison: Univ. of Wisconsin Press, 1964.

Bernstein, Richard J., "Wittgenstein's Three Languages", *Review of Metaphysics*, 15 (1961), pp. 278–98. Repr. in present volume.

Black, Max, (1) *The Nature of Mathematics: A Critical Survey*, London: Routledge and Kegan Paul, 1933.

—— (2) "A Propos of 'Facts' ", *Analysis*, 1 (1934), pp. 39–43.

—— (3) "Some Problems Connected with Language", *Proceedings of the Aristotelian Society*, 39 (1939), pp. 43–68. Repr. in (Black (4)) and present volume.

—— (4) *Language and Philosophy: Studies in Method*, Ithica, N.Y.: Cornell Univ. Press, 1949.

—— (5) Review of (Plochman and Lawson), *Philosophical Review*, 72 (1963), pp. 265–6.

—— (6) Review of (W4), *Mind*, 73 (1964), pp. 132–41.

—— (7) *A Companion to Wittgenstein's 'Tractatus'*, Ithica: Cornell University Press, 1964.

Blanshard, Brand, *Reason and Analysis*, London: George Allen and Unwin; New York: Open Court, 1962.

Bochénski, I. M., *Europäische Philosophie der Gegenwart*, Berne: A. Franke A.G. Verlag, 1947. English trans. by D. Nicholl and K. Aschenbrenner, *Contemporary European Philosophy*, Berkeley and Los Angeles: Univ. of California Press, 1961.

Bogen, James, "Was Wittgenstein a Psychologist?" *Inquiry*, 7 (1964), pp. 374-8.

Braithwaite, Richard, (1) Editor's introduction to (Ramsey (6)).

—— (2) "Philosophy", *University Studies Cambridge 1933*, London: Nicholson and Watson Ltd, 1933, pp. 1-32.

Britton, Karl, (1) "Structure of Language and Structure of Fact", *Psyche* (London), 17 (1937), pp. 67-91.

—— (2) "Recollections of L. Wittgenstein", *Cambridge Journal*, 7 (1954), pp. 707-15.

—— (3) "Portrait of a Philosopher", *The Listener*, June 16, 1955, vol. 53, pp. 1071-2.

—— (4) "Erinnerungen an Wittgenstein", *Merkur*, 1957, pp. 1066-72.

Burkamp, W., *Wirklichkeit und Sinn*, Berlin: Junker und Dunnhaupt, 1938.

Campanale, D., (1) "Ludwig Wittgenstein: *Tractatus logico-philosophicus*", *Rassegna di Scienze filosofiche* (Napoli), 7 (1954), pp. 421-8.

—— (2) *Studi su Wittgenstein*, Bari: Adriatica Editrice, 1956.

Cappelletti, V., "L'imperativo del silenzio. Premessa a un-interpretazione dell' opera wittgensteiniana", *Proceedings of the XII International Congress of Philosophy* (Venice and Padua, 1958), 12, pp. 55-61.

Carnap, Rudolf, *Logische Syntax der Sprache*, Vienna: Springer, 1934. English trans. by A. Smeaton, *Logical Syntax of Language*, London: Kegan Paul; New York: Harcourt Brace, 1937.

Cassirer, Eva, Review of (Anscombe (5)), *British Journal for the Philosophy of Science*, 14 (1964), pp. 359-66.

Chadwick, J. A., (1) "Logical Constants", *Mind*, 36 (1927), pp. 1-11.

—— (2) "On Propositions belonging to Logic", *Mind*, 36 (1927), pp. 347-53.

Charlesworth, Maxwell John, *Philosophy and Linguistic Analysis*, Duquesne Studies, Philosophical Series, 9, Pittsburg: Duquesne Univ., 1959.

Colombo, Giancarlo, (1) Letter, *Tablet* (London), May 15, 1954, p. 478.

—— (2) "Epilogue on Wittgenstein", *Month*, 18 (1957), pp. 356-8.

Copi, Irving M., (1) "Objects, Properties, and Relations in the *Tractatus*", *Mind*, 67 (1958), pp. 145-65. Repr. in present volume.

—— (2) "Tractatus 5.542", *Analysis*, 18 (1958), pp. 102-4. Repr. in present volume.

—— (3) Review of (Stenius (4)), *Philosophical Review*, 72 (1963), pp. 382-90.

—— (4) Review of (W4), *Journal of Philosophy*, 60 (1963), pp. 764-8.

Copleston, F., *Contemporary Philosophy*, Westminster, Maryland: Newman Press, 1956.

Cornforth, Maurice, (1) *Science versus Idealism*, London: Lawrence and Wishart, 1946.

—— (2) *In Defence of Philosophy*, London: Lawrence and Wishart, 1950.

Costello, Harry T., "Introduction to Wittgenstein's Notes on Logic", *Journal of Philosophy*, 54 (1957), pp. 230-1.

Daitz, Edna, "The Picture Theory of Meaning", *Mind*, 62 (1953), pp. 184-201. Repr. in (Flew) and present volume.

Bibliography

Daly, C. B., (1) "Logical Positivism, Metaphysics and Ethics, 1: Ludwig Wittgenstein", *Irish Theological Quarterly*, 23 (1956), pp. 111–50.

—— (2) "Wittgenstein's 'Objects' ", *Irish Theological Quarterly*, 23 (1956), pp. 413–14.

—— (3) "New Light on Wittgenstein", *Philosophical Studies* (St Patrick's College, Maynooth, Ire.), pt. i, 10 (1960), pp. 5–49; pt. ii, 11 (1961), pp. 28–62.

Delius, H., "Was sich überhaupt sagen lässt, lässt sich Klar sagen. Gedanken zu einer Formulierung Ludwig Wittgensteins", *Archiv für Philosophie* (Stuttgart), 8 (1958), pp. 211–54.

Dell'oro, Angiolo Maros, *Fecondità e sterilatà intellettuale*, Padova: Cedam, 1959.

Drudis Baldrich, R., "Consideraciones en torno a la obra de Wittgenstein", *Revista de Filosofia*, 17 (1958), pp. 283–6.

Drury, M. O'C., "Ludwig Wittgenstein: a symposium, II", *The Listener*, Jan. 28, 1960, vol. 63, pp. 163–4.

Eichner, Hans, Review of (W5 (*g*)), *Dialogue*, 1 (1962), pp. 212–16.

"The Essential Nature of Propositions", review of (W4), *Times Literary Supplement*, vol. 60, Aug. 11, 1961, p. 528.

Evans, Ellis, (1) "Tractatus 3.1432", *Mind*, 64 (1955), pp. 259–60. Repr. in present volume.

—— (2) "About 'aRb' ", *Mind*, 68 (1959), pp. 535–8. Repr. in present volume.

Fabri, Albrecht, "Ludwig Wittgenstein", *Merkur*, 7 (Dec., 1953), pp. 1193–1196.

Farber, Marvin, (ed.) *Philosophic Thought in France and the United States*, Buffalo: Buffalo Univ. Press, 1950.

Favrholdt, David, (1) *An Interpretation and Critique of Wittgenstein's Tractatus*, Copenhagen: Munksgaard, 1964.

—— (2) "Tractatus 5.542", *Mind*, 73 (1964), pp. 557–62.

Feibleman, James K., *Inside the Great Mirror: A Critical Examination of the Philosophy of Russell, Wittgenstein and their Followers*, Hague: Nijhoff, 1958.

Feyerabend, Paul, (1) "Ludwig Wittgenstein", *Merkur*, 1954, pp. 1021–38.

—— (2) "Wittgenstein und die Philosophie. 2. Teil", *Wissenschaft und Weltbild*, 1954, pp. 283–7.

Feys, R., "La Raisonnement termes de faits", *Revue Neo-Scholastique*, 1928, p. 259; 1929, pp. 216–17.

Ficker, Ludwig, "Rilke und der unbekannte Freund", *Der Brenner*, 1954.

Findlay, John H., "Wittgenstein's Philosophical Investigations", *Revue Internationale de la Philosophie*, 25 (1953), pp. 200–16.

Flew, Anthony, (ed.) *Essays in Conceptual Analysis*, London: Macmillan; New York: St Martin's Press, 1956.

Freunlich, Rudolf, "Logik und Mystik", *Zeitschrift für philosophische Forschung*, 7 (1953), pp. 554–70.

Gabriel, L., "Logische Magie. Ein Nachwort zum Thema Wittgenstein", *Wissenschaft und Weltbild*, 1954, pp. 288–93.

Gasking, D. A. T., "Anderson and the Tractatus Logico-Philosophicus:

An Essay in Philosophical Translation", *Australasian Journal of Philosophy*, 27 (1949), pp. 1–26.

G(asking), D. A. T., and A. C. J(ackson), "Ludwig Wittgenstein", *Australasian Journal of Philosophy*, 29 (1951), pp. 73–80.

Geach, P. T., (1) Review of (W5 (*c*)), *Philosophical Review*, 66 (1957), pp. 556–9.

—— (2) Review of (W5 (*g*)), *Philosophical Review*, 72 (1963), pp. 264–5.

Griffin, James, *Wittgenstein's Logical Atomism*, Oxford: Clarendon Press, 1964.

Hadot, P., "Réflections sur les limits du language à propos du 'Tractatus logico-philosophicus' de Wittgenstein", *Revue de Métaphysique et de Morale*, 64 (1959), pp. 468–84.

Hamburg, Carl H., "Whereof One Cannot Speak", *Journal of Philosophy*, 50 (1953), pp. 662–4.

Hamlyn, D. W., "Categories, Formal Concepts and Metaphysics", *Philosophy*, 34 (1959), pp. 111–24.

Hannay, Alastair, "Was Wittgenstein a Psychologist?" *Inquiry*, 7 (1964), pp. 379–86.

Harris, Errol E., *Nature, Mind and Modern Science*, London: George Allen and Unwin; New York: Macmillan, 1954.

Harrison, Frank R., "Notes on Wittgenstein's Use of 'das Mystische' ", *Southern Journal of Philosophy*, 1 (1963), pp. 3–9.

Hartnack, Justus, *Wittgenstein og den moderne filosofi*, Copenhagen: Gyldendal, 1960. Trans. from Danish into German by R. Logstrup, *Wittgenstein und die moderne Philosophie*, Stuttgart: W. Kohlhammer, 1962.

Hawkins, D., "Wittgenstein and the Cult of Language", Aquinas Paper no. 27, London: Blackfriars Publications, 1957.

Heller, Erich, (1) "Ludwig Wittgenstein. Unphilosophische Betrachtungen", *Merkur*, 1959, pp. 1101–20.

—— (2) "Ludwig Wittgenstein: a symposium, I", *Listener*, Jan. 28, 1960, p. 163.

Hintikka, Jaakko, (1) "Identity, Variables, and Impredicative Definitions", *Journal of Symbolic Logic*, 21 (1956), pp. 225–45.

—— (2) "On Wittgenstein's 'Solipsism' ", *Mind*, 67 (1958), pp. 88–91. Repr. in present volume.

Horgby, Ingvar, "The Double Awareness in Heidegger and Wittgenstein", *Inquiry*, 2 (1959), pp. 235–64.

Irving, John A., "Mysticism and the Limits of Communication", in (Stiernotte).

J(ackson), A. C., and D. A. T. G(asking), "Ludwig Wittgenstein", *Australasian Journal of Philosophy*, 29 (1951), pp. 73–80.

Jarvis, Judith, (1) "Professor Stenius on the *Tractatus*", *Journal of Philosophy*, 58 (1961), pp. 584–96. Repr. in present volume.

—— (2) Review of (W5 (*g*)), *Journal of Philosophy*, 59 (1962), pp. 332–5.

Jarvis, Judith, and Frederic T. Sommers, Review of (Anscombe (5)), *Philosophy*, 36 (1961), pp. 374–6.

Jorgensen, Jörgen, (1) *A Treatise of Formal Logic*, Copenhagen: Munksgaard; London: Humphrey Milford, Oxford Univ. Press, 1931.

Bibliography

Jorgensen, Jörgen, (2) *Den logiske empirsmes udvikling* (The Development of Logical Empiricism), Copenhagen: Ejnar Munksgaard, 1948.
—— (3) *The Development of Logical Empiricism, International Encyclopedia of Unified Science*, vol. 2, no. 9, Chicago: Univ. of Chicago Press, 1951.

Jünger, Friedrich Georg, "Satzsinn und Satzbedeutung. Gedanken zu den 'Schriften' von Ludwig Wittgenstein", *Merkur*, 15 (1961), pp. 1009–1023. Repr. in Jünger, *Sprache und Denken*, Frankfurt/M., 1962.

Kaufmann, Felix, "Basic Issues in Logical Positivism", in (Farber), pp. 565–88.

Kempski, Jürgen von, (1) "Über Wittgenstein", *Neue deutsche Hefte*, 82 (1961), pp. 43–60.
—— (2) "Wittgenstein und analytische Philosophie", *Merkur*, 1961, pp. 664–76.

Kenny, A., "Aquinas and Wittgenstein", *The Downside Review* (Bath), 77 (1959), pp. 217–35.

Keyser, C. J., Short Notice of (W5 (a)), *Bulletin of the American Mathematical Society*, 30 (1924), pp. 179–81.

Keyt, David, (1) "Wittgenstein's Notion of an Object", *Philosophical Quarterly*, 13 (1963), pp. 13–25. Repr. in present volume.
—— (2) "Wittgenstein's Picture Theory of Language", *Philosophical Review*, 73 (1964), pp. 493–511. Repr. in present volume.

Klibansky, R., *Philosophy in Mid-Century*, 4 vols., Firenze: La Nuova Italia Editrice, 1958.

Kneale, Martha, and William Kneale, *The Development of Logic*, Oxford: Clarendon Press, 1962.

Kneale, William, "Truths of Logic", *Proceedings of the Aristotelian Society*, 46 (1945–6), pp. 207–34.

Kneale, William, and Martha Kneale, *The Development of Logic*, Oxford: Clarendon Press, 1962.

Kraft, Victor, (1) *Der Wiener Kreis. Der Ursprung des Neupositivismus,* Vienna: Springer, 1950. English trans. by A. Pap, *The Vienna Circle*, Philosophical Library, 1953.
—— (2) *Erkenntnislehre*, Wien: Springer-Verlag, 1960.

Kraft, Werner, "Ludwig Wittgenstein und Karl Kraus", *Die neue Rundschau*, 1961, pp. 812–44.

Laguna, Theodore de, Review of (W5 (a)), *Philosophical Review*, 33 (1924), pp. 103–9. Repr. in present volume.

Langer, Susan K., (1) "A Logical Study of Verbs", *Journal of Philosophy*, 24 (1927), pp. 120–9.
—— (2) *Philosophy in a New Key*, Cambridge, Mass.: Harvard Univ. Press, 1948.

Langford, C. H., "On Propositions belonging to Logic", *Mind*, 36 (1927), pp. 342–6.

Lawson, Jack B., and George Kimball Plochmann, *Terms in their Propositional Contexts in Wittgenstein's 'Tractatus': An Index*, Carbondale: Southern Illinois Univ. Press, 1962.

Lazerowitz, Morris, "Tautologies and the Matrix Method", *Mind*, 46 (1937), pp. 191–205.

Bibliography

Levi, Albert William, *Philosophy and the Modern World*, Bloomington: Indiana Univ. Press, 1959.

"The Limits of What Can Be Said" (review of Stenius (4)), *Times Literary Supplement*, vol. 59, Dec. 23, 1960, p. 831.

Lindemann, H., " 'El Círculo de Viena' y la filosofía científica", *Minerva* (Buenos Aires), 1 (1944), pp. 123–51.

McCall, Storrs, Review of (Maslow (1)), *Dialogue*, 2 (1963), pp. 114–15.

Mace, C., *British Philosophy in Mid-Century*, London: George Allen and Unwin, 1957.

McGill, V. F., "An Evaluation of Logical Positivism", *Science and Society*, 1 (1936–7), pp. 45–80.

McGuinness, B. F., "Pictures and Form in Wittgenstein's Tractatus", *Filosofia e Simbolismo* (*Archivio di Filosofia*), Roma: Bocca, 1956, pp. 207–28. Repr. in present volume.

MacIntyre, Alasdair, "Guide through a Maze" (review of Black (7)), *The Guardian*, Oct. 23, 1964, p. 13.

McTaggart, J. Ellis, "Propositions Applicable to Themselves", *Mind*, 32 (1923), pp. 462–4.

Malcolm, Norman, (1) *Ludwig Wittgenstein: A Memoir*, Oxford and New York: Oxford Univ. Press, 1958. Trans. into German by A. Sjögren, *Ludwig Wittgenstein, Ein Erinnerungsbuch*, München-Wien: Oldenbourg, 1961.

—— (2) "Ludwig Wittgenstein: a symposium, III", *The Listener*, Feb. 4, 1960, vol. 63, pp. 207–8.

Maslow, Alexander, (1) *A Study in Wittgenstein's 'Tractatus'*, Berkeley and Los Angeles: University of California Press, 1961.

—— (2) Letter (concerning Rhees (4)), *Philosophical Review*, 73 (1964), p. 290.

Mays, W., (1) "Note on Wittgenstein's Manchester Period", *Mind*, 64 (1955), pp. 247–8.

—— (2) "Wittgenstein's Manchester Period", *Manchester Guardian*, March 24, 1961, p. 10.

Metz, Rudolf, *Die philosophischen Strömungen der Gegenwart in Grossbrittanien*, 2 vols., Leipzig, 1935. English trans. by J. Harvey, J. Jessup, and H. Sturt, *A Hundred Years of British Philosophy*, London: George Allen and Unwin; New York: Macmillan, 1938.

Moore, George Edward, (1) "An Autobiography", in (Schilpp (1)), pp. 1–39.

—— (2) "Wittgenstein's Lectures in 1930–33", *Mind*; pt. i, 63 (1954), pp. 1–15; pt. ii, pp. 289–316; pt. iii, 64 (1955), pp. 1–27. Also, "Two Corrections", *Mind*, 64 (1955), p. 264. Repr. in (Moore (3)).

—— (3) *Philosophical Papers*, London: George Allen and Unwin, 1959.

—— (4) *The Commonplace Book of G. E. Moore, 1919–1953*, ed. by C. Lewy, London: George Allen and Unwin; New York: Macmillan, 1962.

Moore, Willis, "Structure in Sentence and in Fact", *Philosophy of Science*, 5 (1938), pp. 81–8. Repr. in present volume.

Mora, José Ferrater, (1) *Diccionario de filosofia*, 3rd ed., Buenos Aires: Editorial Sudamericana, 1951.

Mora, José Ferrater, (2) "Wittgenstein, a Symbol of Troubled Times",
Journal for Philosophy and Phenomenological Research, 14 (1953), pp.
89–96.

Morrison, James C., *Meaning and Truth in Wittgenstein's Tractatus*, dis·
sertation, Pennsylvania State University, 1964.

Muirhead, J. (ed.), *Contemporary British Philosophy*, London: George
Allen and Unwin; New York: Macmillan, 1924.

Mure, G. R. C., *Retreat from Truth*, Oxford: Blackwell, 1958.

Nerlich, G. C., (1) Review of (Stenius (4)), *Philosophical Books*, 1 (1960),
pp. 13–16.

—— (2) Review of (Maslow (1)), *Philosophical Books*, 3 (1962), pp. 10–11.

Nygren, Anders, "From Atomism to Contexts of Meaning in Philosophy",
in *Philosophical Essays Dedicated to Gunnar Aspelin*, Lund: GWK
Gleerup bokförlag, 1963, pp. 122–36.

O'Brian, George Dennis, *Meaning and Fact in the Philosophy of Wittgenstein*, dissertation, University of Chicago, 1961.

Ogden, C. K., and I. A. Richards. *The Meaning of Meaning*, London: K.
Paul, Trench, Trubner; New York: Harcourt Brace, 1923; 6th ed.,
1953.

Palmer, H., "The Other Logical Constant", *Mind*, 67 (1958), pp. 50–9.

"The Passionate Philosopher", *Times Literary Supplement*, May 1, 1959,
pp. 249–50.

Passmore, John, *A Hundred Years of Philosophy*, London: Duckworth, 1957.

Pauler, A., Logikai alapelv és mathematikai axióma (Logisches Grund-
prinzip und mathematisches Axiom), *Athenaeum*, 22 (1936), pp. 18–78.

Pears, D. F., "Logical Atomism: Russell and Wittgenstein", in (Ayer,
et al.).

Pinsent, David, "Excerpts from the Diary of David Pinsent, 1912–14", on
deposit at Trinity College (Cambridge).

Pitcher, George, *The Philosophy of Wittgenstein*, Englewood Cliffs, N.J.:
Prentice-Hall, 1964.

Plochmann, George Kimball, "A Note on Harrison's Notes on 'Das
Mystiche' ", *Southern Journal of Philosophy*, 2 (1964), pp. 130–2.

Plochmann, George Kimball, and Jack B. Lawson. See (Lawson and
Plochmann).

Popper, Karl R., (1) "Ein Kriterium des empirischen Charakters theo-
retischer Systeme", *Erkenntnis (Journal of Unified Science)*, 3 (1933),
pp. 426–7.

—— (2) *Logik der Forschung*, Vienna, 1935. English trans., *The Logic of
Scientific Discovery*, New York: Basic Books, 1959.

—— (3) *The Open Society and Its Enemies*, vol. 2, London: Routledge and
Kegan Paul, 1945; 2nd ed., 1952; 3rd ed., 1957; 4th ed., 1962.

—— (4) "The Nature of Philosophical Problems and their Roots in
Science", *British Journal for the Philosophy of Science*, 3 (1952), pp.
124–56. Repr. in (Popper (6)).

—— (5) "Philosophy of Science: A Personal Report", in (Mace), pp.
155–91.

—— (6) *Conjectures and Refutations: the Growth of Scientific Knowledge*,
London and New York: Basic Books, 1962.

Bibliography

Preti, G., "Realismo ontologico e senso comune", *Rivista critica di storia della filosofia*, 8 (1953), pp. 533–44.

Proctor, George L., "Scientific Laws and Scientific Objects in the *Tractatus*", *British Journal for the Philosophy of Science*, 10 (1959), pp. 177–93. Repr. in present volume.

Quinton, Anthony, "Linguistic Analysis", in (Klibansky) vol. 2, pp. 146–202.

Ramsey, Frank P., (1) Review of (W5 (a)), *Mind*, 32 (1923), pp. 465–78. Repr. in (Ramsey (6)) and present volume.

—— (2) "Universals", *Mind*, 34 (1925), pp. 401–17. Repr. in (Ramsey (6)).

—— (3) "Mathematical Logic", *Mathematical Gazette*, 13 (1926–7), pp. 185–94. Repr. in (Ramsey (6)).

—— (4) "Facts and Propositions", *Proceedings of the Aristotelian Society*, sup. vol., 7 (1927), pp. 153–70. Repr. in (Ramsey (6)).

—— (5) "The Foundations of Mathematics", *Proceedings of the London Mathematical Society*, 25 (1926), pp. 338–84. Repr. in (Ramsey (6)).

—— (6) *The Foundations of Mathematics and Other Logical Essays*, London: Routledge and Kegan Paul, 1931.

Rescher, Nicholas, Review of (W5 (c)), *Modern Schoolman*, 33 (1956), pp. 120–2.

Review of (W5 (a)), *Times Literary Supplement*, 21 (1922), p. 854.

Rhees, Rush, (1) Review of (Cornforth (1)), *Mind*, 56 (1947), pp. 374–92.

—— (2) "Ludwig Wittgenstein: a symposium, IV", *The Listener*, Feb. 4, 1960, vol. 63, pp. 208–9.

—— (3) 'Miss Anscombe on the Tractatus", *Philosophical Quarterly*, 10 (1960), pp. 21–31.

—— (4) "The Tractatus: Seeds of Some Misunderstandings", *Philosophical Review*, 72 (1963), pp. 213–20.

—— (5) "Some Developments in Wittgenstein's View of Ethics", *Philosophical Review*, 74 (1965), pp. 17–26.

Richards, I. A., and C. K. Ogden. See (Ogden and Richards).

Riverso, E., *La costruzione interpretiva del mondo, analizzata dall epistemologia genetica*, Napoli: Istituto Editoriale del Mezzogiorno, 1956.

Russell, Bertrand, (1) "The Philosophy of Logical Atomism", *Monist*, 28 (1918), pp. 495–527; ibid., 29 (1919), pp. 33–63, 190–222, 345–80. Repr. by Department of Philosophy, Univ. of Minnesota, and in (Russell (6)).

—— (2) "Logical Atomism", in (Muirhead). Repr. in (Russell (6)) and (Ayer (2)).

—— (3) "The Limits of Empiricism", *Proceedings of the Aristotelian Society*, 36 (1935–6), pp. 131–50.

—— (4) *An Inquiry into Meaning and Truth*, London: George Allen and Unwin, 1940.

—— (5) "My Mental Development", in (Schilpp (2)).

—— (6) "Ludwig Wittgenstein", *Mind*, 60 (1951), pp. 297–8.

—— (7) *Logic and Knowledge*, ed. by R. C. Marsh, London: George Allen and Unwin, 1956.

—— (8) *My Philosophical Development*, New York: Simon and Schuster, 1959.

Bibliography

Russell, Bertrand, and Alfred North Whitehead, "Introduction to the Second Edition" and "Appendix C", *Principia Mathematica*, vol. 1, 2nd ed., Cambridge: Univ. Press, 1925.

Ryle, Gilbert, (1) "Logic and Professor Anderson", *Australasian Journal of Philosophy*, 28 (1950), pp. 137–53.

—— (2) "Ludwig Wittgenstein", *Analysis*, 12 (1951), pp. 1–9. Trans. into Italian by F. Rossi Landi, *Rivista di filosofia*, 43 (1952), pp. 186–93. English version reprinted in present volume.

Schilpp, Paul A. (ed.), (1) *The Philosophy of G. E. Moore*, Chicago: Tudor Publishing Co., 1942.

—— (2) *The Philosophy of Bertrand Russell*, New York: Tudor Publishing Co.. 1944.

Schwyzer, H. R. G., "Wittgenstein's Picture-Theory of Language", *Inquiry*, 5 (1962), pp. 46–64. Repr. in present volume.

Sellars, W., (1) "Being and Being Known", *Proceedings of the American Catholic Philosophical Association*, Washington, D.C.: Catholic Univ. of America, 1960, pp. 28–49.

—— (2) "Naming and Saying", *Philosophy of Science*, 29 (1962), pp. 7–26. Repr. in (Sellars (4)) and present volume.

—— (3) "Truth and 'Correspondence' ", *Journal of Philosophy*, 59 (1962), pp. 29–56.

—— (4) *Science, Perception and Reality*, London: Routledge and Kegan Paul, 1963.

Shapere, D., "Philosophy and the Analysis of Language", *Inquiry*, 3 (1960), pp. 29–48.

Shoemaker, S., "Logical Atomism and Language", *Analysis*, 20 (1960), pp. 49–52.

Shwayder, D. S., (1) *Wittgenstein's 'Tractatus': A Historical and Critical Commentary*, a thesis deposited in the Bodleian Library, Univ. of Oxford, 1954.

—— (2) Review of (Stenius (4)), *Mind*, 72 (1963), pp. 275–88. Repr. with omissions in present volume.

—— (3) "*Gegenstände* and Other Matters: Observations occasioned by a new Commentary on the *Tractatus*" (the commentary is (Griffin)), *Inquiry*, 7 (1964), pp. 387–413.

Sloman, Aaron, Review of (Griffin), *Philosophical Books*, 5 (1964), pp. 8–10.

Sommers, Frederick T., and Judith Jarvis, Review of (Anscombe (5)), *Philosophy*, 36 (1961), pp. 374–6.

Stebbing, L. Susan, (1) "Logical Positivism and Analysis", Annual Philosophical Lecture, *Proceedings of the British Academy*, 19 (1933), pp. 53–87.

—— (2) "Language and Misleading Questions", *Erkenntnis (Journal of Unified Science)*, 8 (1939), pp. 1–6.

Stenius, Erik, (1) "Verklighetens avbildning i språket", *Eros och Eris Kulturessäer tillegnade Rolf Lagerborg*, Stockholm, Bokforleget Natur och Kultur, 1944, pp. 286–97.

—— (2) "Den språkliga beskrivning", *Ajatus*, 16 (1950), pp. 69–101.

—— (3) "Linguistic Structure and the Structure of Experience", *Theoria*, 20 (1954), pp. 153–72.

Stenius, Erik, (4) *Wittgenstein's Tractatus: A Critical Exposition of Its Main Lines of Thought*, Oxford: Blackwell, 1960.

—— (5) "Uppbyggnaden av Wittgensteins Tractatus logico-philosophicus" (The Structure of Wittgenstein's *Tractatus Logico-Philosophicus*), *Ajatus*, vol. 19, pp. 121–38.

—— (6) "Wittgensteins 'Kritik av det rena språket' ", *Societas Scientiarum Fennica Årsbok—Vuosikirja*, 38B, no. 5, Helsingfors, 1960, pp. 1–14.

—— (7) Letter, *Times Literary Supplement*, vol. 60, Feb. 17, 1961, p. 105.

—— (8) "Wittgenstein's Picture-Theory: A Reply to Mr. H. R. G. Schwyzer", *Inquiry*, 6 (1963), pp. 184–95. Repr. in present volume.

Stern, J. P., *Lichtenberg, A Doctrine of Scattered Occasions*, Bloomington: Indiana Univ. Press, 1959.

Stiernotte, Alfred (ed.), *Mysticism and the Modern Mind*, New York: Liberal Arts Press, 1959.

Stigen, Anfinn, "Interpretations of Wittgenstein", *Inquiry*, 5 (1962), pp. 167–75.

Stolte, Dieter, "Logik ist die Hölle. Zu Ludwig Wittgensteins Schriften", *Monat*, 14 (1961–2), pp. 66–70.

Storer, Thomas, "Linguistic Isomorphisms", *Philosophy of Science*, 19 (1952), pp. 77–85.

Trentman, John, "A Note on Tractatus 4.12 and Logical Form", *Graduate Review of Philosophy* (Univ. of Minnesota), 4 (1962), pp. 29–33.

Urban, Wilber Marshall, *Language and Reality*, London: George Allen and Unwin; New York: Macmillan, 1939.

Urmson, J. O., *Philosophical Analysis: Its Development Between Two World Wars*, Oxford: Clarendon Press, 1956.

van Peursen, C. A., "Edmund Husserl and Ludwig Wittgenstein", *Journal for Philosophy and Phenomenological Research*, 20 (1959), pp. 181–97.

Vines, S. (ed.), *Whips and Scorpions: Specimens of Modern Satiric Verse, 1914–1931*, London: Wishart, 1932.

Waismann, F., (1) "Logische Analyse der Wahrscheinlichkeitsbegriffs", *Erkenntnis* (*Journal of Unified Science*), 1 (1930–1), pp. 228–48.

—— (2) "Über den Begriff der Identität", *Erkenntnis* (*Journal of Unified Science*), 6 (1936), pp. 56–64.

—— (3) "Was ist Logische Analyse?" *Erkenntnis* (*Journal of Unified Science*), 7 (1939–40), pp. 265–89.

—— (4) "Notes on Talks with Wittgenstein", *Philosophical Review*, 74 (1965), pp. 12–16.

Warnock, G. J., (1) "The Philosophy of Wittgenstein", in (Klibansky), vol. 2, pp. 203–7.

—— (2) *English Philosophy since 1900*, London: Oxford Univ. Press, 1958.

Wasmuth, Ewald, (1) "Das Schweigen Ludwig Wittgensteins; über das Mystische im *Tractatus logico-philosophicus*", *Wort und Wahrheit*, 7 (Nov., 1952), pp. 815–22.

—— (2) "Ludwig Wittgensteins tystnad. Om 'det mystiska' i Tractatus logico-philosophicus' " (The Silence of Wittgenstein. On 'the mystical' in *Tractatus Logico-Philosophicus*), *Credo*, 36 (1955), pp. 118–25.

Bibliography

Weiler, Gershon, (1) "On Fritz Mauthner's Critique of Language", *Mind*, 67 (1958), pp. 80–7.

—— (2) Review of (W4), *Philosophical Books*, 2 (1961), pp. 16–18.

—— (3) Review of (W5 (*g*)), *Philosophical Books*, 3 (1962), pp. 25–7.

Weinberg, Julius, (1) "Are There Ultimate Simples?" *Philosophy of Science*, 2 (1935), pp. 387–99. Repr. in present volume.

—— (2) *An Examination of Logical Positivism*, London: Kegan Paul; New York: Harcourt Brace, 1936.

Whitehead, Alfred North, and Bertrand Russell. See (Russell and Whitehead).

Wholstetter, Albert, "The Structure of the Proposition and the Fact", *Philosophy of Science*, 3 (1936), pp. 167–84.

Wienpahl, Paul D., "Wittgenstein and the Naming Relation", *Inquiry*, 7 (1964), pp. 329–47.

Wiplinger, Fridolin, "Ludwig Wittgenstein. Sprache und Welt in seinem Denken", *Wort und Wahrheit*, 1961, pp. 528–41.

Wisdom, John, (1) "Logical Constructions", *Mind*, pt. i, 40 (1931), pp. 188–216; pt. ii, pp. 460–75; pt. iii, 41 (1932), pp. 441–64; pt. iv, 42 (1933), pp. 43–66; pt. v, pp. 186–202. Pt. i is reprinted in present volume.

—— (2) "Ludwig Wittgenstein", *Mind*, 61 (1952), pp. 258–60.

Wisdom, J. O., "Esotericism", *Philosophy*, 34 (1959), pp. 338–54.

Wolter, Allan B., "The Unspeakable Philosophy of the Late Wittgenstein", *Proceedings of the American Catholic Philosophical Association*, Washington, D.C.: Catholic Univ. of America, 1960, pp. 168–93.

Wood, A., *Bertrand Russell, the Passionate Sceptic*, London: George Allen and Unwin, 1957.

Wright, Georg Henrick von, (1) "Logistisk filosofi" (Logistic Philosophy), *Nya Argus* (Helsingfors), 31 (1938), pp. 175–7.

—— (2) *Den logiska empirismen. En huvudriktning i modern filosofi* (Logical Empiricism. A Leading Movement in Modern Philosophy), Helsingfors, 1943. Finnish trans. by H. Kinos, *Looginen Empirismi*, Helsinki: Otava, 1945.

—— (3) "Ludwig Wittgenstein, en biografisk skiss", *Ajatus*, 18 (1954), pp. 4–23.

—— (4) "Ludwig Wittgenstein, A Biographical Sketch", *Philosophical Review*, 64 (1955), pp. 527–45. Repr. in (Malcolm (1)).

—— (5) *Logical Studies*, London: Routledge and Kegan Paul, 1957.

—— (6) *Logik, filosofi och språk*, Helsingfors: Söderström, 1957. Trans. into Finnish by Tauno Nyberg and Jaakko Hintikka, *Logiikka, filosofia ja Kieli*, Helsinki, 1958.

Zdarzil, Herbert, "Die Selbstaufhebung der Philosophie. Persönlichkeit und Werk Ludwig Wittgensteins", *Hochland*, 53 (1960), pp. 107–15.

Zemach, Eddy, "Wittgenstein's Philosophy of the Mystical", *Review of Metaphysics*, 18 (1964), pp. 38–57. Repr. in present volume.

Index of Proper Names

Index of *Tractatus* References

Index of Tractatus *References*